OF THE

SACRED SCRIPTURES,

WITH EXPLANATIONS AND REFLECTIONS

REGARDING

THE INTERIOR LIFE.

By MADAME GUYON.

Translated by
T. W. DUNCAN.

WIPF & STOCK · Eugene, Oregon

Wipf and Stock Publishers
199 W 8th Ave, Suite 3
Eugene, OR 97401

The Mystical Sense of the Sacred Scriptures
By Madame Guyon
ISBN 13: 978-1-55635-794-7
Publication date 1/9/2008
Previously published by G. W. McCalla, 1913

ADVERTISEMENT.

THE original French edition of this work was published in 20 small octavo volumes, at Cologne, in the years 1713-15. That it has not hitherto appeared in an English dress is a matter of no small astonishment when we consider the remarkably eventful life of its pious author, the great merits of the work itself, and the peculiar method of its production.

In that wonderful book, her Autobiography, Madame Guion thus writes:—

"Thou wast not content to make me speak, my God! Thou didst move me moreover to write the Holy Scripture. It had been sometime since I had read at all, not finding in myself any void to be filled, but, on the contrary, rather too much fulness. When I began to read the Holy Scripture, it was given me to write the passage I read, and instantly thereon its explication. Whilst writing the passage I had not the least thought of the explication, but, immediately that it was written, I was impelled to explain it, writing with inconceivable swiftness. Before I wrote I knew not what I was going to write, and I saw that I was writing things that I had never known; I was illumined to see that I had in me treasures of wisdom and knowledge I had not even known of. Had I written? I remembered nothing whatever of what I had penned, and neither the ideas nor figures remained to me. I could not make use of any part of it for the help of souls; but our Lord gave me at the time I spoke to them, without any study or reflection of mine, all that was needful for them.

Advertisement.

"Thus our Lord made me go on with the explication of the whole of the Sacred Scriptures. I had no other book but the Bible, and never made use of any but that, without even seeking for anything. When, in writing upon the Old Testament, I made use of passages of the New to support what I had said, it was without seeking for them, but they were given me along with the explication; and the same with the New Testament, I therein made use of passages of the Old, and they were given me in like manner, without my seeking for anything. I had no time to write except in the night, for I found it necessary to speak the whole day, without any reliance on myself (no more for speaking than for writing), and without being any more concerned about my health or life than of myself. I had only one or two hours' sleep every night, and with that I had the fever almost every day, generally a fourth part. And yet I continued writing without inconvenience, without caring whether I lived or died. He, to whom I belonged without reserve, did with me all that He pleased, without my mixing myself with His work. Thou didst quicken me Thyself, O my God! and to me so entire a dependence and obedience to Thy will was necessary, that Thou wouldst not suffer the least movement of nature. Did the least thing enter therein, Thou didst punish it, and it fell immediately.

"Thou didst make me write with so much purity, that I was obliged to leave off and begin again as Thou wast pleased. Thou didst try me in every way; all at once Thou didst make me write, then cease immediately, and then resume. When I wrote during the day, I was suddenly interrupted, and often left words half-finished, and Thou didst give me afterwards what Thou pleasedst. What I wrote was not in my head; that part was kept free. I was so disengaged from what I wrote that it was, as it were, strange to me. If I gave way to reflection I was punished for it, my writing was stopped immediately, and I stood still until I was enlightened from above. All the faults in my writings come from my not being accustomed to

Advertisement.

God's operation, being often unfaithful therein, and believing I did well to continue writing when I had time, without feeling the immediate impulse of the Spirit, because I had been ordered to finish the work; so that it is easy to see some places clear and consistent, and others which have neither taste nor unction. I have left them such as they are, so that the difference may be seen between the Spirit of God and the human and natural spirit. Yet I am ready, however, if ordered, to adjust them according to my present light."

*   *   *   *   *   *   *

"I still continued writing with inconceivable rapidity, for the hand could scarce follow fast enough the Spirit which dictated; and through the whole progress of so long a work, I never changed my manner nor made use of any other book than the Bible itself. The transcriber, whatever diligence he used, could not copy in five days what I wrote in one night. Whatever is good in it comes from Thee alone, O my God! whatever is otherwise, from myself, I mean from my infidelity, and from the mixture that I have unwittingly made of my own impurity with Thy pure and chaste doctrine. At the beginning I committed many faults, not being yet trained to the working of the Spirit of God that made me write. For He made me cease writing when I had time, and could do so conveniently, and when I seemed to be greatly in want of sleep, it was then He made me write. When I wrote during the day, it was with continual interruptions, for I had not time to eat, on account of the great number of people that came to me; I was obliged to leave everything when it was required of me; and, to crown all, the girl that served me in the state I before spoke of, without any reason, came suddenly to interrupt me, just as it was her humour. I often left the sense half finished, without being concerned whether what I wrote was connected or not. The parts that may be defective, are so only because sometimes

I wished to write when I had time; and it was not grace that was the source then. If these places were frequent it would be pitiable. At last I accustomed myself, by degrees, to follow God's manner, and not my own.

"I wrote the Canticles in a day and a half, and received visits besides. The rapidity with which I wrote was so great, that my arm swelled up and became quite rigid. During the night it caused me extreme pain, and I did not think I could write any longer. There appeared to me, as I slept, a soul in purgatory, who pressed me to ask her deliverance from my Divine Spouse. I did so, and she seemed to me to be immediately delivered. I said to her, if it is true that thou art delivered, heal my arm, and it was instantly healed, and in a fit state for writing.

"Here I may add to what I have said about my writings, that a considerable part of the book of Judges happened by some means to be lost. Being desired to render that book complete, I wrote over again the places lost. Afterwards, when the people were about leaving the house, they were found. My former and latter explications, on comparison, were found to be perfectly conformable to each other, which greatly surprised persons of knowledge and merit, who attested the truth of it."

This work, then, born in the Augean stable of a great apostacy, hated or neglected for nearly two centuries by the so-called Christian Churches, we recognise as of celestial origin, and seek to rescue from unmerited obscurity. The translator of the present volume has been led, from the exceptional nature of the work, and the peculiarities of the author's French, to aim at a literal, rather than a classical translation.

AUTHOR'S GENERAL PREFACE.

I. *That the essence of religion is interior and spiritual, being founded upon the spirit of simplicity, of truth, and of justice. The angel having fallen away from it, and having caused the fall of man, in order to precipitate him into death,—Jesus Christ has come to re-establish him in life and innocence, through this spirit of truth, justice, and simplicity, which, with what depends upon it, forms the essence and interior of the Christian Religion.*

II. *The obstacles opposed to the essential of religion are only removed by stripping, abandon, faith, hope, and charity, which come back to its interior spirit, manifested in Jesus Christ, set forth in all Scripture, and which in this work it has been our aim to discover and to inspire in all.*

III. *Precautions against being mistaken in putting a wrong meaning on some parts of Scripture or of the following books upon certain subjects. Exhortation, Prayer, and Protestation of the Author.*

§ I.

ALL the evils that are committed in the world are caused only by irreligion. The beauty and principles of the Christian religion are not known; a religion so admirable, that were it fully comprehended, it would command the respect and love of all men.

But how can it be known by those who do not practice it, and who have not entered into it, since those who appear to make a particular profession of it, are so absolutely ignorant of it, that they make it consist not in what it is, but in what it is not, neglecting the *essential* but to stop at the accident, and leaving the *foundation* and the *spirit* only to attach themselves to its body and exterior.

The Christian religion as taught us by Jesus Christ and his disciples has nothing but what is great, sublime, and divine, although hidden under the most simple and common things. That which is the simplest and most common in appearance, is what has most of the Spirit of God, and consequently what is the most exalted; since things are only great inasmuch as their principle is elevated, not according to the caprice of those who give the names of greatness and lowness to what pleases them, calling that great and worthy of honour which is the least so, and the most vile, and having shame and confusion for what is most honourable.

Jesus Christ was not content to overturn these vain opinions of men by his words, he has done so much more by his example. He enhanced the nobleness of poverty by the choice that he made of it, and exposed the baseness of riches by the contempt he had for them. He showed that what men, deceived by their false imaginations call meanness, was a veritable greatness, and that what they consider as something great, ought to be but the object of our scorn. In fine, in order to establish truth upon the earth, he found it necessary to overturn all things, or rather to reinstate them in their primal order, which lying and vanity had ruined.

God in creating the world, veritably established religion, which was the worship of Truth and Justice, and which was due but to Him alone; but the angel in the heavens began through vanity to be usurper and idolater at the same time, wishing to rob God of what was due to Him, in order to attribute it to himself. Pride had no sooner seduced the superb angel than it overthrew him, and forcing him out of his natural order, gave him another, or rather, threw him into a disorder opposed to his nature, and for him a state of violence, which must last as long as his pride and revolt. If God had desired to re-establish His truth in this rebellious angel, in whom pride reigns, He would have subverted his false being of vanity, to replace it in His truth, and then he would have re-entered into his natural being, out of all violence, and this state would be no other than a state of truth, which, stripping him of his usurpations, would restore to God what belonged to Him, and the angel would be reinstated in his state of religion.

Hardly had pride subverted the simple and natural order of

the angel in the heavens, than this same angel, now become devil, son of vanity and father of falsehood, brought it upon the earth, vomiting thereon this monster, whose violent poison infected the whole world soon after its creation.

God created man in truth and simplicity. This was a communication of Himself and a participation in His being which He gave to man. This man was created in religion, inseparable from truth, which consisted in worship due to one only God, and in perfect innocence, which is an effect of the simplicity and truth communicated to him at his creation. This truth and this simplicity formed the fundamental principle of the religion of Adam, by which he rendered a continual worship to God, and a worship of justice, such as God could exact of him. The worship of justice, founded on simplicity and truth, kept him in innocence, for it is impossible to remain in simplicity and truth if we do not dwell in innocence, and he who loses innocence, must necessarily lose truth and simplicity.

Religion then is nothing but *an humble worship of justice and truth, which makes us regard God as God, and the creature as creature*, remaining in the place proper to us, and this state is necessarily accompanied by *innocence*, for it maintains man in the order in which God has placed him, and in absolute subjection to His will, which is the true innocence, excluding all wickedness and sin, which can only be caused by revolt and disorder.

Man was in this state of religion and innocence, of truth and simplicity, when the angel, envious of his happiness, wished to render him companion of his punishment by making him accomplice in his crime; this is why he inspired him with lying, which had no sooner entered into man, than it banished from him truth and simplicity, and overthrew religion and innocence. And it was this loss of truth and simplicity which has been the source of all sin, which has subverted religion, and has introduced into the world idolatry and so many pernicious sects; has banished innocence, and in fine, has drawn man out of his natural order, to throw him into a state of violence, which is a perpetual death, for life consists only in truth and simplicity.

God not desiring to leave man in this disorder, in the fulness of time has sent His only Son, by whom He had breathed the Spirit into man in creating him. He has sent, I say, this Son to reinstate man in his natural order of truth and simplicity; an order of justice which would keep man in his place, and which, stripping him of all his usurpations, banishing lying and multiplicity, makes him restore to God all that he owes Him, and re-establishes in him the worship of religion and innocence, replacing him in his natural order, and causing him happily to lose this state of violence and death, to enter into one of liberty and life.

This great principle being thus established, it is easy to see that everything which simplifies us and brings us into truth, necessarily brings us into the foundation of religion and into innocence. Every other road is but wandering. This is why Jesus Christ having come into the world, has taught us nothing else by his words and examples, but simplicity and truth. Has he not said himself that he was come to bring this *Spirit of Truth*, but *that the world could not receive it?* The world, as the world, cannot receive truth or simplicity, because it lies in disorder and confusion, and must necessarily be destroyed, that man through the truth may be re-established in his natural order, in his religion and innocence. Let people seek for refinement in devotion as much as they desire; all that is not simplicity and truth, cannot be the true religion nor the perfect innocence.

Religion and innocence, then, are founded on simplicity and truth, and truth is found only in the Christian religion, which is nothing else but truth and simplicity. It is nothing but truth in itself, since it keeps us in the order of our creation, and in the will of God, making us render to him a worship of justice, and stripping us of all the usurpations of lying, to hold us in innocence through the stripping of everything not our own. But what can we have or what have we of ourselves, if it is not nothingness? And all the rest is it not God's? It is also nothing but simplicity, since its end is to withdraw us from our too multifarious occupations, to attach us to our *sole necessity*, and to cause us, calming our natural agitations, to enter into the repose and unity of God, without which we could not resemble Him, nor consequently be united to Him.

§ II.

If what I say here be examined, no difficulty will be had in comprehending the reason why so much mention is made in the Holy Scriptures of *strippings*. Therefore I have enlarged so much in treating of them, and in describing *abandon, faith* and the *interior spirit*, this state of the Will of God under these

General Preface.

different passages of the soul. Although this may seem useless to those who are not acquainted with it, it is nevertheless the spirit of the Christian religion.

It is this road of *stripping* which conducts the soul into truth and into the essential of the Christian religion, preventing all illusions, deceits, heresies, all the sins which are but winding ways; in fine, it is what places the soul in truth, stripping it totally of everything that hinders it from being God's in the order of its creation and entire innocence.

It must here be observed that the grace of redemption, which Jesus Christ has merited for us, brings us into truth and simplicity, rendering us *true worshippers of the Eternal Father in spirit and in truth*, which is the chief worship in religion. The spirit of prayer is there, on which everything must revolve. This *stripping* is also a spirit of sacrifice leading us to destroy ourselves by the homage that we render to the greatness of the one only and Sovereign Being. It is for this cause that Jesus Christ has once offered himself up on the cross, and that he unceasingly offers himself up on our altars. So that sacrifice, the spirit of religion, united to adoration in spirit and truth, forms religious worship, which is only wrought by the *stripping* through which man is placed in truth and simplicity.

I pray it to be observed that it is impossible to reach truth save through the loss of the prejudices, reasonings, and thoughts which conceal it from us; it must be so naked that we cannot cover or decorate it without rendering it unrecognisable. No more can we proceed to unity by multiplicity; we must then go to it by simplicity. Now this simplicity enters into our souls, not by discourse or reasoning, which are multiplied, but by the simple practice of the three Divine Virtues, which, when they have taken possession of the three faculties of the soul, simplify it; *Faith* simplifies the understanding; *Hope*, the memory; and *Charity*, the will; and it is those three virtues that are admirably exercised by *worship* made *in spirit and in truth*, by the sacrifice of religion, by simple prayer, which makes us adore the simple Spirit of God.

Behold then the spirit of the Christian religion, which is no other than the Spirit of Jesus Christ, and this is what we call the *Interior Spirit;* and I affirm that all those who do not enter into the interior, into the spirit of religion and of Jesus Christ, are but the bodies of inanimate Christians, and have not the Christian spirit and life. Jesus Christ was unceasingly occupied in his interior; he was in the perfect unity; and he has prayed his Father for us that we might be made participants in this unity. "*My Father*," said he, "*may they be one as we are one, and may all be consummated in unity.*" We can only arrive at this unity by simplicity, and by the loss of multiplicity; for unity causes simplicity, and simplicity leads to unity.

It is a matter of extreme consequence to make known to Christians this spirit of religion, so clearly evident throughout all the sacred writings, that all who will read them and the explication here given, without any prejudice, will perceive that they tend but to establish us solidly therein through truth and simplicity, which are wrought by total *stripping* and by *abandon* to the conduct of Jesus Christ, who is come as our *way*, our *truth*, and our *life*.

This whole work revolves on these three principles, and all that it contains is but to make us follow this Saviour as *the way*, to listen to him as *the truth*, and to allow ourselves to be animated by him as *our life*.

What then ought to inspire us more to apply ourselves to the reading of the Sacred Scriptures, is this, that they teach us this spirit of religion and all its perfection, in its beginning, its progress, and its consummation, as we shall see by the explications that I shall give of them without doing any violence to the text, and without giving it a foreign sense or spirit. It will not be difficult there to discover the essential of the worship due to God alone in truth and simplicity, which we there get as from the fountain-head, whether we take the Old or New Testament.

Moreover we there also happily find all the means to enter and advance therein. We admire there the example and conduct of the ancient patriarchs and prophets, who have left their footsteps for us to follow: We read there the words of Jesus Christ, and of the Evangelists and Apostles: It is there that we learn the excellence of the sacrifices of our religion, and particularly that of the holy eucharist, which eminently contains all the others; the necessity of prayer, the efficacious manner of making it, the spirit of true worship, the totality of *stripping* and *abandon;* in a word, all that is included in simplicity and truth, and everything that can contribute thereto. But what is most important, we there learn to make a just discernment between the *exterior* and *interior* of our religion, in order not to separate the one from the other.

General Preface.

The principal part of the Christian religion is its spirit or interior, a spirit of truth and simplicity, and which banishes equally multiplicity and lying; for as this spirit emanates from God himself, who is simple, without mixture and without division, it is necessary that it be simple, one and upright, that it may place man in the truth of everything of God and nothing of the creature; that it may render the soul so upright for God, that it cannot come out of this uprightness as long as it dwells in truth, so that there is not the least turning of the soul from God, or of God from the soul, and this is what makes its innocence. This uprightness for God is accompanied by righteousness for the neighbour. This then is what I call the true interior spirit, which is no other than the spirit of the Christian religion.

If we make use of a great many terms, such as *abandon*, *destitution*, *death*, *loss*, *annihilation*, and the rest, they are but expressions of the states through which God causes the soul to pass, to reduce it into perfect simplicity and truth, into innocence and the spirit of religion; but the essential is, the spirit of unity and simplicity, which, placing us in the order of creation and redemption, unites us to God without a medium as to our First Cause.

The state of worship in spirit and in truth, which is wrought by simplicity, is then the interior and the spirit of the Christian religion. There is besides this, religious worship, which is not only included in the state of adoration, but there is implied the state of sacrifice and of continual destruction, which is performed by the entire *stripping* of everything; and this it is which composes the interior of the Christian, as it did proportionately that of Jesus Christ.

There is still the exterior of the Christian, having connexion with the interior, and which is exterior sacrifice and worship. Now this exterior, as well as the interior, brings man into *strippings*, making him suffer equally all that happens to him in the spirit of sacrifice; and detaching him from all exterior objects, it makes him do outward acts of worship, putting the body as well as the spirit into a state of worship. This is the essential of our religion, the rest contains only the accessories, to which, nevertheless, we ought to submit and apply ourselves by the obligation imposed upon us by natural and Divine laws.

The sole object I have in view in undertaking this work, is to discover to those who read it, the beauties of our religion, and to inspire them with the desire of becoming *worshippers of God in spirit and in truth.*

§ III.

I pray it to be observed beforehand, that when I speak of *faith* in several places, especially in St. Paul, that I do not mean in the explication that I give of it, the common faith of the church, and general amongst all Christians; but faith which is this interior spirit, exempt from all multiplied operations of the mind or heart, which is content to receive in a passive manner the workings of its Divine Mover, and suffering His operations both gratifying and crucifying. But by these multiplied operations I do not mean good works, nor that they are useless, since faith would be void without them. I am very far from excluding *them*, since I lead the soul into the ways of orison, sacrifice, and continual prayer, which are the *principal good works;* but I only wish to cut off from the exercise of faith all the multiplicity of the reasonings and reflections of self-love. O faith, how pure thou art, how naked and simple, and how agreeable thou art thus to the eyes of God!

As Scripture never contradicts itself, taking things in the sense I have just expressed, it will be easy to reconcile the doctrine of St. Paul upon faith, with that of St. Peter and St. James, who were obliged to write because of the bad turn which had been given to St. Paul's epistles. When then I exalt faith above works and good practices, I am to be understood to mean only passive faith which is animated by a pure charity.

When the *stripping* of virtues is spoken of, I believe I have sufficiently shown in the body of the work, that God, wishing to divest the soul of the propriety in good, often strips it of the facile usage and pleasant and easy practice of the virtues, and takes away even certain outward observances to cause the soul to lose its attachment to them, and to enter into perfect indifference; but he takes them away from it in an outward manner perceptibly, and for a time only, but that He may restore them to it in the sequel without any propriety, and in perfect disengagement.

Let us enter then, my brethren, into the spirit of this work without any air of prejudice or criticism, and we shall learn to become true Christians, not only in appearance, but in reality.

O God, imprint these truths upon the hearts of those who

read them. Make them see, acknowledge, and taste of the truth, the beauty, and the grandeur of the Christian religion and in what it consists. Thou hast expressed it so admirably in all Thy Scriptures, by Thy patriarchs and prophets, by Thyself and by Thy apostles; let it be now *that the true worshippers worship the Father* according to the promises Thou hast made to us, *in spirit and in truth; for God is spirit and He desires worshippers in spirit!* O truth, too little comprehended and still less practised!

It is Thine, O Child-God, simple and innocent, who camest to bring truth and simplicity upon the earth at a time when they were entirely banished from it, and to make for Thyself true worshippers, and who hast been Thyself the foundation stone of the spiritual edifice of the Christian religion, whose legislator and institutor Thou art; it is Thine, I say, to imprint on all the hearts of those who will read this work, the interior spirit of our religion. Do this, O Divine Child! Imprint upon them Thy qualities, and seal them with Thy seal. Inspire them with Thy spirit and life, which consists in truth and simplicity. Make us all children, Thou who hast said, that if we become not as little children, that is to say, simple and innocent, we shall never enter into the kingdom of heaven. Thou canst do it, O Adorable Infant; and I hope that Thou wilt do it by this work, which has nothing but what is simple, and which for that reason will be understood only by the simple and the little ones, and not by the great and high minds of the age.

Dear reader, if anything gives offence to you in this work, whether it be in the expressions or the sentiments, or in some places which you may not understand, do not make it your study to criticise it, but rather to become humble and little, and you will understand and receive everything with much fruit. Excuse, moreover, the defects of a person who makes no profession of science or ability; but who has her spirit and heart entirely submitted to the Church, to whose correction she has hitherto and will always submit her writings.

AN ADDITION TO THE PREFACE

BY THE SAME AUTHOR AND UPON THE SAME SUBJECT.

THE Holy Scriptures possess an infinite depth and many different senses. The great men of learning have clung to the *literal* and other senses; but no one has undertaken, that I know of, to explain *the mystical sense* or *interior*, at least entirely. It is this that our Lord has caused me to explain here for the use of souls who desire with all their heart to enter not only into the exterior of Christianity, but to participate in the most profound grace of the Christian, which is the *interior*. I am obliged to declare that I have done nothing but lend my hand to Him who conducted me inwardly; so that whatever is good therein, must be entirely attributed to Him; if there is anything that cannot be considered such, I have unwittingly mixed my false lights with those of the Holy Spirit. I beg the reader, however, not to adhere scrupulously to the letter, and to be persuaded, that there will be many things that he will not understand since they will surpass his experience; let him not judge of them on that account, but making use of the first means given him, let him labour with all his might to enter into perfect love, into a spirit of faith, and a total *abandon* to the conduct of Jesus Christ, and then he will soon experience the things he is ignorant of at present. The more he believes in the all power of God and his love for men, the more he lets himself be conducted to God by a blind *abandon*, the more he will love purely, the more also will he be enlightened as to the truths that are contained in the mystical sense of the Divine Scriptures. He will discover then with infinite joy that all these experiences are there described in a manner simple, yet clear; he will find himself happy in meeting a guide to pass over the Red Sea, and the frightsome desert that follows; but he will not comprehend his perfect felicity until he be arrived at the promised land, where all his past labours will appear to him but dreams. Transported with so great a happiness, he will not believe it to have been too dearly bought by all the troubles he has borne, even though he should have suffered many far greater.

I pray the reader also to note, that of so great a people that came out of the land of Egypt, there arrived only two persons into the promised land. How comes this? from want of courage, regretting unceasingly that they had left. If they had been courageous and faithful, only a few months would have been necessary to arrive there; but murmuring and despondency made them remain on the road forty years. It happens as much thus to persons whom God desires to conduct by the interior. They regret, not the onions of Egypt, but the sensible sweetnesses when they are desired to walk in a purer and barer road; they do not wish so delicate a food as manna, they desire something more sensible; they revolt against their Conductor, and far from profiting by the goodness of God, they raise His anger and kindle His fury; so that they make for themselves an extremely long road, and turn round about the mountain; if they advance one step, they fall back four, and the greater part do not arrive at the promised end by their own fault.

Let us take courage, my dear brethren, let us endeavour to reach the goal without ever being discouraged by the difficulties we find on our way. We have a sure Guide, who is this *cloud* during the day, which, concealing from us the brightness of the sun, leads us the more surely; we have during the darkest night of faith the *pillar of fire*, which guides us also. What is this *pillar of fire*, if not sacred love, which becomes the more glowing, as faith appears the more obscure and dark? Let us be content with this hidden *manna* of the interior, which will nourish us much better than the grosser meats that our senses so ardently desire. Let us choose the mystic *tomb* and not that of *concupiscence*.

Besides all these beautiful figures which the Old Testament proffers us to conduct us into the interior, Jesus Christ has come himself to show us a real and a sure road. It is no longer mysterious and admirable figures, it is a living model, it is the words of truth; Jesus Christ is the *way* by which we must walk, he is the *truth* that instructs us, the *life* that animates us; he has given us in reality what our ancient fathers had but in figure. If nevertheless they followed the road of the *interior*, how much more ought Christians to walk therein who have so palpable an example in the whole life of Jesus Christ. He teaches us nothing else in the Gospel as we shall see. It can be said that the *interior* is the spirit of the Gospel, as outward practices are its letter. The apostles continued to teach it to us by their examples and writings. Let us walk then in this way so pure, so simple, so sure, though we may not feel the assurance, and we shall walk according to the will of God.

GENESIS.

WITH EXPLICATIONS AND REFLECTIONS REGARDING THE INTERIOR LIFE.

CHAPTER I.

1. *In the beginning God created the heaven and the earth.*
2. *The earth was without form and bare, and darkness covered the face of the abyss. And the Spirit of God was borne over the waters.*

God created the heaven and the earth in the beginning, and He created them by the Word; for it is by Him that everything has been made, and without Him has there been nothing made: He was at the beginning in God. This is a beautiful figure of the regeneration or re-creation of the soul sunk in the nothingness of sin. It is from this frightful chaos that God draws the sinner to create him anew; but He does it only by Jesus Christ. For as from the beginning the first step towards conversion is this new creation, and as St. John assures us that from the beginning was the Word, and that everything has been made by Him, and without Him has there been nothing made, it must also be said that from the beginning of the Christian and spiritual life, as well as in its progress and consummation, everything is wrought by Jesus Christ, who is "the Way, the Truth, and the Life." God, then, by His Word regenerates and re-creates this soul which was as annihilated by sin. And how does He do this? Here is the order expressed in this first verse of Scripture, which, relating what happened at the beginning of the ages, points out to us the conduct of God in the conversion of the sinner, which is the first step and entrance into the Christian way, both spiritual and interior.

In the first place, *God creates the heaven and the earth.* This marks the two renewals that must be wrought out by penitence, the exterior and interior; for we must quit sin not only of the body, but also of the heart and spirit. But as outward conversion must always depend on that of within—that is to say, on that of the heart and spirit, represented by the heaven—it is here said that God created the heaven and the earth. He begins by the heart and spirit, then He reforms the outer. The first stroke of conversion is made within. God creates this spirit, drawing it out of the horrible chaos where it lay; then He frees the body from sin. He gives this heart a secret proneness to be in Him who is, and without whom it can never exist; then He leads the exterior to quit the engagements that keep the heart in death and non-being, drawing it away from the sole and sovereign Being, to place it in created nothings.

Nevertheless this *earth*, after its creation, remains *void and without form;* that is to say, deprived of all good; whatever it may be, it is only clothed with some form and appearance—and that is all. There is yet no plant, but only a great *void*, and an extreme dearth. This is the exterior state of man in his conversion. It is added that *darkness was upon the face of the abyss*—that is to say, that this spirit and heart, like a deep abyss impenetrable to all but God, are so enveloped in *darkness*, that the poor soul does not then know what to do; it sees within itself nothing but the darkness and horrors that sin has spread there; it sees out of itself but *void* and sterility; it finds itself deprived of all good, and surrounded by every evil.

Nevertheless, although this is the case, the *Spirit of God* does not cease to *move over the waters*. What are these *waters*, if not the tears of penitence, over which grace rests, and is diffused in spite of the *darkness of ignorance* (which is the remains of sin), and the frightful vacuity of all good?

3. *Now God said, Let the light be made; and the light was made.*

This bountiful Spirit, who has brooded over the waters of penitence, seeing the grief of this ignorant sinner, sends him in the midst of his darkness a ray of His light. *God said let there be light, and there was light.* A certain lustre that emanates from God Himself, and which is nothing else but a ray of His wisdom, strikes this blind spirit, who, feeling his darkness dispersing little by little, begins to comprehend that the Word of God is an efficacious word. It is speech, and it is light. For created light is the expression of the Uncreated Word, as the Uncreated Word is the source of the light communicated to the creature. This is why the Divine Word is called the splendour of the saints; for He is a word full of light, shed abroad on them. Thus God, to create all things out of nothing, has but to speak; for His speech is His Word, and His Word is His light. God speaks then in this new creature; and what is the first word He says to it? It is, *Let there be light;* and this word is no sooner spoken than *there is light;* this darkness of ignorance is changed into a light of truth, which increases little by little, as the rising sun disperses by degrees the darkness of night. This light is a light of grace, which is the light effected by Jesus Christ, and not yet Jesus Christ the Light. It is then we can say, in the highest sense, that they who were in the darkness of sin and ignorance have seen a great light, and that the sun has risen upon those who dwelt under the shadow of the death of sin.

It is easy to see that all this is done by the grace of the Redeemer, and the bounty of the Creator.

4. *God saw that the light was good; and He divided the light from the darkness.*
5. *He called the light Day, and the darkness Night: and of the evening and the morning there was made one day.*

Scripture adds, that *God saw that the light was good;* that is to say, that this light having emanated from Himself, and being mixed with no impurity of the creature, was good, and that it was working good effects in this new creature. For it is by its means that the new creature begins to discover its first cause, and to conceive the desire of returning to Him. Thus a light shed abroad in so obscure a place, discovers the place which it leaves—the ray manifesting itself, and at the same time the abode of its original.

God has no sooner shed His lights of grace upon a heart, and the heart has no sooner responded to them by its fidelity, than, seeing the good use the soul has made of them, and the goodness of this light diffused in those dark places, He begins to *divide the light from the darkness.* Until then it was a day of gloom or of luminous darkness; but now God divides His light from our darkness, so that this mixture may not spoil it. This beautiful *light* is faith, the gift of God, coming to take possession of a soul. At the beginning, only illustrations are distinguished clearly, on account of the heavy night in which the soul lies. Not that this beautiful light is clearer and more abundant in its first illustrations than afterwards, although it may be more perceptible. It is quite the contrary; but the profound darknesses of the soul cause it to be better distinguished, although it may not be so lively as afterwards.

God then divides His light from our darkness; and it is then that it becomes purer, more extended, and more eminent, although it may seem to grow dark for man; who, on account of the division that has just been made between what is God's and what is his own, perceiving nothing but his own darkness, believes himself to be in a greater obscurity. Nevertheless, he never was more enlightened nor more luminous in his highest region; but as he is exposed before God, who, like an immortal sun, sends His light unceasingly upon him, and as he renders back to God this same light with much fidelity, everything appears obscure on his side; just as we see the moon, when most exposed to the sun at the time of her conjunction, shedding so much the less light upon the earth the more she receives of it, and appearing dark when her sun regards her the most nearly and strongly; and, on the contrary, rendering so much the more light to the earth when she is in her fulness, and receiving less from the sun. It is thus also with the soul illuminated by the divine light; when the Divine Sun sheds upon it His ardent and burning rays, it is so strongly correspondent to its God, that it perceives not His brightness and splendour; whilst, when His light is smaller, and when it receives less from its sun, it is then that it diffuses more. This is the difference between distinct and perceptible knowledges (however sublime they may appear), and the general and indistinct light of faith.

It is added, however, that the *evening and the morning made but one day*. This is understood in two ways: One, that a continual alternation of light and darkness makes but one day, the day of faith, partly luminous and partly obscure; the other, that the light, commencing as the light of life, which is that of the *morning* of the interior life, and alive with brightness and splendour, and the *evening*, signifying the state of death, extinction and stripping, make *one* complete *day*, the day of faith and of the interior Christian.

6. *Then God said, Let the firmament be made in the midst of the waters, and let it divide the waters from the waters.*
7. *And God made the firmament, and divided the waters which*

were under the firmament from the waters which were above the firmament; and it was so.

8. *And God gave to the firmament the name of Heaven. And of the evening and the morning was made the second day.*

The days of penitence being passed, *God said, Let the firmament be made in the midst of the waters*—as much as to say, Let the course of these tears be now stopped, let the heart and spirit be made firm, and let these first tendernesses be separated from the waters, which, although holy, are nevertheless procured by the *sensible.* Let these *waters be divided* from those of my grace, so that they may be pure, and without mixture.

The *waters which are above the firmament* are the waters of grace, all pure, clear, and spotless, which submerge and overflow the soul in such a manner, that they purify it in an abyss of delights. Then the waters of bitterness and grief are placed under, and the superior part, represented by the region above the firmament, finds itself plunged in a torrent of delights; whilst the lower part, the earth, is inundated with the waters of bitterness and grief. And it is these two waters thus divided— the *day* of consolation and the *night* of grief—that compose the *second* spiritual *day*, which is no other than the second period of the interior Christian.

9. *And God said, Let the waters under the heaven be gathered together into one place, and let the dry appear; and it was so.*
10. *And God called the dry, Earth, and gave to the mass of waters the name of Sea; and God saw that that was good.*

These waters of bitterness and griefs which had spread over all the soul *are gathered together into one place;* they now retire to the limits marked out for them, and these limits surround the heart. Then *what is dry appears*, and the soul begins to enter into new regions which it had not yet discovered since its conversion. This is when the dry and arid is discovered, and is much more difficult to bear than the waters of bitterness. For these waters, which before covered all the earth, were still mingled with sweetness; but they are no sooner shut up in their limits than they become sea *(mer)*,—that is to say, full of bitterness *(amertume)*, and all that they covered before is reduced into dryness.

Chapter I.

God gave the name of Sea to this mass of waters; for, in the division made, all sweetness seems to have retired and mounted up to the superior waters, and there remains in the inferior nothing but what is bitter, which is so closely gathered into one place, that [these waters] have much more bitterness there where they are collected, than they had before in their greater extent. *This dry (land),* says Scripture, *was called Earth.* This signifies, that it is only then that man begins to enter into the knowledge of himself, and of the vileness and baseness of his origin. Now this is done by means of this great dryness and aridity, which is produced only by God withdrawing all the waters that covered it, as much the sweet and celestial waters as those of bitterness and grief; and having drawn to Himself into the supreme region of the soul the sweet waters of grace, withholding from them the power of descending upon the earth—that is to say, the lowest parts of ourselves, in which resides the *sensible*—the dry and arid must necessarily there be discovered; but this is done in a painful manner, because the waters of bitterness are there also, not to moisten and refresh as formerly, but to communicate their bitterness without any refreshment, except at certain moments when there falls a heavenly dew, which the sun of righteousness dries up almost immediately. Nevertheless this dew fortifies, sustains, and vivifies.

It is added that *God saw that this was good.* This is said of all the preceding works—not only to teach us that all the works that God does alone, or without resistance on our part, are always good, and that nothing can be spoiled in His actions but by the mingling of the proprietary creature; but more, that each state or degree in which God places the soul possesses a goodness proper and peculiar to it; and that, nevertheless, all have their times and uses very different. For when God had created the waters, and they had spread over all the earth, He said that it was good. Shortly after, however, He changes things, and still says the same, that it is good. That which was good and necessary for one time becomes useless and dangerous for another. It is good for a time that this dry and arid earth be inundated by the waters of grace; but it is very good for another time that it be deprived of them, and that these waters retire into their place, without which their sojourn upon the earth would corrupt them, and hinder the earth from bearing any fruit. We see, then, the necessity there is of allowing God to operate in souls without mixing therewith the confused and precipitate action of the creature, which generally desires to retain the waters by efforts when God wills to withdraw them; or to dry them up of itself, before God does it, under pretext that the state is purer. Oh almighty hand of God! it is Thine to do all things by Thy Divine Word; Thou sayest, and it is done; Thy saying is doing, and all that Thou doest, Thou doest well.

We must then leave it to God to do; He will do it better than we. Oh poor creatures that we are! We believe ourselves able to do what God does, and often even to do it better than He. This is why we meddle with everything, and desire always to keep everything between our hands; but we never advance in anything; on the contrary, our eagerness hinders it from working. God performs His perfect works only upon nothingness, which does not resist Him.

11. *And God said, Let the earth bring forth the green herb, yielding seed, and fruit trees bearing fruit, each according to its kind, and containing their seed within themselves upon the earth. And it was so.*

12, 13. *And God saw that that was good. And of the evening and morning was made the third day.*

When the time has arrived, the moment of the will of God, who disposes the soul, to fill it or render it void according to His eternal designs, God commands this dry and arid earth, hitherto apparently useless, to produce the *green herb*. This is its first production. This soul, in the midst of its aridity, is astonished to see communicated to it a vivifying quality, rendering it able to apply itself to good things with facility. All these plants *bear their seed within themselves*, causing them to be reproduced and multiplied to infinity. They are yet, however, young herbs, feeble actions, and little things, which nevertheless does not prevent them appearing very great to this soul, who knows nothing greater; and who did not even expect this strange sterility to produce so great a good. When then it believes itself possessor of the greatest things, it is still more surprised to perceive, that this same Word, which has produced in it the herb, also *produces trees, leaves and fruits*, which is quite another production from that of simple herbs. These are the most heroic virtues, which bear within themselves the *seed* of an infinity of other virtues which must be communicated by its organism.

Chapter I.

Then the soul begins to discover its grandeur and nobleness, and what is proper to it—what it can aim at, and attain to. It sees this, however, only confusedly; but it is not yet shown how these things are wrought in it, nor who it is that does them. It only comprehends with its confused sight that it is God who is the author of them; but, at the same time, imagines He has done it all on account of its fidelity.

However, it will be necessary for it to comprehend afterwards two things. The first is, that it is by the Word that everything is wrought in it, and that without Him is nothing made; therefore, God employs only His Speech (*parole*), which is nothing but His Word (*verbe*) to operate all things: "*He spake and it was done.*" This was the fault of Moses at the rock of the waters of contradiction. He wished to strike the rock, and it was only necessary for him to speak; for it was given him then to act no longer by the rod of his own operations, but to act by the Word, and to perform everything in God by the same Word. The miracles of souls well advanced in God are done by speech, without any sign or figure, which does not happen to souls still in gifts—they make use of outward actions, it not being given them to act by the Word; for it is only in God himself, and in an eminent manner, that Jesus Christ is communicated and formed in us, which is called the mystic Incarnation. Now the soul can only act by the Word after It is given it in the manner already mentioned; and it is then that speech operates everything, and that saying is doing, and doing saying. But when we, by infidelity, wish to make use of the rod and signs as we did formerly, then we displease God much.

The second thing that this soul must learn is, that these operations of grace are not done by virtue of its merits, but rather with a view to our annihilation, as the divine Mary knew, when, relating the mercies of God, she said, that they had been given, *because God had regarded the low estate of his handmaiden.* He has looked upon its nothingness, and this regard has produced in it the Word, the image of the Father, who is produced in us by His looking upon our nothingness; and in regarding us thus, He begets in us His Word, which is His speech, and in communicating this Word, it is given us to act from Him with speech alone.

This state of the production of all those virtues in the soul for the *third day*, or degree of the interior life; but what is admirable, all these virtues come into the soul and are found established there without it being comprehended how it is done; for without any labour on man's part, but that of letting himself be possessed by his God, and allowing Him to operate in him, he is astonished that God does all things in him and for him, and does them each in its time, but with an order so ravishing, that this astonished soul cries, Oh, how well He does all things! It belongs to Thee, O Eternal and Uncreated Wisdom, to cause all things to be well done; for all that is not of Thee, or comes from Thee, is but lying, error, and deceit.

If this explanation is faithfully followed, there will be seen the course of the operation of God in souls by Jesus Christ from the beginning of their conversion, and the necessity there is of corresponding to it; not, as it is imagined only by a strong activity, but much more by an entire dependence on the conduct of grace, which does not leave for a moment the soul that it has taken under protection, until it has conducted it to its end. We must then allow the Spirit of God to act in us. But it seems that, on the contrary, man labours only to hinder that same Spirit from working in him; for, instead of following the Holy Spirit by the continual renouncing of ourselves and entire resignation to His will, we seem to be desirous of preceding Him by the violence of our operations, and of obliging Him not to conduct us, but to follow us; and as our own conduct is but faults and misery, we endeavour to engage this Holy Spirit of God to walk in the road that we point out, without being willing to abandon ourselves to Him, that He may conduct us into His ways. This is what happens when we unceasingly run counter to this Divine Spirit; when we vex It even, according to the words of scripture, and when, in fine, we quench It entirely. St. Paul warns us to be careful not to use It thus.

14. *God said also: Let luminaries be made in the firmament of the heaven, that they may divide the day from the night, and that they may serve for signs to mark the times and the seasons, the days and the years.*
15. *That they may shine in the heaven, and give light upon the earth. And it was so.*
16. *And God made two great lights: the greater light to rule the day, and the lesser light to rule the night: He made the stars also.*
17. *And God set them in the firmament of the heaven to give light upon the earth.*

Chapter I.

18. *And to rule over the day and over the night, and to divide the light from the darkness: and God saw that that was good.*
19. *And of the evening and the morning was made the fourth day.*

When the third day or degree of the interior is passed, God begins to produce in the soul a new state, which is the *fourth* step of the interior Christian. This is when the soul, in whom until now everything has passed as in darkness and obscurity, begins to receive the light and diverse interior illustrations. In its highest region there is nothing more but light and heat: it has a great many *distinct lights*, besides the general one, and its state is so luminous, that even in the *night*, its time of obscurity, but an obscurity conform to its degree, it continues to have light, although different from that of the *day*. The difference between the light of the day, that is to say, the most luminous state, and that of the night, is, that by the former, objects are better discerned, whilst it itself is less distinct: a great many knowledges are communicated, and many truths discovered, although the nature of the light is not so much seen, on account of its dazzling brilliancy: whilst the latter does not nearly reveal objects, but shows itself only very distinctly. This is what often deceives souls in this degree, causing them to take the day for the night and the night for the day, thus making much more of these lights of darkness than the general one, which, concealing itself, discovers, nevertheless, by its brilliancy objects as they are.

This light of the day, being the Eternal Sun, is nothing but the light of faith, which is not so satisfying on account of its general nature, although infinitely more luminous than that of the other stars. The other lights of the night are all distinct ones—visions, illustrations, everything distinguished and perceived throughout our night of ignorance. All these lights, however, come from God, and being the effects of His goodness and power, we ought to accept them with reverence and humility; but they are, nevertheless, very different from each other. We are so blind that we prefer generally the light of the night to that of the day, and whilst amusing ourselves too much discerning *the stars of the firmament*—that is to say, the distinct lights, these visions, illustrations, and ecstasies—we do not go beyond them to lose ourselves in the general light of faith;

stopping thus to distinguish objects by these faint glimmerings, which deceive us, magnify and change them, and often make them unrecognisable. Oh, strange loss is this that the soul suffers in this degree! This is one of the most important points in the spiritual life; for if the soul is not instructed as to the difference between these two lights, it stops at the latter even to death, and never enters into the open day of faith, where truth is manifested without error and deceit.

Now, the degrees of rising and setting of these lights make known the seasons of the soul—that is to say, the state in which it is—just as the sun distinguishes the times and seasons by the different stay it makes in its signs; and the same with the moon. Thus the first approach of the interior sun produces the first spring of the spiritual life, not yet the eternal spring; its advance makes summer, a state where there is nothing but light and heat; and at length it produces by its warmth fruits, which appear in autumn; but in proportion as it retraces its steps and recedes from us, it leaves us a winter so much the more grievous, as the other seasons had been agreeable; in short, the course of these heavenly luminaries, either approaching or receding, marks the seasons and states of the soul. And as the sun finds again the sign of its zodiac whence it set out, whether it approaches or leaves us, so the soul always re-finds its God, its house and birthplace, although it may experience a fearful obscurity through the retirement of the same light that had at first advanced upon it with giant strides.

God saw that it was good—that is to say, the advantage the soul derives from His divine conduct, which makes Him terminate this fourth day or degree, to cause it to pass into another. If the soul was faithful, would it not go on its way until it arrived at the seventh day, the rest of God in Himself? But, alas! our infidelity makes us stop at the first day, without going beyond; this is why we dwell all our life in a frightful chaos.

It must be observed, that at all the days and degrees it is said, *that the evening and the morning made one day*. This shows how God composes this day or step (which is distinguished from the others), of the commencement and introduction of a degree, and its consummation; and how the beginning of each degree is like a new day opening, and its consummation—a day ended, but ended only to re-commence with greater strength. Each change of day is preceded by a night, which, in terminating, gives birth to the other again. Oh admirable mystery of God's conduct with His creatures! If we had our eyes open to the Divine light, we would discover with infinite joy that there is nothing that takes place in the natural order of creation but is found in some proportion agreeable to the order of grace in the soul. It is this that delights the illumined spirit, making it not only discover God in all creation, but even the wise conduct that He exercises on souls to draw them to Him, so that it sees nothing in nature but what expresses something that takes place within its own interior. Thus it is very true that man is a little world, in whom everything that is done in the great universe is expressed as in epitome; but the reason we do not perceive it is, that we are not wholly penetrated with the light of Truth.

20. *God said again, Let the waters bring forth living animals, that swim in the water, and birds that fly under heaven, over the earth.*
21. *And God created great fishes, and all the animals that live and move, which the waters brought forth, according to their kind, and all the birds according to their kind. And God saw that that was good.*
22. *And He blessed them, saying, Increase and multiply, and fill the waters of the sea, and let the birds multiply upon the earth.*
23. *And of the evening and morning was made the fifth day.*

Until now plants had appeared upon this dry and arid earth; the luminaries had been born and had risen within the soul—that is to say, as much the distinct lights as the general light of Faith, which, although indistinct in itself, yet continues to make manifest truths as they are, provided only that we do not waste our time regarding the light itself, but make use of it to view the objects discovered to us by its means; for if we should amuse ourselves with gazing upon it alone it would dazzle us, and give to the eyes of the spirit a property which, although luminous in appearance, hinders them from discovering objects in their reality, and makes them see everything affected by it. Thus it happens to all those souls who, in place of using this light of faith to discover simply what it manifests to them, desire to reflect upon it, and see into itself, and what it is, and its different effects. Then is the eye dazzled by thus acting contrary to God's designs, who gives us this light only to make us hasten to Him by the way it opens for us. This is what causes all the illusions that take place in the way of faith, which is itself so pure, so straight, and so sure, that there are never any to be feared for the souls who make use of it in the manner already mentioned. It is not the same with the other kinds of lights, which have something diverting in themselves; for as they manifest themselves only, discovering but very few objects, and that in a very limited manner, they cannot show themselves as they are, but rather according to our comprehension, which by its vivacity represents them to itself often, under its former ideas of them, although they may no longer exist, and thus they are imagined unwittingly by the reflection of the spirit. The luminaries of the night are counterfeited by artificial lights. But the light of Faith is of a nature impossible to be counterfeited, for it absorbs in its vast extent even all the other distinct lights, surpassing them all by its clearness. It is the property of faith to surpass all things, to stop at God only; and it is in that its solidity and exemption from deceit consist, if only we use it not to contemplate it alone, but to walk unceasingly by its light.

The soul until now had well experienced all these luminous graces, but its waters have not yet been alive or vivifying. Why is it said that *God created in the waters different animals, each after his kind*, and according to the quality of the waters? The reason is, that, as we have already remarked, there are two kinds of waters, sweet and bitter. The bitter are made alive; for it is only now that the soul begins to discover that there is a germ of life in the bitterness and death that have carried it away, thus causing it to love even the bitterness itself, seeing it altogether of another extent and use from the sweet waters. It is these bitter waters that produce the greatest, rarest, and most precious things upon the earth; and it is now that the soul, having perfect discernment, prefers by its own choice bitterness to the greatest sweetness.

These sweetnesses and graces, however, continue to be living and animated. They are no longer simply lights, discovering the truth of objects without giving them; but they are vivifying flowings bringing into the soul a living principle. Then it feels itself animated by a secret and profound life, which does not leave it for a moment, even in its employments; this life is no other than charity, which is already in this soul in an eminent degree, and produces in it a germ of immortality. It is this that makes the foundation of life and grace, and of the complete and intimate presence of God. This is what operates the intimate union, but not yet the essential.

Besides this, God creates in the bottom of the heart, or rather in the highest point of the spirit, birds which fly in the consecrated airs of Divinity. These birds are sublime and elevated conceptions, but they pass so quickly, and stay so short, that they leave no trace behind; and there is this difference between what is performed in faith and what takes place under the other lights: that the others can be discerned and explained, and remain distinct in the mind: We can tell them when we see them, and make them present with us, in order to relate them. It is different with the former; they pass so quickly, that they leave no trace or remains in the imagination: this is why we can neither picture them to ourselves, nor form any idea of them whatever. Nevertheless as birds, showing themselves only by their flights, remain really in the air, where they are better heard than seen; so also, souls enlightened by the light of Faith possess in themselves these knowledges, without distinguishing them otherwise than by their song—that is to say, when the necessity arises, when we must speak, or write, or otherwise make use of them—then we see that we possess those things without conceiving that we have them; just as the birds remain concealed in their habitations, and manifest themselves only by their voice.

God bids these living animals *increase and multiply*. They increase, and are multiplied to infinity, not according to the cognizance of the possessor; for they are either shut up and hid in the waters, or lost in the air, and so high up in the supreme part, that they are completely lost to sight from the lowest.

This is the beginning and consummation of the fifth state, which forms the *fifth* day or degree of the interior Christian.

24. *God said also, Let the earth bring forth living animals according to their kind, the tame animals, the reptiles, the wild beasts of the earth according to their kind. And it was so.*

25. *God made the beasts of the earth according to their kind, the tame animals, and all the reptiles, each according to its kind. And God saw that that was good.*

When the superior part has attained to the highest pinnacle of the sublimest knowledges, then the fifth day is in its consummation, and the soul seems to itself no more to adhere to the earth (for in these last days *it* has no longer been spoken of, but light, knowledge, ardours, and love). When it is thus lost in a sea of life, and in a perfect disengagement from everything material and earthly, it is greatly astonished to see being born from its earth *animals of every kind*, who crowd round its feet, and appropriate the beautiful verdures with which it is decked, to make for themselves pasture grounds. In fine, after having been the throne of God, it finds itself the footstool of animals. Oh, state very different from the others! Nevertheless, 'tis the same God, who did the first, that operates here also. Until then we do not see the use of these things; on the contrary, they appear to spoil the earth, and to detract somewhat from its beauty; it is, nevertheless, its principal ornament, and these animals are something nobler than the plants that decorate it so much, and which now serve for their nourishment. This is the state of man when it pleases God to raise him to the highest pinnacle of his perfection, robbing him for a time of the sight of the beauties He puts into him, to let him see only terrestrial and animal operations. Nevertheless these operations are both living and vivifying; it is necessary that the *earth*, the inferior part, should also produce works of *life*. But, it will be said, all these plants with which it was decked, were they not animated? 'Tis true they had a vegetable life, but they had not a sensitive one. It is this life that must be communicated to the interior soul, no longer for the evil, but for the good; for here it is given to glorify God by the sense, there being nothing in us so poor or so low but can and ought to render some glory to its God. This man, then, who for so long had been *insensible*, is quite astonished to see himself become *sensible* again; and it surprises him all the more, as he had believed himself deprived of sensation for ever. It is necessary, however, that he should become *sensible*, but his sensation will hereafter become so purified, that it will serve him, not contrary to the will of his Creator, but in accordance with it.

Thus, then, *animals of every kind are created upon this earth.* There are carnivorous *beasts* and *reptiles*. What! This imagination that previously represented only agreeable things, luminous, and divine; this spirit that was filled with such sublime knowledges, sees itself full of reptiles and unclean animals! Will it not readily say, like another St. Peter, *I have never eaten*

Chapter I.

anything that is impure or unclean, and I will not do it. But it was said to him, *What the Lord hath cleansed, call not that impure*—that is to say, that these things are good and holy, inasmuch as they have emanated from their Creator; but the only impurity that makes them unclean is within ourselves. God makes use, however, of the troubles that these things cause us, to free us from whatever impurity there is in the *sensible*, in order to spiritualise it by degrees; and He does this only by seeming to sully it. The cattle represent our outward nature, which is extremely troublesome when it is in revolt against its Creator, but becomes extremely useful when entirely subjected to Him. There is nothing in us but in the order of our creation would be very excellent, and it is only rendered hurtful by the abuse sin has made of it. These animals, coming from the hands of God, possessed nothing but what was useful and agreeable, for they were in perfect submission to man, being in the order of their creation; they have only become hurtful to him by his own revolt, which has raised them up against him; the revolt of our spirit causes that of the flesh. But God, out of His infinite goodness, uses this very rebellion of the flesh against the spirit to render subject to Him the spirit, which has no sooner entered into perfect submission to its God, than the flesh is made subject also. *God saw that this was good*, it being of infinite use to man in order to annihilate, humiliate, and destroy him.

Many will be astonished, without doubt, that I should attribute to man states and processes that happened before even his formation, but there need be no surprise if attention is paid to two things; the one is, that (as we have already observed) nothing has passed in the universal world but takes place within man in particular, so that the conduct God has exercised in this great universe, in its creation, is still observed towards man for his reformation into the order of grace; the other is, that all that took place, in the innocence of nature, before the creation of man, who corrupted it, passes within the same man, to reinstate him, by the means of grace, into an innocence abundantly restored by his Redeemer. Therefore, without doing violence to anything, we find that, as the world has had seven ages, including that of its consummation, so also man has seven ages of grace relating to the state of innocence in nature, and which, being consummated in him, render him innocent, through grace, as much as it is possible to be so in this life. We can have no difficulty in believing this, since, according to St. Paul, it is not with grace as with sin, for many are dead to the truth through the sin of one; but grace and the gift of God have abounded much more unto many by the grace of one man, Jesus Christ. The redemption, then, of Jesus Christ being superabundant, has restored to man much more than sin had ravished from him. If it please God we shall explain, moreover, how this is wrought, and how there is nothing in it contrary to the common thought of the Church.

> 26. *And God said, Let us make man in our image, after our likeness: and let him have dominion over the fish of the sea, and over the birds of the heaven, and over the cattle, and over all the earth, and over every creeping thing that creepeth upon the earth.*

When man has arrived at this point, then the *image of his God* is truly renewed in him; this image that had been spoiled and disfigured by sin is found perfectly re-established. What is this image of God? It is none other than Jesus Christ, who, being the living image of His Father, delights to retrace Himself in man, and to fully express Himself there. Thence we can see the design of the creation, and also that of the redemption. God, at the creation, made all things for man, but man He made for Himself. And as He created him after all the other creatures, as *their* crown and end; so there was only God before and after man, that *he* might tend to no other conclusion than Him. Man was the end of all the rest, but he had no other end than God. *God* then *created man in His image*—that is to say, He re-traced in him His image, which is His Son and Word, impressing upon him His Spirit; and as His delights were to dwell with the children of men, and His Son being the only object of His regards, seeing that He can take pleasure in no other than Him (for if He delights in some creature, it is only by His Son), it was necessary that, before taking man into His delights, He should make him *in His image*, imprinting upon him the character of His Word, without which He could not take pleasure in him. This was, then, the end of creation, to make images of the Word in all men, in whom the Divinity would be expressed, and who might represent it, as a spotless mirror represents the object exposed to it.

But man through sin having disfigured this beautiful image,

it was the design of the redemption that God, who delights so entirely in His Word, not being able to suffer men in whom this image had once been graven to perish, and lose at the same time for ever the image of His Word and the characters of the Divinity, was willing that His Word should come to restore it. For it is the Word-God alone that can retrace Himself—none but He can do it—and it was for that He was made man; just as we see that when a mirror has lost the object it reflected, the distant object must needs approach it, without which it could never be represented. It was necessary, then, that Jesus Christ should come into man, so that man, never more losing this Divine object, should no longer lose the image and character of the Divinity. I know that the image of God is graven so deeply in man that he can never lose it, although sin may cover it, and infinitely disfigure and sully it; and it is this that causes God's sorrow for the loss of men, and which renders Him so desirous of their salvation. All that is wrought in the soul is but to discover and renew this image; and its restoration is no sooner achieved, than man is replaced in his state of innocence. It was this that made the prophet-king cry, "I will behold Thy face in justice; I shall be satisfied when Thy glory shall appear." As if he had said, "I will behold Thy face in the justice I have received of Thee, and I shall be satisfied when Thy glory shall appear in me by Thine image which Thou hast there renewed."

It must be observed that God, in creating man, made him king over all the animals, and put them all under subjection to him, so that in this universe he had dominion over all that was not God, and was ruled by Him alone; but when through sin man rebelled against his God, all the creatures that God had subjected to him rose up against him, which made him by his sin thus change not only the particular order of His creation, but the general order of this great universe—I mean in what was subject to him.

27. *So God created man in His own image, in the image of God created He him; male and female created He them.*

God created man in His own image, making him one and simple like Himself. He cannot re-enter this first state of innocence if he does not return to this first likeness in simplicity and perfect unity, which can only be performed by quitting the multiplicity of the creature and its operations, to enter again into the unity of God, which alone can render man perfectly like unto Him.

28. *He blessed them, and said to them, Increase and multiply, replenish the earth and subdue it; and have dominion over the fish of the sea, over the birds of the heaven, and over all the animals that move upon the earth.*
29. *God said again, I have given you all the herbs bearing their seeds upon the earth, and all the trees containing within themselves the seed of their kind, that they may serve you for food.*
30. *And to all the animals of the earth, to all the birds of the heaven, to everything that moves upon the earth and is living, that they may have wherewith to feed upon. And it was so.*
31. *Now God saw all the things that He had made, and they were very good. And of the evening and the morning was made the sixth day.*

God wishes this man to *increase and multiply*—that is to say, that this image of the Word *should spread over all the earth*, so that there may be no place where He may not be delighted by the sight of His image imprinted in His creatures. Before man was created, it is said that the earth was void. How was it void, since there is no place that is not filled with the immensity of God? Ah, it is void in the eyes of God when it does not yet bear these noble creatures that are the living images of His Son. He wills, then, that this image should increase and be multiplied throughout all the earth; and wherefore that, O my Great God? It is, He says, that My delights may be multiplied; for since man bears My image, and My Word has been imprinted in him, all men are to Me places of delight.

God, as it has been said, had made all things for man; therefore He gives him dominion over them. And whence comes this sovereignty of man over all the other animals? It is by virtue of the image of the Divinity within him. This image is the expression of His Word in man. Now Jesus Christ says, "All power is given Me in heaven and earth;" so man, who was His figure and living image, had all power on the earth; and his power was so much the greater as the flowing of the Word was more abundant within him.

Although we lose this power through sin, as well as the image of the Word is disfigured within us by crime, nevertheless, when the image of Jesus Christ is perfectly renewed in us, He possesses complete power over us, and so great, that we will not nor even can any longer resist Him—not from an absolute powerlessness, but from an impotency caused by the order reestablished in us, which having taken away from our wills not only rebellion, but even repugnance to do the will of God, we find ourselves so consolidated by resignation, by the union and transformation of our own will into that of God, that no more self-will is found in us; but we will only what God wills, and the will of God is become our own.

That it is possible for this to happen in this life is incontestable, since Jesus Christ has commanded us to ask in the "Lord's Prayer" that His will be done on earth as in heaven. If we could not experience this losing of our will into God's in this life, as the blessed in heaven possess it, Jesus Christ would not have bid us ask it; for would He have bid us ask a chimera? Or would He have asked it Himself for us when He made that admirable prayer, "My Father, may they be one, as we are one"? It is certain that this perfect unity cannot exist without the total loss of all will in opposition to God. Now it is only in him who has no longer any will or resistance of his own that Jesus Christ can say in the highest sense: "All power is given Me in heaven and earth."

This is a fruit of the Redemption, that man having attained this state, through the application of the blood of Jesus Christ, resumes his right of dominion over the other creatures, of which he is the end; for he rules everything in God, thus possessing everything in himself. This is what God desires to make apparent, when saints have been seen with astonishment to command and render obedient to them the most untameable animals, and even in opposition to the nature of the elements, as when the fire served for bath and refreshment to those whose love of their God made them rather even lose their life than live out of His will, or because they could not live safely without becoming disobedient to Him, or even because they preferred death to not pleasing Him enough.

Oh grandeur!—oh power of Jesus Christ in man, and of man in Jesus Christ, how admirable you are, but how little are you known! We all bear the name of Christians, and yet we are anything but that, since we do not know even what it is to be such. Christians, bearing the most beautiful name that ever was, learn to become Christians, and ye shall learn your greatness and your nobleness; you shall enter into a just ambition to do nothing unworthy of your birth. Oh chivalrous Christians, shedding so much blood for a false point of honour! If you would comprehend what it is to be Christians, how many lives would ye not give (if you had them) to preserve this glorious quality, and to do nothing unworthy of it? But, alas! people are ignorant of the truth and spirit of the Christian religion; they stop only at the superficial, without fathoming its essential, and thus they lose advantages without end. Ah, man is created king, and he would be a king infinitely happy, if he would allow to be renewed in him the image of Jesus Christ. Yet he ever remains a slave, for he makes his royalty consist in leading himself, instead of placing it in the dependence he owes to his God, in submission to His entire will, obedience to His conduct, and, in fine, bearing with reverence all His operations, whether gratifying or crucifying; for it may now be seen, that what has led man up to so high a state, has not been his own industry, but God's goodness alone, and the faithfulness not to resist Him. All that we can do by ourselves is to resist God, and is evil (as we shall see hereafter); and man's fidelity consists in leaving God absolute master of all that he is, interiorly or exteriorly.

And God saw all the things that He had made, and they were very good, for there is nothing better for man than to see in him the image of his God; nor more glorious for God, out of Himself, than to see Himself expressed in man. It is this that causes His ardent love for man; for God delights in beholding Himself in man; and as all His delights in Himself are to contemplate Himself, thus begetting His Word; so all His pleasure out of Himself is to see His image in man, and to form there His Word. This is what St. Paul calls the formation of Jesus Christ in us.

Man, then, ought never to regard himself out of God. If he does this, it becomes the source of his disorders, and he falls into a false presumption, drawing vanity from his vileness, and becoming forgetful of his origin. But, if faithful to look on none but God, in Him he discovers with admiration his own nobleness, without fear of pride; for he sees nothing in himself out of God, but the dust of which he is formed; but in Him he sees himself God by participation; and he sees this in such a manner as to discover at the same time, that if he cease to regard himself in his Source to view himself in himself, and if he desire to attribute anything to himself, he cannot do it without usurpation; so that out of God he would be such a frightful nothing, that he loses all desire of ever more regarding himself. And what is strange, the sight of what he is out of God, does not serve to humble him; on the contrary, he becomes proud in his humiliation, and, self-deluded, he attributes to himself what does not belong to him. It is then of great consequence for man never to regard himself, but to regard solely his God, in whom he can see himself without danger. This contemplation of his God by man, which is nothing but a simple regard, or uplifting of the face of the spirit in God, attracts God's contemplation of man; for the more man contemplates his God, the more he is contemplated by Him. It is the admiration of this great marvel that makes David cry out in a transport of spirit, "O God, what is man to be the object of thy regard!"

Of the states or passages of which we have just spoken, God forms the *sixth* mystic day or degree of the interior Christian; and it is here that everything is finished for man within him. It is the consummation of the works of God in man, since the end of His labours is to retrace the image of His Son. It is now that man quits the road, to rest in the termination, and that he comes out of the mystic days to enter into the eternal and divine day.

CHAPTER II.

1. *Thus the heaven and the earth were finished, with all their ornaments.*
2. *And on the seventh day God completed the work which he had made, and he rested on the seventh day after all the works which he had made.*

It is said that *God finished his work.* What was the fulfilment and perfection of all His works? It was the work of the perfect image of His Word, after which *He rests* in Himself, and causes the soul to rest in Him, where it remains hid with Jesus Christ, its divine original.

But Scripture adds that *God completed the work which he had made*. All these words are necessary, and well express the interior. It is not said only *His work*—seeing that all the good that is wrought in man is undoubtedly of God; and that "no one can say Jesus is Lord, but by the Holy Spirit"—but it is said *His work which He had made*, to show that He had made it alone. Thus also is it with the soul arrived at the state of innocence through annihilation; God is sole operator there, acting sovereignly, without the creature resisting in anything. *And he rested on the seventh day after all the works which He had made;* by which is meant the glory, and also the repose He finds in the deified soul, which can no longer resist Him, and being one in Him, to which He has Himself led it, He has but now to rest in it, and there to take His delights.

3. *He blessed the seventh day and sanctified it, because He had rested on that day after all the works which he had created in order to make.*

God blessed and sanctified the seventh day, because on this very day He had ceased to make all His work, absorbing the soul into Himself, into His divine life, where there is nothing now but repose, although He had created this work to be made; but having arrived at the end of its creation, which is the rest in God, there is nothing now but to remain in this Divine repose in God Himself. There, the work is finished as to the agitation that carried it to its termination; but not as to the activity of enjoyment, which is continued in the repose, and which will endure eternally.

4. *Such was the beginning of the heaven and of the earth; and it is thus they were created in the day that the Lord God made them both.*
5. *And that He created every plant of the field before it appeared out of the earth, and every herb of the field before it grew; for the Lord God had not yet caused it to rain upon the earth, and there was no man to till it.*
6. *But there went up a spring from the earth, and watered the whole face of the ground.*

The beginning of the heaven and of the earth—that is to say, of the two parts of man—is God; and as his beginning, so must be his end. He must re-enter the same place whence he set out. And

Chapter II.

as in our creation everything has been performed by the Word, and nothing has been made without Him; so also in the return of man to his end, all is wrought by Jesus Christ, and nothing can be done without Him. He takes man from the beginning of the road, and does not leave him for a moment until He has brought him with Him into God, provided that we are willing wholly to abandon ourselves to His amiable conduct.

Therefore the Holy Spirit, who delights to instruct us in everything, assures us that *God created the plants without man having laboured at their cultivation.* These plants are the virtues which increase and germinate within the soul (when it abandons itself to God) before ever it works for their acquisition; for the desire itself of acquiring virtue, is a virtue which God puts into the soul by His goodness alone; and we are no sooner enlightened by the true light (which is a fruit of the free gift man makes of himself to the entire will of his God) than we know that it belongs to God alone to put into the soul all the virtues.

What, then, it will be said to me, is the care of the soul, and in what consists its fidelity, if not in the acquisition of virtues? Here is the secret, my Christian brethren: the fidelity of the soul consists in submitting itself unceasingly to its God; and as St. Peter teaches us, "*humbling ourselves under the mighty hand of God*," who alone can work in us all manner of good; in placing all our troubles in His hands—for He himself takes care of us; in renouncing ourselves continually so to remove the oppositions of nature to grace, and in so doing to resign ourselves entirely to the whole will of God, so that by this renouncement and resignation, we may give place to God to act in us in entire freedom. It is in this that man's principal work with grace consists; but for the ornament of virtues, it is God's to make it, and He does so infallibly, provided that we are faithful to coperate with His grace in these two points. And that we may not believe this grace wanting to us, it is said that God has placed a spring, representing his grace, which *rises*, so to speak, *from the earth:* for this grace is near us, always ready to flow out into our hearts. It is added that this was done before *God had caused it to rain upon the earth:* to make us admire the care that God takes of our interior when it is fully submitted to Him, and how that when some means of perfection are wanting to us by His order, there are others supplied. Thus he caused water to spring from the earth to water His plants when there fell none from heaven.

42 Genesis.

> 7. *And the Lord God formed man out of the dust of the ground, and He breathed upon his countenance the spirit of life, and man became animated and living.*

As Scripture has taught us the spiritual origin of man, which is God himself, it now desires to show us also his natural origin; therefore it teaches us of what substance he was formed, so that he may see what he is by his nature. All that is good in him is of God and belongs to Him; all that he is by himself is only vileness and baseness. Nevertheless, as there are two states in man, the one of his creation, in the natural order; the other of regeneration, in the spiritual; it is certain that, after God has formed the interior man of the dust, which is the state of his own abjection, to which he is reduced in the vileness and baseness of the clay—his origin, He out of this dust creates a new man, and then breathes into him His own *spirit*, and not a particular spirit, so that there is no other spirit than God's animating and moving him; but this is only wrought through annihilation.

> 8. *Now the Lord God had planted from the beginning a delightful garden into which He put the man whom He had formed.*

God forthwith places man in the *paradise of delights*. By this is meant the sweetness of the passive state of light, of love, and of the sensible presence of God, which is the greatest of all the joys that can be had in this life.

> 9. *The Lord God had also brought out of the ground every kind of tree, beautiful to the sight, and whose fruit was pleasant to eat, and the tree of life in the midst of the paradise, with the tree of the knowledge of good and evil.*
>
> 10. *There flowed out of this place of delights a river, which watered the paradise, and thence divided into four streams.*

In this passive state everything flourishes in the soul, and the *trees* of its faculties are found all laden with the practice of virtues, without the soul knowing how they have been produced in the earth of its heart. These *fruits are delicious*, for then the practice of virtues is very agreeable.

The tree of life is in the midst. This tree of life is God

Himself, who is the source of all life, and who vivifies by the Spirit of His grace the root of the man who has the happiness to be united to Him, so that he may bear nothing but the fruits of life. *The tree of the knowledge of good and evil* is Jesus Christ, who, being the Divine Wisdom, knoweth, as saith the prophet, "to refuse the evil and choose the good," and perfectly to discern in what both consist. Men for the most part are ignorant of this discernment; they "call the evil good, and the good evil:" they call the darkness light, and the light darkness. Their error and deception come from their trusting to their own lights, in place of asking from Jesus Christ the communication of His wisdom. This tree of the knowledge of good and evil must not be wanting in the paradise where man was to live, since this knowledge was absolutely necessary for him to conduct himself well. But he was to be contented with what the Divine Wisdom had communicated to him, which was more than sufficient for his conduct, and not to carry his ambition to desire to penetrate secrets that God willed to be concealed from him, and whose curious and magnificent research served but to blind him.

The river that watered the paradise of delights, which is the interior flower-garden of our soul, is the grace that flows into the heart of the just: and this grace *is divided into four portions*, either because it takes different names, according to its different effects, although it is always the same grace in its source; or to be diffused over all the faculties and actions of man, thus these four rivers come forth from the place of delights to water the earth; which shows us, moreover, that the grace has been merited for us by Jesus Christ, and that the very graces given to Adam after his fall were accorded to him in view of Jesus Christ, and by the merit of His redemption.

11. *The first is called Pison: this is that which compasseth the whole land of Havilah, where there is gold.*
12. *And the gold of that land is excellent; there is also bdellium and the onyx stone.*
13. *The second river is called Gihon; this is that which winds through all the land of Ethiopia.*
14. *The third river is called Tigris, which goeth towards the Assyrians. And the fourth river is Euphrates.*

The first of these rivers is the first grace given us by the means of baptism; it is thence that there comes *very excellent gold*, which is pure charity, and which is there communicated to us; *bdellium* signifies hope; and the *onyx stone* faith. Now it is certain that with this first grace infused into us by baptism, the three Divine virtues are also infused. The *second* is a river that *winds about* in the earth of our soul and its faculties, and it is the augmentation of grace which increases by diverse windings, for it grows by degrees, until it has conducted us to its limit. *The third* designates the gratuitous graces given for others; thus the Tigris (Heddekel) *goes to diffuse itself over the Assyrians*—that is to say, over entire peoples. *The fourth* marks to us the final perseverance which conducts to the eternal life, and the particular effect of which is to bring us back efficaciously into our birthplace; being a grace not only sanctifying, but also of consummation.

15. *The Lord God then took the man, and placed him in the paradise of delights, to till it and keep it.*
16. *And He gave him this commandment, saying, Eat of the fruits of all the trees of the paradise.*
17. *But eat not that of the tree of the knowledge of good and evil. For in the day that thou eatest thereof, thou shalt surely die.*

After *God has put man into* this *paradise of delights*, which is the centre of his soul, and has given him His grace to overflowing, and a grace which protects him everywhere, so that he cannot fall away without a notable infidelity; after, I say, having loaded him with such great gifts, He desires him to *dress and keep the paradise*. It is in this that the soul's fidelity consists, to dress and keep what God has confided to it.

What is this *keeping*, my dear brethren? Learn it of Jesus Christ: "Watch and pray," said He, "that ye enter not into temptation; for the spirit is willing, but the flesh is weak." We must, then, keep this earth by watching, and watching on God continually; for this is the kind of watching that God desires of us, that it may be always sustained by prayer, as David said, "I will watch on thee, from early dawn; for it is in vain that we watch over the safety of our city, if the Lord keep it not Himself." But, it will be said, if I keep not watch over myself, and thus neglecting myself, I am content to wait on God alone, I shall be surprised by mine enemies. It is quite

Chapter II.

the contrary; for so soon as we forget ourselves to think only on God, the love that He bears to us makes Him take the more care over us; for He never allows Himself to be conquered in love, although He suffers Himself to be conquered by love. Are we not much better guarded by the strong and mighty Protector than by ourselves? Whatever care we may exercise watching over ourselves, it is certain that a stronger than we would disarm us, and seize upon the very things we were guarding so carefully. But if we put all our affairs into the hands of God, shall we not be able to say with the utmost confidence, like another St. Michael, "Who is mightier than God?"

God wishes also that we *cultivate* this delicious paradise of our interior. And what is this cultivation? Our Divine Master will teach us: "Deny yourselves (says He), and take up your cross daily." To deny ourselves unceasingly in all that nature might desire contrary to God, and resign ourselves correspondingly, so as to bear equally the many crosses, pains, and difficulties that God permits to happen to us,—this is the work of man, who, aided by the abundant waters of grace, which fail him never, dwells in the order of the will of God, and arrives thus at his end.

God permits man to *taste of all* those delights represented by the *fruits*—that is to say, of all the virtues—*but He forbids him that of the knowledge of good and evil*, which is the usurpation of our own conduct to the prejudice of the reign of Jesus Christ over us. *If you taste of it*, He says, *ye shall die;* for it is thus that we seize upon what belongs to God alone, and attribute it to ourselves, regarding as a fruit of our cares what comes from His pure goodness. And as every tree that is not grafted into Jesus Christ cannot bear good fruit, so all good fruit comes necessarily from Him, in whom we are grafted, that He Himself may bring forth fruit in us. Now he who desires to conduct himself, and who would withdraw himself from the dominion of Jesus Christ, attributing to himself by his reflection the good that God does in him by Jesus Christ our Lord, seizes upon it with complacency; and it is thus that in so marvellous a state of grace we give entrance to sin, curiosity, and self-looking into the goods of God, bringing death to it.

Although it is said, *the day that thou eatest thereof thou shalt die*, the soul does not die, on that account, the very day it commits the usurpation (I mean here not the death of sin, but the state of mystic death). It does not die, I say, this very day—it would be too happy—but it is condemned to die, and it is from that time that its punishment begins: as Adam did not die immediately after he had sinned, but he was from that moment destined to death, into the labour of which he straightway entered. It is said in the text, *ye shall surely die:* which means that God is not content with a half death, nor a thousand deaths, or mortifications, but it is necessary that a real and veritable death follow, without which there is no true death, but only an image of it.

> 18. *And the Lord God said: It is not good that man should be alone. Let us make for him an aid like unto him.*

This can be understood of the human nature that God has desired to unite to the Divine in Jesus Christ by the person of the Word His Son. For a God cannot suffer or satisfy, and man being too feeble to merit with justice the redemption of a world, the human nature has been given as an *aid* to the Divine, so as to work most perfectly the redemption of the human race by the Man-God. It is also the figure of the union of Jesus Christ with His Church, which, like a fruitful mother, must yield Him an infinity of children as the fruit of His blood, and also as a faithful spouse, must contribute with Him to their sanctification and salvation. It is moreover the symbol of the gracious union that God makes of certain persons in this life, to perpetuate it in the Heavens, rendering them companions in destiny, in labours, and crosses, and making them act in concert, and with uniformity of grace, as much for their perfection as for the salvation of many.

> 19. *And the Lord God formed out of the ground every beast of the field, and every bird of the heaven, and brought them unto Adam to see what he would call them. And the name that Adam gave unto every animal was its true name.*
> 20. *He called every animal by its proper name, the birds of the heaven and the beasts of the earth. But for Adam there was found no aid like unto him.*
> 21. *And the Lord God caused a deep sleep to fall upon Adam, and while he slept, He took out one of his ribs, and put flesh in the place thereof.*

The power of Adam over all the animals in the state of innocence, is a proof of the submission of all the creatures to man, and of that of man to his God: as their revolt is also a mark of his own. *God brings all the animals to Adam that he may give them names* agreeable to their nature, to show that He made him king of the animals as well as of his faculties, senses, and passions, over which the innocent man ruled absolutely: but the criminal man being subject to his passions, it is the same with all the rest. Adam being the figure of Jesus Christ, it was to Him as Adam that the *animals* (representing the animal part of man and its die r ent passions) were to be rendered subject: and the *name* so suitable that He gives them, is the sure witness that it is Jesus Christ alone who can subject to Himself the passions of man, in rebellion through sin: so also the *birds of the heaven* designate the noblest parts of the soul, its faculties, and all that belongs to them: everything being re-instated in the order of its creation only through the grace of the Redeemer.

Scripture adds, that although Adam, figure of Jesus Christ, had given so fit names to the animals, and they were all subject to him as their king, the birds of the heaven as well as the beasts of the earth, *yet he had no aid like to him.* This is explained of Jesus Christ in two ways: the first that although everything had been made by Him as the Word, and without Him was there nothing made, nevertheless this Divine Word had no *aid* like unto Him: for although He was the image of His Father, and the source and origin of all creatures, He had extended His image only in the creation of man, and this image after its corruption resembled Him no longer. And even although the human nature at the time of Adam's innocence was a living image of the Word, it is certain that it had not the perfection of that of Jesus Christ. God then in saying *Let us make an aid like unto him* had in view the hypostatic union of the Word and the human nature which was an *aid like unto Him,* but so fit, that they were to work together for the salvation of the human race, which could not be wrought without their union, the greatest of all the works of God. This aid was rendered so like unto Him, that of two natures so different in themselves, as the Divine and human, there was made but one person alone in Jesus Christ.

The other manner of explaining it is of Jesus Christ and His Church. Before the birth of the Church, there was found no aid like to Jesus Christ, but after its formation there was a veritable aid to Jesus Christ and such as works with Him for the salvation of men, having with Him but one sole and only will.

Could it be more like Him, this all holy *aid*, than to be "glorious without spot or wrinkle or any defect?"

But how was this aid formed? *God sent a sleep* to the new Adam. This sleep came to Him on the bed of the cross; there from His opened side came forth a daughter and spouse whose beauty was so perfect, that she possessed nothing unworthy of Him who was her Father, as He was also to become her Husband. The union of Jesus Christ and His Church is so close, in order to work with one accord, and in the one same spirit and will for the salvation of men, that whoever belongs not to the Church cannot appertain to Jesus Christ, and none can belong to Him that is not a child of His Church. By the bond of this marriage, as unique as legitimate, no one is a true son of the Church, if he is not a child of Jesus Christ: and no one is conceived of Jesus Christ, but must be brought forth by His Church.

Now as Jesus Christ was in the ideas of God from the creation of the world, and as all the graces that were accorded to men since they had need of a Redeemer, were given them in view of His merits, the Church likewise was from that time associated with Him for the regeneration of as many children, as were to be born from the blood of the Saviour, which in this sense was shed from the beginning of the world, and for the sanctification of all the chosen whom God the Father had given to His Son as the price of his death.

22. *And the Lord God formed woman out of the rib which He had taken from Adam, and brought her to him.*

23. *And Adam said: Behold now bone of my bones, and flesh of my flesh: she shall be called drawn from man, for she was taken out of man.*

24. *Therefore shall the man leave his father and mother and cleave unto his wife, and they shall be two in one flesh.*

25. *Now Adam and his wife were then both naked, and they were not ashamed.*

It was from the side of Jesus Christ, opened upon the cross, and from the blood and water that flowed out, that the Church was drawn. This union of Adam and Eve was also the figure of the mystical marriage of the soul with Jesus Christ: it is in the sorrows of Calvary, and not in the sweetnesses of Tabor that

Chapter II.

it is made: and the union of the soul with its Heavenly Spouse becomes so close, that it is then that Jesus Christ says: *It is flesh of my flesh and bone of my bones*. For it becomes so much one spirit with the Word, that it finds within itself nothing now but the Word, and as it came out from Him, it finds itself united to Him without a medium, and sees itself having for spouse Him who before was its Father. This union of the soul with Jesus Christ becomes so intimate, that although wrought in the most extreme crosses and griefs, nevertheless, these pains, far from breaking the union, draw it all the closer.

It is added, that *God gave this woman to Adam:* which shows that this union can never be wrought by the creature, being a work of God alone, and not of the will of man, who has no other part therein than that of acceptation and faithfully following all the Divine movements.

What, then, is to make the soul faithful in corresponding to what the Spouse has done for it, and to enjoy the ineffable delights of the marriage of the Lamb? It must *leave its father and mother*, without which the spiritual marriage will never be consummated in it. Who is this *father* and this *mother*, if not the old Adam and the corrupt nature, which must be left absolutely? It is in quitting ourselves by renouncement, which operates the total death, that we reach the marriage of the Lamb, and we will never arrive there by any other way. Those who are all full of themselves and imagine themselves arrived at this spiritual and divine marriage, are infinitely deceived. And if Jesus Christ was obliged to leave the bosom of His Father to espouse our nature, do we believe ourselves able to espouse Him without quitting ourselves? No, it can never be.

It is also added, that *they were both naked*, to wit, Adam and his wife, and *they were not ashamed:* which shows the perfect destitution of all self-will, self-sight, of all our own turnings and windings, of all self-righteousness, which is the state of a soul that has wholly forsaken itself. These souls live in so great a forgetfulness of themselves, that they are not ashamed of their spiritual nakedness, that is to say, of the extreme poverty of spirit and of the profound abjection to which they are reduced, not being able to see it or think of it, on account of their absorption and loss in God, which is a state of transformation and may be well called a state of true innocence.

CHAPTER III.

4. The serpent said to the woman, ye shall not surely die.

5. But God knoweth that so soon as ye shall eat of this fruit your eyes will be opened, and as gods shall ye know good and evil.

6. And the woman saw that the fruit of this tree was good to eat, and beautiful and pleasant to the sight. And she took of the fruit, and did eat, and gave of it to her husband, who did eat of it with her.

Self-love under the figure of the serpent, desires to show the soul the advantage there would be in going to God by another road than that of blind *abandon* to His conduct, without regard to self: and that if they would throw off obedience to God and the total abandon (in which they are in an entire destitution through the loss of their will into God), they *would know* all things, would be assured of their ways, and would not die.

The inferior part, represented by the *woman, looks upon this* fruit of science and knowledge, which appears to her much more beautiful than this ignorant innocence, in which she is kept by the grandeur of her grace: she *presents it to her husband*, denoting the superior part: he accepts and tastes of it: and by so doing, he withdraws his will from that of God, throws off His sway, comes out of his blind *abandon*, and sins in reality.

7. Then the eyes of both were opened, and they knew that they were naked, and they twined fig leaves together to cover themselves.

The eyes of both were *opened* by sin: these poor deluded ones fell into confusion, *and saw that they were naked*, for having lost their innocence, which served for clothing to them, and possessing no good of their own, since all the good that was in them belonged to God, there remained for them only a shameful nakedness, which they endeavoured to *cover*, not being able to bear it themselves, and fearing to appear before God.

8. And they hid themselves amongst the trees of the garden from before the face of God.

9. The Lord God called unto Adam, and said unto him: Where art thou?

Chapter III.

In this they commit two notable faults: first, that after their fall they remove themselves still further from God, for they *are ashamed of themselves:* second, that they have recourse to artifice to *cover themselves,* and believe they can fully hide their nakedness by their own industry, which consists only in feeble actions of virtue, like to leaves. To go away from God after the fall, is to come out of the way of abandon to resume and commit ourselves to the human guidance. But God, whose goodness is infinite, goes to seek for them, calls them back from their wanderings, *asks them where they are,* and what has become of them.

> 10. *And he answered, I heard Thy voice in the Paradise, and was afraid because of my nakedness, and hid myself.*

He *fears* to appear before God, *for he is naked.* This is the false humility of those who withdraw from the *abandon* after their fall, under pretext that they are not worthy of remaining in it, or of any longer treating so familiarly with God.

> 11. *And the Lord said: How hast thou learned that thou art naked, unless thou hast eaten of the tree whereof I commanded thee not to eat.*

God admirably instructs these two, showing them that their shameful nakedness comes only from their disobedience, and from their having desired to penetrate His conduct, the knowledge of which is reserved for Him alone. Therefore the serpent promised them, that when they had this knowledge they would be like to God. To be desirous of knowing where God conducts us, and the secret of His designs over us, is to forestall His rights, and to do Him an injury: on the contrary, to blindly abandon ourselves to Him, is the most sure witness of love, and the true worship that renders to Him His due.

> 17. *God said unto Adam: Because thou hast hearkened unto the voice of thy wife, and hast eaten of the fruit of which I forbade thee to eat, the earth shall be cursed in thy work; by labour shalt thou live from it all the days of thy life.*
> 18. *It shall bring forth for thee thorns and thistles, and thou shalt eat of the herb of the field.*

Here is the punishment of the superior part for having followed the temptation of the inferior and self-love. These prevaricators are condemned to *labour* with many toils and very little fruit, the earth being cursed in their work: that is to say, that this beautiful interior field, which under God's cultivation yielded infinite fruits, scarcely produces anything more than thorns from the time it falls into the hands of Adam.

> 19. *In the sweat of thy face shalt thou eat bread until thou return into the ground from which thou wast taken. For dust thou art, and unto dust thou shalt return.*

God condemns these two parts, or souls, to many toils and pains, until through total annihilation wrought by death, rottenness and the dust, they have returned as into the state of nothingness, in which they were when God created them: then will he make new creatures of them.

> 22. *God said: Behold Adam has become like one of us, knowing good and evil. Let us beware that he put not forth his hand upon the tree of life, lest taking of its fruit, he eat thereof, and live for ever.*

This passage admirably shows how this *knowledge of good and evil*, which is that of the works of God in us, preserves the self-life of the soul, and prevents its interior death: therefore God drives Adam from the place of delights, so that *he may no longer put forth his hand upon this tree*, and that there may remain to him no knowledge that maintains his life and hinders his death; for the remedy for his evil can only be found in his death, by which, losing his proper and infected life he re-enters into the divine life, which had been communicated to him by the original justice. If he did not die to himself, he could not live again in God. The trouble and concern after the fall, and which end often in despair, are the effects of a false humility. When we are so greatly afflicted and distressed after some fault, there must be a great deal of pride and self-love in us. As on the contrary, it is the fruit of a true humility to remain calm and tranquil in our abjection, after having fallen into some shortcoming even of consequence, quietly abandoning ourselves to God, to be raised again out of His mercy, submitting ourselves by a great sacrifice to all the uses it will please Him to make of it.

CHAPTER IV.

13. *Cain said unto the Lord: My iniquity is too great to be pardoned.*
14. *Thou drivest me this day from off the earth, and from Thy face shall I be hid. A fugitive and a vagabond shall I be throughout all the world, and every one that findeth me shall slay me.*

What is it to *fly from before God*, if not to withdraw from the *abandon*, to wander as a *fugitive* in all the human ways, and to go astray on the earth in the paths of vanity, after quitting the Supreme Truth, who is God alone, and the infallible attachment that held us to Him in total *abandon?* Truly, whoever strays thus from the Almighty protector, is exposed every moment to the fury of his enemies.

CHAPTER VI.

2. *And the sons of God saw the daughters of men that they were fair, and they took unto themselves wives of all that pleased them.*
3. *And God said: My spirit shall no longer dwell with man, for he is flesh, and his time shall be not more than an hundred and twenty years.*

The sons of God are the productions of His grace in souls, and which are all pure in His hands, but they are no sooner in man, than they are changed by the mingling of the creature, which rashly desires to alloy the productions of nature with those of grace, and in order to better succeed in it, it seeks in nature *whatever is most pleasing to it;* and in attributing it to grace, it gives to nature what appertains to grace, and to grace what is of nature. God, angered at the abuse that is made of His graces, withdraws them, and declares, that *His spirit will no longer dwell with man, because he has become wholly carnal and earthly:* the effect of which is that He takes from man all that belongs to Himself. Nothing now remaining to the creature but the operations of nature, it finds itself so hideous, that it begins to hate itself very greatly: and it would wholly despair of ever possessing the spirit of God, if there was not given to it a light, assuring it that we can come out of ourselves to enter into God: since there is a *time* for man, that is to say, a time which God shortens even, when man is left to himself, in fine, when man is man, which is well expressed by these words: *the time of man will not be more than one hundred and twenty years:* as if to say, I have set limits to his corruption. This promise leads him who desires to be faithful to his God, to yield himself up as speedily as he can be quit of himself by a continual renouncement; and it is that hope of one day being able to quit himself by a perfect renunciation, that creates all man's confidence after the sin.

4. *Now in those days there were giants upon the earth. For the sons of God having taken to wife the daughters of men, their children became the mightiest of the age and men of renown.*

The giants and monsters of pride come only from the mixing of the human and the divine. All the great men of renown in the world have been those who made fleshly wisdom triumph, concealed under a little spirituality. Oh the frightful monster! You will see persons puffed up and elevated like *giants* by the estimation they have of themselves, on account of their natural talents accompanied by some spiritual maxims: and who nevertheless are buried in nature, and in the secret esteem of their own conduct. They are, however, the extraordinary men, and of great reputation. But as for those who by dint of self-renunciation have become wholly annihilated, as for them I say, they are unknown: they are not even distinguished from other men. And how would they be distinguished amongst those *giants*, since they are so little, that they appear when near them only as ants, which they tread under foot with contempt, and regard often as useless things upon the earth? But, oh God, Thou "who resisteth the proud and giveth grace to the humble," Thou sheddest it abundantly on these little valleys fitted to contain it, whilst these pompous and superb mountains cannot receive a drop without allowing it to flow down upon these little ones, who acknowledge themselves so much the more unworthy of it, the more they are filled with it.

Chapter VI.

5. *And God saw that the wickedness of men was extreme upon the earth, and that all the thoughts of their hearts turned to evil continually.*
6. *And He repented to have made man upon the earth, and it grieved Him to the heart.*
7. *And He said: I will cut off from the earth man which I have created, from man even to the animals, from the reptiles even to the birds of the heaven; for it repenteth me that I have made them.*

The expression of Scripture is admirable. Can God *repent* or be susceptible of *grief?* It is to express how much He holds in horror the abuse that is made of his graces, and how much the mingling of the flesh with the spirit displeases Him. God has an extreme desire to communicate His graces to men: He has His hands always filled ready to heap them upon them: they are, as says the Spouse, "all of gold beautifully fashioned and full of hyacinths:" denoting by that, that the excess of His love makes Him distribute His graces with so much profusion, that He cannot withhold them. But, inasmuch as His liberality is great on behalf of men, so the abuse they make of His favours offends Him so much that *He is grieved at heart*. And why? for He bears all men in the depths of His heart, as He says Himself: so that the ingratitude of man and the abuse of His graces, are what wound Him most. What then does He do? He takes away from this man all that He had given him: and with the very arm by which He had conferred favours on him, He takes the avenging blade, to *exterminate* in man himself all that He had wrought there. Oh ungrateful man, it is thy pride and propriety that make of God the creator God the avenger, and oblige Him to leave nothing in thee that He does not destroy, from the greatest to the smallest things.

8. *But Noah found grace before the Lord.*
9. *Noah was a just man, and perfect amongst all those of his time, and he walked with God.*

In a whole world there is found one man alone simple and little, who *found grace in the eyes of God*. And wherefore found he this grace? The reason is given by scripture in a few words: it is, *that he was just:* and this justice prevented him from ravishing from God what belonged to Him, and from being guilty of the crimes of the other men, who were criminal, being unjust, stealing from God His property to make a miserable alliance of it with nature and corruption.

It is said also of Noah, that he was *perfect amongst all the men of his time.* Whence came this perfection? It was in his *walking* always *with God:* he abandoned himself to Him, following His conduct, remaining attached to His ways, and filled with His presence. This is what formed the perfection of Noah, and would form that of all Christians if they were truly willing to walk likewise. But the opposite of that, the forgetting of God and the passion of conducting ourselves in our own will, causes all the evils, and effects the loss of men.

13. *God said unto Noah: The end of all flesh is come before me. They have filled the whole earth with iniquity, and I will destroy them with the earth.*

As man sins upon the earth, that is to say, as he abuses the body given him, making it serve sin in place of subjecting it to the spirit, God punishes him *with the earth,* using the body itself for its proper punishment, and often punishing sin by sin itself, which happens when God by a just decree delivers man to himself, and leaves him a prey to his passions: as it is said in a Psalm: "So I gave them up unto their own hearts' lust, and they walked in their own counsels."

22. *Noah then performed all that the Lord commanded him.*

Before being received into the ark of Salvation, which is God Himself, we must have *kept all His commandments,* and obeyed all His will, not only as to exterior actions, but also as to interior purity, which can only be acquired by the observation of the law of spirit and life.

CHAPTER VII.

1. *The Lord said unto Noah: Enter into the ark, thou and all thy house; for thee have I found just before me amongst all this generation.*

Chapter VII.

Throughout a whole world there is found only one *just* man worthy *to enter into the ark*,—which is God Himself. Yet there are so many people amongst us, who believe they are in God. We must be just to enter therein, that is to say, to have usurped nothing from God, or to have restored to Him all the usurpations we had made, leaving Him in Himself, and all that belongs to Him, to remain in our nothingness. This then is the justice we must have in order to be received into God by a most intimate union.

12. *The rain fell upon the earth for forty days and forty nights.*

20. *The water rose fifteen cubits higher than the summit of the mountains which it had gained.*

21. *All flesh that moved upon the earth was consumed by it, the birds, the animals, every beast, every reptile that creepeth upon the earth, and every man.*

22. *And every thing that lived, and breathed upon the earth, died.*

23. *There remained but Noah alone, and they that were with him in the ark.*

This is a beautiful figure of what takes place in the interior state, in which *everything* human and natural, whatever it be, must be entirely *submerged and drowned in the waters* of bitterness and grief, so that Noah, representing here the root of the soul, may remain *saved alone*, and may pass into God Himself. But it is necessary that these waters *rise above the highest mountains*, that is to say, that the faculties of the soul may be submerged by them. But if this state is grievous and afflicting for him who experiences it, consolation ought to be had in one thing, which is, that sin is drowned with the sinner, and *that there remains now only the just alone*, which is no other than man pre-eminently justified by his loss and annihilation.

The deluge marks also the passions and tumult of the age. All are submerged therein with the exception of those who are in God as in an ark, where they live in safety. There are few of these latter, although they may be of every sort, that is to say, of every sex, age, and condition.

We know that the ark is also the figure of the Church.

CHAPTER VIII.

1. *And God remembered Noah, and every beast, and all the cattle that were with him in the ark, and caused a wind to blow over the earth, and the waters began to recede.*
2. *The fountains of the deep and the cataracts of heaven were closed up, and the rains that fell from heaven were stopped.*
3. *And the waters flowed over the earth from one side to the other, and began to decrease after one hundred and fifty days.*
4. *And on the twenty-seventh day of the seventh month, the ark rested upon the mountains of Armenia.*

God remembers this root and centre of the soul which He had preserved alone, and unknown, amidst so strange an inundation. How comes it that Scripture makes mention here only of Noah and the beasts, and does not speak of his family? It was because all Noah's family was included in himself, and everything is saved in him : so likewise the noblest productions of the soul are saved by means of the centre. By the losing of the centre of the soul into God Himself, are lost there also all its operations, and its faculties, which seem cut short and altogether swallowed up, so much so that they lose their functions: but it is only for their salvation that God causes their loss in this manner; and He saves them only on account of the soul: therefore no distinction is made for them.

God remembers also *all the beasts:* that is to say, all that belongs to the inferior part, so as to rescue it from oppression and ruin.

It is then that *this overflowing of the waters is stopped.* It is not now the inundation of the waters of grace: they are the waters of wrath and indignation, and the torrents of vengeance, that have overflowed. But, oh Goodness of my God! Thou willest only the loss of the criminal: Thou willest only the extinction of sin in its root and branches: and Thou overwhelmest it thus only to preserve the just in true justice: that is, this beautiful portion of Divinity distributed in the soul, almost disfigured by its corrupt nature and the sin that surrounded it. The deluge is only to drown what is bad in this corrupted nature, but God preserves whatever is good, which comes immediately from Himself, and is represented by the beasts saved in the ark.

Chapter VIII.

But how does God stay this deluge, and what means does He take for this? He sends a living and vivifying *breath* of His Spirit, which dries up the waters of iniquity and gives life again, according to this beautiful passage, "Thou sendest forth, O Lord, Thy Spirit, they are created: and Thou renewest the face of the earth."

When this wind of Salvation begins to blow upon the soul, it *agitates* it at first in such a manner that it cannot at all discern whether it blows for its salvation or its ruin: when suddenly it is astonished to see *that the ark rests upon the mountains of Armenia.* That is to say, that peace and tranquility begin to appear upon the highest point and part of the spirit, where God discovers Himself by a little ray of His wisdom, making this soul comprehend that its loss is not without resource, and that there is some hope of salvation for it.

6. *And after forty days Noah opened the window of the ark, which he had made, and sent forth a raven,*

7. *Which went forth to and fro, until the waters were dried up off the earth.*

The raven signifies the proprietary soul full of its own will, which stops at everything it meets: everything forms a rest for it, but a deceiving rest, for it immediately finds unstableness there.

8. *He sent also a dove after the raven to see if the waters had ceased to cover the earth.*

9. *But the dove found no rest for the sole of her foot, for the waters covered the whole earth; and Noah put forth his hand and took her and brought her back into the ark.*

But the *dove* represents the abandoned soul, already lost and transformed in God, which comes forth from Him to act abroad if such is His will; I mean, that it comes out of its mystic repose, when Noah, in this place representing God, sends it abroad for the good of the neighbour: however, as there is nothing for it upon the earth, it finds no rest for its feet, that is to say, upon which it can lean: therefore, without stopping at anything, it returns into the mystic repose, where the Divine Noah, putting forth His hand, receives it into Himself.

This represents the annihilated state, in which the soul finds nothing more for it upon the earth.

10. *And he stayed yet other seven days: and again he sent forth the dove out of the ark.*

Seven days afterwards, representing the years of the perfect annihilation, it is *put forth again out of the ark:* and then it everywhere finds its resting place, as in the ark itself, all the world having become God for it: then it rests everywhere without stopping in any one place: and this is now the Apostolic life.

11. *And she returned unto him in the evening, bearing in her mouth an olive branch, whose leaves were green: so Noah knew that the waters were abated from off the earth.*

It bears everywhere the sign of peace, but without retaining anything of it for itself: it *carries it to* the Divine *Noah*. This soul in the Apostolic life takes nothing to itself of what it does for God: but with an admirable fidelity, it *brings* back to Him the *olive branch:* and it is then that it, and all its like, who were also shut up and confined in the ark, can come forth from it in all safety, and have no more need or means of protecting themselves from the deluge. They are no more straightened or sustained by anything created, and everything is salvation for them without any assurance of it. It is on this account that it is known that *the waters are abated from off the earth:* and that there is nothing more to be feared for these souls upon the earth, unless that by some dangerous turning back to themselves, they should give entrance to infidelity, which is, however, difficult in this degree.

15. *Then God spake unto Noah and said unto him,*
16. *Come out of the ark, thou and thy wife, thy sons, and thy sons' wives.*

This represents the care that God takes of souls that are abandoned to Him, and who think only of living in repose in the ark of perfect resignation. He warns them of everything in its time. This is why the care that Noah took of sending out the dove would appear useless and offensive to Providence, if it were not so mysterious as it is. Learn, oh souls, who are in the ark of God by His order, that is to say, in the mystic repose, that we must not come forth from it, for the practices of the Apostolic life, except by the same order of God, which He will point out to us every moment by His providence.

20. *Now Noah built an altar unto the Lord, and took of every animal and of every clean bird, and offered unto Him a burnt offering upon that altar.*

21. *And the Lord smelled a sweet savour, and said: I will no longer curse the ground for man's sake.*

It is then that the sacrifices of the soul have a *sweet smelling savour* for God; there is nothing more unclean or impure in them. Whilst the soul is in the ark, that is to say, in the divine repose preceding the permanent Apostolic life, it *offers* no *sacrifices*, everything having ceased with it. But from the time it is set at full liberty, it then *offers sacrifices*, whose odour is a sweet smelling savour to God: which had not been until then: for it is not said before this that the sacrifices had been of a good odour before God. Now the odour of this sacrifice is so agreeable to Him, on account of its purity and simplicity, that He is constrained to swear that He *will not any longer curse the ground:* the little faults of this soul, says God, will not any longer be disagreeable: for it is innocent, and there is no more malignity in it: there remains only to it the feebleness of its origin: I will not again take away from it this life, for it is not corrupted like the first, and it exists in me.

CHAPTER IX.

1. *And God blessed Noah and his sons, and said unto them, Be fruitful, and multiply, and replenish the earth.*

It is then that we *multiply upon the earth* by the souls that we win to Jesus Christ, to justice, and to the interior.

2. *I have brought into your hands every animal, everything that creepeth upon the earth, and every fish of the sea.*

3. *Every moving thing that liveth shall be meat for you.*

Man is re-established in a state of innocence after the afflictions of the deluge, and enjoys the advantages of it, shown by the *power* he receives over *all the animals*, and the freedom of *eating of everything*.

4. *Only of the flesh with the blood thereof shall ye not eat.*

Nevertheless there is given him a new commandment: no longer to eat not of the fruit of knowledge, or of flesh: but only *not to eat the flesh with the blood,* nor the blood separately. This division of the flesh from the blood marks the separation of the spirit from sense, which must never be united again, except in the perfect order of God, after their purification.

9. *I will establish my covenant with you, and with your seed after you.*

Then God makes a covenant with man, by the most intimate union, transforming him into Himself. This is the spiritual marriage, and cannot any more be broken.

Therefore God gives a token and sign of this covenant, and sets it in the heaven: that is to say, He renders this soul so immovable, and so strong over everything, that it can no more fear the deluge: for its transformation renders it as stable as the heaven itself is invariable, and keeps it covered from every attack.

12. *God said, This is the token of the covenant that I will establish with you, to endure for perpetual generations.*

This is the immovability, and *permanent* state of a soul, in union and transformation.

13. *I will put my bow in the clouds to be the token of the covenant which I have made with the earth.*
14. *And when I bring clouds upon the earth, then will my bow appear in the clouds.*

Though the soul be *covered with the clouds* of outward afflictions, *this sign* of thorough immovability will not cease to appear: on the contrary, it will be in the clouds themselves that it will be most remarked: thus the rainbow appears only in the cloud. This is the infallible mark of the transformed state : all those who have not yet attained to it, experiencing from time to time vicissitudes, and their immovability being not yet permanent for ever.

20. *And Noah was an husbandman, and began to till the ground, and planted the vine.*

Noah is the figure of our Lord Jesus Christ, who comes once more to *cultivate* our *earth*, which was become wild again through sin, and submerged by the waters of the deluge: barren as it was, He now renders it fruitful : He gives facility to the exterior to employ itself in every kind of good. But how does He cultivate it, and what does He plant there ? *The vine*—the figure of charity. Jesus Christ coming into the soul that has arrived in God through the loss of everything, and incarnating Himself in a mystical manner, *plants there the vine*, that is to say, in the sense of the Spouse, He there ordains charity. Now, as grapes have the property of giving everything to others, without retaining anything to themselves, so perfect charity empties the man who is filled with it, and does not allow him to possess anything that he does not distribute.

21. *And he drank of the wine, and was drunken : and he appeared naked within his tent.*

As Jesus Christ comes into the soul only to render it a participant in His states, He causes it to bear them all in a marvellous order. Jesus Christ *drank of the wine* : He drank it in the cup, and was drunken. This is understood in two ways : firstly, of the shame that He bore, as saith the Prophet, " even to being filled full of it : " secondly, of the wine of the wrath of God, which was poured forth upon him for the sins of men. It was from this dreadful cup that he asked his Father to exempt him ; " Let this cup pass from me," said he : "nevertheless let Thy will be done."

He looked upon His passion in two ways, or rather, He separated two liquors in His cup. The first was that of the shame and sufferings : and it was this that He desired to be filled full of : as He witnessed to His disciples, " that He had a great desire to eat the Passover with them before suffering." In this Passover He drank this first cup, and was so drunken, that from that moment He thought of nothing else than anticipating the torments. The other cup wsa that of the garden, and was the wrath of God upon the sins of men. Oh this was so fearful, that after drinking it, He changed this wine into blood, and sweated the blood over His whole body, as if to say, O Eternal Father, just God and avenger of a crime which merits still more chastisement and indignation than what Thou makest to appear! I drink all Thy wrath, and change it into my blood, so that my blood may assuage it on behalf of men! Let the first cup, which is that of suffering, pass to my chosen and well beloved ones: for it is only of that I say to them: "Drink of it all of ye and be drunken, my friends." But as for the cup of Thy fury, let it terminate in me, or rather, let it pass beyond, and let it go everywhere to exterminate sin, sparing the sinner."

When Jesus Christ comes into a soul truly annihilated, and no longer living in itself, but in whom He alone lives, He completes in it what was wanting in His passion, that is to say, He makes in it an extension of this same passion, and generally He intoxicates it with His first cup: but He reserves the last for the chosen souls, and He makes them drink it at two different times: one is, when He exterminates their proprieties and annihilates them; it is then that such a soul experiences nothing more in itself but the wrath and indignation of God. The other time is when it has become another Jesus Christ; oh, then it drains this cup of fury for the sins of others like Jesus Christ: but with so much horror, for God, whilst His indignation lasts, conceals from it that this is for others, and only discovers it to it afterwards, or at the most, in asking its consent. For God usually asks the consent of the soul, before making it suffer for the neighbour; and it is then that the soul is moved to sacrifice itself to the justice of God, and to all His will.

The *nakedness*, in which Noah appeared in his drunkenness, marks the state of nakedness in which the souls must remain that are intoxicated by afflictions, shame, and ignominy, as well as those who drink the cup of the wrath of God. He holds them in such an entire stripping of all the sensible and perceptible graces, of all the gifts and communications, that served them as a garment to hide what might cause them confusion, that at last they often appear in their own eyes and those of others, shamefully naked. There is seen in those persons nothing now but feebleness and impotency: being stripped by the power of God, all their miseries, which were concealed under the abundance of graces, are discovered: in fine they appear to the eyes of the creature in a most abject state. This is the state of Jesus Christ himself upon Calvary, who, not content with being intoxicated with shame and ignominy, was willing to be *naked:* and this exterior nakedness, shameful in appearance, was only the figure of the stripping of his soul, which was so great, that he even cried: "My God, my God, why hast Thou forsaken me?" Thou who art my only sustenance, why hast Thou abandoned me? As he is the example of the stripping of souls in the state of sacrifice in which He keeps them, He must also be their only consolation.

22. *And Ham, the father of Canaan, saw the nakedness of his father, and told his two brethren without.*
23. *But Shem and Japhet stretched a garment upon their shoulders, and went backwards and covered their father's nakedness.*

There are two classes of persons who *see* these souls in their *nakedness.* Some like Ham laugh at them, murmur against them, and take occasion thereby to decry the Spirit of God, seeing these persons now so feeble after having been so strong. Others, on the contrary, *covering them with the mantle of their charity,* excusing their faults, and regarding them in their source, as a stripping caused by the abundance of the wine of bitterness, grief, and shame, with which they have been intoxicated, consider that as an effect of the goodness of God, who is destroying in them sin and all its appendages, in order to dwell there alone: and these receive the blessing of God, whilst the former are punished for their temerity. We must excuse all that is excusable, and lean rather to the side of mercy than to that of severity.

CHAPTER XI.

1. *All the earth at that time was of one speech and one language.*

This is the uniformity of the souls who have come out of the deluge, who truly all speak but one language, being all taught of God: and who have but one speech, since it is the same Spirit that speaketh in them.

Genesis.

4. *They said, Let us build to ourselves a city and a tower whose top will reach heaven; and let us make to ourselves a name before we be scattered over all the earth.*

This is the picture of souls who aspire to be holy by their own works, and believe themselves able to succeed in it by their natural efforts, without perceiving their mistake. These subtlely presumptuous people amass together, and pile up practice upon practice, in order, say they, to render ourselves holy. They look for everything from their own efforts: and without considering what they are doing, they think to give law to God. Therefore Scripture says, they built of bricks and slime, showing by that, that it was all of the invention of man.

5. *Now the Lord came down to see the city and tower which the children of Adam built.*

God lowers Himself to *see* their temerity, the vanity of their works, and the productions of their caprices; because He Himself did not build.

7. *And He said: Come then, let us go down into this place, and let us there confound their language, that they may no longer understand each other.*

They change their language, because that having withdrawn from simplicity in action, they also withdraw themselves from simplicity in discourse, and God suffers them to lose this first language of innocence, which was no longer conformable to their works. This was then the beginning of trouble and confusion. Acting in the selfhood produces all the trouble and confusion of the interior. Men having lost the language of God, which is simple and unique, have all a different one.

8. *So the Lord scattered them abroad from this place over the face of the earth; and they left off building the city.*

9. *Therefore was this city called Babel; that is to say, Confusion.*

From that time they are no more united. *The Lord scatters them:* and most frequently they are constrained to *leave* everything, not being able to make any progress, nor to make themselves understood by others, nor to hear God. God recedes from them, and *scatters* them on account of their interior *confusion*, caused by their proprietary practices. The ark, constructed by the order of God, was the abode of peace: *Babel*, built by men, was the habitation of trouble and *confusion*.

29. *Abram's wife was called Sarai.*
30. *She was barren, and had no children.*

Sarai is barren in her own country: likewise the soul that is still in itself, cannot be fruitful.

CHAPTER XII.

1. *The Lord said unto Abram, Get thee out of thy country, and from thy kindred, and from thy father's house, and come into a land that I will show thee.*

This is the figure of the calling of the soul to *come out* from itself. God *speaks to it* in the depths of the heart, and instructs it that there is another *land* than that which it inhabits: and that if it is faithful to follow Him by total *abandon*, He will show it to it, and introduce it therein.

2. *Out of thee will I bring a great people: I will bless thee, and make thy name great, and thou shalt be blessed.*

God promises moreover to this soul, that when it shall have arrived at this land, which is the repose in God, it will possess a *great nation*, and will be *glorified*. He only asks of it for all this that it abandon itself to Him by the renouncement of itself, and that it allow itself to be conducted to Him in an entire destitution.

3. *And I will bless them that bless thee, and curse them that curse thee: and in thee shall all families of the earth be blessed.*

Who will not admire how much God is concerned about the souls who abandon themselves to Him, how He Himself takes in hand their defence, how that on their account He shows mercy to so many people, and the *blessings* that they draw down upon all the persons united to them ! This is so real and so true, that those who have experienced it will be ravished to see it so well pointed out under these figures, and will be charmed to see the wholly natural order in which all these things are expressed even in the ancient Scripture.

4. *So Abram departed, as the Lord had commanded him.*

Such a strict obedience as this of Abram's marks the fidelity and promptitude with which the soul ought to *come forth* from itself to follow God.

7. *The Lord appeared unto Abram, and said to him, Unto thy seed will I give this land.*

God's promises are always infallible, although they may not be performed according to the conception of him to whom they are made. Those persons who, at the beginning and during the way, have interior words or promises, ought not to stop at them, nor give their judgment on them, nor make any interpretation of them. The truth of these words is in God, and they are only rendered true for us in their accomplishment, which is very often altogether contrary to our expectation.

7. *Abram built an altar unto the Lord, who had appeared unto him.*

8. *And he passed from thence towards the mountain on the east of Bethel, and pitched his tent there, having Bethel on the west; and Hai on the east; and in this place he again built an altar unto the Lord, and called upon his name.*

9. *Abram journeyed still further, advancing towards the south.*

This *altar* which *Abram built to the Lord in the place where He had appeared to him*, instructs us that we must always offer to God sacrifices of all the graces He imparts to us, and in the very place that He gives them, receiving them only to send them back with fidelity to their origin. There are few souls who act like Abram: every one appropriates the graces of God, and retains them in Himself. This goes even so far, that we are often afflicted when He withdraws them ; we complain of it to ourselves as if He were robbing us of something of our own.

Nevertheless He only takes what belongs to Him : if we were not proprietary, although God should withdraw His favours, we would not even pay attention to it: and as we would not stop at them on their reception, but on the contrary go beyond them all, we would thus, without reflection, suffer them to be taken back again to Him who gave them. Yet we see nothing but persons lamenting over the abstraction of consolations and sensible graces, and making this pass for great interior pains ; when, nevertheless, it is no other thing than great *propriety*.

You will tell me, without doubt, that you are not afflicted at the privation of these gifts, but that what grieves you is that you fear to have given cause for this by your infidelities. Oh deceit of nature, how well you conceal yourself under pretexts ! If, my brethren, it is the fear of our infidelities that afflicts us, let us humble ourselves for these very infidelities which have given cause to God to act thus, and at the same time, let us be delighted that He should deprive us of His goods, and that He should not bestow them on us, for fear we may abuse them : we ought also to have a holy joy that He does justice to Himself. This then is the disposition of the truly humble soul ; far then from bewailing and being alarmed at these privations, and continually tiring the directors with them, we ought to be humbly joyful at these abstractions, and never desire anything other than what we possess.

It is also said that *Abram built an altar in another place :* to show that he went from sacrifice to sacrifice ; and it is added, that he *journeyed still further towards the south*—to show that he went beyond all things to go to God alone.

10. *And there came a great famine over that land.*

The abandoned soul must, like Abram, remain faithful—not to be at all astonished at the aridities, and seeing only afflictions and crosses in a road, in which God seemed to promise nothing but sweetnesses ; it must follow God indefatigably through all its bitternesses, without ever stopping or being discouraged.

11. *Abram said to Sarai his wife,*
13. *Say, I pray thee, that thou art my sister, that they may treat me well on account of thee, and that my life may be saved on thy behalf.*

This apparent fault of Abram, by which he seems to dissimulate somewhat, and to expose the honour of his wife to preserve his own life, teaches us by the use that God makes of it, the care that He Himself takes of correcting the faults and wanderings which fear and weakness cause those souls to commit, when they do not come out of the *abandon*, and do not quit the way He taught them since they gave themselves to Him. This Divine conduct over Abram, and this permission appear so admirable to those who are in the light of truth, that an infinity of volumes would be necessary for its full explanation.

17. *And the Lord plagued Pharaoh and his house with great plagues because of Sarai, Abram's wife.*

God *punishes Pharaoh* for an innocent fault, which, according to appearance, was more in Abram than in him; and He recompenses Abram for a shortcoming apparently real. Who will penetrate the secret judgments of God? But who can sufficiently admire the surety of the *abandon* when everything seems most desperate? Oh! God saves both the life of Abram and the honour of his wife, on account of the faith of this patriarch who had fully abandoned them to Him.

CHAPTER XIII.

1. *And Abram went up out of Egypt, he, and his wife, and all that he had, and Lot with him, into the south.*
2. *And Abram was very rich, and possessed much silver and gold.*
3. *And he returned by the same road that he had gone, from the south even to Bethel, unto the place where he had pitched his tent, at the beginning, between Bethel and Hai,*
4. *Where the altar was which he had built, and he there called upon the name of the Lord.*

There is nothing in Scripture that has not an admirable signification. It is said that *Abram went towards the south;* this is, as we have explained, that he always went to God: and yet it is added, that he *returned by the same road, and came from the south even to Bethel.* What does this signify? There appears a contradiction; yet there is none. The reason is that all the roads lead to God. He who stops at none, and makes use of everything he meets, and all that happens to him to hasten to God with eagerness, finds Him assuredly.

It is added also, that he possessed a *great deal of riches;* but he brought them to the place of the *altar,* that is to say, that he sacrificed them all to God, and that he advanced equally towards Him by whatever road there was, whether he was conducted by prosperity or by adversity; everything was for him *one road* to proceed to God and to *call on His name.*

6. *The land was not sufficient to bear them together, for their riches were very great, and they could not dwell together.*

7. *Wherefore there arose a strife between the herdsmen of Abram and those of Lot.*

Too abundant interior *riches lessen peace* and union between the servants, who are the passions. These cling to them and lean upon them: and tasting them naturally, imperfect zeal arises.

8. *Abram then said to Lot, Let there be no strife, I pray thee, between thee and me, nor between thy herdsmen and mine, for we are brethren.*

9. *The whole land is before thee. Separate thyself, I pray thee, from me; if thou goest to the left, I will go to the right, and if thou choose the right, I will take the left.*

10. *And Lot lifted up his eyes and beheld all the country along Jordan, which, before God destroyed Sodom and Gomorrah, appeared a goodly land, well watered even as a Paradise of delights.*

Abram, who had peace in himself and peace with his God, could not bear *strife between his herdsmen and those of* his kinsman, and above all for the goods which he held from God alone, and to which he was so little attached that he was ready to sacrifice them a thousand and a thousand times. His *abandon* and indifference were so great, that he *gave the choice of country* to his nephew, although the preference was due to him. *Lot,* being very far distant from this faith and *abandon* and disengagement of Abram, *chose for himself the most delightful place.*

How many of these persons are there who seek in the service of God the delights of the spirit, in place of seeking there only death, renouncement, the cross, and bitterness! The issue will well show how much more advantageous it was for Abram to abandon himself to God, than for Lot to choose.

11. *The two brothers separated from each other.*

God is not content with drawing the soul out of itself: He *separates it* also from everything that could retard it, however good it may be; thus Abram might have been hindered in the way of God by the affection that he entertained for Lot, or might have been in danger of taking some natural satisfaction in his company.

14. *The Lord said unto Abram, after Lot had departed from him, Lift up thine eyes and look from the place where thou art, to the north, to the south, and to the east, and to the west.*
15. *For all the land which thou seest, to thee will I give it, and to thy seed for ever.*

Oh excessive goodness of God—recompensing a soul so soon as it leaves itself in something out of love for Thee! With what tenderness does He speak to Abram *after he had separated himself from Lot!* A good thing which serves us for support and company, hinders the communication of God, and stops the course of His graces. These promises, reiterated to Abram, were only performed according to the letter four hundred years after they were made, and after bloody battles between the people of God and their enemies; to instruct us to give neither sense, nor time, nor manner, nor anything determinate to the interior words spoken in the hearts of the servants of God.

16. *I will multiply thy seed as the dust of the earth; so that if a man can number the dust of the earth, so shall thy seed be numbered.*
17. *Arise, walk through the land in the length of it and in the breadth of it: for I will give it unto thee.*

God is admirable in His rewards, even temporal ones: He measures these, as well as the eternal, according to the nature of the renouncements made out of love to Him. Abram has no sooner separated himself from his nephew to do God's will, than God promises him, as the price of the sacrifice of one single man, the most numerous race that ever was. This great nation was promised him for this first renouncement, as the sacrifice that he made of Isaac merited his having Jesus Christ in his posterity. When we separate ourselves from the creatures for the love of God, whether from friends according to the flesh, or even from imperfect spiritual ones, God gives us for that an inconceivable number of friends of another kind, who are our friends in Him and for Him. For the children and nephews that we have abandoned for His love, He gives us an innumerable multitude of spiritual children; as it is promised in Isaiah, "Sing, O Barren, thou that didst not bear, for more are the children of the desolate than the children of the married wife."

The earth that *God promised* then to Abram was not only the material earth that he saw, but it was also the earth of his heart, which is the reward promised to the meek. It is as if God had said to him: Immediately that thy heart is disengaged from everything that could attach it to the earth, it will possess itself in perfect freedom, which will have no more limits than thine eyes can have in this land which I destine for thee; and as thou canst not see anything here which does not belong to thee, so likewise art thou master of all things by the fidelity of thy renouncement.

CHAPTER XIV.

11, 12. *The conquerors, having taken the spoil, took Lot, Abram's brother's son, who dwelt in Sodom, with all that he possessed.*

16. *And Abram brought back with him all the spoil that they had taken, and Lot his brother, with all that he possessed, the women, and all the people.*

Abram is rewarded for having separated himself from Lot, and Lot is punished for having parted from Abram. Souls who leave all for God, receive from Him new favours with the highest peace and tranquillity. But they who, through interest or distrust, separate themselves from the just, have for their lot only war, trouble, and chastisement. Lot represents those who separate themselves from the souls of faith and *abandon*, to live in assurance in the strong city of reason and leaning upon the creature, where, nevertheless, they find themselves still more in danger: as much on account of the instability of the creatures, who cannot sustain them, as that God justly abandons them to themselves on account of their presumption.

The *help* so opportune that *Abram renders to his nephew*, marks the care that the abandoned souls take of those even who separate from them, and how they yet continue to succour them in time of need.

18. *And Melchizedek, King of Salem, offered bread and wine, for he was priest of the Most High.*
19. *And he blessed Abram, saying, Blessed be Abram of the most high God who has made heaven and earth.*

It belongs to the only *Melchizedek, priest* of the *living God*, to *bless Abram*: for He alone knows and approves the pure and sublime way of the *abandon*. This is representative of the true priest, who gives to the soul a double refection after the combat, namely, of the word of life, and the holy eucharist.

20. *Abram gave to Melchizedek the tenth part of all he had taken.*

This soul of faith, seeing that he who is given as a guide for it is the priest of the Lord, submits to him, and recognises him as such, and gives him the tithe of all it possesses, which is, to obey him, for the love of God, and as God Himself.

22. *Abram said to the King of Sodom, I swear by the most high God, possessor of heaven and earth,*
23. *That I will take nothing of all that is thine, from a thread to a shoe latchet, lest thou shouldest say that thou hast made Abram rich.*

This is the generosity of abandoned souls who walk in the way of faith, to *refuse all riches* and all the supports of the faculties, only to have God alone. They reject all the rest, and raising themselves by a holy boldness, even to the heaven, they find nothing worthy of themselves out of God, who, as their only treasure, enriches them with Himself.

CHAPTER XV.

1. *After these things the word of the Lord came unto Abram in a vision, saying, Fear not, Abram: I am thy protector and thy exceeding great reward.*

Man could not give God a stronger proof of his love than in despising everything else to content himself with Him alone; therefore God hastens to witness to him His complacency by words of the extremest tenderness, assuring him that He is his protector, and that He Himself will be *his reward*. Oh inconceivable happiness—God Himself will be the compensation for these little things which we quit for Him! Truly, oh Paul, there is no comparison between the ills of this life and the glory which shall be revealed in us; for what could enter into comparison with the possession of a God?

2. *And Abram answered: Lord God, what wilt Thou give me? I shall die childless,*
3. *And the son of my servant will be my heir.*

This faithful servant seeing himself near his end without having received the fulfilment of the divine promises, and continuing to abandon himself, seeks nevertheless some means of being assured of the future, which is designated by the *heritage;* and he thinks of taking measures himself.

4. *The Lord said unto him, This shall not be thine heir, but he that shall be born of thee shall be thine heir.*
5. *And He brought him forth abroad, and said, Look now towards heaven, and tell the stars, if thou be able to number them: and he said unto him, So shall thy seed be.*

God, whose goodness is infinite, quickly proceeds to frustrate all the measures that Abram's weakness had made him take, by a new assurance which He gives him of the care of His providence; but as this poor abandoned one had re-entered a little into himself by the care that he desired to take for the future, God draws him out still further, and by a simple comparison *of the stars*, He shows him the effects of His power, again assuring him that His promises are infallible, and that He is almighty to fulfil them.

6. *Abram believed in the Lord; and his faith was imputed to him for righteousness.*

Faith is what God looks at most: thus the *faith* of this person, continuing his *abandon* and leaving himself in God's hands, is considered by Him more than all the actions of righteousness not sustained by so great a faith; for this is a faith animated by an excess of love. Then faith and *abandon* suffice him for every thing; and he has nothing more to do than to live in them.

7. *God said unto him again, I am the Lord that brought thee out of Ur of the Chaldees, to give thee this land to possess it.*

In order to so much the more exercise his faith, and to maintain him in the *abandon*, God gives him new assurances of His promises; but this soul, not being yet permanently established in *abandon* and faith, vacillates, and through infidelity demands signs, without considering that they are as much opposed to the perfection of faith as to its state of destitution, and that stopping the creature at something created, they hinder it from having only the support of the goodness of the Creator.

8. *Abram said, Lord God, how shall I know that I am to possess it?*

12. *And when the sun was going down, a deep sleep suddenly fell upon Abram, and a horror of great darkness seized him.*

God gives him a sign, but in a manner sufficiently showing him that his distrust has displeased Him: for nothing is so much opposed to faith and *abandon* as signs. The Divine moment must decide in everything, and the soul wait for this moment without seeing anything, without troubling itself to foresee anything for the future, not even when the time of the promises appears past. And the only way to avoid being deceived is to halt at nothing but at this moment of God's will, who is always infallible in His execution.

13. *Know of a surety that thy seed shall dwell in a strange land, and shall be reduced to slavery, and afflicted with diverse evils for four hundred years.*

As renouncement, faith, and *abandon* lead God to give great rewards, that it seems He has not wherewith to recompense these heroic virtues, otherwise than in giving Himself: so the least distrust, or desire for a sign, which is so much opposed to them, draws down His indignation, and obliges Him to threaten and punish even him whom before He had desired to recompense with Himself. Oh how mysterious this is, and how necessary for our instruction! for it is certain that often the faults that we commit against faith and *abandon*, for which we are immediately reprehended, strengthen faith more by the use that God makes of them than a pursued fidelity which has never experienced any weaknesses.

God then in a manner threatens Abram regarding his posterity, as the promises He had made were for the same posterity. The *horror and great darkness* point out the bad effects of signs and assurances that we seek for through infidelity, and which, casting the soul into fear and hesitation, form an obstacle to the graces of God, and to His Divine light.

> 14. *They shall come out of this land afterwards enriched with great goods.*
> 17. *When the sun went down, there was a great darkness.*
> 18. *And that day God made a covenant with Abram.*

Nevertheless God continues to fulfil His promises after seeing them dearly paid for, and the soul having re-entered the *darkness* of faith, as it is said that *after the sun went down it was dark*, God renews His *covenant* with it, and continues on its behalf the cares of a particular providence.

CHAPTER XVI.

> 1. *Sarai, Abram's wife, had yet borne no children.*
> 3. *And she took her maid Hagar, an Egyptian, and gave her to wife unto her husband.*

The inferior part, represented by the *wife*, tiring of so long a *barrenness*, and of so obscure and bare a road, seeks amongst strangers what she does not find with herself; and provided that she has a little support, she does not trouble herself where it comes from.

4. *Hagar, seeing that she had conceived, despised her mistress.*
5. *Then Sarai said to Abram, Thou wrongest me.*
6. *Abram answered her: Thy maid is in thy hand, do with her as thou wilt.*

She is not long in experiencing its penalty: for this support, which she has desired to take, is a *servant*, to whom she has given an advantage over herself, and who makes use of it to despise and wrong her. Then she sees her mistake, and complains to the superior part, whom she had made a participant in her fault, the latter re-establishes her in her place, and restores to her her authority, which she had allowed to be usurped.

11. *The Angel of the Lord said unto Hagar: Behold thou hast conceived, and wilt bear a son, and thou shalt call his name Ishmael, for the Lord hath heard thy affliction.*

Hagar represents the ways of multiplicity and activity, which we prefer to faith, because of the latter's apparent sterility. Although she is only a servant, she is yet to become mother of a great people in *Ishmael*, but of a people all full of trouble, wars, and divisions, and who obtain nothing but at the point of the sword: God recompenses thus *her affliction*.

13. *Hagar called upon the name of the Lord that spake to her, saying, Thou God seest me; for surely, she said, I have looked upon him from behind who sees me.*

God bestows some favours on these multiplied souls, but He only suffers them to *see* Him *from behind*, that is to say, in His gifts and images: and they can never arrive at union with Him by this way.

CHAPTER XVII.

1. *The Lord appeared unto Abram, and said unto him, I am the Almighty God, walk in my presence and be thou perfect.*
2. *I will make a covenant with thee, and will multiply thy seed even to infinity.*

God shows the soul abandoned to Him that He is *almighty*,

and that it ought to be content to *walk before Him*, in order to please Him in all things, seeing that this is the way to become *perfect*. He protests to it at the same time, that He will *unite Himself* to it, and will render it *fruitful;* which is, in the first place, to honour it with His Divine union; then to enrich it with the productions of its own fruitfulness.

3. *And Abram fell on his face on the ground.*

This soul being instructed to no longer desire signs, thinks only of being annihilated, knowing that the most fit disposition for serving God's designs is annihilation, and that the true preparation for the supernatural is nothingness.

4. *And God said to him, It is* I WHO AM. *I will make a covenant with thee, and thou shalt be the father of many nations.*

After the mystic annihilation, God communicates Himself quite in another manner from formerly: for He gives to a heart perfectly submitted to Him, the greatest and most complete *knowledge* that can be had here below of His Divine Majesty; saying that HE IS, and that nothing is without Him nor out of Him. He also renews *the union* and His promises.

5. *Neither shall thy name any more be called Abram, but thy name shall be Abraham: for a father of many nations have I made thee.*

6. *Kings shall come out of thee.*

It is then that there is *given the new name*, to wit, after the annihilation: a name that no one knoweth but he that receiveth it: a name given by the Lord from His own mouth, and consequently with everything necessary to complete its meaning. The promises are reiterated for a *numerous generation*, even exalting the merit and quality of the persons included in them, for it is added: *Kings shall come out of thee:* and it is said elsewhere that "he is the father of us all."

7. *And I will establish my covenant between thee and me, and thy seed after thee in their generations, for an everlasting covenant, to be a God unto thee, and to thy seed after thee.*

He assures this abandoned soul, after it has reached this

point, and has received the new name, that *He* will henceforth be *its* God, and the God of all the abandoned souls that will issue from it. It is then that there is established the true stability: and there are no more changes for this soul. God says that *He is their God*, and that His covenant with them will be permanent, durable, and everlasting. He is their God, for He commands them as a sovereign, and nothing resists Him in them any longer, their will being lost in His own: and they do His will on the earth as the blessed in heaven.

10. *Every man child among you shall be circumcised.*

12. *The child of eight days shall be circumcised among you: the slaves born in thy house, as well as those thou hast bought, or which are of a foreign nation.*

God gives a commandment as the sign of the covenant. He expresses to us by it that in order to enter the way of *abandon* we must labour by *circumcision*, or the cutting off of all that gave us life in Adam. The beginning of the way of the spirit is this continual mortification and renouncement of everything that maintains the carnal and animal life; by this we know God's people. There is no longer any difference between *bond and free*, for all conditions are equal for those who abandon themselves to God.

By *the child born in the house*, is represented him whose life has been innocent: there seems no retrenchment necessary for him: nevertheless there is, and all are obliged at the beginning to renounce everything of the life of Adam in order to give place to the life of Jesus Christ. *The slave* signifies those who, having groaned under the tyranny of sin, must, whenever they give themselves to God, suffer circumcision. I confess that this circumcision is more passive on their part than active: which happens thus, because that, when they are fully abandoned, God Himself operates with sword in hand, cutting off their uncircumcision, without being arrested either by the grief, fears, or tears of those who must suffer these wounds. The more inveterately old sensuality becomes, like the foreskin, the more it resists the knife, and circumcision is so much the more severe. Those then who pretend to be abandoned, and who nevertheless have not suffered the knife nor the cutting off of their own life; or who, having only the name thereof, wish to preserve everything, and to lose nothing, are as much excluded

Chapter XVII.

from the number of the true abandoned ones as from that of the truly circumcised.

> 15. *God said again unto Abraham: Thou shalt no longer call thy wife Sarai, but Sarah.*
> 16. *I will bless her, and give thee a son by her.*

God having renewed the centre of the soul and the superior part by the resurrection of the spirit after its mystic death, drawn as it has been from the region of the shadow of death, and established in the new life, typified by the new name: He now also renews the inferior part, *changing its name*, and making it participate in the renewal of the superior. Therefore some time after changing Abram's name *He changes Sarai's*, and makes to her the same promises as to her husband; He adds that she will bear him a son.

> 17. *Then Abraham fell on his face to the earth, and laughed, saying in his heart, Shall a man that is an hundred years old have a son; and shall Sarah, that is ninety years old, bear?*
> 19. *But God said to him, Sarah thy wife shall bear a son, and thou shalt call his name Isaac, and I will make with him and with his seed after him an everlasting covenant.*

The superior part, which had believed the promises made for itself, hesitates when there is promised that of its reunion with the inferior there is *to be born a son*, for whom all the promises have been made, knowing the feebleness of this inferior part, and regarding it as out of God, it *doubts* it, and at the same time the Divine power: pleading reasons derived from the long experience of their weakness, impotency, and sterility. These two parts live contented in their poverty, and desiring nothing more, hope for nothing more. This is the state of repose in God, preceding the Apostolic life. This *Isaac* that is to be conceived, is Jesus Christ formed in the souls: but He is only born when there is no longer anything in them that can create a just hope of conceiving Him. This infant is only conceived in the complete despair of all natural succour, and in a perfect disinterestedness for all supernatural gifts: so that, as says St. Paul, "the excellency of the power may not be attributed to man, but to God."

18. *And Abraham said unto God, Oh that Ishmael might live before Thee.*

20. *God said unto him, I have heard thee also regarding Ishmael: I will bless him and will multiply him exceedingly; twelve princes shall come out of him, and I will make him the chief of a great people.*

Abraham by these words represents most perfectly the souls of faith that are in total nakedness. When they reflect upon their state, so poor and so destitute, Oh that it *might please God,* say they, for us to employ ourselves in holy activities, instead of remaining thus useless, and *that this Ishmael,* representing the multiplied practices, *might live* from *God* Himself. But God, seeing this error, affirms that He *has blessed* this way in everything He could, as much as it is capable of, and that it will possess great advantages: yet it is not to be that of His people, because it is the way of a people, not freed from the flesh, and His people are to be in Jesus Christ. For this reason He allows those who are to beget this people, so dear to Him, to attain even a hopeless age, so that they who will be born of them, as says St. John, "may be born, not of blood, nor of the will of the flesh, nor of the will of man, but of God."

As there is not a word in Scripture that may not serve for our instruction, it must be observed, that all the promises made for *Ishmael* are confined and limited to a certain *number:* but those made for *Isaac,* who is the figure of faith and *abandon* to God, are without limit: for he includes in his posterity nothing less than God Himself. Nothing less than God can be the recompense of a soul of faith: thus He Himself says to Abraham, " I am thy exceeding great reward."

CHAPTER XVIII.

1. *The Lord appeared to Abraham as he sat at the door of his tent, in the Valley of Mamre, in the heat of the day.*

This passage marks the assiduity of a soul to attract God and to preserve his possession, when it has found Him in the repose of contemplation. *Abraham sat in the Valley of Mamre:*

Chapter XVIII.

to sit, this is to be in repose; we must be in repose that God may manifest Himself—be in repose *in the valley* of humiliation and annihilation.

> 2. *And lifting up his eyes he beheld three men near him.*
> 3. *And He said, Lord, if I have found grace in Thy sight, pass not by the tent of thy servant.*

This soul is not at all desirous of allowing its Beloved to depart, who has honoured it with His visit: on the contrary it longs to retain Him for ever. In this love that it has for its God, it believes everything to be God, and would treat every one as God Himself. It is then that He communicates Himself to it in such a manner, that it finds Him in everything. Thus Abraham treated those strangers who presented themselves before him, as God Himself: he is so filled with God, that he cannot say anything else. He speaks to three as to one: *Lord*, he says, *if I have found favour in Thy sight, pass not by the tent of Thy servant*. It is the same with this soul; it finds God in everything, and everything is God for it.

> 6. *And Abraham hastened into the tent unto Sarah, and said, Make ready quickly three measures of fine meal, knead it, and make cakes upon the hearth.*
> 7. *And Abraham ran unto the herd, and fetched a calf tender and good, and gave it unto a young man, and he hastened to dress it.*
> 8. *And he took butter and milk with the calf that he had dressed, and set it before them.*

Those who are worthily touched by the love of God in the passive way of contemplation, find nothing difficult when His glory is in question; nothing costs them an effort to give Him proofs of their love: thus they do everything with *speed* and activity, without, however, interrupting their repose; their liberality equals their love. Such was that of Magdalen at the house of Simon the leper.

> 9. *And when they had eaten they said unto him, Where is Sarah thy wife?*
> 10. *In a year she shall bear a son. And when Sarah heard this, she laughed behind the tent door.*

12. *Saying to herself, After I am old, and my lord is old also, shall I yet have this pleasure.*

Their liberality is rewarded by the assurance of the near fulfilment of the promises: but they who are not made firm in God *hesitate*, returning from time to time to their doubts and distrusts, caused by reflections on their incapacity and weaknesses. As for those who are thoroughly established in God, they cannot hesitate or doubt any more. But, oh how rare these are upon the earth! Where shall we find them?

What Sarah says: *After I am waxed old shall I have pleasure?*—meaning that she did not think to make use of marriage any more, shews that she regarded it still in a human manner and not in God.

13. *But the Lord said unto Abraham, Wherefore did Sarah laugh, saying, How could I have a child, being so old?*
14. *Is there anything too hard for the Lord?*

Abraham firmly fixed in the state of *abandon* and faith is the father of all those who have entered therein after him. He doubts no more: therefore he has no part in Sarah's fault: he believes it incumbent upon him to hope even against hope. This is the just praise that St. Paul bestows upon him. The Lord complains to him of the hesitation of his wife, bringing to his recollection that *nothing is impossible for God*. It is thus that He delights to exercise faith and *abandon*, granting things only when they are most despaired of. But the creatures not yet wholly drawn out of themselves *doubt* like Sarah, on account of looking at things from the side of reason; in place of which the souls of pure faith regard them only from the side of God, to whom nothing is difficult.

15. *Sarah denied it, and said, I laughed not, for she was afraid. It is not so, said the Lord, for thou didst laugh.*

This creature still existing in herself, being reprehended for her doubt, desires to *justify herself;* and endeavouring to do so, inconsiderately falls *into lying*. *Sarah* commits two faults: the one, of lying; and the other, that in order to excuse herself, she accuses God: for if it *be not true* that she laughed, she casts the lie back upon the Lord Himself who chides her for it. It is thus also with persons who are continually excusing themselves. They accumulate fault upon fault in their replies and hesitations, and then they cast back the fault upon God Himself, accusing Him of cruelty, or complaining that He abandons them and does nothing for them. But the soul of faith remains firm and constant in all His providences: and by this fidelity it draws the regards of God upon it with His greatest graces: thus St. Paul says, that "it was by faith that Abraham was blessed."

17. *And the Lord said, Shall I hide from Abraham that thing which I do:*
18. *Seeing that Abraham shall surely become a great and mighty nation, and all the nations of the earth be blessed in him.*

God could not *conceal anything* from His servant now established in naked faith and reposing in Him. He cannot but discover to him His secrets: and as he has the spirit of God, so also does he know what passes within the heart of God, and even the most hidden things of conscience, discerning immediately their states by a secret odour and a divine taste.

20. *The cry of Sodom and Gomorrah is great, and their sins have become very grievous.*
21. *I will go down now, and see whether their works are according to this cry which has come up to me. I will know whether it is so or not.*

Let us admire the manner in which God punishes sinners. He desires to *examine* everything Himself: for He seeks only to show mercy: He warns His friends of it, that they may prevail with Him if it is possible. But to bestow favours on His creatures, He anticipates them; and to reward, He does not examine things so minutely: for His mercy surpasses His judgment.

23. *And Abraham drew near and said, Wilt Thou destroy the just with the wicked?*
24. *If there be fifty just persons in that city, shall they perish with the others? And wilt Thou not rather spare the place on account of these fifty just persons should they be be found there?*

Two of these angels go to Sodom, and the third, representing God, remains with Abraham, who always speaks to Him as to the Lord. We ought here to admire the ardent and efficacious manner in which the friends of God supplicate Him on behalf of His enemies. They lay themselves before Him as their advocates. They take God by the strongest and most touching points, making it appear to Him that there are some *just* persons, so that on their account He may pardon the criminals. But what are so few just among so many guilty? Nevertheless if they had been found, they would have saved the city. The servants of God press Him still by His justice itself, pointing out to Him, that He has never caused an innocent one to perish for the guilty. 25. *That be far from Thee, said Abraham, to do after this manner, to slay the righteous with the wicked; and that the righteous should be as the wicked, that be far from Thee.*

> 27. *Since I have taken it upon me, I will speak again unto the Lord, although I am but dust and ashes.*

The humility of him who supplicates in a profound *annihilation*, looking for nothing from other source than from the goodness of God, is of great weight before Him to obtain what is sought. Thus God promises him (verse 32) *that should only ten just persons be found in this city, it should not perish;* whilst Abraham, admiring the infinite clemency of God, dares not push his supplication further, doubting not but that Lot and his family are pardoned.

> 33. *And the Lord departed when He had left off speaking to Abraham, and Abraham returned to his own place.*

Two things are to be remarked here: the one, that as God cannot refuse anything to His best friends, and as, moreover, there are sinners in a final impenitence on account of their obstinacy, He does not permit His favourites to ask Him anything other than what He can and will grant them. It was for this reason that Abraham's prayer finished as above: and that God refusing him nothing, did not relinquish exercising His justice on this impious city. The other thing to be observed is, that persons who have attained this permanent state in God can only pray what He wills, and according as He Himself moves them, having no longer any other interests than His. This is visible in Abraham, who, forgetting all self-interest, and everything regarding flesh and blood, to abandon all to God, does not even enquire what will become of Lot his nephew in the vengeance that God will take on the city of his habitation. So much is he assured of God's goodness and justice. His own interests are nothing more to him than those of others, and everything has become for him one in God.

Abraham returns after this prayer *unto his place*, which is the repose in God, in which he was before seeing the three angel travellers.

CHAPTER XIX.

1. *There came two angels to Sodom at even, and Lot sat in the gate of the city, and when he saw them, he rose up to meet them, and bowing himself to the ground, he worshipped them.*

In the midst of so corrupt a city as *Sodom*, there is found one man who dwells in the repose of contemplation, and whom God delivers from the ruin destined for the wicked. *Lot* in his repose (for he is *seated*) marks the contemplative soul: and as being Abraham's kinsman, he is of the race of souls abandoned to God, so also he does what Abraham did on the preceding day, although in a much lower degree: for he still *sat at the gate of the city*, marking only an incipient contemplation, and yet little distant from the tumult of action: but Abraham seated at the door of his tent designates the repose in God free from all commerce with the creatures.

12. *The angels said unto Lot, Hast thou here any of thy relations, son-in-law, or sons, or daughters? Bring out of this city all that belong to thee.*

A contemplative soul, especially at the beginning, has yet a great many things binding it in commerce with the creatures, of which it has difficulty in ridding itself. This is why the angels are obliged to press Lot. But words are not efficacious enough; for the steps of these persons, although full of apparent fire and ardour, are yet slow and tardy as to the performance when there are many difficulties to surmount. It is necessary that God or His angels *take them by the hand* in order to protect them from the fall and ruin which would overwhelm them, if they did not come out from it speedily.

16. *And seeing that he still lingered, they took him by the hand, for the Lord was merciful to him, and they took also his wife and two daughters.*

17. *And they brought him out of the city, and said to him, Escape for thy life, look not behind thee, neither stay thou in all the plain, but escape to the mountain lest thou perish with the others.*

If God did not act thus, these persons are so little courageous, and still so feeble and attached, that they would never succeed. God, wishing to draw them from everything created, and to *conduct* them by His providence, bids them *look not behind them, nor stop at all.* These are the faults of persons in this state: either they look behind them, by reflection, or they stop at something less than God, through some reserve. The angels counsel them to leave off all commerce with the creature, *to get up upon the mountain*, which is the highest degree of contemplation.

18. *Lot answered them,*
19. *I cannot escape to the mountain, lest some evil befall me, and I die.*
20. *But here there is a city near to flee to. It is a little one, and it will save my life.*

Those persons who hesitate, *are fearful of their loss*, excuse themselves at first, and desire by measures of prudence to place themselves in safety. They propose a *city*, which they choose in order to be assured of a manner of life in which they can preserve and conduct themselves, not yet being able fully to trust themselves to God, and to abandon themselves wholly to His providence. They make even a specious pretext of the *littleness of the city*, as if to say: I prefer a lower and more sure way than these great states where there is more danger. They wish also to make God enter into this design by asking Him: *Is it not a little one*—this city that we ask for our security? Is it not the way of humility, which will give *life* to my soul?

Chapter XIX.

21. The Angel answered him, I have heard thee concerning this thing. I will not overthrow this city for which thou hast spoken to me.

God *hears* the prayers of these wavering souls, on account of their feebleness: and *grants them* what they ask, even miraculously. This enraptures them, thinking that this request was agreeable to God, and advantageous for themselves: since He performs miracles on their behalf: but it is quite the contrary, it being only granted them on account of their weakness.

26. Lot's wife looked behind her, and was changed into a pillar of salt.

The soul that is not far advanced enters on reflection, and *looks behind it*, against God's commandment. Nothing is so necessary in this way as to go on without reflecting: and God, in order to make an example, *changes this* feeble *woman* into a *pillar of salt;* showing thereby that *the salt*, that is to say, our own wisdom, prudence, and foresight is useless in a way where abandon and faith must alone conduct: and that all the measures that we are desirous of taking by ourselves, serve only to create a stoppage in the interior road, far from contributing some means of advancement therein.

29. And it came to pass, that when God destroyed the cities of the plain, He remembered Abraham, and delivered Lot from the overthrow of the cities in which he dwelt.
30. Lot then withdrew into a mountain with his two daughters.

God, for the sake of the perfect contemplative soul, delivers him who was only beginning, from the overturning of the city he had chosen for habitation. Lot, by his prayers, or rather on account of Abraham, is inspired to *go up into the mountain,* where he dwells in *a cave with his two daughters:* this is the representation of the solitude of the contemplative.

33. They gave wine unto their father, and made him drink that night.

He believes himself covered from everything, having with him his *two daughters*, to wit, silence and retreat; but he sees not that because he trusts too much in himself, they will be the cause of his loss : God permitting it thus to shew him that it is in vain he thinks of taking care of himself if God Himself does not protect him, and to lead him by this to total *abandon*, into which he wishes to make him enter.

CHAPTER XX.

1. *And Abraham went to Gerar and dwelt there some time.*
2. *And he said of Sarah his wife, She is my sister. Abimelech King of Gerar sent for Sarah, and brought her to him.*
3. *But God appeared to Abimelech in a dream by night, and said to him: Thou shalt surely die if thou touchest the woman thou hast taken, for she has an husband.*
4. *Now Abimelech had not touched her. And he said, Lord, wilt Thou slay an innocent nation dwelling in ignorance.*

Abraham told no lie, saying that *Sarah was his sister*, since as he explains further on, she was truly his sister, being the daughter of his father although not the daughter of his mother : not, however, the immediate daughter of Terah the father of Abraham, but of Haran his brother. Thus Sarah was the granddaughter of Terah, and Abraham's niece : and Abraham could say that she was his sister, seeing that she was the granddaughter of his father, and that in Scripture the words son and daughter are often used for grandson and granddaughter. The fault that he would seem to have committed would be to so often expose the life and honour of his wife. But besides the fact that a man of so great a faith does nothing but by the particular order of God, who moves him to act thus, there is more than that—that God permitted those things as they happened, in order to show to every one both the great faith of Abraham and the altogether particular protection of God over those who trust themselves to Him. It will be said that if Abraham's faith was great, and if the conduct of God was particular over him, He ought to have made him aware that Abimelech would not touch his wife, should he declare her as such. To that it is easy to reply, that besides that this is the

Chapter XX.

manner in which God usually acts toward the souls whom He conducts by faith, to wit, making them go and come as He wills without, however, giving them any certitude of what is to happen, and that it is to exercise so much the more their faith and *abandon* that He thus conceals His designs from them: besides this, God desired to signalise His protection of those who unreservedly abandon themselves to Him, and to declare Himself on their behalf, in a striking manner, to serve for ever as an example to the souls of faith and to encourage their confidence.

5. *I have done this with a simple heart and pure hands.*
6. *God said unto him, I know that thou hast acted in this with a simple heart: therefore have I withheld thee from sinning against me, and have not suffered thee to touch her.*

It is certain that many people are persuaded of not being guilty on account of their ignorance, and nevertheless they are truly so. For to prevent sin two things are necessary—ignorance, and simplicity of heart: the latter is the most necessary. Therefore *God said* to Abimelech that *He had not permitted him to sin against Him, because of the simplicity of his heart.* God would sooner perform miracles incessantly than permit a person, who would go to Him in simplicity, to sin against him in ignorance, not only in sins of the spirit, but even material ones, according as it is added: *I have not suffered thee to touch her.* But it usually happens that those who sin through ignorance have the heart corrupted by other sins which they knowingly commit: therefore having no simplicity of heart, but on the contrary having the heart corrupted in everything, they sin even in things that they do not know to be sin, by reason of the depravity of their heart. From which it can be inferred, how much uprightness and simplicity of heart are advantageous for us. This is what God asks principally from us. It is simplicity which renders the heart pure and upright: and such a one as appears to commit faults does not do so, because of the simplicity of his heart: whilst those, who appear outwardly just, sin on account of the artifice and duplicity with which they act, and which is the source of hypocrisy.

9. *And Abimelech called Abraham, and said to him, Wherefore hast thou treated us thus? What evil have we done*

> *thee that thou has brought on me and on my kingdom a great sin?*
> 11. *Abraham replied, I said to myself, surely they fear not God in this place, and they will slay me for my wife's sake.*
> 12. *And yet indeed she is my sister, being the daughter of my father, although not the daughter of my mother.*

The reproach that Abimelech makes to Abraham shows the innocence and simplicity of heart of this king, and the fear he had of displeasing God, which obliged the Lord to perform a double miracle in order to save the honour of Sarah and preserve this prince from crime. I have cited these passages designedly to make apparent the fidelity of God towards His little creatures when they are willing fully to trust themselves to Him, and abandon themselves to His care, always preserving a sincere desire of pleasing Him, and a real aversion to sin.

> 16. *And Abimelech said unto Sarah, I have given to thy brother a thousand pieces of silver that thou mayest always have a veil for thine eyes, before all with whom thou art, and wherever thou goest: and remember that thou hast been taken.*

Beauty, however chaste, may be violated if it have not a holy modesty which leads it to conceal itself. So holy a woman as Sarah had need of advice on this point for having affected to appear a maid, and not a wife: and a prince gives it to her wisely, although in an age in which God had not yet caused His law to be written, which ought to be graven only on the heart. How much more are similar cautions necessary for Christian women who suffer themselves to be seduced by the vanity of the age? And how much ought the guides of souls to be firm and inflexible in reprehending the immodesties and nudities which scandalise the Church so greatly? It is not sufficient to have the heart pure: exterior modesty is necessary to prevent the sins which others would commit on account of beauty too much exposed, although its possesser may have a heart very far removed from crime. *The veil*, which Abimelech gave to Sarah, is of the highest instruction for Christian women, who ought always to go veiled, particularly to churches. This is the counsel of St. Paul. We cannot have too much reservation on this point: for the exterior is often a sign of the corruption or purity of the heart.

This *veil* has also a mystical sense altogether divine. It is that God caused a veil to be given to Sarah who was of her time the most favoured woman of God: to teach two things to interior persons; first, that they ought to preserve the gifts of God under the veil of silence and retreat; and secondly, that God makes use of naked faith as a veil to cover the gifts and favours He imparts to souls, and to keep them secure when He believes that His graces may expose them to be taken in the snare of the DEMON through vanity. Therefore Abimelech in giving Sarah wherewith to buy herself a veil said to her, *remember that thou hast been taken.* From that time there was no more danger for Sarah; as there is no more for a soul when naked faith has been communicated to it. That is its sure guard; for concealing from it its graces and virtues, it keeps it free from danger of taking some vain satisfaction in them, and consequently thus giving entrance to its ruin.

CHAPTER XXI.

1. *The Lord visited Sarah, as he had promised, and fulfilled his word.*
2. *For she conceived, and bare a son in her old age at the set time that God had spoken.*

Behold the *fulfilment* of God's promises, *in the time* that He hath appointed; and not always according to our views. The true interior life is begotten by faith, signified by Abraham; and it is brought forth by *abandon*, designated by Sarah. Abraham is then the father of all the interior souls; for "he is the father of all those who believe," according to St. Paul; and the interior and mystical life has its origin in faith.

3. *Abraham called the son that Sarah bare to him, Isaac.*
4. *And he circumcised him on the eighth day as God had commanded him.*
7. *Sarah nourished him with her milk.*

This interior infant is no sooner born, than faith begins to purify it, by *retrenchment;* whilst trust and abandon sustain it by their *milk.*

8. *The child grew, and they weaned him, and Abraham made a great feast on the day that he was weaned.*

When this interior new born child has been for sometime sustained by the sweet milk of sensible trust, it is weaned from it as to the savoury flow which caused the delights of its spiritual infancy, in order to have it no more but in essence. It cannot but experience grief at this; but faith is rejoiced and *makes a solemn feast* of it, for this first stripping causes the child to *grow* and advance in age in the spiritual life.

9. *And when Sarah saw the son of Hagar the Egyptian playing with Isaac her son, she said to Abraham:*
10. *Cast out this bond-woman with her son, for the son of a bond-woman shall not be heir with Isaac my son.*

When *Abandon* sees this little interior one which has been newly weaned from the sweetnesses and the milk of the spiritual life, going to seek amusement with the active and multiplied life; then it says to faith: *Cast out* entirely all that remains of the particular method and of multiplicity; and let my son have no commerce with those who are attached to them without being willing to pass beyond; for, being slaves of their own inventions, *they never inherit* God Himself, who is the heritage reserved for the free man, who is *my son*, and whom I shall conduct straight to God by my total *abandon*, so that he may find in Him alone his everlasting portion.

11. *This appeared hard to Abraham, because of his son.*

Abraham would preserve in his house this multiplied son, for he is also *son* of faith; but he is the son of faith in a manner comprised, possessed, and mixed with something of propriety; and not in a manner spiritual, imperceptible, and lost in God.

12. *But God said unto him, Hearken unto Sarah in all that she saith to thee; for out of Isaac shall thy seed come.*
13. *And also the son of thy bond-woman will I make the chief of a great people.*

God gives faith to understand, that it must abandon this son, who dwells much in nature, and must blindly follow all that *abandon* will bid it do. He declares to it that this must be the rule of its house; because it is from the son of *abandon* and faith that *its posterity must proceed*.

For this reason when scripture speaks of *Ishmael*, it separates him from Abraham, saying that he will be the *father of a great nation;* but when it speaks of Isaac, it affirms that in him Abraham will be the father of an innumerable nation, shewing that it is by this only son of blind *abandon* that faith can establish its posterity.

14. *Abraham rose up in the morning, and took bread and a vessel of water, and put them on Hagar's shoulder, and sent her away with the child. And she departed and wandered in the wilderness of Beersheba.*

Faith is contented with giving provisions to the multiplied life, for it cannot do without them; and these provisions are *bread* and *water*,—some support and nourishment, and some flow of sensible grace, so that it may be able to walk; but so soon as the water begins to fail, being its support, that is to say, the sweetness of grace, it loses courage. Hagar and her son *wandered in the desert;* which is, that the multiplied have never a fixed and straight road, as those who walk by simplicity and *abandon*. They go wandering from place to place, from subject to subject, from way to way; and so soon as the water of sensible grace fails them, they fall into discouragement, cease to walk, and stop short.

15. *The water in the bottle being spent, she left her son lying under one of the trees that were there.*

16. *And going away from him the length of a bow shot, she sat down, saying, I will not see my child die, and lifting up her voice, she wept.*

She *leaves her son under a tree*, that is to say, all her hope in the things of the earth; and then going away from him, she weeps for the loss that she believes she has sustained of all her productions. Must *I see perish*, says she, what I have produced with so much pain? But as the affliction of these souls makes them return to God, they cry to Him, and they sit down; which means that being weary of their inquietudes and groanings, they remain a little in repose; then God fails not to send them new graces and sweetnesses, so as to sustain them, and to make them pursue their road; without which they would abandon all.

17. *God heard the voice of the lad.*
19. *And at the same time He opened the eyes of Hagar, and she saw a well of water, and she went, and filled her vessel, and gave the lad drink.*
20. *God dwelt with him; he grew and dwelt in the wilderness and became an archer.*

The Lord *hears the voice of the lad*, this is to remember the good which this multiplied soul has endeavoured to do, and to console it by the compassion He has for its weakness. He causes it to *find water;* for everything is done in these souls by activity: thus have they only earthly water, and *they must go and fetch it themselves* and carry their own provision. This is what those do who are laden and filled with practices and anxieties and a multitude of thoughts. God continues to accept their little cares and to be with them; but He prepares them for war, and their industry has a great part in all they do. They live on what they take by labour or in the combat: nothing can better mark the active life than all this.

33. *But Abraham planted a wood in Beersheba, and called there on the name of the Lord, the Everlasting God.*
34. *And he dwelt for many days a stranger in the land of the Philistines.*

Abraham, father of believers and the man of the greatest faith that ever was, called on the name of God in all places; because he was in continual prayer, he left everywhere the marks of his invocation, of his prayer and sacrifice. Scripture here calls the Lord the *everlasting God*, to give us to understand that being always God, He must always be worshipped, prayed to, and called upon as God; and that thus our worship and prayer are to become everlasting. Therefore Jesus Christ has said Himself, "that we must pray always, and faint not," and St. Paul desires us to pray without ceasing. It is the state of faith solely that can render prayer continual.

God exacts yet another thing from the souls of faith, which is, that they be as *strangers* upon the earth, so that stopping at nothing created in the world, whether corporeal or spiritual, they may go direct to God. And it is to be for us a figure of the disengagement in which faith places the soul, that *Abraham remains* thus a *stranger upon the earth*, having no fixed abode.

God asks not this external from all the souls of faith, although He may exact it from some whom He desires to render true children of Abraham. But as for the internal, He wishes it from all persons who are conducted by faith and *abandon;* without which their state would not be true, but imaginary. The other souls conducted by gifts, and not by blind faith, are established in themselves, and are firmly there in repose, and very contented; but the souls of faith have no repose, since they entirely quitted themselves, coming out, like other Abrahams, from their country, the place of their parentage, to go into another land, which is God; giving themselves entirely up to be lost in their Creator; going on unceasingly—without resting, until they have returned unto the abode of their origin, according to the promise made to them when faith took possession of their hearts. For, from the time that it seizes upon them, it suffers them to take no repose, neither in themselves, nor in anything created; and it gives them to understand that everything must be looked at out of themselves, and that if they are faithful in following faith, however hard it may appear to them, they will not fail to succeed.

CHAPTER XXII.

1. *After these things God tempted Abraham and said to him:*
2. *Take Isaac thine only son, who is so dear to thee; and go unto the land of Vision, and there offer him to me as a burnt offering upon one of the mountains that I shall shew thee.*

God tempts Abraham, to make the last trial of his faith, and to test him to the utmost in total nakedness, and in the stripping of all supports; not only of human props, of which He had already stripped him previously, making him come forth from his country, but also of supports taken in God even, in all His benefits and promises. He spares nothing; and to render the thing more severe and this faith more magnanimous, to prove and purify his love, and to rid him of all self-interest, and of all foreign attachment, although most legitimate, He says to him: *Take thy son;* this word is very sweet: not only thy son, but thine only son: how very dear to him must he then have been! He continues:—*thy son whom thou lovest so tenderly;* to make even his love serve for its liveliest grief. He names him by his name, *Isaac;* placing before his eyes all the sweetness of this amiable victim, so as to make him conceive so much the more of the greatness of his loss and to render it more sensible to him. Then He adds, *come and sacrifice him to me upon a distant mountain.* Is it not that the length of the road may try his faith the more? Isaac, who has always represented the passive life, or contemplation, is to perish: faith must sacrifice this life, and give it the deathblow, so that there may remain nothing more that can hinder the total loss into God.

But far from so severe a temptation diminishing the faith of this Patriarch, it takes again even a new vigour; and although so surprising a commandment as is given him, is contrary to that which God had given to every one not to shed human blood, and must horrify him, according to reason, in the fear of committing a parricide. Yet faith bears all that; and trusting itself to God above reason and faith, it sets about executing what has been commanded it. By this incomparable faith, Abraham offered his Isaac although he had received the promises for him, and he was his only son; and he offered him after God had said to him, that it would be from Isaac that his descendants would go forth: But he thought to himself, that God could well resuscitate him; therefore he was given him as a mysterious figure. It is thus that St. Paul extols the greatness of this sacrifice.

It is by these wise excesses that God sometimes tries the greatness of the faith of those perfectly abandoned to Him. The active life loses courage for a little thing; by the failing of the water of sensible grace it is afflicted and halts; but faith cannot be shaken even by the loss of what is dearest to it: It must immolate itself, whilst activity grieves over the loss of its productions. This difference between these two ways is very real, and it could not be better explained than in these parts of scripture, where we can see by the difference of these two sorts of courage the distinction between these two ways, as it may be noticed in the course of the whole history of Abraham, Hagar, Isaac, and Ishmael.

3. *Abraham then rose up while it was yet night, and prepared his ass, and took with him two of his servants, and Isaac*

Chapter XXII.

his son; and having cut the wood necessary for the burnt offering, he went unto the place where God had commanded him.

Oh surprising promptitude of Abraham, or of faith, in obeying! He waits not until the day be come; he sets out *when it is yet night*. The night marks equally his diligence and the obscurity of his faith, denuded of all lights, and signs: Faith disposes of everything itself: it causes itself to be accompanied by *servants*, but they cannot aid it in this. It *prepares the necessary wood for the sacrifice,* so that there may remain no pretext for eluding obedience, although in a matter which reason might regard as suspicious in many points. Oh fidelity and generosity of faith! It is truly on good grounds that it is the source and origin of a great people and of an innumerable multitude of saints so much the more admirable before God as they are the more hidden from men.

4. *On the third day he lifted up his eyes, and saw the place afar off.*

Oh admirable perseverance of naked faith exempt from reflections and windings, which so long a road could not make to waver, no more than the presence of so amiable a son, of whom Abraham must be the innocent parricide. All natural and divine reasons—ought they not to hinder him from pursuing this road, and make him turn back,—the fear of being deceived, of being mistaken, of committing a crime against God and a cruelty against so dear a son? But how very far removed from these reasonings is naked faith! It does not even regard them, it has no eyes to look upon them. The command alone of God sufficeth it, and it is sufficient for it to believe what He has commanded without even examining whether it believes it or not: it has only ears to hear. Oh Faith, which removest mountains, thou makest to be done even more impossible things!

5. *He said unto his servants, Await me here with the ass: my son and I only go yonder to worship, and will return again to you.*

He does not take his *servants* upon the mountain which is to be the place of sacrifice; they would be too incapable for that, and would be scandalised at it. Let us by no means discover the secrets of the interior to those who serve God yet as hirelings. The ways of the purest faith can be trusted to those who, as its friends, serve it already without interest; but the extreme *abandons* are only for children, who as *Isaacs* merit learning the sacrifices which have God for their author, and of which they are to be the victims. Perhaps also Abraham left his servants for fear that from a false pity, they might trouble or hinder the execution of this generous and in appearance rash design.

> 6. *And Abraham took the wood for the burnt offering, and put it upon Isaac his son; and he took the fire in his hand and a knife, and they went both together.*

Which ought we here to admire,—the inflexibility of faith, pitilessly *loading* this poor victim, or rather the generosity of this soul in accepting the cross that is to consummate its sacrifice, represented so naturally by the wood which it is made to carry? Faith, the cross, and the burnt-offering go in company, and walk in concert to conduct the soul to suffering.

The *fire* and the *knife* must be united in order to immolate it and reduce it to ashes. Oh admirable figure of the interior, sustained by the word of Jesus Christ! "I am come," said He, "to bring fire upon the earth, and what do I wish except that it burn:" and further, "I am not come to bring peace, but the sword." The knife must kill, and the fire burn; and it is naked faith that commits in the soul all these ravages.

> 7. *Isaac said unto his father, Behold the fire and the wood, but where is the victim for the burnt offering.*

This question of Isaac's shows the ignorance in which faith conducts the soul until it has arrived at the place of suffering. Abraham's reply expresses the *abandon* to providence, which accompanies faith: and the docility of Isaac in making no further enquiries, marks the soul's fidelity in suffering itself to be blindly conducted by faith and abandon. But it would be a little thing for this generous soul—this innocent victim to allow itself to be led thus in obscurity, if, when it sees its death near and its loss inevitable, it changed conduct.

> 8. *Abraham replied, My son, God will provide for Himself a victim for His burnt offering.*

Chapter XXII.

9. *And having come to the place which God had showed him, Abraham built an altar, arranged the wood, and bound his son Isaac, and laid him upon it.*

This dear victim must let itself be *attached* to the cross by the bonds of faith: it must lower the neck under the knife without hesitating or lamenting. All this takes place in deep silence and profound death, which permits not the least relief to nature, not even a single sigh or groan. Oh truly, although the natural death of Isaac did not then follow, his mystic death was certainly accomplished, all hope having been taken from him, and all desire for life extinguished in him. The extinction of his own life in order to live no longer but in God, was the just price of this great sacrifice which he had accepted with his whole heart. Likewise the death of the ram was the figure of the mystic or mysterious death represented in Isaac; since this was really a mystic and mysterious death, as much on the part of Isaac with regard to Jesus Christ, as on the part of the ram that died for Isaac.

10. *And he took the knife in his hand, and stretched forth his arm to slay his son.*
11. *The Angel of the Lord cried unto him out of heaven, Abraham, Abraham! and he answered, here am I.*
12. *The Angel said, Lay not thine hand upon the child, and do him no harm. Now I know that thou fearest God; since to obey me thou hast not spared thine only son.*

The sacrifice was also entire on the part of faith: for Abraham, *lifting his arm*, was sincerely willing to immolate this son so dear to him. The manner and time which God makes use of to prevent the execution of this strange design, are admirable in showing the conduct that He exercises over souls of this degree. In the first place He waits for the very extremity before succouring them, for there are no longer either signs or assurances for them, but only the Divine moment, which causes things to happen and to be known only the instant that they are to be performed, and no sooner. In the second place, He makes them walk by this very thing in an entire loss: and in order to take from them everything distinct, He makes known to them things only as they happen.

This is also to try the purity of their love, which fears not to lose all to do the will of God, even to committing apparent crimes through an excess of *abandon* and trust in His wisdom and power. This promptitude of God in succouring the souls of *abandon* and faith in the extremity of their need, augments their *abandon* and faith: and this *abandon* and this faith cause Providence to redouble His care over these persons so wholly abandoned to Him: thus are they truly the souls of Providence.

> 13. *Abraham lifted up his eyes and perceived behind him a ram caught by the horns in a bush, and he took him, and offered him up as a burnt offering in his son's stead.*

God often appears to desire the sacrifice of everything, although in the execution He is contented with the least part, thus He accepts the *ram instead of Isaac*.

> 15. *The Angel of the Lord called unto Abraham out of heaven the second time, and said to him,*
> 16. *I swear by myself, saith the Lord, that since thou hast done this, and for love of me hast not spared thine only son,*
> 17. *I will bless thee, and will multiply thy seed as the stars of heaven, and as the sand that is on the sea shore: and thy posterity shall possess the gates of its enemies.*

God does not delay rewarding so liberal a sacrifice as this of his servant. And as this mystic death has been achieved by the real death and destruction of the victim—the ram, which was the figure of it, having been annihilated and reduced to ashes: so does God bestow upon this faithful soul new favours, and much greater than the first. It must be observed, that since immolation and sacrifice have been spoken of, all promises have ceased, and Scripture says nothing approaching to them: on the contrary these holy patriarchs walked in death: and by this very immolation all the promises that had been made to them appeared vain and useless, since they saw that everything was going to be destroyed for them: but naked faith has no more regard for blessings and past favours, nor for what has been promised to it: if it remembers them, this remembrance augments its death; for the soul cannot see them in itself, nor take anything of them for itself. But so soon as the sacrifice is finished, and the soul annihilated, God restores to it all its goods, and much more than it had before, but quite in another manner: for it has them no more in propriety, and it regards them no more as its own, but as belonging to God and being in Him.

When it is said to Abraham, that *his posterity will possess the gates of its enemies*, it is to signify that the soul which formerly had enemies extremely adverse and cruel to it, finds itself through its annihilation so strong over them, that it rules them, and holds them subject and as it were imprisoned: for to possess the gates of the place where the enemy is shut up is to hold him prisoner, and to become his master. So also these souls can no more fear the demon, since God, to whom they have unreservedly abandoned themselves by a generous love, has rendered him subject to them.

18. *All nations shall be blessed by him that shall come out of thee, for thou hast obeyed my voice.*

This expresses the inconceivable blessings God bestows on others on account of those persons so fully abandoned to Him. The greatest blessing is to make use of them for the formation of Jesus Christ in hearts: for it is *by Him* that *all the holy nations are blessed*. Therefore, as St. Paul remarks, "when God made His promises to Abraham and his son, He said not, to thy sons, as if speaking of many, but to thy son, as speaking of one alone who is Jesus Christ.

CHAPTER XXIII.

1. *Sarah lived one hundred and twenty-seven years,*
2. *And she died in the city of Arba. Abraham mourned for Sarah and wept for her.*

After faith and *abandon* have operated the mystic death, there must yet be lost this same *abandon*: it must die, not as to what there is real in it, which is even so much the more perfect, the more it is hid in God: but as to what it perceptibly had, and as to the facility of producing actions from it; for that being yet an obstacle to annihilation, it must be taken away. It is thus then that *abandon* dies, represented by *Sarah*, that is to say, that this soul, through having abandoned itself, loses all power of doing so any further: for it enters into God, where it dwells in total destitution, and where *abandon*, which had until now aided it to enter therein, leaves it. It costs it some *tears*, seeing that it can no more abandon itself: for it takes that as a more certain sign of its loss: but when it is established in destitution and loss into God, the pain ceases, and *abandon* being no longer perceived, is purer than it ever was before.

3. *Abraham said to the Children of Heth,*
4. *I am a stranger and a sojourner with you, give me as one of yourselves possession of a burying-place, that I may bury my dead.*
5. *The Children of Heth answered him,*
6. *Hear us, my lord, Thou art as a prince of God amongst us: choose of our sepulchres what pleases thee.*

There are Princes of God, and there are Princes of the world. Those of the world have authority only in their estates, and yet they are usually the slaves of those they rule over: since without them they can neither subsist nor defend themselves, nor undertake anything: but the Princes of God, who, as His children have entered into His freedom, are sovereign and mighty in the very place of their exile. They rule every one and are ruled by none. They are *as strangers with* men: but they are independent of the same men, and have a certain authority and gravity which surprise and oblige those who see them, and who do not comprehend this mystery, to look upon them with respect. The reason is that they bear the stamp of Divinity, as Princes bear the marks of their human authority. *Abraham*, whom the excess of his faith rendered *a stranger* and wanderer in the world, so that he might have no other country save heaven, who left his hereditary possessions in his fatherland, that God Himself might become his heritage,—Abraham, I say, is Sovereign Prince wherever he dwells. His independence makes itself known on all occasions. He enriches everybody, and receives nothing from any one, as he said to the King of Sodom, that "it should not be said that any one had enriched Abraham." Oh how rich he is who has God alone for his portion! It is the property of faith to impoverish in order to enrich, and to strip of everything so that God Himself may be our riches. David had experienced this happy state of denuded faith when He said: "The Lord is the portion of my inheritance;" adding afterwards: "the lines are fallen unto me in pleasant places: yea, I have a goodly heritage."

CHAPTER XXIV.

1. *Abraham was old, and already well advanced in years, and the Lord had blessed him in all things.*
2. *And he said to his eldest servant,*
3. *Swear unto me by the Lord, the God of heaven and earth, that thou wilt not take a wife unto my son of the daughters of the Canaanites, amongst whom I dwell,*
4. *But that thou wilt go into my country, and to my kindred, there to take a wife unto my son.*

This marks the perseverance of faith, and as since it has established the soul in God, it draws down upon it all kinds of blessings, for the soul essentially united to God is loaded in God Himself with all manner of good; and as faith alone can conduct the soul into God Himself, it is by it that the soul is *blessed in all things.* But so ample a blessing is only accorded to it when it is already *very old,* I mean in its consummation.

The *country of the Canaanites* is the figure of the corrupted world. It is never there that faith makes an alliance: it loves to ally itself to the people that fear God, although they may be in multiplied ways: hoping that, as they have already quitted sin, it will the more easily be able to reduce them to its unity. It calls for this purpose all its old servants. The *eldest servant* of faith is prudence, which is the first faithful servant that serves it on its road, and which, nevertheless, would become afterwards most troublesome to it, if it did not know to change it, as will be shown further on. This *servant* is the eldest and the most necessary to faith at its beginning, for it leads it to abandon itself to God by a holy prudence, which causes us, seeing our affairs going wrong in our own hands, to put them into the hands of God by a total *abandon.* It is this prudence which, according to the sage, is "the knowledge of the holy:" this then must be the office of a true prudence. Faith, however, seeing that prudence, which has been so useful to it up to this point, is becoming extremely hurtful when, after the abandon to God, it desires to unite itself to human foresight, calls it in the person of *Eliezer*, and makes it *swear* that it will never make an alliance of the already advanced interior life with the world: which could not be without making the most detestable of all mixtures; but that it will *go into the country* of the children of God, although still multiplied, which is the place whence faith itself takes its origin, so that it may there ally *its son*, the interior and already mystical life, born of *abandon* and faith.

> 5. *The servant replied, If the woman will not come into this country with me, must I bring back thy son into the land from which thou camest.*

Careful Prudence takes its precautions afar off, and would desire, in case there should be found no souls willing to enter into the interior ways (which is the alliance that faith desires to make), to *bring back* the already advanced interior man, figured in *Isaac*, into the multiplied ways sooner than leave him alone in the one and simple way: although God had drawn him from them in his father even before his birth. For faith is what takes hold of the soul in multiplicity to conduct it into unity; and communicating to it the germ of its own life, places it beyond the power of ever returning to its ancient origin, at least without violating God's order over it, and going contrary to His will.

> 6. *Abraham said unto him, Beware that thou bring not my son into that country again.*
>
> 7. *The Lord, the God of heaven, who brought me out of the house of my father, and out of the land of my kindred, who spake unto me, and sware unto me, saying, Unto thy seed will I give this land: He shall send His Angel before thee, that thou mayest take a wife unto my son from thence.*

Faith, which never abandons this soul until it be in God, where, after seeing all lost, it re-finds everything in perfect unity, says firmly: *Beware*, Oh prudence, of ever conducting my son into the country of multiplicity, *out of which God has drawn us* in His infinite goodness. I have this confidence, that the *Lord of heaven* and earth, *who has taken me from my father's house*, from the way and commerce with the creatures in which I was born, *and who sware unto me to give me this land* of repose in God, and not only to me, but also to all those of my children who will follow the same way by which I have conducted my Isaac —the model of souls abandoned and sacrificed to the supreme will of God: The Lord, I say, *will send his angel before thee*, and will dispose all things, so that the spouse and faithful companion destined for my son, may enter into the same way with him, and may likewise possess the land of peace and repose in God, which they must leave to the posterity to be born from them. The angel here spoken of is Providence; it is then that there begins the spiritual alliance.

8. *And if the woman will not be willing to follow thee, then thou shalt be clear from this my oath: only bring not my son thither again.*

9. *The servant bound himself by oath to perform what Abraham had commanded him.*

Faith says to Prudence, that *if this woman*, whom it is sent to choose, *will not come, it is freed from all oath*, provided that *it bring not back* its son, and that it leave him in repose and union, for that being chosen for the Divine repose, they must never, under any pretext whatever, return to multiplicity. This agrees with what is said elsewhere: " If ye keep my covenant, then ye shall be a peculiar treasure unto me above all people: ye shall be my priestly kingdom, and the holy nation that shall be consecrated to me." Upon which prudence swears to faith never to draw the abandoned soul from its way.

10. *And the servant took ten camels from the flock of his master, and took with him of all his goods, and he departed, and went into Mesopotamia, to the city of Nahor.*

He loads *ten camels*, representing the ten commandments of the law to be given to Moses, and which are observed interiorly by the mystics in a much more perfect manner than are the exterior, expressed simply by the letter. He loads them *with all his master's goods*, that is to say, with a great increase of graces which this way had drawn to it: so that love, faith, confidence, and all the virtues were so many riches that covered and sweetened the rigour of the law: they bring to her, moreover, all the goods of the house that is offered to her, so that concealing from her nothing of all the advantages of this way so simple, yet so rich, they may be able easily to attract her to it, and make her enter therein with pleasure. Mesopotamia is the country where people fear God though in multiplicity. Thence are drawn the docile persons, so as to introduce them into the country of peace and union.

> 11. *And he made his camels rest without the city by a well at even time, at the time when the women went out to draw water.*
>
> 12. *And he said, Lord God of Abraham my master, I pray Thee, help me this day, and show mercy to my master Abraham.*

The arrival of him who is sent to draw this woman (figure of the soul) from her multiplied state, is made in *the evening:* marking by that, that she was already in a repose half begun, or approaching repose, being at the end of the day of her activity; for God sends thus, when it is time, some person who points out the simple way. He seeks her *near the well,* that is to say, in the very practice of prayer, where she endeavours with all her strength, as do the young souls, to draw up the water of grace. *He makes the camels rest without the city:* to show that the graces coming of the passive faith, are not given in the tumult but in repose. And afterwards, addressing God, he makes his prayer to Him, in which this servant, albeit so wholly God's, speaks not of himself; he *entreats* Him only by *his master Abraham,* and on his behalf: for he knows that faith can obtain everything.

> 13. *Behold, I stand here by the well of water: and the daughters of the men of the city come out to draw water.*
>
> 14. *Let it come to pass then that the damsel to whom I shall say, Let down thy pitcher that I may drink: and who will answer me, Drink, and I will give thy camels drink also; let the same be she that Thou has destined for thy servant Isaac. Thereby shall I know that Thou hast showed mercy unto my lord.*

Chapter XXIV.

He asks of God that amongst so many persons following the same way, He may make known to him her whom He destines for the repose. But the condition in his prayer is wholly admirable and mysterious. He sees that all that can make the soul come forth from the country of multiplicity, to make it enter into the divine unity, is charity; that this charity is to be united to the abandoned soul, and that it is it that causes it to exist in a well purified love, although in the obscurity of faith. Therefore it is only charity which Eliezer seeks for Isaac, not an ordinary charity, but an abundant charity, fit to *water the flock* of Jesus Christ, included in Abraham. This is a mystery which would require a volume for its explication. And as the generosity of love performs more than is asked of it, this charity finds water to give to all according to their wants. This part of Scripture is enrapturing, seeing that everything relates so fitly to the interior conduct. It was necessary that the *wife* of Isaac be mother and nurse of the people of faith: therefore she is to be charity, that is to say, to give us in her person and conduct an excellent figure of it.

15. *Hardly had he finished these words, when, behold Rebecca appeared, daughter of Bethuel, the son of Milcha the wife of Nahor, Abraham's brother, bearing her pitcher upon her shoulder.*

16. *And the maid was very beautiful, neither had any man known her; and she went down to the well, and filled her pitcher and came up.*

Oh promptitude of God in hearing prayers made with faith when they are so just! The young girl came then immediately that Eliezer had finished his prayer.

She was very beautiful: for nothing is so beautiful as charity, which renders itself agreeable to all. She was a *virgin;* for charity is always pure; and having her origin in God Himself, she preserves herself always chaste in the midst of the creatures, without sullying herself by their commerce. She *went down to the well, and filled her pitcher:* charity is always accompanied by humility, which in emptying itself grows full: and like a fountain, the more it empties itself of its waters, the more the source, which is God Himself, communicates to it new waters. This is what makes these two virtues, represented under this mystery, absolutely necessary for the soul destined to *abandon* and unity in God, for the fidelity of charity consists in being always full for others, and retaining nothing for itself; and the perfection of humility is to empty itself unceasingly of the waters of grace, communicated to it, and to return them to God as pure as it receives them from Him.

Scripture says that Rebecca *returned again:* marking by that that although charity is beneficent to all, nothing, however, stops her: and that although she may go away quickly, she does not cease showing what she is, by doing good so soon as it is asked of her, and even sooner than that.

17. *The servant went before her, and said to her, Give me, I pray thee, a little of the water thou bearest, that I may drink.*
18. *And she answered, Drink, my lord, and letting down her pitcher upon her arm, she gave him to drink.*
19. *She added, I will draw water for thy camels also.*
20. *And she poured water from her pitcher into the trough, and ran to the well to draw another, and drew for all the camels.*

Who will not admire the grace and promptitude with which she does everything? She *wishes* even *to give water to all the camels*, for it is charity that waters and vivifies the law, represented by the camels. She does not cease until she has filled them with her water, for the law without her would be void: she has no sooner *emptied* her pitcher than she goes to fill it from the source, from whence she draws all her goods. Charity does not content herself with words: she comes from them to deeds, truly *giving water to all the camels*, as she had offered.

21. *Still the servant looked upon her without saying anything, to see whether the Lord had made his journey prosperous or not.*

He *contemplated her*, says Scripture, so well: for he was of the house of faith, of which even the servants are contemplatives. He looked upon her in silence, showing the repose and silence of contemplation; and he contemplated thus in silence, *to see whether the Lord had made his journey prosperous or not.* He does not interrogate this young girl: he does not make use of the multiplicity of discourse to be enlightened as to his

Chapter XXIV.

doubt: he only employs repose, by which he is better instructed than he had been by all the cares. Likewise did he also hesitate before speaking to her.

22. *And after all the camels had drunk, he drew out golden ear-rings, weighing two shekels, and bracelets of ten shekels weight.*

He gives to her of his riches, to make known to her by deeds, much more than by words, the way and country to which he desires to attract her. But what are the presents he makes to her? *ear-rings;* to make her comprehend, that there is now no other thing necessary for her but to hear and be silent; and that that is the practice of the country to which he wishes to conduct her. He gives her also *bracelets* for her hands; so as to make her understand that faith, silence, and good works, must be inseparable from charity; from all this she is to learn to hear, to act, and to be silent. She accepts this pledge as a mark that she is disposed to enter on this way, if obedience permit it to her. The ear-rings are of *gold*, to mark the purity with which we must listen to God: they only *weigh each one shekel*: showing that we must listen only to God Himself and His holy will: but *the bracelets* weigh *several shekels of gold:* for virtues and good works must be multiplied. The attention must be fixed on God alone: but practices are extended towards all.

23. *And he said to her, Tell me, I pray thee, whose daughter thou art? Is there room in thy father's house for me to lodge?*
24. *She said to him, I am the daughter of Bethuel, the son of Milcha, the wife of Nahor.*
25. *There is with us straw and provender enough, and room to lodge in.*

Prudence, which never hastes, leads the servant to enquire of this young girl *who she is:* she tells him; and he asks her, *if there is room to lodge in her father's house?* Charity, which is never empty, assures that at the house of her father (who is the figure of God) there is wherewith to *provide for all*, and infinite space to lodge and well receive all who have recourse to her.

26. *And the man bowed down his head and worshipped the Lord.*

27. *And he said, Blessed be the Lord, the God of my master Abraham, who has not failed to show mercy on him according to His truth, and who has led me straightway into the house of my master's brother.*

Prudence *worships* God, admiring how faith is never destitute of truth, and how God makes everything succeed happily with it, for there is nothing which conducts so direct as this same faith. This servant is all astonished that for having blindly followed it, he has been *conducted by a straight road* to the most desired place, and that he has found much more than he had dared to hope. This is what leads him to render justice to the truth of the way of faith, and to proclaim how straight and sure it is. He does not know what most to admire, the providence of God in providing for everything at the proper moment, or the generosity of faith in undertaking everything in obscurity and without assurance. He sees too how God blesses faith with so many graces that he cannot forbear being struck with it and constrained to worship God in all His ways.

29. *Rebecca had a brother called Laban, and he ran out to the man, unto the well.*

31. *And he said to him, Come in, thou blessed of the Lord, why remainest thou without? I have prepared the house, and room for thy camels.*

Laban seeing the pledges given to his sister, and which are the witnessings of the way of faith, comes out and seeks him who teaches her, to make him *enter into the house*. It happens as much thus to persons of good will when they obtain knowledge of these ways: they long to possess them and to introduce them to themselves: they receive them with pleasure, and protest that they have prepared with their best the *house* of their heart for their reception.

33. *They set meat before him, but the servant said, I will not eat until I have told mine errand.*

They hasten quickly to *give him meat to eat;* but he, instructed in the ways, says: *I will not eat until I have told mine errand:* for such is the will of the Lord. Oh faithful servant, forgetting his own interests and pressing needs to think only of executing the desires of God.

34. *And he spake to them thus, I am Abraham's servant.*
35. *The Lord hath blessed my master very greatly, and hath made him rich and powerful.*
36. *And Sarah his wife bare unto him a son in her old age, to whom my master hath given all that he had.—Etc.*

When he expatiates upon *the riches of his master* and the favours that God has bestowed upon him, he extols the magnificence of this way, and how much God blesses it, making it appear elevated above all others. For, although prudence has very little experience of faith in its progress, nevertheless it is obliged to admire it in its successes. He declares its origin, and shows that there is nothing hidden for it, for faith having *given all* that it possesses to it, has convinced it of its truth. He adds that abandon is the mother and nurse of this same way.

He imparts to them all the secrets of faith, so as to constrain them by that to give themselves to it, by making the recital of all Abraham had said to him, and all that had passed near the fountain.

50. *Bethuel and Laban answered and said, It is God that speaketh here; we can only answer thee what pleaseth Him.*
51. *Rebecca is in thine hands; take her with thee that she may be the wife of thy master's son, as the Lord hath ordained it.*

The efficacy of grace is so great in the mouth of an interior person, that they *cannot* refuse him anything, nor *reply to him;* and *they are constrained to confess* that all comes *from God*, whom it is difficult to resist. These relations are then constrained by a gentle violence to give their consent, after which charity is truly united to the way of abandon. And at the same time there is made the all divine spiritual *marriage* of the Bridegroom and Bride, who are united to finish their course in the interior way, and to lose themselves happily in God.

53. *The servant brought forth vessels of silver and gold, and*

raiment, and presented them to Rebecca; and he made presents also to her brethren and to her mother.

Then God displays all His riches to decorate and enrich His spouse.

But although He is almighty, He wishes, however, the consent of the spouse before making her wholly abandon her first way, denoted by her father's house; and causing her to embrace this one, which introduces her by simplicity into the depths of the interior.

58. *And they called Rebecca, and said unto her, Wilt thou go with this man? and she said, I will go.*

She agrees willingly, *replying* without artifice. This single word, *I will go*, suffices to express everything in a soul beginning to be instructed in the ways possessed by faith, and which are all simple.

60. *And they blessed Rebecca, and said unto her, Thou art our sister, be thou the mother of thousands of millions, and let thy seed possess the gate of those which hate them.*

Rebecca's relations having received considerable presents on account of her, teaches us how advantageous it is to be united to charity; for we participate also in its felicity, and all those connected with persons so cherished of God, receive singular graces by it. They afterwards *bestow a thousand blessings* upon this dear sister, *wishing her fruitfulness*, and that *she may possess the gates of her enemies*, which is the very blessing God gave to Abraham, and has been explained above (chap. xxii. ver. 17).

62. *Isaac walked in the road leading to the well of the Living and Seeing.*

63. *He had gone out to meditate in the field at even, and lifting up his eyes, he saw the camels at a distance.*

Isaac went towards the well of the Living and Seeing, that is to say, near the spring that is in God, who alone lives and sees. He walked in God; for the breadth of his soul was not straitened. He had come forth out of himself to better occupy himself with God alone. It was in this admirable intercourse that all-pure charity was brought to him, to be united to him by an indissoluble bond. He goes to meet her when he perceives her. Pure love is only granted to a soul when, having come out of itself, it occupies itself with nothing but God; and this happens only *towards the evening*, in the latter period of life, and after great labours.

> 64. *And when Rebecca perceived Isaac, she came off her camel.*
> 65. *And she forthwith took her veil and covered herself.*

She *comes off her camel* to go to him still more speedily; but she *covers herself with her veil*, which is fidelity; and thus equipped she goes to be united to him.

> 67. *Then Isaac brought her into the tent of Sarah his mother, and took her for his wife: and he loved her so much, that he moderated his grief, which the death of his mother had caused him.*

But what does Isaac? He does not amuse himself admiring the beauty of Rebecca, being already advanced in the way of faith, which has nothing sensual: but *he takes* her straightway *into the tent of his mother;* which is to make her enter into total *abandon*, which has been always represented by Sarah. And this *abandon* is the disposition immediate to union and to the enjoyment of the spouse. Therefore he makes her take that way. But having known the merit of charity, which renders the soul one in God alone, *he loves her so much that he forgets by that his grief caused by the death of Sarah*, which was the loss of abandon, which then became useless to him, being confirmed by charity in perfect destitution in God.

CHAPTER XXV.

> 1. *Abraham took another wife, named Keturah, who bare him six sons,*
> 5. *But he gave to Isaac all that he possessed.*
> 6. *He made presents to the sons of his other wives, and separated them during his life from his son Isaac, sending them into the country looking towards the east.*

Abraham had yet other children, but they had no part in the inheritance. Faith has many children to whom it gives some goods; but the *one Isaac*, son of naked faith and blind *abandon*, is the inheritor of all its riches. Those of the other ways have a share as servants, and have not a like habitation with him: Isaac is treated as an only son, and has nothing less than God Himself for heritage, since God was the possession of faith and *abandon*, of whom he is born. No soul ever arrives at the enjoyment of God, before being stripped of all support and all self-interest.

8. *And Abraham began to fail and died in a good old age.*
9. *And Isaac and Ishmael carried him to the Cave of Macpelah in the field of Ephron,*
10. *And buried him there, as he had done Sarah his wife.*

Abraham, the image of faith, having united his son to charity after conducting him by *abandon* and naked faith into God Himself, *begins to fail*, and faith itself *dies*. This patriarch having passed in substance into his son, and through him into all his descendants, all view of faith and all use of this light remain as dead and buried for the soul arrived in God Himself: because that all means, even the most necessary and most holy, finish when we have arrived at the last end. Then there is nothing for this soul to do but to enjoy pure charity in God Himself with an admirable purity and simplicity. And this is what precedes the Apostolic life, which is one and multiplied. For as God acts in everything without coming out of Himself or His unity, so also do these souls act outwardly without coming out of their unity in God. *Abandon* and faith are left at the same place, to wit, on arriving in God Himself.

Isaac remains with his spouse in this same place after the death of his father; since there could not be other abode for such a soul than that, though it should traverse the whole earth; for it might go throughout all the world without coming out of its place: thus it is added, that (v. 11) *after the death of Abraham God blessed his son Isaac, who dwelt near the well of the Living and Seeing.*

21. *Isaac prayed the Lord for his wife, for she was barren; and the Lord heard him, and Rebecca conceived.*

Charity reunited in God alone is in so perfect a repose, that she thinks no more of producing fruits abroad if she was not awaked from her gentle slumber by the occasions which providence gives rise to; for she possesses in herself all the blessings. *Isaac* her spouse *prays*, and *God immediately hears him*, giving him two children who become two very different peoples. Angels are lost in heaven: an apostle perishes in the company of Jesus Christ: and charity seems here to conceive and to bring forth a reprobate.

But as everything contributes to the glory of God and to the good of the chosen ones, according as a holy people is conceived in the bowels of charity, she conceives also a perverse people to try the former and make it suffer. To conceive and bring forth the race of the predestined, is to conceive and bring forth persecution and crosses. This nation, so holy, was persecuted before coming to the light, and suffered rude attacks before being born. There is no place exempt from the cross for the predestined, God makes them find it everywhere, it is born with them, it grows with their steps, and must be upon them until they expire.

22. *But the two children with which she was big struggled within her womb; which caused her to say, If this was to happen to me, why did I conceive? She went to inquire of the Lord.*

The soul not yet rendered firm in the experience of the ways of God *is afflicted* at seeing persecutions being born: and her grief obliges her to *consult the Lord.* This is the pious custom of the saints, to have recourse to God in their doubts and troubles; for all their trust is in Him. The example of all the patriarchs in this point shames Christians, who for the most part consult only the world or passion.

23. *God answered her, Two nations are in thy womb, and two peoples will come out of thy bowels, which shall be divided the one against the other; and the one people shall overcome the other; and the elder shall serve the younger.*

God consoles her, representing to her that it is necessary for it to be thus; and that after He has permitted the wicked to try the predestined, then they will be subjected to them; and the predestined who appear the *smallest* on account of their humiliations, will become *masters of their enemies.*

24. *When the time was come that she should be delivered, behold she was big with twins.*

There were found then *two children* in the same womb, the persecutor and persecuted; and by exchange master and servant. He who persecutes is the slave of his passions, whilst the persecuted enjoys an admirable freedom and peace. The good and the wicked have truly issued from the same womb of Divine power by the creation, and yet the wicked do not cease opposing God and the good. Sin alone makes this division.

25. *He that came out first was red and all covered with hair, and was called Esau. The other came out after him, holding in his hand his brother's heel: therefore was he called Jacob.*

The persecutor *comes out first*, whose aspect is as fierce as his disposition is to become; and as he is to be inhuman and cruel, he bears even upon his body the marks of a natural ferocity.

27. *When they grew, Esau became a cunning hunter, and loved to till the ground. But Jacob was a simple man dwelling in tents.*

Esau exercises his cruelty upon the animals which he takes *in the chase:* but Jacob, gentle and *simple*, tastes the repose of solitude, and imitating Jesus Christ beforehand, he exercises himself in retreat and prayer before applying himself to external employment. Grace leads to retreat and repose, until the Divine calling obliges us to put ourselves forward.

28. *Isaac loved Esau, for he ate of what he took in the chase; but Rebecca loved Jacob.*

Isaac loved Esau with some interest. It is so rare that one acts from pure grace, without any pursuit of self. The most holy are sometimes mistaken in the choice of their friendships: this choice is never perfect when interest, however so little, is mixed in it. But charity *loved Jacob*, because he was after God's heart; and having no self-interest, her love was accompanied by justice and sustained by equity.

30. *And one day Esau said unto Jacob, Give me of this red pottage which thou hast made ready; for I am very faint.*

31. *Jacob answered him, Sell me then thy birthright.*
33. *And Esau sware unto him, and sold him his birthright.*

This is an admirable conduct of God, making His creatures, even the most rebellious, serve His designs. Everything happens as if it was not premeditated, and by the most natural providences. God permits Esau to dispossess himself of the *right* that he had over his younger brother, and *to sell it to him* for a little sensuality, which is, to eat a mess of *pottage*. All this, which appears so unreasonable and inconsiderate, serves God's design, who never violates our freedom, but who conducts all things gently to their ends.

CHAPTER XXVI.

1. *And there came a famine over that land, as there was one in the time of Abraham. And Isaac went to Gerar to Abimelech, King of the Philistines.*
2. *For the Lord had appeared unto him and said to him, Go not into Egypt, but dwell in the country which I shall show you.*
3. *Sojourn in this land, and I will be with thee, and will bless thee; for unto thee, and unto thy seed, I will give all these countries, and I will perform the oath which I sware unto Abraham thy father.*
4. *I will multiply thy children as the stars of the heaven, and all nations of the earth shall be blessed in him that shall come out of thee.*

At whatever degree of grace the soul may have arrived, it often experiences privations, which are kinds of *famine;* but there is a time when they are no longer painful, because, although the famine may be over all the earth, that is to say, in the sensible part, we yet continue to have wherewith to provide for every need, which happens when the soul has no more will (of its own) for then it no longer suffers, because the will of God fully satisfies it. There is another *famine*, namely, the total privation of the very things that appear necessary: and it is not this that is here spoken of, at least with regard to Isaac; but we may take this famine for the state that comes when God wishes to drive the soul out from itself, and to cause it to be totally lost in Him. In this case it was this latter dearth which led Isaac to leave the place where he dwelt by the command of God. But where *does he go?* into a strange land; because for sometime he finds himself a *stranger* to himself. He dwells there as a pilgrim, not being permanently there, as he will be in the place that he is afterwards to possess.

God *forbids* him *to go into Egypt*. This part is most instructive for us, namely, that in the time of privations, and even of the most extreme famine, we must not sustain ourselves, nor preserve ourselves from the pain that we suffer, by multiplicity and our own efforts; but we must dwell in the place where God has placed us with much patience, until He withdraws us Himself. God, however, assures that He will be with the soul entirely abandoned to Him, in whatever place it may go to, and in whatever disposition it may be. Is not this too much for an afflicted soul, this assurance that God gives it? He again assures it that He will *give* it *the promised land*, which is the soul's permanent state in God, and is called transformation.

He will give it not only to Isaac, but to all those who, like him, will offer themselves up unreservedly to His whole will; and He even promises that there will be a great number of his descendants that will follow the same road with him. When there is said, that *all the nations of the earth will be blessed in him who will come out of Isaac*, Jesus Christ is meant, in whom all the graces and blessings are comprised.

6. *Isaac dwelt then in Gerar.*

7. *And the inhabitants of that country asked him of Rebecca: and he answered them, She is my sister.*

Isaac makes the same reply as his father did on a like occasion, by saying that *Rebecca is his sister*, and making use of this to preserve his life. Although there appears to be a falsehood here, it is nevertheless certain that he did not lie; for brother in Hebrew signifies relative, and they were accustomed to give the names of brother and sister to relatives of the nearest degrees, such as Rebecca and Isaac, who were

Chapter XXVI.

blood-relations. Thus in the Gospel, even the relatives of our Lord are called his brethren. This conduct, which appears human, covers great mysteries. It is sometimes given to interior persons to penetrate them: and far from that obscuring the majesty of the Word of God, it serves even to make it honoured by the greatest faith.

8. *Abimelech, King of the Philistines, was looking out of a window, and saw Isaac sporting with Rebecca his wife;*
9. *And calling him he said to him, It is truly seen she is thy wife; wherefore saidst thou, she is my sister?*

This charity of Abimelech in judging favourably of *Isaac*, condemns the rashness of those who censure everything immediately, and who are scandalised at the most innocent actions done in a holy freedom.

10. *And Abimelech charged all his people,*
11. *He that toucheth this man or his wife shall surely be put to death.*

Who will not admire God's protection of persons wholly abandoned to Him? He takes care of all their wants; He makes people take the greatest precautions for their safety, and even causes their advantages and blessings to spring from their faults. Isaac's wife, was she not more secure after the king's charge than before?

12. *Then Isaac sowed in that land, and received in the same year an hundred-fold; and the Lord blessed him.*
14. *This stirred up the Philistines' envy against him.*

This is the progress of the Apostolic life; after the soul has for a long time enjoyed the repose in God Himself, it proceeds to *sow its seed*, the fruits of which do not so soon appear, but which afterwards *yields an hundred-fold*.

This *attracts the envy* of the common souls, on account of not seeing a like success to their labours; because, working for themselves, or at least mingling something of their own interest in their most holy functions, they have not a blessing approaching that of the disinterested persons. It is God Himself who labours when we labour only for God, and if it is He who labours, how will He not bless His work?

15. *They stopped up all the wells which the servants of Abraham his father had digged, and filled them with earth.*

These proprietary persons persecute the Apostolic souls, *stopping up the wells* which faith, represented by *their father, had digged.* They endeavour to destroy the source of the waters they diffuse, and which has been digged by the purest faith, accusing them of evil doctrine; for not being able to condemn their morals, they attack their faith, endeavouring *to cover it with earth*, that is to say, with things maliciously invented, which they add to their pious and solid discourse.

17. *Isaac departed thence, and came to the valley of Gerar to dwell there.*
18. *And he caused the wells to be digged again which his father Abraham had digged, and which the Philistines had filled up after his death; and he called them by the same names which his father had given to them.*

These servants of God are often obliged to leave, and to go and *dig other wells*, which always contain the waters that faith has found, and which are always ready to water those who are so happy as to be the spiritual children of these persons who know how to dispense them. We may also observe the fidelity of Isaac in making no innovation or change in what has been established by faith, not even *the names*.

19. *They digged also in the bottom of the valley, and found there a well of springing water.*
20. *But the shepherds of Gerar strove with those of Isaac, saying, The water is ours. Wherefore he called the name of this well " Injustice."*

In the works done for God, too many people are found who *attribute* them to themselves, and who desire the glory of them as did these shepherds, who had not known that there was *springing water* in this place until Isaac had discovered it. He has no sooner found it, with much labour, than they dispute it with him, maintaining that it is theirs. But Isaac, as a perfect model of virtue, does not contest with them; he withdraws peacefully and abandons the well to them, practising the Gospel even before the Gospel. Perfect charity is known by detachment from what is dear and useful to us; and whoever prefers not peace to interest will lose charity for it also.

> 22. *Going from thence he digged another well, for which there was no dispute: wherefore he call it "Breadth," saying, Now the Lord has made room for me, and hath caused my goods to increase upon the earth.*

He withdraws twice for the same reason, and only takes possession of the water that no one disputes with him, because to him peaceful and tranquil waters were necessary: and as his soul had wide scope within, no more must it find anything outwardly that would limit or straiten it. The preacher of the Gospel must be thus also, above all he who preaches the most interior Gospel. He must dig his wells in places sheltered from debates and contests, and by no means quit these places until God gives the opportunity. For as his soul is at large, without anything straitening it, no more must he be under restraint in his ministry. The purity of faith and the Gospel, being drawn from God Himself, who is all peace, we must dig wells only in the places where the water is received wholly pure, and where we can possess it quietly.

> 24. *On the following night the Lord appeared to him, and said, I am the God of Abraham thy father; fear not, for I am with thee. I will bless thee and multiply thy seed because of Abraham my servant.*

The Lord appeared unto him the night after he had found these tranquil waters: and to re-assure him still more against oppositions, *He said unto him, Fear not: I am the God of thy father, and I am with thee.* He gratified him also by this appearing, making known to him how much he approved of his practising beforehand what His son has since taught us: "And I say unto you, that ye resist not evil." We cannot forsake for God anything, however little, but He recompenses it Himself: and the more we renounce ourselves, the more He approaches us.

> 25. *He built an altar in that place, and called there upon the name of the Lord: and there he pitched his tent, and commanded his servants to dig a well.*

This Divine assurance leads these Apostolic men to offer

sacrifices to the Lord in this place of peace which they have found ; and to pitch their tent there, to dwell there, and to produce there all the fruit that God desires.

32. *The same day Isaac's servants came and told him of the success of the well which they had digged, telling him that they had found water.*

33. *Therefore he called this well "Abundance."*

God overwhelms the labour of His Apostolic workers with blessings, promising them to multiply their children of grace even to infinity on account of their faith. Thus this *well*, formed in tranquility, furnished waters in so great *abundance*, that it merited bearing this name. Whoever labours by the order of God does not fail to find in Him the source of living waters.

CHAPTER XXVII.

6. *Rebecca said to Jacob her son, I heard thy father tell Esau thy brother, saying,*

7. *Bring me something from thy hunting, and prepare it for me, that I may eat of it and bless thee before the Lord before I die.*

8. *But, my son, follow my counsel.*

9. *Go thou to the flock, and bring me two of the best goats thou canst find, that I may make savoury meat for thy father, for I know he loveth it.*

10. *And after he has eaten, he will bless thee before he dies.*

This procedure of Rebecca is so divine, that it is easy to judge from her example that a soul established in God alone, and confirmed in charity, acts by Divine inspiration even when it seems to err. God uses the affection of the mother, and the faithfulness of the son in remaining in his solitude, to execute His designs and effect His promises. According to the laws that God had established with regard to these patriarchs, everything depended on the blessing of this father; and God causes this blessing to fall quite naturally upon Jacob. There was no lie in all this; the truth was found there as much on the side of nature as in the order of grace: Jacob having acquired the natural birthright over his brother, and possessing it still more by the pre-eminence of his interior, since he dwelt in continual union with God, and as he was to become the father of interior and deified souls, and God Himself was to be born of him, he could say with truth to his father Isaac that he was his eldest son.

11. *Jacob answered her, Thou knowest that my brother Esau is an hairy man, and I am a smooth man.*
12. *If then my father should feel me and perceive it, I fear I shall seem to him a deceiver, and thus I shall draw down upon me his curse, and not his blessing.*
13. *His mother said to him, My son, upon me be this curse, only hearken to me, and fetch me what I have told thee.*

Jacob's fear proceeded from his candour. Interior and innocent souls fear the least turning more than death: obedience, however, re-assures them. Moreover, an interior and truly abandoned soul, as Jacob, is contented with stating its reasons; then it abandons itself without further reasoning or fearing. All persons of faith and *abandon* follow the same conduct: so also does Providence cause everything to succeed happily for them, even to their faults and follies. But in this particular case of Jacob's, there was nothing but what was most mysterious.

15. *Rebecca took Esau's best raiment, and put it upon Jacob.*
16. *And she put the skins of the kids of the goats upon his hands and upon the smooth of his neck.*
21. *And Isaac said unto Jacob, Come near, I pray thee, that I may feel thee my son, whether thou be my very son Esau or not.*
22. *And Jacob went near unto Isaac his father; and he felt him, and said, The voice is Jacob's voice, but the hands are the hands of Esau.*
23. *And he recognised him not.*

God *hides* these interior souls *under the skin of Esau*, that is to say, under the appearance of the commonest life. There is nothing on the exterior, nor on their dress, that can distinguish them; *speech* alone can make them recognised. Creatures speak as creatures, but the deified souls have only the words of God in their mouth, and they have all one and the same language. All can have the skin and raiment of Esau, but the deified souls alone can have *the voice of Jacob*. It is impossible to make these souls speak another language than that which God teaches them. They are accommodating with every one, and conform themselves easily to all that is desired according to God; but for their language, none can make them change it. It is always the same. Oh holy patriarch Isaac, how wouldst thou *know* Jacob *by the touch*? Didst thou not know indeed that the voice alone could distinguish him? But, perhaps knowing God's design, when thou recognisedst the voice of Jacob, thou sufferedst things to proceed according to the order of Providence: although we must hold to Scripture, which says, that *thou didst not know him*, God permitting it thus for the accomplishment of His designs.

27. *Isaac then blessed him and said to him,*

29. *Be lord over thy brethren, and let thy mother's sons bow down before thee. Cursed be he that curseth thee, and let every one that blesseth thee, himself be blessed.*

He gives him *authority over his brethren and the children of his mother*. It is in this that the contemplative life is truly elevated above the active life, and ought to be preferred to it, according to the witness of Jesus Christ himself given on behalf of Magdalene: "Mary, said He, "hath chosen the better part which shall not be taken away from her."

This place also truly marks how sensible God is to the cry raised by the lovers of themselves against these interior ways, and the persecutions they excite against the contemplatives: He threatens those with *His curse* who ill-treat them, and will *load* those *with His blessings*, who respect and imitate them, for there are none whose love is more purified, there are none more dear to Him; so much so that he calls them "people after His own heart," and considers them as the "apple of His eyes"; because abandoning themselves unreservedly to His whole will, they give place to Him to reign sovereignly over them.

Chapter XXVII.

31. *Esau presented to his father what he had prepared from his hunting, saying, Rise, my father, and eat of thy son's venison, that thou mayest give me thy blessing.*
32. *Isaac said to him, who art thou? He answered, I am Esau thy first-born.*
33. *Isaac was greatly amazed, and astonished beyond measure at what had happened; he said, Who then is he who has already brought me what he had taken in the chase, and has given me to eat of everything before thou camest? and behold I have blessed him and he shall be blessed.*

Isaac's astonishment was extreme. Prophets have not always the spirit of prophecy, and their natural actions serve in God's hands to accomplish His mysteries. It is, however, credible that he knew then the marvel of the secret concealed underneath, which caused his firmness in not changing what he had done, and persisting in always subjecting Esau, representing the active life, to Jacob signifying contemplation.

34. *And when Esau heard the words of his father, he cried with a great and exceeding bitter cry, and said unto his father, bless me, even me also, my father.*
35. *And he said, thy brother came with subtlety, and hath taken away thy blessing.*

Isaac does not repent even of this mistake, no more than Rebecca of this apparent fault; for the souls that are in God cannot see anything out of God: therefore they cannot attribute anything to the creature, but, mounting higher, they make use of everything in a Divine manner. One of the surest signs that a person is truly God's, is this rare immovability of spirit in things even that cause the most confusion.

36. *And Esau said, He is rightly named Jacob, for hath he not supplanted me these two times?*
37. *Isaac answered him, I have made him lord over thee, and all his brethren shall serve him.*

The name of *Jacob*, signifying to supplant, had been given to this patriarch on account of his having laid hold of his brother's heel in birth. Here Esau uses it to complain of his brother surprising him by artifice. It is true that Jacob takes place above him; but justly so, since it is due to him by so many titles. Notwithstanding Esau's complaints, Isaac yet continues to confirm what he had done, declaring anew that he *subjects* the active life to the contemplative. For although the active life is necessary, and has also its fruits, nevertheless it regards the contemplative as its perfection and end; since all good works tend only to the enjoyment of God, who is the portion of contemplation. Therefore it is said that *the elder shall serve the younger:* because the active life is the first that is practised: but it is as much inferior to the contemplative which follows it, as the means are inferior to the end for which they are destined.

> 41. *Esau always thereafter hated Jacob, because of this blessing which he had received from his father, and he said in his heart, The time of my father's death draweth nigh, and then will I slay my brother Jacob.*
> 42. *And when Rebecca heard this, she said to Jacob,*
> 43. *Believe me, my son, arise, flee thou to Laban my brother, to Haran.*

The advantage which the contemplative souls have over the active ones attracts the jealousy of the latter, who being pained at seeing them preferred, excite persecutions against them: which is the true mark that they seek themselves much in their pious labours, and not solely the interests of God.

But charity here signalises her all-heavenly prudence, by separating these two brothers on account of the difference of their ways, which can indeed agree together when they are united in one person with the subordination which God institutes for the good of many: but which harmonize with difficulty in diverse persons who go not by the same ways, because the multiplicity and bustle of the active people cannot bear the simplicity and repose of the contemplatives.

> 46. *Rebecca said to Isaac, I am weary of my life because of the daughters of Heth. If Jacob take to wife a daughter of this land, I have no more wish for life.*

It often happens that the active life makes an alliance with the human and sensual life. Persons unwittingly mingling prayer with activity, act usually in a very human and natural manner, and are sometimes more dangerously buried in nature than recognised sinners. Now charity, who is the mother of the active life, as well as the contemplative, *complains of this alliance*, which causes her extreme grief, and enfeebles her so greatly in the soul possessing her, that insensibly *it destroys her life*. Therefore she says: *I am weary of my life;* as if saying, I am ready to perish in this soul because of this unhappy mixture.

But although that displeases her much, it is quite another thing when the human life is united to the contemplative: for the malignity of nature even turns into corruption the delights of the spirit, and it could not be believed how far its infection goes when it is mingled with spirituality. It is quite otherwise than in the first souls, and so much the more dangerous as it conceals itself under the most beautiful pretexts. This causes charity to say: if *Jacob* (the contemplative soul) *allies himself* with nature to produce fruit from the flesh and the spirit, which are impure fruits, *I have no more wish for life*. It is certain that the spiritual persons, who become carnal, extinguish the life of charity in a much more cruel manner than the greatest sinners and imperfect souls do. Therefore St. Paul gives this warning: "Beware that after having begun by the spirit, ye finish not by the flesh."

CHAPTER XXVIII.

1. *And Isaac called Jacob, and blessed him, and said unto him, Thou shalt not take a wife of the daughters of Canaan.*

2. *But go thou into Mesopotamia, which is in Syria, to the house of Bethuel, thy mother's father; and take a wife from one of the daughters of Laban thine uncle.*

3. *And God Almighty bless thee, and make thee fruitful and multiply thy seed, that thou mayest be the chief of many peoples.*

Isaac, *after blessing his son*—the model of the true contemplatives and souls abandoned to the conduct of their God—forbids him to ally himself with the human and carnal life, which would be incompatible with his grace. He directs him on the contrary to *come out* of himself, denoted by his leaving the place where he dwells, *and to take to wife a daughter of his mother's family*, as if he said: far from making an alliance with the human or carnal life, take no other spouse than her who is connected with charity. Thou must make a new alliance with her: for although she has given thee birth, thou mightest lose her if thou didst not preserve her alliance. We must be united to pure love, and not to natural love, human or carnal. If thou actest thus, thou wilt receive a thousand blessings, and so divine a marriage will be followed by a posterity as pure as abundant.

Jacob will be in the latter ages *the father of many nations*, as he has already been in the preceding ones, with regard to all the great contemplatives who have distinguished themselves from the rest of men. But he will be so quite in another manner when this spirit will have spread over all the earth, and the world has been renewed by it. Oh God, do Thou send this interior spirit over the whole earth, and it will be created anew! Let this same spirit rest on the waters of Thy common grace, and it will communicate to them a most abundant fruitfulness. If the interior spirit, which is but charity and prayer, animate not the faculties of our soul and their productions, they are barren in themselves, and unfruitful for others; but if this spirit of life actuates us, our works are truly worthy of God; and the regard with which He looks upon them, causes Him to give them His blessing, by virtue of which they sanctify ourselves, and contribute to the sanctification of many others.

11. *Jacob came to a place where he wished to rest after the sun was set, and he took of the stones that were there, and put one under his head, and slept in that place.*

The soul, amorous of its God and united to him, finds nothing that hinders it from *reposing* in Him. Its journeys never interrupt its repose, nor does its repose hinder its walk. *Jacob* stops in the middle of the road, and makes his bed there. *He takes* the very *stones found there* to serve for his pillow: he chooses one of them *to support his head;* and this stone was the figure of Jesus Christ, his only support. He softly *reposes* upon this earth; because it is the earth of repose and contemplation promised to the spiritual race, that is to say, to all the

Chapter XXVIII.

contemplative souls, who love better to repose upon this earth, though hard, than upon strange ground.

Such have always been the children of so holy a father when they have said by David: "How shall we sing the Lord's song in a strange land"? How could we rest in a multiplied way, we who are born for unity and the repose of contemplation?

Jacob *sleeps*, and enters into ecstasy *after the setting of the sun:* the excess which leads the soul into the pure divine light, is only caused by the extinction of natural light; and it is necessary that what is acquired give place to what is to be infused.

12. *And he saw in a dream a ladder, whose foot rested upon the earth, and the top of which reached to heaven: and angels of God were ascending and descending by this ladder.*
13. *He also saw the Lord resting upon the top of the ladder, who said to him, I am the Lord, the God of Abraham thy father, and the God of Isaac. To thee and to thy seed also will I give the land on which thou sleepest.*

Jacob, sleeping in a mystic sleep, *sees a ladder going from this earth* of repose *up to heaven; and God resting upon the top of the ladder.* This ladder, resting with its foot upon this earth of repose, and which served at the other end for repose to God Himself, marks the degrees that must be ascended in order to proceed from the repose of contemplation up to the repose in God alone. The distance is great. These souls, although wholly *angelic, ascend and descend:* for even the degrees of ascent often become for them degrees of descent, either apparent or real: but everything is equal for such a soul by the excellent use it knows to make of them,—abandoning to God everything that regards it. *The top* of this ladder *is in heaven* and in God Himself; since Scripture says, that God rested upon the top of the ladder. This means, that these steps, representing the ways of ascent and descent variously conducting to God, all cease when one is arrived at Him alone, just as a ladder would be useless to a person who by its aid had ascended to where it reached.

The Lord was resting upon the ladder. He who supports the whole world, and sustains it by His almighty arm, can He lean upon anything? Yes, truly; for He finds a delicious repose in souls who, by their perfect annihilation, by the loss of all means, have arrived at the last degree of their origin, which is God.

With what complacency would God not repose in a soul which reposes no more but in Him? This is to repose in Himself, since this soul has no longer anything out of Him.

This mysterious *ladder* also teaches us by God resting upon its summit, that as souls having come out from Him by the creation, come by these steps of descent upon the earth of an impure life; so also to return into Him, they must re-ascend by the way they have descended. This thought has caused many mystics to say, that the soul, to re-enter into God by a perfect union, must have attained to the purity of its creation; which is understood by the loss of all spot and propriety. This is very well expressed by this ladder, where to arrive at God, the same degree must be attained which was left in descending from Him,—which is quite natural.

It was here God promised that *this land* of repose *would be given* not only to these first mystics, but also *to all their descendants;* and that all the persons who would walk in this same way, and who like Jacob would rest in contemplation, would be able to ascend the whole ladder and arrive at God. Therefore the Lord said to Jacob: *They will possess the land on which thou liest*; for this was the place whereon the ladder was set: otherwise, the promise would have been a small affair taken in the strict letter, since he could rest only on a very small piece of ground.

14. *Thy seed shall be multiplied as the dust of the earth. Thou shalt spread abroad from the east to the west, and from the north to the south, aud all nations of the earth shall be blessed in thee, and in him that will come out of thee.*

He promises him that this interior people will become so *numerous that it will equal the dust of the earth.* This expression, the dust of the earth, can be understood as to number, or as to the quality of this people. According to number, God represents to him that it will be so multiplied, that some of them will be found in all places, and that in all nations there will be this interior people; which has been indeed verified, and is and will always be true: for there is no place where some are not found. According to quality, they are souls so annihilated that they are reduced into the dust of their nothingness; therefore Scripture says not: they will be multiplied as much as the dust, or more: for that would signify but the

Chapter XXVIII.

excess of number; but it says, *as the dust*, expressing very well their annihilation.

> 15. *I will be thy protector wherever thou goest; I will bring thee again into this land, and will not leave thee until I have fulfilled all that I have said unto thee.*

God assures him that He Himself will *protect him*, and *bring him back*: showing by this that it is He who conducts souls abandoned to Him, in all ways, until He brings them back into Himself, their birth-place.

> 16. *And Jacob awaked out of his sleep, and he said, Surely the Lord is in this place and I knew it not!*

When he *awoke from his mystic sleep, he said that God was there and he knew it not;* not that he didn't know that God was everywhere; but because the souls of this degree are so absorbed in peace and union, and faith conducts them so nakedly, that they possess God without thinking they possess Him, and without having any knowledge of it, with the exception of some moments, when He makes Himself a little perceived, which is as when one awakens from a deep sleep. Faith and *abandon* blind them, as the too great light of the sun dazzles, so that they cannot distinguish anything of Him. It is as a person seeing in the atmosphere and breathing it without thinking that he sees it and breathes it, on account of his not reflecting upon it. These souls, although wholly penetrated by God, do not think of it, for God hides from them what they are; therefore is this way called *mystic*, meaning secret and imperceptible.

> 17. *And he was seized with fright, and cried, How terrible is this place! Surely this can be no other than the house of God, and the gate of heaven.*

Scripture says *that he was afraid, and cried, How terrible is this place!* This followed on the knowledge given him of the extreme sufferings through which these chosen souls must pass to arrive at the gate of heaven: for otherwise, what was there dreadful in this gate, and should he not sooner have entered into admiration and transports of joy, discovering the abode of glory? Yet, on the contrary, he cries, How terrible and dreadful is this place! This can be nothing less than the house of God and the gate of heaven. Should he not rather have said in the usual manner: Oh how desirable this place is! How lovely and charming it is, since it is the house of God and the gate of heaven? But as at this moment he comprehended more than he was to express, he was contented to say that. He knew all that he must suffer, and the strange ways through which God conducts souls to bring them to the gate of heaven; but he said no more, because there are secrets of which it is not permitted for man to speak.

18. *And Jacob rose up early in the morning, and took the stone that he had put for his pillow, and set it up for a monument, and poured oil upon the top of it.*

20. *And he made a vow, saying, If God remain with me and lead me in the road that I go, and give me bread to eat, and raiment to put on;*

21. *And if I return to my father's house in peace, the Lord shall be my God;*

22. *And this stone which I have set up for a monument shall be called the house of God.*

This *monument* was to be a memorial to posterity of what had happened to Jacob in this place, and what he had there known.

It is the property of the knowledge we receive in this so obscure a way, to cause fear and hesitation. Moreover, in the way of faith and abandon, we should stop neither at visions, words, favours nor anything assuring, for this assurance would retard the course: therefore Jacob, well instructed both for himself and for us, without stopping at what he had seen, or even what God had said to him, and courageously going beyond all things to halt only at the divine moment of providence, who is the only assurance without assurance of abandoned souls, says to himself: *If the Lord remain with me, and if* by His providence *He conducts me*, so that He protect me from sin *in* so dangerous and intricate a way; then shall I confess Him as my God. But although I blindly abandon myself to His providence, and desire no other conduct than His during all the way, yet cannot I have complete assurance and experience that He is my God, until I be in the peace of *my father's house*, that is to say, in the repose of my origin, because the obscurity of this way would always keep me in some inequality.

But how can a *stone* be called the *house of God?* It is because the stone being the sign of the mystic repose, where everything is hidden, the soul which, by a rare felicity has passed over all the mystic deserts and has arrived in God Himself, cries for itself and others that the mystic way is assuredly the habitation of God.

CHAPTER· XXIX.

9. *And while Jacob yet spake with the shepherds, Rachel came with her father's sheep; for she tended the flock herself.*
10. *And when Jacob saw Rachel, the daughter of Laban, his mother's brother, and the sheep of Laban, he rolled the stone from the well's mouth, and watered the flock.*

It is here *Jacob*, who *gives water* for the use of *Rachel;* and it was Rebecca who gave it for the servants and camels of Isaac. This difference marks for us a profound mystery: neither Jacob nor Rachel, at the time the water was poured out, was yet sufficiently prepared for the spiritual marriage: Rachel had yet no tincture of the spiritual life; therefore Jacob himself must make the waters flow, for it is to him, on account of his father, that the promise had been made. Moreover, Rachel was to be barren; and although she contributed with Jacob to the birth of two numerous enough tribes, yet the source of living water, Jesus Christ, was not to issue from her, but from Jacob, who, for this reason, gives the water—the figure of the graces of salvation and perfection which were to be communicated by the Saviour of the world. But Rebecca, being a source whence was to issue the pure and vivifying water, which is Jesus Christ, could water the peoples in the person of Eliezer and on behalf of Isaac. Jacob performs the office of shepherd to Rachel, for he is in Jesus Christ, or rather Jesus Christ is in him, the legitimate Shepherd, who is to water his flock with the water from the rock.

11. *And Jacob kissed Rachel, and lifted up his voice and wept.*

He *kisses her* as a sign of the union he makes with her, associating her by this kiss to the way and life of faith. He *sheds tears* on account of the presentiment he has that although she is most beautiful and extremely virtuous, yet she will never have the advantage of producing Jesus Christ in souls: the love that Jacob bore for her, being mixed with the natural, could alone hinder this production, which shows that a greater purity and more complete stripping is necessary for the Apostolic life, than for every other life however holy it may be, and although it appear full of virtues.

20. *Jacob served Laban seven years for Rachel; and this time seemed to him only a few days, so great was his love for her.*

The natural love that Jacob bore *for Rachel* was a weakness which God permitted in this holy patriarch: so the *seven years that he served* in the hope of espousing her were not counted, and *they appeared but a few days*. But these kinds of weaknesses in souls of this fortitude serve also the design of God, contributing to their annihilation, so as to render them fit for the cross, and at the same time to dispose them for the Apostolic life, which is given by the cross, represented by Leah. The sweetnesses of contemplation alone (denoted by Rachel) can never produce this life divinely fruitful on behalf of souls. It must be the cross that gives it. Prayer must be joined to the cross in order to bear these fruits of grace: the cross pours out the blood of Jesus Christ into the womb of prayer so as to render it fruitful; and prayer sheds upon our crosses the Spirit of God, whom it attracts from heaven to sanctify them.

21. *After that he said unto Laban, Give me my wife, for the time has arrived when I must espouse her.*
22. *Laban got ready the marriage feast.*
23. *And in the evening he took Leah his daughter into Jacob's chamber.*

God, who is full of goodness, agreeably deceives us. He first makes us love interior sweetnesses, and then when we think of attaching ourselves to them and of living contented with them, He substitutes the cross in their place. Interior consolations (figured by Rachel) being always agreeable, the

Chapter XXIX.

soul through infidelity and feebleness becomes attached to them in a disorderly manner. God, however, suffers it to love them for a time, and bestows them abundantly: but it is to dispose it to suffer the cross He prepares for it.

24. *Jacob found in the morning that it was Leah.*
25. *And he said to his father-in-law, How hast thou treated me thus? Have I not served thee for Rachel? Why hast thou deceived me?*

By day it is Rachel we love, that is to say, whilst the illuminative state lasts: *by night* it is Leah we possess, when the obscurity of faith has arrived. Faith loves Leah because of her fruitfulness: nature loves Rachel because of her beauty. Leah is blear-eyed; but she is as agreeable in the repose of the night as Rachel; she is even taken for her. The cross is ugly when it is regarded with reflection, but the soul that possesses it in the repose of union without reflecting upon it, finds there as many pleasures as amidst the greatest sweetnesses. Self-love, then, which served God for sweetnesses, and expected to possess them for ever, finding nothing else but distaste and the cross, complains of it to God Himself. What, it says, is this the reward Thou hast promised me for my long services? I believed that afterwards Thou wouldst load me with spiritual pleasures: and behold Thou sendest me only afflictions and bitterness! Whence comes to me this so unlooked for change?

26. *Laban answered him, It is not the custom of this country to give the youngest daughters before the first-born.*
27. *Pass the week with her, and I will give thee the other afterwards for the time of seven other years which thou wilt serve me.*
28. *Jacob accepted her; and after seven days he espoused Rachel.*

God, full of compassion for this soul, consoles it and says to it: Suffer only for some days the afflictions that I apportion to thee: and afterwards will I give thee in real and intimate possession the sweetnesses which thou hast only outwardly and for some moments. But grief must precede this pleasure; for the cross in My sight possesses the *birth-right* and it must pass before the intimate and lasting pleasures; for all the enjoyment of this life is a very little thing, and I grant it to thee only on account of thy weakness; but after thou shalt have tasted of this eternal sweetness, which I promised thee, thou must yet *serve me seven years*, so as to repay with some labours a good that cannot be estimated.

> 30. *Jacob having at last obtained the so much desired nuptials, preferred the love of the second to the first, and served Laban yet seven other years.*

Souls not advanced in the ways of truth prefer the love of delights to the love of the cross: and this is what greatly retards their progress. God permits all this in Jacob to instruct us: since as the great Apostle declares, "There is nothing in Scripture that is not written for our instruction."

> 31. *When the Lord saw that Leah was little esteemed, He opened her womb, whilst her sister remained barren.*
> 32. *She conceived, and bare a son whom she called Reuben, saying, The Lord hath looked upon my humiliation, and now my husband will love me.*

The cross, so little agreeable and so little loved, is always *fruitful:* which makes an enlightend soul prefer it above everything else; but sweetnesses, which cause only an apparent pleasure, have a veritable *barrenness*, whilst the cross, under the form of bitterness preserves inexpressible advantages.

The cross, represented by *Leah*, expresses the joy she has of being a mother, in the hope that *her husband*, the soul to whom she is united, seeing her fruitfulness, will entertain for her all the esteem that is due to her. Nevertheless, she is not carried away by it, recognising that all comes from God, who has given her this advantage so as to raise her from her natural *abjection*, and faithfully consecrating to Him all the glory of it. The cross must be judged by its fruits: the senses cannot taste them, but the spirit discovers them by faith.

> 34. *She conceived again.*
> 35. *And the third time she bare a son, and she said, Now will my husband be more united to me, seeing I have given him three sons; therefore she called his name Levi.*

It is a strange thing that the cross, which has so many

advantages, has so much difficulty in making herself loved. Behold her here producing the priestly race and all that there is of the greatest: yet hardly can she make herself loved. The first time she gives birth she aspires to nothing but to render herself less despicable: at the second, she hopes to render herself worthy of being loved: but the third time, after producing Levi, who is the Royal Priest, she believes she has made herself to be desired, and that the soul to whom she has been given, having become wiser, will long to be united to her.

> 36. *She conceived again for the fourth time, and she bare a son and said, Now will I praise the Lord: therefore she called him Judah, and left off bearing.*

But, *at the fourth time*, she only *gives praises to the Lord*, which is to announce *Jesus Christ* in *Judah*, from whom he was to proceed. And as in Jesus Christ there is found the end and consummation of every desire; so after having given Judah *she left off bearing*.

The cross, enraptured at so noble a production, which she sees born from her, holds herself so high above everything created, that she speaks no more of Jacob, and shows no more desire to possess him, as at the other times; but only with a bold flight at the sight of so admirable a production, she cries: Oh, this time *I will praise the Lord*, having nothing more upon the earth that can arrest my desire! The cross could not produce anything greater than the salvation of all the world, which she has truly given birth to, when, by the blood which Jesus Christ has shed upon the cross, peace has been made between things in heaven and things on the earth.

CHAPTER XXX.

> 1. *And when Rachel saw that she was barren, she envied her sister; and said unto Jacob, Give me children or else I die.*
>
> 2. *And Jacob's anger was raised; and he said to her, Am I God, who hath withheld from thee the fruit of the womb?*

Sweetnesses, although spiritual, would desire to have the

advantage of the cross ; and tiring of their barrenness, they say to the soul which possesses them : *Cause some production to be born* of us, *else we die;* why should the cross have all the advantage? They would wish either to exist no longer, or to participate in the fruitfulness of the cross. The soul, seeing the little solidity of this way of sweetnesses, grows angry, and shows it that *God* alone can *make it fruitful.* The cross and consolation are trials which exercise differently the same person, just as these two wives, who were the figure of them, exercise Jacob their husband. To be faithful in these trials, we must receive them equally from *God's hand,* and regard them only in Him.

3. *And she said, Behold my maid Bilhah, go in unto her ; and she shall bear upon my knees, that I may also have children by her.*
4. *And she gave him Bilhah her handmaid to wife.*
5. *And Bilhah conceived, and bare Jacob a son.*

Rachel, seeing that she cannot produce anything on account of her barrenness, has recourse *to her servant.* So the soul in the sweetness of contemplation, seeing herself powerless, has often recourse to a servant by whom to obtain productions, making use of some exterior works of charity, which she appropriates to console herself for her barrenness, and to provide for herself a natural support.

14. *And one day Reuben went into the field in the days of wheat harvest, and found mandrakes, which he brought to Leah his mother. Rachel said to her, Give me of thy son's mandrakes.*
15. *Leah replied; Is it not sufficient for thee to have taken away my husband without desiring also to have my son's mandrakes? Rachel answered, I am willing that he sleep with thee this night, provided thou givest me of these mandrakes.*

The whole illuminative life is yet but a life of infancy and feebleness, considering the life of faith which is to follow it. Rachel is so childish that she prefers the pleasure of seeing and and smelling *mandrakes,* plants beautiful to the sight, and of an excellent odour, to the real possession of her husband. Effeminate souls full of sensual inclinations resemble her in

Chapter XXX.

that: they prefer the sweet to the solid, which is the possession of God in Himself above all gifts.

> 16. *And when Jacob returned from the field in the evening, Leah went out to meet him, and said to him, Thou must come with me, for I have purchased this favour by giving my sister my son's mandrakes.*
> 17. *And God heard her prayers; she conceived and bare a son for the fifth time.*

The strong and generous souls who have been rendered such by the cross, willingly give up all delights and everything that is from without, for the real possession of the spouse, as did Leah: so God blessed so just a choice by a new fruitfulness, giving her yet two sons and one daughter. This marks also how the soul which has abandoned all for God, *runs* with pleasure *to tell Him* that she merits *possessing Him, having acquired it* by the destitution of all gifts.

> 22. *The Lord also remembered Rachel, and hearkened to her, and made her fruitful.*
> 23. *She conceived and bare a son; and she said, The Lord hath taken away my reproach.*

God, whose goodness is infinite, and who leaves nothing without recompense, treats the feeble souls according to their feebleness. He had pity upon Rachel, *and made her a mother*. This teaches us that these souls of graces and sensible favour having become riper towards the end of their career, bear some fruit; but it approaches neither in quantity nor quality to that produced by the souls who have been conducted by a way as mighty as it has been crucified. Then they are extremely rejoiced at this production, and say that God has raised them from their lowliness.

> 25. *And when Joseph was born, Jacob said to his father-in-law, Let me go now, that I may return to my country and my own land.*

The way of lights and sweetnesses has no sooner become fruitful, and outwardly produces some mark of its beauty, than the soul, all enraptured to see such beautiful fruits, because they retain the beauty of their mother, earnestly desires to come forth from this first way to introduce them into that of *abandon*. Therefore *Jacob presses Laban to allow him to go;* as if he apprehended that his children might contract something foreign by a longer sojourn in this land, which would be a dangerous mixture.

CHAPTER XXXI.

3. *And the Lord said unto Jacob, Return unto the land of thy fathers, and to thy kindred, and I will be with thee.*

God, who had a particular care over Jacob, and who with paternal attention kept him under the conduct of His providence, Himself bids him *return to the land of his fathers:* this is lest he should be tempted to enter into other ways on account of his great riches. He promises him a second time *that He will be with him* in all his labours until He has conducted him to his origin and to the place of repose in God. Until that time some change is always to be feared.

8. *The lambs of various colours were the reward of Jacob.*

Jacob's sheep were of various colours; to teach us, that until the soul has permanently arrived in God, there is always some change in it, and it varies incessantly, being sometimes in one state, sometimes in another; sometimes in peace, at other times in trouble and agitation. It is only the state of the soul in God which varies no more: for it has come to the purity and simplicity of its origin.

13. *I am the God who appeared unto thee at Bethel, where thou anointedst the stone, and where thou madest a vow. Get thee out speedily from this land, and return to the land of thy birth.*

Remember, says the Lord, *the stone* where thou *madest a vow unto me*, and where I promised to conduct thee. It is there I wish to lead thee back, for that is thy birth-place, where I desire to reconduct thee so as to lose thee in Me, and make thee flow again into the source whence thou art sprung.

18. *Jacob took all that he had acquired in Mesopotamia, and went on his way.*
19. *And when Laban had gone to shear his sheep, Rachel stole her father's idols.*

Jacob took everything that was his, and left nothing ; but it is easy to see from *the theft of Rachel*, how far removed the souls of lights are from the perfect stripping of those conducted by crosses. The former have always some idols or attachments which they carry with them, which the others have not. Leah takes nothing but her children, and God suffices her for everything.

22. *And it was told Laban on the third day that Jacob was fled.*
23. *And immediately he pursued him for seven days, and overtook him at Mount Gilead.*
24. *But God appeared to Laban in a dream, and said to him, Take heed that thou speak not harshly to Jacob.*

Who will not admire the care God takes of souls abandoned to Him. He prevents on their behalf even the least accidents, not sparing even *revelations* or miracles to protect them from the ill-treatment of their persecutors, as is seen here by the admirable manner in which God delivered Jacob and all his family from the anger of Laban.

37. *Jacob said to Laban:*
38. *Thy sheep and thy she-goats have not been barren, and the rams of thy flock have I not eaten.*
39. *That which was torn of beasts I brought not unto thee; I bare the loss of it; and thou didst require of me all that was stolen.*
40. *The heat of the day consumed me, and the frost by night, and sleep fled mine eyes.*
41. *Thus have I served thee in thy house these twenty years.*

Behold the qualities of the good shepherd, who does no hurt

to the flock, who suffers nothing to be taken by the enemy; who exposes himself for the sheep, and who gives his life for them; who burdens himself with all their interests, and who takes upon himself all the hurt that can be done them. There will not easily be found in all Scripture a figure more full of the Shepherd JESUS, than that seen in Jacob; nor of the qualities that all true shepherds ought to possess. But let no one flatter himself he is able fully to perform all these great duties if he is not like Jacob, strong in God by a profound interior.

CHAPTER XXXII.

1. *And Jacob went on his way, and the angels of God met him.*

This consolation given by *the angels*, is to prepare the soul for great combats it must sustain before entering into God. It is no longer the persecution of the creatures it is to apprehend, it is God Himself; but first must be sustained the attack of earthly enemies, who are only the forerunners of another combat, which is not feared, because not known: a visible combat is feared which is only apparent; and a real combat is not feared, because it is unknown.

6. *Esau, thy brother cometh to meet thee, and four hundred men with him.*
7. *Then Jacob was greatly afraid and distressed.*

We often distress ourselves about an imaginary evil, whilst we remain firm and constant in real combats: thus *Jacob fears* extremely *the meeting with Esau*, who nevertheless will do him no evil; but he does not yet dread many other combats which God prepares for him, although by His particular assistance he is to come out happily from them.

9. *Jacob prayed to God thus: God of my father Abraham, God of my father Isaac, Lord which said unto me, Return into thy country, and to thy birth-place, and I will bless thee.*

10. *I am unworthy of all thy mercies, and of the truth which thou hast manifested in the fulfilment of the promises thou didst make to thy servant. I crossed this river of Jordan having but my staff, and now I return with two bands.*

The manner in which Jacob returns to God in his affliction shows how useful pain and affliction are. They bring God's favours to remembrance; not only to serve for some consolation, but also to redouble confidence. Jacob represents to God all *His promises:* he does not complain: he lays before Him only all the blessings He has bestowed on him, pleading that they may not be rendered useless.

He asks of Him His help in a manner so powerful and so tender, that the words related in the text express it more than all we can say of it. The perplexity and grief in which he finds himself well represent a soul returning by the way of faith and *abandon* into God its origin: for then it is in doubts and pains; the fear of death seizes upon it, it appears to it inevitable. But what death does it fear? The death caused by sin. It knows that it has often been victorious over this enemy, whom it has ruled and supplanted; but seeing itself about to fall into his hands, it does not doubt but that he will avenge himself: and being assured that he will not spare it, it seems to have no power to evade its loss. Then this poor soul, pressed on all sides, reminds God that it is He who has made it enter upon this way, and that it is to blindly obey Him that it has bound itself to it; that it has wholly abandoned itself to Him; after which it prays Him to protect it. It represents to Him also that its *fathers* have walked by the same way, and that it is on that account He has declared Himself their God. It humbles itself before Him, and puts Him in mind of His *truth.*

11. *Deliver me from the hand of my brother Esau, for I fear him exceedingly, lest he smite the mother with the children.*

12. *Thou hast promised to bless me with riches, and to multiply my seed as the sand of the sea, which cannot be numbered.*

It is a beautiful expression, *to smite the mother with the children.* Sin smites *the mother*—righteousness acquired by grace; and also *the children*, the virtues and good works. Now this soul pressed with anguish sees itself on the eve of losing both. It forgets all the other goods, and thinks only of its own righteousness, which it sees itself on the point of losing: it freely gives up the other goods, that is to say, it consents to the loss of heavenly inclinations and favours. It is just that all that be ravished from it by sin, which here appears inevitable to it; but its very integrity and its fruits—the divine virtues, ah! this is what it cannot consent to lose. No, poor afflicted soul, thou wilt have more fear than hurt: there is nothing for thee to be afraid of; for God will prevent the disaster thou art threatened with.

13. *Jacob passed the night in that place; and he put aside out of all he had, what he had designed to be offered to his brother Esau.*

23. *And he sent over the brook all that he possessed.*

24. *He remained alone in that place. And there appeared at the same time a man, who wrestled with him until the morning.*

25. *And when he saw that he could not prevail against Jacob, he touched the sinew of his thigh, and it shrank immediately.*

Jacob, as I have said, hazards all his goods and *remains alone*. Oh poor man, you think you have only to fight an enemy that you can even appease by your presents; you have already escaped the pursuit of your father-in-law (signifying the creature); you think, according to your own judgment, to elude likewise the other enemies: but you do not know you must combat God Himself, and that it is He who comes to attack you. Now this combat is the last and most severe of all. To maintain a combat against God, to sustain the weight of God's strength, is a thing that experience alone can make understood. It always costs something this war, as to Jacob, who became lame by it.

26. *This man said to him, Let me go, for the day breaketh. Jacob replied, I will not let thee go until thou hast blessed me.*

27. *And he said unto him, What is thy name? And he said, Jacob.*

28. *The man said to him, Until now thou hast been called Jacob, but hereafter thou shall be called Israel; for if thou hast been mighty against God, how much more so wilt thou be against men.*

This combat being the last of all, after having borne it, *the name must be changed*, and the new name is given, as to Abraham and Sarah. This is clear in the Old and New Testaments. But this soul here loses its own righteousness, and its own strength, to be invested with the strength of God: thus this name of Israel given him, signifies *mighty against God*, as if it was said, strong as God, and with the strength of God Himself. For this reason all Jacob's children and his people, who are to be God's spiritual people, are to be called the people of Israel, clothed with the strength of God Himself: thus it is said to this people in Exodus: "The Lord shall fight for you, and ye shall hold your peace," meaning, that He Himself fights in them, and that they have but to keep themselves at rest. And in the book of Samuel: "Thou comest to me with a sword, and with a spear, and with a shield: but I come to thee in the name of the Lord of Hosts." This soul, then, clad with the strength of God, no longer fears either men or demons: for having borne the combat with the very God, what is there more to fear?

> 31. *As soon as Jacob had passed this place, which he had called Penuel, he saw the Sun rising; but he was lame of one leg.*

After these terrible combats *the Sun rises:* the creature being still further destroyed and drained off, melted and annihilated, comprehends more truly what God is, true *Sun* of all beings, although it can still less comprehend Him, the excess of its absorption into Him rendering Him still more incomprehensible to it, although it knows Him better than it ever did. These persons, happy enough to have sustained with faithfulness the Divine Combat, may appear to the eyes of the creatures still more feeble than they were formerly believed to be, but in truth they never were stronger, since by the loss of their own strength they have entered into the strength of God; thus Jacob, although become lame, bears the name and fulfils the meaning of Israel—*mighty against God.*

CHAPTER XXXIII.

> 10. *Jacob said to Esau his brother, I have seen thy face this day, as though I had seen the face of God. Be then favourable to me.*

11. *Take this present which I have offered to thee, and which I have received from God, who gives all things.*

When the new name has been given, and the soul is well advanced, *it sees* all things in *God* and *God* in all things. Sin, which before gave it so much fright, terrifies it no longer; all hell itself could not dismay it, because it can no longer see anything distinct from God Himself, where there is no sin, but perfect Holiness. This manner of expressing itself, so simple and natural, is so appropriate to the soul of this degree, that although it would, it could not do otherwise. Let those who do not comprehend this believe it not impossible. It must be thus, because the soul that has been received into God can no longer see these things but as God sees them, without fear, without trouble, without emotion, without malice, without fault, taking part in His Divine Attributes in proportion as it is received into His Unity. Jacob shows also to Esau that everything which he gives him is from God, because it is He who gives all things. It is the property of those persons established in the Divine Truth to attribute nothing to themselves, but to refer all to God.

CHAPTER XXXV.

1. *And God said unto Jacob, Get thee up quickly unto Bethel, and dwell there, and there build an altar unto the Lord who appeared to thee when thou fleddest from thy brother Esau.*
2. *Then Jacob, having gathered together all his household, said unto them, Cast out from you the strange gods that are in the midst of you; purify yourselves, and change your garments.*

God bids the soul, after so many fatigues and combats sustained on the road, *go* to the place of its origin, where He conducts it with so much goodness by His admirable providence, *and build there an altar.* But before the superior part of the soul is received into God, it must have attained to the purity of its creation; and for this state all propriety must be taken away, and all faults and spots cut off from the inferior parts, represented by *Jacob's family*.

It is necessary that everything be extremely *clean*, and *have changed garments*, and have become quite different by renovation. Jacob does nothing for himself in preparing for so great a good; for it was solely the work of God who had conducted him by this road, and who was bringing him back to his origin; but he commands the inferior part to *leave* everything *strange* and proper to itself, so that nothing may further retard this happy loss into God.

Let us remark, too, that in so holy a family as Jacob's, there are still found some *idols;* and perhaps some of his servants were idolaters. What place is there so holy, what soul so pure, in which there is not mixed some impurity?

> 3. *Let us arise, and go up to Bethel, and there build an altar unto God, who hath heard me in the day of my affliction, and who hath been with me on my way.*
>
> 7. *And he built there an altar, and called the place the House of God, for there God had appeared unto him when he fled from Esau his brother.*

Then the soul is apprised of God's faithfulness, and it knows how *He has conducted it*. Then it is delivered from the true afflictions and pains of the spirit, and from all inquietude, although it is still reserved for good crosses; but these will be crosses it will bear like Jesus Christ and with him, and which it can bear in all security.

It is the property of this soul to render back everything to God in the same place, and in the very manner He has given it. Then there is made the pure sacrifice, which is favourably received.

> 9. *God appeared unto Jacob the second time,*
> 10. *And said to him, Until now thou hast been called Jacob, but hereafter shall thy name be Israel.*
> 13. *And God withdrew from him.*

God again blesses Jacob, and confirms to him his new *name*. The state is given to the soul a long time before it is confirmed in it. We have for a long time the transitory dispositions; then the state is given; but confirmation in the state is a much later thing, and a much more eminent grace. Confirmation is here given to Jacob when God repeats to him so positively, *thy name shall be Israel.*

It is added that God *withdrew*, or disappeared, from Jacob's eyes. This signifies how God, having raised the creature's capacity in order to elevate it up to Himself, lowers Himself also towards it without ceasing to be what He is; but this is only to take it, carry it away, and lose it into Himself, disappearing so much the more from the eyes of the spirit as He causes it to be lost in Himself.

16. *And setting out from that place, he came in the spring time to the road leading to Ephrath, where Rachel travailed.*

18. *And feeling that death was coming upon her by reason of the violence of her pain, being ready to expire, she called her son's name Benoni, that is to say, son of my grief: but his father called him Benjamin, that is to say, son of my right hand.*

19. *Thus died Rachel, and she was buried in the way to Ephrath, since called Bethlehem.*

The soul confirmed in God is entirely separated from all natural and spiritual feelings; should there remain ever so little, God makes them *die* as He did Rachel. Scripture does not say that Jacob wept for her: for being then well established in the will of God, he could not be afflicted at this loss, which he saw in God Himself to be advantageous for him. For this is a light of this state, which shows that God does everything for our advantage, and that everything contributes to our greatest good. Behold, then, this soul deprived of everything it had dear to it in nature; there remains nothing to it but God alone and the cross; but the cross is no longer painful to it; it has known its value too well not to esteem it; and it is too strong in God to have any difficulty in bearing it. There remains, however, a secret love for Rachel's productions, because they are sweet and amiable, and those of the cross are somewhat wilder. Moreover, the fruits of sweetness and union contain within themselves their beauty, and they show outwardly all that they are; but the fruits of the cross are bitter at first; they are only sweet and admirable in their continuations, for they terminate at nothing less than the production of Jesus Christ.

CHAPTER XXXVI.

6. *And Esau took his wives, and his sons, and his daughters, and all the persons of his house, and his cattle, and all his beasts, and all his substance which he had got in the land of Canaan, and went into the country from the face of his brother Jacob.*

15. *The sons of Esau were Princes, Prince Teman, Prince Omar.*

Who can sufficiently admire how God conducts things by the wisdom of His providence? The child of wrath *separates himself* from the chosen of God, the nation of the flesh removes itself from the generation of the spirit, and the active way is divided from the contemplative. *Esau goes into another country*, leaving the chosen nation in peaceful possession of the region of repose.

But Esau was at once great upon the earth; people spoke of him only. As for Israel, he remains little in the eyes of men and great before God; he has only the cross, which will follow him even to the tomb, and by which he will triumph in Jesus Christ.

CHAPTER XXXVII.

3. *Now Israel loved Joseph more than all his children, because he was the son of his old age; and he made him a coat of many colours.*

4. *And when his brethren saw that their father loved him more than all his brethren, they hated him, and could not speak peaceably unto him.*

The history of Joseph is a living expression of a predestined soul; and the various incidents related of him in the sacred text admirably mark the various states through which one of the most chosen souls must pass in order to arrive at the perfection destined for it. God makes it first pass through a state of spiritual *infancy*, in which it receives only sweetness and caresses. It seems as if God was occupied only in decorating and embellishing it and neglecting the others. This attracts, indeed, the jealousy of other persons, who see that all the favours are for it. But how dearly they will be sold to it!

> 9. *Joseph related to his brethren also another dream which he had: It seemed to me in my dream that the sun and moon and eleven stars worshipped me.*

God Himself makes known to it by *dreams* and visions something of its future elevations; and this simple and innocent soul *tells it to its* spiritual *brothers*, but who are far removed from simplicity. Thus do they attribute to pride and idle fancy what comes from the Holy Spirit.

> 17. *And Joseph went after his brethren, and found them in Dothan.*
> 18. *When they perceived him afar off, before he came to them, they resolved to kill him.*
> 19. *And they said one to another, Behold this dreamer cometh.*
> 20. *Let us go and slay him, and then we shall see what his dreams will be worth to him.*

Amongst jealous brethren there are found some who, having strayed from the way of truth, take everything amiss, and who, pretending to punish a crime, which exists only in their imagination, wish to *take the life* of an innocent person. Such are these false zealots, who, in order to extinguish interior ways, accuse those who teach and maintain them of pretended crimes, designing thereby to *destroy the life*, if not of the body, at least of the spirit and reputation.

> 21. *Reuben, hearing them speak thus, endeavoured to deliver him out of their hands, and he said to them,*
> 22. *Slay him not, and shed not his blood, but cast him into this pit in the desert, and preserve your hands pure.*

The sweetnesses of spiritual infancy are hardly passed than the strangest crosses are prepared. We see ourselves exposed to the most extreme persecutions. Joseph is as a sheep amid a pack of wolves; but God, who continually takes care of souls who give themselves to Him without reserve, finds some defender to draw them from the hands of their enemies.

23. *And immediately when Joseph had come to his brethren, they stript him of his robe of many colours which covered him,*

24. *And cast him into this old pit, where there was no water.*

26. *And Judah said unto his brethren, What profit is it if we slay our brother, and conceal his blood?*

27. *Come, and let us sell him unto the Ishmaelites, and let not our hand be upon him, for he is our brother and our flesh. And his brothers were content.*

This poor lamb suffers himself to be *stripped*. It is thus also with souls destined to a great interior. The first stripping is performed in them by the privation of gifts and sensible graces, represented by their *coat of many colours*. The soul, seeing these things taken away from it, believes, from this first stripping, that it has come to its end, and that it is going to lose its life. It would, indeed, be thus if God gave the power to its enemies.

This soul, conducted by *abandon*, allows everything to be done to it, without saying anything or complaining; it seeks, however, on every side for some help to come to it, as did the prophet king when in this state he said, *I have lifted up mine eyes to the mountains to look whence my help will come.* Then he adds, filled with truth, *My help can only come from the Lord, who has made heaven and earth.* There is no other help for the soul but the Lion of the tribe of Judah, who delivers it from the approaching death to make it endure a thousand and a thousand deaths. Oh, my God, it is thus that Thou deliverest Thy dearest friends! Thou retardest their death to make them suffer an infinity of deaths. Every day feeling the rigours of death makes persecuted persons take courage in bewailing their distresses; and when they believe he is going to impart to them of his sweets, which is the loss of this life, he removes himself from them. It is a continual game of death's to show himself to those persons and to hide himself from them. St. Paul has expressed it for all when he said, *Through all our life we cease not to be exposed to death for Jesus' sake.*

28. *Then there passed by Midianite merchantmen; and they drew and lifted Joseph up out of the pit, and sold Joseph to the Ishmaelites for twenty pieces of silver: and they brought Joseph into Egypt.*

Joseph is sold even by his liberator. From a free man he becomes a slave. He was free in the sweet and peaceful love of God in which he lived; now he is sold as a slave. And to whom is he sold? To sin. Sold to sin! Oh, what a change! He is sold to sin, so that sin may exercise its tyranny over him; but he is not on that account rendered subject to sin. The state of *being sold* to sin and of being made its slave is very different from that of subjection to sin. St. Paul explains it of himself: *I am*, says he, *sold to sin;* and then he says that he is in *bondage under the law of sin which is in his members*. This is the distinction he makes between these two states.

29. *And Reuben returned to the pit, and not finding the child,*
30. *He rent his clothes, and came and said to his brethren, The child is no more, and what will become of me?*

There is always found some soul of too natural a tendency who would draw us from the conduct of providence: they would desire it seems, out of charity, to *draw* us *from the pit*—that is to say, from the cross, from *abandon*, from the loss by which God conducts us; but God by His providence knows so well how to act His part, that none can draw us out of His hands.

31. *After that they took Joseph's coat and dipped it in the blood of a goat which they had killed.*
32. *And they sent it to his father.*
33. *And he recognised it and said: It is my son's coat, a cruel beast hath eaten him.*

Those who strip us in the order of Providence, of gifts and sensible graces, *dip* them *in blood;* for all these sweetnesses and benefits of God are changed into apparent cruelty; but it is a cruelty only superficial, and having nothing real but the figure. Everything becomes blood and carnage for such a soul: everything is a cross to it, but outwardly only; for within, it is in peace through *abandon*.

Spiritual persons, hearing what is told of the apparent disaster of these souls, believe them lost, and say like Jacob, "These poor interior ones have been deceived, the *cruel beast has devoured them.*" Credulity finds a place even in the holiest souls, who, adding faith to calumny, believe at first that the *Demon* has *devoured* these simple persons, having caused them to fall into his illusions.

34. *Jacob rent his clothes, and covered himself with sackcloth, and wept for his son many days.*
36. *Meanwhile the Midianites sold Joseph in Egypt to Potiphar, an officer of Pharaoh's, and captain of his guard.*

These holy ones are afflicted, *weep*, and *do penance* for these abandoned persons, so as to entreat God's mercy. Jacob had not wept for Rachel, who was so dear to him, and he is so greatly afflicted for Joseph. The reason is, that regarding things in God, Rachel's death was useful and necessary, and he saw in that only the death of a truly lovely form, but which he desired only in God's will; whereas he is here surveying the disaster of a spiritual soul believed to be lost under the dominion of the Demon, although really it is holier than ever. Jacob saw only the tragic and bloody exterior, and he knew not that his son was full of life and repose.

Joseph is again *sold* a second time. Does it not seem as if he were born only for slavery and the cross? But as a noble soul finds its liberty in the fetters, so a soul abandoned to God is never freer than when it appears more a slave.

CHAPTER XXXIX.

1. *And Joseph was brought down to Egypt; and Potiphar, an officer of Pharaoh, captain of the guard, an Egyptian, bought him from the Ishmaelites, which had brought him down thither.*
2. *And the Lord was with Joseph, and he was a prosperous man.*

Is it not a conduct worthy of God's right hand to preserve so great souls under an exterior so lowly and reviled? *God was always with Joseph*, as He never leaves these dear abandoned ones, and they are never better than when they are most despaired of by every one; for it is then that God exercises a particular protection over them, which they experience so sensibly, that they cry out of the depth of bitterness with the prophet-king: *The Lord is my light and my salvation*, whom could I fear?

3. *His master saw that the Lord was with him, and that He blessed him in all his actions.*

God mortifies and vivifies, and he sustains by the very hand that he strikes with. He gives mortal wounds; but he puts the balm at the arrow's point, so that we cannot tell which is the most sensible—the grief, or the pleasure. It is a pleasure full of grief; it is a grief full of pleasure. Oh God, dost thou not always kill thus!

6. *Now Joseph was of a fair countenance, and very agreeable.*
7. *And a long time afterwards his mistress cast her eyes upon him, and said to him, Sleep with me.*
8. *But Joseph looked upon this crime with horror, and answered her,*
9. *How can I commit so criminal an act, and sin against my God?*

Thou hast, oh Lord, redoubled blows, in which thou minglest much bitterness! There are times that Thou probest and poisonest the wound. Oh why dost Thou not kill entirely? Might we not dare to call Thee cruel, since Thou preservest life only to have the pleasure of killing once again? But who could complain of Thee, save those that do not know Thee? Thou appearest lovely to those very ones who experience only Thy severities, no longer feeling the sweetness of Thy love.

12. *His mistress took him by his cloak, and said to him, Sleep with me? Then Joseph left his cloak in her hands, and fled, and got out of the house.*

Here is the grievous blow: he must perish, or sin. It seems, O God, that thou hast only given a little respite to Joseph with Potiphar in order to prepare him for harder blows.

Chapter XXXIX. 157

These are Thy master-strokes. Joseph is subjected to sin; but, nevertheless, he triumphs over sin. These are thy salutarily-poisoned arrows, which mortally wound without killing. This is a calamity to be avoided *by flight*. Yes, Joseph, thou wilt avoid the reality of sin, and not the appearance; for thou wilt pass for a sinner.

13. *And when this woman saw his garment in her hands, and that she had been despised,*
14. *She called the people of her house, and said to them, They have brought in this Hebrew slave to mock us. He wished to force me, and when I cried out,*
15. *He has left his cloak with me, and has fled.*

Thou must pass for a criminal although thou art innocent. Thou wilt be accused of the crime thou hast not committed, and thou wilt be looked upon as guilty by all. Thou wilt even be punished for it. This is a degree through which God makes many souls pass; and this advances and finishes their death, because the exterior cross joined to the interior, the pain of destitution, of abandonment, of the confusion they bear, consummates all the sooner their mystic death. There are others in whom the crosses being great and heavy, both inwardly and outwardly, God is content with that, particularly if these persons are not destined for the conducting of others.

19. *And his master, too ready to believe the accusations of his wife, was greatly enraged.*
20. *And he caused Joseph to be put into the prison, where the King's prisoners were kept, and he was shut up.*

It does not end here for Joseph. Those even whom he has obliged the most must believe in the calumny; he must pass several years in prison abandoned by all, and held as guilty. But oh, Joseph, thou art a prisoner and innocent: thou hast lost nothing of thine integrity: thou art happier an innocent prisoner than David a guilty king. Oh what a beautiful parallel might be drawn between these two persons, so that God's conduct over abandoned souls might be observed! He will cause it to be done at the time He pleaseth. Some remain innocent and are punished as guilty; others with the punishment have also the sin. Joseph becomes more a slave in proportion as he is more innocent. David yet continues to reign, although afflicted, punished, and guilty.

21. *But the Lord was with Joseph, and showed him mercy, and gave him favour in the sight of the keeper of the prison.*
22. *And the keeper of the prison committed to him the care of all the prisoners; there was nothing done there but by his order, the keeper entrusted to him everything,*
23. *And looked not to anything whatsoever under his hand, for the Lord was with Joseph, and made him prosper in all things.*

God's goodness is signalized in mingling the greatest bitternesses with sensible sweetnesses. So long as our Lord does not abandon the soul, and it is assured of His aid and presence, there is nothing so severe but becomes sweet; but when He conceals Himself, and we lose this so sweet a Presence, which consoles in all afflictions, oh, it is then that grief is extreme.

The innocent soul rules over all the world, and is never subject to it. Joseph, a prisoner and in chains, becomes the governor of the other prisoners. This is how these faithful servants of Jesus Christ in the midst even of their afflictions, continue to aid others; and when they are more afflicted in their ways, they would introduce every one to them, and make them walk therein. It is the effect of the truth contained in this way, to have a complete certainty of it for others, although we may have no assurance of it for ourselves.

CHAPTER XL.

1—5. *Two officers of the King of Egypt, his chief butler, and his chief baker being in prison, had each a dream on the same night, the interpretation of which was to be different.*
8. *They said afterwards to Joseph, We have had a dream, and we have no one to explain it to us. Joseph answered them, And who is the interpreter of dreams? Is it not God? Tell me what ye have dreamed.*

Chapter XL.

God, for the sake of these persons so fully abandoned to the conduct of His providence, often gives to sinners some extraordinary light so as to lead them to communicate it, and that thus they may be instructed of the ways He takes with souls, and that these poor wandering ones may come out of the captivity of sin. Joseph's reply is truly worthy of a faithful abandoned one, who, attributing nothing to himself, refers everything to God. This is what gives us a holy boldness, and leads us to undertake everything, leaning upon the Divine strength, from which we derive our origin, as Joseph derived it from Israel; nevertheless, little advanced souls attribute this often to pride and rashness.

12. *This is the interpretation of thy dream: The three branches are three days.*
13. *After which Pharaoh will remember the service thou hast rendered to him, and will restore thee to thy former charge.*
14. *—I pray thee only to remember me when this happiness shall come to thee.*
18. *He said also to the other, This is the interpretation of thy dream: The three baskets signify that thou hast but three days yet to live.*
19. *After which the King shall cause thy head to be cut off.*

The same word of God is often a word of life and a word of death; it renders liberty to some, drawing them out of the slavery of sin; and it innocently causes death to others afterwards from the bad use they make of it. It was not Joseph's word that caused the death of the baker, since the cause of it lay in the sin of him who had committed it—it warned him only that his death was nigh; but he took no measure to avoid it. We can escape sin by our own cares, sustained by God's grace and by penitence; but life comes from God alone: therefore Joseph prayed the butler when he would be re-established in favour *to remember him*, and the word of God he had announced to him, which very often the propriety causes to be forgot. The word of God is a seed, but hidden, however, in the ground, and bearing fruit in its own time.

21. *Pharaoh restored the chief butler to his place again, and he continued to give the cup to Pharaoh.*

22. *And he hanged the other, which verified the interpretation, which Joseph gave of their dreams.*

23. *Nevertheless the chief butler, when he found himself restored to favour, thought no more of his interpreter.*

God here brings to view His faithfulness in sustaining His word, which he has put into the mouth of His servants; and although its execution be delayed for some days, it is nevertheless found always true. But when one is in prosperity, one easily *forgets* him from whom the word has proceeded, unless God by a particular providence brings him to our remembrance. God also is pleased to permit this forgetfulness so as to augment the merit of His servants, by prolonging their sufferings; and to exercise so much the more their faith and their *abandon*, the more He seems to forget them.

CHAPTER XLI.

1. *Two years afterwards Pharaoh had a dream.*

9. *Then the chief butler remembered Joseph, and said to the king: I confess my sin.*

10. *Being in prison with the chief baker,*

12. *We had both a dream on the same night;*

13. *And a young man, an Hebrew, who was in the same prison,*

14. *Told us all that has since happened.*

Awaking and *remembering* God are admirable means to draw a soul out of prison, out of captivity and the shadow of death. After having had some hope of issuing out of its poor and destitute state, it passes yet several years in a total destitution and in an entire oblivion. There no longer even remains to it any hope, and it thinks only of remaining thus, like the eternal dead, who are thought of no more; it endeavours only to bear this state with *abandon*, and to be contented with it, seeing itself in the will of God, but it does not think ever to come out of it.

14. *Joseph was immediately brought out of the prison by the*

command of the king; and they shaved him, and made him change his raiment, and presented him before the king.

When it is buried in this manner in the oblivion of death, it is all astonished to see its *prison* opened, to see itself approached and stripped of this state of death, the marks of slavery taken from it by degrees, and itself *covered with the robe* of life and liberty. For sometimes this soul is as half asleep; it does not know whether it sleeps or wakes, whether it is a dream or reality, when suddenly it sees itself *drawn out of this obscure and gloomy place*, and placed in the open day of the true light. Then it knows the truth of its change, and so much the more as it is brought to *appear before the King*. It is then from this moment placed in the resuscitated life, but it is not yet established in the resuscitated state, which has many other advantages. God makes use of this very word, which had been hid in the earth of forgetfulness, to draw this soul out of death and eternal oblivion, as the Son of God by His word drew Lazarus from the tomb.

15. *And Pharaoh said unto Joseph: I have dreamed a dream, and there is none that can interpret it. I have heard it said that thou hadst a singular gift of interpreting them.*
16. *And Joseph answered him, and said: It will be God and not I who will give a favourable interpretation to the king.*

There was no person in all Egypt *who could interpret* Pharoah's dreams; for what passes in the heart of God is only known by the Spirit of God. Joseph's reply shows that it is only self-renunciation and the loss of all desire to be anything which leads such a soul to attribute nothing to itself. On the contrary, persuaded that it is but a feeble instrument, and that God can do everything without it, it declares itself with a frankness worthy of so high a truth. *God*, without it, can perform all that He does by it; and if He uses it, all the glory must be rendered to Him. Therefore, it leads the creature, beforehand, to render all the glory of it to God, and to regard no good done out of Him.

17. *Pharaoh then related to him what he had seen. It seemed to me, he said, that I stood upon the bank of a river,*

18. *From whence came up seven fat-fleshed and well-favoured kine, and they fed in the meadows.*

This *bank of the river* represents the waters either of Baptism or penitence, out of which a soul comes forth very beautiful, and in a most perfect fatness. *The seven kine* or the *seven years* which they signify, are the usual time that souls remain in the acquisition of virtues. They appear then all *beautiful*, and no defect is seen in them, because God gives them so many graces that they are as in a most abundant *pasture*, where they become strong, fat, beautiful, and very agreeable.

19. *Afterwards there came up seven others, so horrible and so lean that I have never seen their like in Egypt.*
20. *And these latter devoured and swallowed up the first.*

Those years, so agreeable and so sweet, and so well watered with calm and tranquil waters, having passed, the soul is much astonished, when thinking on nothing less, to see them *devoured* by these other *years* that follow them, but of so great sterility and famine, that without the provisions that had been made, death from hunger must occur. It must be observed that Scripture does not say that *the lean kine* killed the fat, but that they *devoured them*, which shows that, in this time of so strange an avidity, all the graces and virtues of the other years are contained therein, although nothing of them may appear outwardly, just as the fat kine were contained within the lean, although nothing of them appeared without.

21. *They appeared in no wise filled with them, but, on the contrary, they were as lean and frightsome as at first.*

These *lean* kine continue to be *as hideous* and disfigured after devouring the fat ones as they were before. Oh, this is the mystery hidden from men not divinely enlightened, and revealed to the little ones; it is even hid from those in whom it takes place. There appears outwardly only ugliness and deformity, and all the beauty of the king's daughter is hidden within her during these seven years. There appear only defects on all sides; everything seems to be void of grace, as these kine are of flesh. Nevertheless, it is certain that there never was more of it; but it remains hidden in the frightful belly of dryness until the day of manifestation. The beauty of the first years make the others appear *so ugly* that *Pharaoh*, who represents the world, *avers that he had never seen their like in all his kingdom.*

25. *Joseph answered: God has made known unto Pharaoh what He is about to do.*
26. *The seven good kine signify seven years of abundance which will come.*
27. *The seven ill-favoured kine mark the seven years of famine that are to follow them.*
30. *The famine will be so great that it will cause all the abundance which preceded it to be forgotten.*

The souls of grace soon judge of what comes from God by the experience they have of it. Thus *Joseph* immediately *assures* the King that his dream is divine. It is the property of the time of *abundance* to take away all thought of the *famine* and *sterility* that is to follow it, and it is also usual for persons in their trials to forget all the good they had possessed. Nothing of it remains to them any more, because God so effaces all trace of it outwardly that it seems as if it had been only a deception, and they had never really belonged to God. Nevertheless, they were never more His. Confessors even doubt them. It is only such an experience and light as Joseph's that can discover the mystery; for this famine must consume all the earth, and nothing remain, so that the great want may destroy the great abundance; for if there remained anything this would not be entire loss, and this mystery would not be accomplished. Thou must then, Oh soul, expect to lose, without reserve, all that thou possessest, and thou must measure the greatness of thy loss by the greatness of thy possession. The more thou hast been beautiful and agreeable, and the object of the admiration of peoples, the more thou must become ugly, deformed, and the object of their horror and contempt. Oh, conduct of my God! To make the soul return to its origin it must lose all Thy gifts. Thou grantest them to it to make it come out of sin and to make it return into its heart, from which it had strayed, and Thou takest them away from it to make it come out from this same heart and to lose it into Thee. Thy gifts drive away sin, and fill the soul with Thy graces, and Thou drivest Thy gifts from it to fill it with Thyself! Oh, truth too unknown!

33. *Now therefore let Pharaoh look out a man discreet and wise, and set him over the land of Egypt.*

34. *And let him appoint officers in all the provinces, who during the seven years of plenty that are to come may gather into the public granaries the fifth part of the fruits of the earth.*

The enlightened director, foreseeing what must happen, obliges the soul to lay up as much provisions as it can, for the more that it profits by the first graces, given to it in abundance, it will be the better for it. I confess that its loss will also be all the greater; but although it lose everything belonging to itself, yet all is found again in God, preserved in His sacred *storehouses*. Therefore, it is a matter of consequence to choose a skilful and experienced director, to whom we may trust the conducting of everything.

37. *This counsel pleased Pharaoh and all his ministers.*

38. *And he said to them: Where can we find a man so full of the Spirit of God as this?*

39. *He said then to Joseph: Since God hath shown thee all that thou hast told us, how can we find one wiser than thou, or like to thee?*

In the choice of a director we must always prefer him who has most of *the Spirit of God*. Pharaoh gives us an example of it. Far from laughing, as some do, at the advice given them for their good, and of which they never profit, he took for conductor, in an affair of this importance, the very one who had given him *this counsel*, and caused everything he commanded to be punctually followed out.

41. *And Pharaoh said unto Joseph: See, I have set thee over all the land of Egypt.*

42. *And Pharaoh took off his ring from his hand and put it upon Joseph's hand, and arrayed him in vestures of fine linen, and put a gold chain about his neck.*

The power which the king gives him *over all Egypt* marks the authority of direction. Now Joseph is established and confirmed in the state of Resurrection. Not only is freedom given to him, but he receives it with many other advantages which he had not before his captivity whilst he was with his father. God restores to the resuscitated and renewed soul all the graces He had rendered to it before its disaster, and there is added to them an infinity of others which it never would have thought it ought to hope for.

> 43. *And he made him ride in the second chariot which he had; and they cried before him, Bow the knee; and he made him ruler over all the land of Egypt.*

Who would have told Joseph two years before, when he thought only to finish his days in an obscure prison, that he was to be *governor of all Egypt?* Who would have told this abandoned soul, destitute, and covered with darkness and the shadow of death, that so great an evil was to produce so great a good? It could not have believed it; yet it has been found most real.

> 45. *He also changed his name, and called him in the Egyptian language, The Saviour of the World. And he gave him to wife Asenath, daughter of Potiphera, priest of On.*

Behold then the resuscitated soul! see it confirmed in its resurrection, and loaded with graces. It is then that it arrives at the purity of its origin; it is then also that *the new name* is given to it, as to all the fathers: Thou shalt be no more called Joseph, but *the Saviour of Egypt.* It is always after the resurrection, and when the soul has arrived at its origin, that the new name is given to it, that is to say, that the perfect renewal is made; and it is then that there is celebrated the marriage of the Lamb.

> 45. *And Joseph went out over all the land of Egypt.*
> 46. *And Joseph was thirty years old when he stood before Pharaoh, King of Egypt.*
> 50. *Before the famine came, Joseph had two children by his wife Asenath.*
> 51. *And Joseph called the name of the first-born Manasseh: for God, said he, hath made me forget all my toil, and all my father's house.*

It is also always at this time that the Apostolic life commences when we do not begin it of ourselves, but when we enter into it only by the command of God; which is so well figured in *Joseph* after this renewal *making the tour of all* the provinces of *Egypt.* We must be renewed before operating. Jesus Christ, our Divine model, passed thirty years in his hidden life before appearing in public; and he did so only after experiencing the temptation in the desert. This relation of the ancient figures to their divine truth will enrapture all who penetrate it.

From the time of this renewal we begin to beget *children* to Jesus Christ. Joseph here *forgets all past labours,* as in poverty he forgot all the graces he had received. This is the property of each of these states.

52. *He called the name of the second, Ephraim, saying, God has made me fruitful in the land of my poverty.*

Joseph, well instructed in interior ways, acknowledges that all his blessings have come to him from his poverty; because it is in the time that the seed remains hid in the ground that it rots, sprouts, and bears much fruit.

CHAPTER XLII.

21. *Joseph's brethren said one to another, It is rightly that we suffer this, for we have sinned against our brother—Therefore does God afflict us thus.*
22. *And Reuben answered them, saying, Spake I not unto you saying, do not sin against the child; and ye would not hear? Therefore, behold, also his blood is required.*

God always makes the wicked feel sooner or later the punishment merited by the persecution they cause to the good; and that also is useful to them, because it makes them return into themselves.

23. *And they knew not that Joseph understood them, for he spake unto them by an interpreter.*
24. *But as he could no longer restrain his tears, he turned himself about a little, and wept.*

The goodness of a heart that is God's cannot be enough admired: he could not see his greatest persecutors suffer the least thing without being afflicted at it, more than they are themselves.

CHAPTER XLIII.

8. *Judah said unto his father:*
9. *I will be surety for the child; of my hand shalt thou require him. If I bring him not unto thee, and set him before thee, then let me bear the blame for ever.*

So long as it is only Reuben who asks Benjamin from Jacob he is not willing to give him, because he was not inclined to trust him to the conduct of men; but as soon as God explains Himself by the mouth of *Judah*, who is the one He has chosen to be the father of His Son, then Jacob gives him without difficulty, abandoning him thus to the conduct of Providence. The children of men act quite differently. They blindly trust themselves to other men—to a lawyer, to a doctor, to a friend, to a coachman—and they believe they would lose themselves if they fully trusted God.

32. *They served Joseph apart, and his brethren by themselves; and the Egyptians that did eat with him by themselves, for it is not permitted the Egyptians to eat with the Hebrews, for that is an abomination to the Egyptians.*

The saints, full of the Spirit of God, have admirable consideration not to offend men in what is immaterial. *Joseph* finds the means not to repel the *Egyptians*, and yet to regale his brethren in his company and in their presence, causing them all to be *served apart* on different tables, although in the same place; and thus, honouring both, he had the consolation of eating with his brethren and with the Egyptian lords, and, what is more, of entering in that into the will of God; but all that was not without mystery. Joseph's brethren were not of an interior elevation equal to his own to sit at table with him; he sends them only meats that had been served before him, so that they might have part in the fulness of his grace and in the unction of his spirit; and the best part fell to *Benjamin*, who was the most united to him, as well by spirit as by blood.

CHAPTER XLIV.

18. *Judah said to Joseph,*
32. *Rather let me be thy slave, since I became surety for the lad, saying unto my father, If I bring him not back unto thee, let me bear the blame for ever.*
34. *For I cannot return unto my father unless the lad be with us.*

This courage of *Judah* in giving himself up for his brother already marks beforehand that He who should give Himself up for all men would be born of him, and thus giving himself as a hostage for a single man he was the figure of Him who was to become the ransom for all. What does it also express to us by his not wishing to *return to his father except the child be with him,* if not that Christ, of the tribe of Judah, desires not to reascend unto His Father until He conduct there with Him the human nature freed from its captivity, and His dear people whom He will have redeemed?

CHAPTER XLV.

4. *Joseph spake gently unto his brethren, and said to them, I am your brother whom you sold into Egypt.*
5. *Fear not, neither grieve ye for having sold me into this land, for God has sent me before you into Egypt to preserve your life.*

A soul of this degree never attributes to its persecutors the persecutions that have been made against it, but, seeing everything in God as an admirable order of providence, it turns all to *God*. Joseph was most faithful in acting thus. This is what makes us love our enemies as much as our friends, for we never stop to look on the evil they do, but on the good that results from it. In this sense the commandment given us by Jesus Christ to love our enemies is found so easy by those penetrated with a lively faith, who have the taste of His love, that we could not help doing it even though He should not have commanded it.

> 8. *It was not by your design that I have been sent hither, but by the will of God, who hath made me as a father to Pharaoh, the lord of all his house, and the prince of the whole of Egypt.*

Joseph, however, confesses that that was not the *design* of his brethren when they persecuted him, but the will *of God*, who causes everything to be conducted according to His eternal design.

He gives them, moreover, to know something of *God's designs* over him, and of His impenetrable conduct of the chosen, whom He humbles only to raise again; and also of the truth of his dreams, of which they saw the fulfilment.

> 13. *Tell my father of the greatness of my glory, and all that ye have seen in Egypt; haste ye and bring him to me.*

Joseph does not say this out of ostentation, but because he knows that his father is acquainted with the secrets of the mystic life; and he gives him proofs of his state by the favours he distributes to all, and by the gifts he makes to him.

> 23. *He sent silver and raiment for his father, with ten asses laden with all the riches of Egypt.*

These *ten asses* laden with *all the riches of Egypt*, are, as I have already said previously (ch. 24 v. 10), the ten commandments of God; but enriched and set off by an admirable practice, performed in God Himself, and known only to the most advanced interior persons.

> 24. *He also sent away his brethren; and when they were setting out he said to them, See that ye fall not out by the way.*

This counsel of charity is so necessary to all, that really it is only union with the neighbour joined to trust in God, that prevents ennui and chagrin in so long a journey as that of the interior, and that makes everything succeed happily.

> 26. *And when Jacob heard that his son Joseph was alive, and that he ruled throughout all the land of Egypt, he started as from a profound sleep, and could not believe it.*

Although Jacob was instructed by his experience of the mystic way, of its reverses, and of the successes by which God vivifies after having mortified; yet he believed he was dreaming, so much was he surprised at so strange a conduct. It is in vain for us to be warned of the surprising routes through which God causes souls to pass: when we see their effects, we yet continue to be in astonishment and distrust.

> 27. *But when he saw the chariots which Joseph his son sent to him, his spirit revived.*
>
> 28. *And Israel said, It is enough; Joseph my son is yet alive: I will go and see him before I die.*

But seeing the fruits of the state, they can no longer doubt, and they must say: Assuredly, this soul *lives* in God; and *that is sufficient*.

CHAPTER XLVI.

> 3. *God said to Jacob, I am the Almighty, the God of thy father. Fear not, but go into Egypt, for I will make thee the chief of a great people in that land.*

As Jacob had hesitated at so strange an occurrence, God reassures him, putting him in mind of *His omnipotence.* He declares to him that this is one of His master-strokes; and that being the *God of his father*, whom He delivered from the knife that was raised to slay him, it is He Himself who enjoins him to *go into Egypt.*

I am the Almighty, the God of thy father. These words are so expressive to make known God's power and faithfulness in what He does on behalf of the abandoned souls, that I cannot help repeating them. Who will fear to abandon himself into His hands, since He calls Himself *the Almighty God* of these souls who are abandoned to Him without reserve? Is not everything secure for them, although in the midst of the greatest despair?

> 4. *I will go with thee, and will bring thee back also when thou returnest, and Joseph will close thine eyes.*

This promise was not only for Jacob; but also for all those who, like him, would fully abandon themselves even *to go into Egypt* for the love of God; that is to say to quit the region of peace, and go by the will of God into the land of trouble and corruption, according as it is necessary and as God requires it. It is so clear that God spoke in the person of Jacob to the abandoned souls, true children of Israel, and not to him personally, since at the same time that He promises to bring *him back from Egypt*, He assures him that he will die there, predicting that Joseph *will shut his eyes*. God, after making the souls that are abandoned to Him go into the Egypt of trial and temptation, never fails to *reconduct* them into their region of repose.

> 29. *When Jacob had arrived, Joseph mounted his chariot, and went to meet his father, and he fell on his neck, and embraced him, and wept.*

It would not have been a complete resurrection for *Joseph* if God had not restored *his father* to him, that is to say, if He had not conducted him into his origin: and this is what happens, as I have said, after the resurrection, when the soul finds itself reunited to God its origin, with the purity in which it had issued from Him.

CHAPTER XLVIII.

> 14. *And Israel stretched out his right hand, and laid it upon Ephraim's head, who was the younger, and his left hand upon Manasseh's head, guiding his hands wittingly; for Manasseh was the first born.*

17. *And Joseph held up his father's hand, to remove it from Ephraim's head unto Manasseh's head.*
18. *And Joseph said unto his father, Not so, my father; for this is the first born; put thy right hand upon his head.*

This *change of hands* which Israel made was not without mystery: he gave the birthright to the younger; because the nearer we approach God, the more ought we to become children; and the greater we are in ourselves and before men, the less are we before God. Therefore Jacob, by the spirit of prophecy, affirmed that the little one would be preferred to the great: which Jesus Christ has so often declared himself.

19. *But Jacob refused, saying, I know it, my son, I know it well. He also shall be a chief of great peoples, and his seed shall be multiplied; but his brother, who is younger than he, shall be greater than he.*
21. *And Israel said unto Joseph, Behold I die: but God shall be with you, and bring you again unto the land of your fathers.*
22. *Moreover, I have given to thee one portion above thy brethren.*

This repetition of Jacob's: *I know it, my son, I know it well*, shows with what understanding he did that, assuring that the infant people, that is to say, living in the simple state, would become very much *greater than the other.* Jacob again assures Joseph of the confirmation of his state in which he is established, promising him that *God* will be always *with him;* which marks the confirmation in grace: and because of the persecutions and sufferings he had borne, *he gives him a portion of his goods above his brethren*, signifying by that how much God preferred him to the others.

CHAPTER XLIX.

1. *And Jacob called unto his sons, and said, Gather yourselves together, that I may tell you that which shall befal you in the last days.*

Chapter XLIX.

Jacob announces to his sons what was to happen touching the interior kingdom and coming of Jesus Christ.

4. *Reuben, unstable as water, thou shalt not excel:*
8. *Judah, thy brethren shall praise thee; thy hand shall put thine enemies under the yoke; thy father's children shall worship thee.*

He had said to Reuben, that all the *strength* coming of man, *would flow away like water;* but for *Judah*, in whom there was contained Jesus Christ, chief of all the true interior souls, he assures him that *his brethren*, the devout and not mystical souls, *will praise him;* that he *will triumph over his enemies* in Jesus Christ, who has destroyed all. For the truly mystical souls have no power of their own; all their strength is in God alone. This expression, *the sons of thy father*, by which he seems to distinguish them from his brethren, marks that he means to speak of the souls entirely abandoned to the supreme will of God, who are the true children of Israel who will worship God with a worship worthy of him; for it is only these worshippers who worship in spirit and in truth.

9. *Judah is a young lion. Thou art risen, my son, to carry off the prey. In reposing thou art couched like a lion and a lioness. Who will rouse him?*

This word *lion* shows his strength; but he calls him a *little lion*, to show that his strength is in his Father and in his nature: his Father is his son, and his son is his Father. This is the Lion that none can conquer.

Thou art indeed *risen to carry off thy prey*, since thou containest in thyself nothing less than the blood of a God by whom the whole world—earth and heaven—is to be conquered.

But to show that he speaks of interior souls, who carry off the prey because they remain victorious on every point, he explains it thus: My son, *in reposing* in the mystic sleep, *thou art couched* in God *like the lion and the lioness*, who fear nothing, because of their boldness and their strength: for the lion rests secure in his strength; and this soul reposes safely in God, who is its strength. Therefore he adds, *Who will rouse him up?* Meaning, who would have the courage to come where this soul is? Could all hell *trouble the repose* of a soul that is permanently in God?

This couching can be also understood of the repose of the Word incarnated in the womb of Mary, for he was couched within her chaste form as the lion in his cavern.

10. *The Sceptre shall not be taken away from Judah, nor the Prince from his race, until he that is to be sent is come; and it is he that will be the expectation of all nations.*

The sceptre shall always remain in his house, because he is master of all the world in this state, his kingdom being God alone: by the state of union and simplicity, he possesses a kingdom within himself through the interior peace, which renders him master of his passions. But when *He that is to be sent shall come*, which is done by the mystic incarnation, in which the Word is given in the state of transformation, then this kingdom will be taken away, for this soul no longer possessing itself, Jesus possesses all within it; and all possessions of its own and all kingdoms are reunited in Him. Thus is He the *expectation of the nations*, and of the souls called to participate in this happiness.

11. *He shall wash his garments in wine, and his clothes in the blood of grapes.*

This wine is no other than the blood of Jesus Christ; for these souls have no longer any purity proper to them, nor merit peculiar to themselves; but they have everything in Jesus Christ: thus do they expect nothing of themselves, nor by any effort on their part: but with whatever misery they may be covered, everything is found cleansed in the blood of the grape Jesus Christ, who has been under the wine press, and who has given Himself to His friends as the wine. There is nothing, then, to be feared any more for these souls made white in the blood of the Lamb.

12. *His eyes are more beautiful than wine, and his teeth whiter than milk.*

His eyes more beautiful than wine, signifies the power of His charity, looking upon the wretchedness of men to succour them. They denote also the knowledge joined to charity, being lost in the Divine love. The purity of His actions, represented by *the teeth*, surpasses all that can be said of them, for they are done in innocence.

> 22. *Joseph is the fruitful son; he will be multiplied more and more. His countenance is beautiful and agreeable.*
>
> 24. *He has placed his bow in strength, and the chains of his hands and arms have been broken by the hand of the Almighty God of Jacob. From thence is gone out the shepherd and the stone of Israel.*

The abandoned soul dwells in its strength although surrounded by feebleness; because it *has placed* all the *bow* of its strength *in the Almighty*, who is its God. But after the years of its trials and captivity are passed, the hands of God, who is *the Almighty One* of Jacob, *loose its arms and hands*, and render them fit for great things.

From thence is gone out the shepherd of Israel. This can be understood in two ways; first, that his hands being loosed, the shepherd issues from this deliverance: for it is after the soul has been set at liberty by the resurrection and renewal that it is fit to conduct others. The other, that from the Mighty One of Jacob, who is God, is gone out the conductor of the interior people, Jesus Christ, the true shepherd.

By *the stone of Israel* is meant the foundation. This foundation is also Jesus Christ, foundation-stone of the spiritual edifice, which has only worth and stability because founded upon Jesus Christ, firm stone and living rock, and not upon the sand of self-inventions: another explanation is, that Israel being the father of souls abandoned to God, all this race is founded upon him as upon the stone.

> 25. *The God of thy father will help thee; and the Almighty will load thee with blessings of the Heaven above, with blessings of the deep that lieth under, with blessings of the breasts, and of the womb.*

The God of thy father, the God of Israel and of the true abandoned ones, and *the Almighty*, He to whom nothing is difficult, *will load thee with blessings from Heaven above:* meaning, that they will not only have the graces and favours of heaven given in the state of passivity of light and love, where everything comes assuredly from on high, the certitude being given with it; but they will also have *the blessing of the deep underneath*, that is to say, temptations and distresses, which are the appendages of the abyss. This is understood also of the interior hell through which such chosen souls as these pass (at least some), and which, with all its consequences and infernal vapours (which have nothing but what is horrible), yet continues to be, for those who know how to make the use of it that God designs, *a blessing* as much and even greater than the first.

The last *blessing* is distinguished into two kinds; the one of *the breasts*, the milk of which represents the facility of aiding spiritual children in this way, and nourishing them with this spiritual milk of contemplation; the other *of the womb*, by which is meant the production of these same children in Jesus Christ. For the grace of spiritual generation is different from that of nourishment and education. The first begets in Jesus Christ, but cannot nourish: the second nourishes, but does not beget: but the two together form the perfection of the apostolic way: therefore this so complete a blessing is reserved for Joseph, who is in that state.

26. *The blessings given thee by thy father are sustained by those he has received from his fathers, until the desire of the everlasting hills is come. Let these blessings be upon the head of Joseph,—of him who is as a Nazarite amongst his brethren.*

The blessings given by Jacob to Joseph are sustained by those which Jacob has received from his fathers; because they are fortified by the faith and *abandon* from which he derives his origin, and this is what must sustain his blessings. He certifies also by these words, that his ancestors have walked in the same way, and that they uphold so extraordinary a blessing by the example of their life *until the desire* of these souls, who have appeared like mountains and *hills* by the eminence of their holiness, *be accomplished*, that is to say, be reduced into unity, when all desire is lost.

But the truest sense is, that the example of his ancestors must sustain abandoned souls in so strange a way, until Jesus Christ, *the desire* of the saints, *be come* to be their preacher and model; and until by the mystic incarnation wrought in the soul, it exists in Him alone without mediums, even the most holy.

This blessing *will be above Joseph's head;* because although

Joseph is very elevated in the mystic life, nevertheless Jesus Christ is infinitely more so; and there is nothing so elevated that is not below Him, since He is the beginning and end of every way.

CHAPTER L.

16. *Thy father before dying commanded us,*

17. *To make this petition to thee from him: I pray thee to forget the crime of thy brethren, and this heinous wickedness they have committed against thee. We pray thee also to pardon this iniquity of the servants of God thy Father.*

19. *And Joseph replied unto them: Fear not: can we resist the will of God?*

20. *Ye thought to do evil against me; but God has changed it into good, so as to elevate me as ye now see me, and to save many people.*

These Hebrew brethren feared vengeance, for they knew not the generosity of persons in whom God reigns alone, and how forgetful they are of the injuries done unto them. This is what leads them to take the title of *the servants of God the Father of Joseph*, so as to engage him to pardon them, well knowing that nothing was more efficacious with so holy a man as to bring God to his remembrance, above all under this amiable quality of father.

But Joseph, established in the state of the Will of God, which is the highest perfection, speaks to them as a man well instructed in his ways, and says to them, that everything has taken place *in the Will of God*, which none can resist. He adds: *Fear not: can we resist this Divine Will,* which conducts everything infallibly, and which even makes use of the evil wills of men to attain its end, which changes evil into good, and elevates the soul by that which was intended to abase it? Sin even, whose nature is so hurtful to us, in the hand of God becomes useful to us; because He makes everything turn into good.

Oh Divine Will, from which everything derives its origin, and in which everything terminates as in its end, how few souls Thou hast that are perfectly abandoned to all Thy commands!

M

EXODUS.

WITH EXPLICATIONS AND REFLECTIONS REGARDING THE INTERIOR LIFE.

CHAPTER I.

8. *There arose a new king over Egypt who knew not Joseph.*
9. *And he said unto his people: Behold, the people of the children of Israel have become great, and are mightier than we.*

God has not been content to give, in diverse persons, particular examples of the conduct He exercises over souls abandoned to Him, but has also given an entire people in the same states, so that His chosen ones may learn from a general and more visible example that all must travel the same road.

No one is exempt, for all called to the mystic life (who are properly the chosen people) must pass through captivity and reverses. Was there a more prosperous people than this whilst Joseph was alive? All the best things in the kingdom were at their service. Yet behold them captives, and the worst treated of all captives. All souls that are to be conducted by this way are placed at the beginning of the spiritual life in the midst of infinite and equally ineffable joys—for there is not upon earth such heavenly blessings as these persons participate in—but when, through so many favours, God has assured Himself of the faithfulness of this people, it is then He makes them undergo the severe captivity. And none can be exempt from it, since Jesus Christ, the first of the predestined and chief of the abandoned ones, has Himself been pleased to come forth from the delights of His Father's bosom to render Himself of all men the most captive.

All must travel this road—the holy Patriarchs were the figure of what was to be accomplished in Jesus Christ, the saints of the new law are as so many copies of it, and the Saviour is the divine model and original of all.

But why must all pass this way? Is it to remain always unhappy? No; it is to enjoy the land promised to Abraham, to Isaac, and to Jacob, and which is no other than the possession of God. Oh! how much must be done to possess it, and what sufferings can merit it?

God uses Pharaoh to cause these souls to enter into captivity. But he is not alone in this employ; he sets task-masters over them: men, demons, and nature are the *Egyptians* to whom they are in bondage. They overwhelm this poor people with labours, thinking, by thus oppressing them, to prevent them from multiplying.

The same thing is still done. It is believed that the Interior Life can be extinguished by dint of persecution and crying it down; but it is just then that it multiplies. The more those persons who teach it are decried, persecuted, or calumniated, the more persons are found joining them in order to pursue the same path; and by its very persecution it is established and increased, just as the Church was founded and spread by the blood of the martyrs. The demons also, by their cruel temptations, take a part in it, and this is most painful at the commencement by reason of the feebleness of nature, which finds itself overwhelmed under the burden. But the more this soul is laden on all sides with weaknesses and miseries, the more it rises again like the palm tree and the more it multiplies itself.

13. *The Egyptians hated the Israelites, and sorely afflicted them.*

15. *And they made their lives bitter with hard bondage in labours of mortar and brick, and in all manner of service in the field; with which they were oppressed.*

The hardest persecution for this people to bear is to see themselves obliged to *labour at the earth* and for it, after having been raised so nobly to the conversation and table of God. All their work is nothing but earth; they seem to have become nature itself, and wholly earthly. Then their enemies *laugh* to see them engaged at a work so contrary to their birth, education, and hopes. This derision and hatred of the people of the world has always exercised the souls of prayer; but a day is coming when they will soon know their own folly and the wisdom of the righteous.

> 16. *The king of Egypt issued this commandment to the midwives of the Hebrew women: When ye deliver the women of the Hebrews, as soon as they have given birth, if it be a male child, ye shall kill him; but if a daughter, ye shall suffer her to live.*

It is strange that the hatred that is entertained against interior persons does not end with them, but people desire also to prevent their productions, and to destroy them from their birth. How many persons are there, even amongst the most enlightened, who eagerly strive to turn beginners from this way? Although they be as *the kings* of the earth, and appointed of God to be the fathers of souls, yet they continue to oppose them, even believing that by so doing they are performing a great good. But if they do not sanction the sacred and most sure abandon, at least let them not condemn it, and let them suffer those souls to enter therein who are happily beginning to relish it, lest they draw down upon themselves the reproach of Jesus Christ, *that they will neither enter into the kingdom, nor allow others to go in.*

The male children denote the courageous souls who are fit to be abandoned to the impenetrable conduct of God, and *the daughters* are the figure of the feeble and timid persons who are too full of self-love and their own interests to abandon themselves to God in a path so full of the cross. People are quite willing that these should *live*, for they love to live with them; but they condemn the others *to death*, because proprietary and interested love cannot bear the generosity of pure love.

> 17. *But the midwives feared God, and did not do what the king of Egypt had commanded them, but saved the male children alive.*

Often the very persons that are employed to turn the souls of grace from their way, *having the fear* and love *of God*, allow themselves happily to be gained over, and by their *preserving this heavenly life*, they receive it themselves in consideration of their simplicity of heart and as the fruit of their docility. Far from taking away the life of these innocent sheep, they begin to walk with them in the same path, and God recompenses them with His graces in such a manner that they grow daily in Him.

20. *God dealt well with those midwives:*
21. *And because they had feared God, He established their houses.*

This singular expression, that God *establishes their houses*, shows that He Himself works at their spiritual edifice, placing them in the passive way, which is the *recompense* of the good they had done in the active, and is granted to all those who are submissive enough to allow themselves to be introduced therein, when the Spirit of God calls them to it.

22. *Then Pharaoh gave this commandment unto all his people: cast into the river every male child that is born, and preserve only the daughters.*

The persecution would be too light if it stopped there; the Prince of this world must make use of all his inventions to destroy the cherished people of God. He bids then *his own*, who are the wicked and the devils, *kill every male child that is born*—to stifle this way at its birth in the souls who are entering therein, causing them either to die to grace by force of temptations, or to their way, leading them to quit it through distrust or fear of perishing therein, or, finally, to the civil life, by destroying their reputation. This is what happens but too often. These poor abandoned ones are either *cast into the river*, which is a place of inevitable death, or they are exposed to extreme dangers. But as for the *daughters*, the people in the active way, Oh, they are never touched. They are secure in their way; neither persecution, nor temptation, nor slander ever attacks them. On the contrary, the endeavour is to elevate them upon the *debris* and ruin of the others. Beware, it is said, of attacking those souls so strong in themselves (though in truth very feeble), *keep them* for ourselves.

CHAPTER II.

1. *And sometime afterwards, a man of the house of Levi espoused a woman of his tribe,*
2. *Who conceived and bare a son; and seeing that he was a beautiful child, she hid him three months.*

It was right that he who was to become the conductor and director of the people of Providence, should himself be a child of Providence. It is this child, exposed to the impetuosity of the waves, who is to be the shepherd of Israel. God, who conducts everything by His wisdom and goodness, bestows outward *charms* upon this *child*, which would take away all power from the mother to deliver him to the execution. *She hides him* as long as she can, during a time in which the death of many innocents accompanied the birth of Moses, who was to be the most striking figure of Jesus Christ: and this was the presage of the martyrdom of so many little saints, which was to follow the nativity of the Saviour of the world.

3. *As she saw that she could no longer keep him hid, she took an ark of bulrushes, and plastered it with slime and pitch, and put the little child therein; and she laid it amongst the reeds at the river's brink.*
4. *His sister, however, stood afar off, to see what would happen.*

This mother seeing that she must yield to superior force, as an intelligent woman, prefers to trust God alone, rather than the compassion of men: taught of God, she knew that all the children of Providence must be *exposed* to the mercy *of the waters;* and that it is in the extreme peril in which *abandon* holds them, that God is pleased to cause His goodness to shine forth the brightest by the unheard of miracles of His Providence.

This poor innocent one *is* then *exposed* thus: and *his sister remains near*, to be the spectator of Providence. What could she expect but to see him carried off soon by the waves? Or what else had she to hope for this innocent abandoned one, but death, and the waters for a burial-place? His death appeared so certain, that they had placed him living in the coffin, from which God only could draw him.

It was necessary that so great a director should early serve his apprenticeship by his own experience. This God caused him to do from *his cradle;* and the very cradle is his tomb. It can't be said whether this cradle is his coffin, or this coffin his cradle. But God, who only shows the miracles of His Providence in the last extremities, brings life to him out of the very danger of death.

> 5. *At the same time, Pharaoh's daughter came to the river to bathe, followed by her maids, who went along the river's side. And seeing the ark amongst the reeds, she sent one of her maids to fetch it; and she brought it to her.*
> 6. *And having opened it, she found within the little child crying; and she was touched with compassion, and said, This is one of the Hebrews' children.*

The daughter of him who so unjustly condemned the children of the Hebrews to death becomes the mother of this one, and in him gives life and birth to an entire people, who were sought to be exterminated.

> 7. *The child's sister having approached Pharaoh's daughter, said unto her, Shall I go and call to thee a woman of the Hebrews, to nurse the child for thee?*
> 8. *She answered her, Go. And the maid went and called the child's mother:*
> 9. *And Pharaoh's daughter said unto her, Take this child and nurse it for me; and I will recompense thee for it. The mother took the child and nursed it. And when he was strong enough, she gave him to Pharaoh's daughter,*
> 10. *Who adopted him for her son, and called him Moses; for, she said, I have drawn him out of the water.*

But as there is nothing wanting to the succour which Providence brings in order to conduct all things to their end, and every man to the vocation to which he is called, by an unlooked for event *this child* of Providence is provided with his own *mother* for *nurse:* for it would be a little thing to be born a child of Providence, and to commence life by abandon, if it was not likewise continued, and if the life was not of a manner worthy of the calling.

This mother did not *give him up* until he had grown, for it was necessary that he should be so firmly established in his way that neither the grandeurs of the court nor the dangers of life might be able to turn him from it. He appears Egyptian outwardly, and passes for *the son* of the princess: and he is Hebrew really at heart. How many people do we see who appear to live in the world in the commonest manner, but who yet contain within themselves treasures of grace? Oh, how necessary it is not to judge by appearances! The judgments of God are infinitely removed from ours; and according to the profound counsel of St. Paul, "The true Jew is not he who is only so outwardly; nor is the true circumcision that which is visible in the flesh: but the true Jew is he who is so in secret, and the true circumcision is that of the heart, which is in spirit, and not according to the letter; and the praise of this Jew comes from God, not from men."

Moses also in that was the figure of Jesus Christ, who, whilst appearing outwardly only a man, was yet inwardly the true God; and who, under the semblance of a sinner, was the Holy of Holies. These ravishing figures are filled with ineffable mysteries. For example: Who does not see under the shadow of the history of the child Moses, so carefully delivered by Providence from Pharaoh's cruel persecution, the Gospel light of the child Jesus so marvellously preserved from the envenomed rage and carnage of Herod?

11. *When Moses had grown up, he went forth to see his brethren, and looked upon their affliction. And finding one of his Hebrew brethren being maltreated by an Egyptian,*

12. *He looked on all sides, and seeing no one, he slew the Egyptian, and hid him in the sand.*

13. *And on the morrow he found two Hebrews striving with each other. And he said to him who was in the wrong: Wherefore strikest thou thy brother?*

14. *He answered him: Who hath made thee a prince and a judge over us? Wilt thou slay me as thou didst slay the Egyptian yesterday? And Moses was afraid, and said, How has that been discovered?*

Nothing can prevent a soul of this character from defending the cause of the flock of Jesus Christ, even should his life be at stake. He despises greatness, and even life itself, when it is the issue to declare himself on the side of the children of God. As long as there is no occasion for so doing, this faithful friend of God remains like the rest in the common life; but when he finds it necessary to declare himself, oh, then is he sparing of nothing. This here is a great point of faithfulness,—to remain concealed so long as one is not obliged to declare on behalf of the truth: but is the truth attacked? then all must be risked for its defence.

Moses has hardly left his mother, and gone out into the world, than he performs the office of shepherd: for as God desired to make him the conductor of others, He had advanced him in his cradle, and rendered him fit from his nursing to become an apostle. He draws then a sheep from the oppression of the enemy; and by an apparent homicide performs an act of justice; for he does this act in the will of God, destroying God's enemy, the whole perverse nation of which he was one day to become the exterminator. Let it not be asked who constituted him shepherd; he was appointed such by God Himself, to be altogether both the figure and imitator of Jesus Christ, the true Shepherd, and the Shepherd of shepherds. His brethren were to understand by that that it would be by his hand that God would deliver them: but they comprehended him not, as St. Stephen has remarked (Acts 7, 25).

15. *Now Pharaoh, having heard all that had happened, sought to put Moses to death. But Moses hid himself, and fled into the land of Midian: and when he came there he sat down near a well.*

The defence of the truth is always followed by the persecution raised by its avowed enemies. Moses was no exception. He also was obliged *to flee*, and thus take part in the lot of the interior and faithful souls, which is to be persecuted for righteousness sake, even to being constrained to flee. But why does he flee in the design of God? It is in order to fill the office of shepherd.

16. *Now the priest of Midian had seven daughters, who had come to draw water; and having filled the troughs, they wished to water their father's flocks.*

Chapter II.

17. *But there came up shepherds who drove them away; and Moses rose and helped the maids, and watered their sheep.*

We have seen how all those whom God had chosen for this divine ministry, have begun by *watering the flocks:* but Moses, who was not a particular shepherd, but the general shepherd of the whole flock, not only waters it, but also begins by *defending* it. Such ought to be the true shepherds of the sheep of Jesus Christ: not only must they give them water, but also preserve it for them, defending them against those who, out of envy, would hinder them from drinking of it.

18. *And when they had returned to Reuel their father, he said to them: Wherefore are ye come back sooner than usual?*
19. *And they answered him: An Egyptian has delivered us from the violence of the shepherds; and has also drawn water with us, to give our sheep to drink.*

God often sends to abandoned souls a Moses, who *gives them water*, and *delivers them from the oppression* in which they are kept by unworthy and ignorant *shepherds*, who hinder them from drinking of the water from the source. Wherever these persons are found that are called to *abandon*, and under whatever violence they mourn, when they are faithful, God never fails to send them a shepherd capable of conducting them into the way of the Lord: and which is wrought by providences no less admirable than infallible. *The daughters of Jethro return early to their father*, that is to say, to their origin, on account of their having found a good shepherd, who, giving them pure waters, has caused them to advance.

21. *Moses sware unto Reuel to remain with him, and he espoused his daughter, who was called Zipporah.*

If Providence was kind towards Reuel, to send him Moses to feed and water his flocks, It was no less so towards Moses, to cause him to find in this very house a faithful companion, who, understanding her calling, and being in the same way with him, was to contribute to the spiritual generation. Moreover, he was made to find there a sure retreat, and wherewith to live during the time that he was to be removed from his people.

22. *She bare him a second son, whom he called Eliezer, saying*

the God of my father, who is my protector, has delivered me from the hand of Pharaoh.

To attribute everything *to God* and his providence, even *children*, and all our productions, is the sign of a soul enlightened of God by a lively faith, and the just acknowledgment which it owes to His succour.

23. *And it came to pass that many years afterwards the king of Egypt died. And the children of Israel, groaning under the burden of the labours with which they were overwhelmed, cried unto the heavens. And the cries caused by their exceeding great misfortunes came up unto God.*
24. *And God heard their groanings, and He remembered the covenant which He had made with Abraham, Isaac, and Jacob.*
25. *And the Lord looked upon the children of Israel, and had compassion for their troubles.*

Whilst God was thus conducting the shepherd of Israel, He still left the flock in a very hard bondage. *Pharaoh died*, but *the labours* of this poor people were not diminished. *They cried to God, and He had compassion on them. He remembered the covenant he had made* with the souls of faith, of pure sacrifice, and of perfect *abandon*. *Abraham* was the father of faith, *Isaac* marked pure sacrifice, and *Jacob* perfect *abandon*. All interior souls must proceed by naked faith, by pure sacrifice, and by perfect *abandon*, if they would arrive at the purity of their creation.

Naked faith is a faith with neither sign nor support for the reason and mind.

Pure sacrifice is a total sacrifice; not only of all that belongs to us and is in us, but also of all that we are, as much in the order of nature as in that of grace.

Perfect abandon is a state of complete destitution in God's hands, so that He may do in us and with us His whole will, either exteriorly or interiorly, with no exception, for time or for eternity.

God remembers these ways, the purest and most necessary for the soul to be received into Him: and He is willing to deliver this poor people from the captivity that oppresses them, and from serving the Lord in liberty and in purity.

CHAPTER III.

1. *And Moses kept the sheep of Jethro his father-in-law, priest of Midian. And he led his flock to the far end of the desert, and came to the mountain of God called Horeb.*

While Moses was thinking only of *keeping the flock of sheep* which God had entrusted to him in the house *of his father-in-law* as to a particular shepherd, he was elevated to a higher union with God, *approaching nearer to the mountain* by a more sublime loss into Him.

2. *And the Lord appeared to him in a flame of fire which issued from a bush. And he saw the bush burning without it being consumed.*

God speaks to him *in a bush from a flame of fire:* God was in the flame, and the flame was in the bush. This *flame* denoted the love that God has for interior souls, in spite of their weaknesses. It pleased Him to bestow a large share of it on this shepherd, whom he had chosen to conduct a very numerous flock; for the first quality of the shepherd is love, causing him to expose his life for his sheep.

This flame is *surrounded with thorns*, for those have much to suffer who have the conducting of souls. One cannot conceive of the crosses that are prepared for them, nor *the thorns* and persecutions that they must suffer.

This bush *burns, and is not consumed.* This is the symbol of the love of the shepherds, which must be always equal, without ever growing tired or feeble. The extent to which this holy shepherd had been filled and inflamed by it appears further on, when, seeing his people on the point of being smitten of God for their sins, he stayed His just wrath by this prayer, inspired by the purest and most violent love (Ex. xxxii. 32): "*Lord forgive them this fault, or if Thou wilt not forgive them, do Thou blot me out of the book which Thou hast written.*"

4. *And when the Lord saw that Moses turned aside to see, He called to him out of the midst of the bush; and said, Moses, Moses. And he answered, Here am I.*
5. *And God said, Draw not nigh hither: take off thy shoes*

from off thy feet, for the place on which thou standest is holy ground.

As if the Lord said to him: *Approach not* a love so pure and so disinterested, a charity so extended and equal toward all, until thou art stripped of all particular affection. This is the final stripping that I still require of thee, to wit, that thy affections, represented by thy *feet*, be perfectly naked, so that thou mayest be able to have a just equality for this entire people, and may judge them in justice and holiness; *for the ground* of love *is* altogether *holy*.

6. *Moreover He said, I am the God of thy father, the God of Abraham, the God of Isaac, and the God of Jacob.*
7. *I have seen the affliction of my people which are in Egypt, and have heard the cries which they send up by reason of the severity of their taskmasters.*
8. *And knowing their sorrows, I am come down to deliver them out of the hands of the Egyptians, and to bring them up out of that land into a good land and large, into a land flowing with milk and honey.*

God again puts Moses in mind of naked faith, pure sacrifice, and perfect *abandon*, adding, that He is the God of this people of faith, sacrifice, and *abandon*. He also says to him, *I am the God of thy father*, to show him that he himself has sprung from this source and origin.

He announces to him, moreover, that He will *withdraw* these souls *from the captivity* to which they are reduced by the multiplicity of the works they are overwhelmed with, and will introduce them into the promised land, which is the region of peace and repose in God. He declares to him also, that the affliction of this people (*oppressed* by external works), and their desire for liberty, *have come up unto Him*, and that it is by his means that He will deliver them.

10. *Come, and I will send thee unto Pharaoh, that thou mayest bring forth my people the children of Israel out of Egypt.*
11. *And Moses said unto God, Who am I, to go unto Pharaoh, and to bring forth the children of Israel out of Egypt.*
12. *And God said unto him, I will be with thee.*

Chapter III.

Moses excuses himself in the sight of his meanness, finding himself incapable of conducting so great a people in so difficult a road as that of blind *abandon*. But what appears to him the most impossible, is to draw this people from the vexation of their taskmasters, and *to bring them out from the dominion* of Pharaoh. This is what is most difficult, to draw souls from practices and methods to introduce them into the desert of faith; therefore, God assures him that *He will be with him*, and that He himself will perform this great work; and that the visible protection which He will give to the word of Moses will be the infallible sign that God has sent him.

13. *And Moses said unto God, Behold, when I come unto the children of Israel, and shall say unto them, The God of your fathers has sent me unto you; and they ask me, What is his name? what shall I say unto them?*

Moses does not find it to be enough to say to the children of Israel, that the God of faith, sacrifice, and *abandon* has sent him: he desires to know *the name of this God*, so powerful as to be able to conduct this innumerable people by so strange a way. God, willing to instruct this faithful shepherd in all things, is not offended at this request. What, then, does He say to him?

14. *The Lord said unto Moses, I AM THAT I AM. Thus shalt thou say unto the children of Israel, I AM hath sent me unto you.*

I am that I am: I am the Being of beings, the Being from whom everything else bearing the name of being is derived. I am He who alone is something, everything being nothing out of Me. Whoever can call himself, or believe or know himself to be something, is not yet fit to be of My people. I require a people of truth, so annihilated, that they are in the truth of *nothing*, as I am in the truth of *all*. Thus is it necessary only to say this to the children of Israel: *I Am has sent me unto you;* so that, putting them in mind of their *nothingness* and of My *all*, they may have less difficulty in abandoning themselves to My conduct, in ridding themselves of their own inventions, and in coming out of the land of the industry of man, to follow the way of *abandon*, which will conduct them surely to Me.

15. *God said again unto Moses, Thus shalt thou say unto the children of Israel, The Lord the God of your fathers, the God of Abraham, the God of Isaac, the God of Jacob, has sent me unto you. This is my name for ever, and this is my memorial unto all generations.*

Thou shalt say unto them that *the God* who led *their fathers*, who always walked by the way of *abandon, sends thee* to be their visible conductor; but that it is I who shall perform everything, for I am that I am, and without Me does nothing exist. *This name shall last me for ever, and shall be my memorial to all generations.* Is not this as if He said: He who alone is, and who is the All-Being, has no need of a name to distinguish Himself from other beings; since there are none out of Him. His being is His name, and His name is His being; and as His being comprehends everything, so His name expresses everything. Creatures, who are at bottom veritable nothings, covered with a little dependent being, lent to them by God, have need of names to distinguish themselves; but He who absorbs in Himself all things, has need of no other name than that of Being; for everything that in some manner exists, is either Himself, or is held so closely to Him by the essential root of its origin, that it is nothing out of Him. This ineffable name *serves* God *as a memorial* to His people; and also to discern this same people— that is to say, to distinguish these dear children, who well know to attribute all to Him and nothing to themselves, from those who act differently. Those who appropriate something to themselves rob Him of His name; therefore, He assures Moses that at this name alone His people will obey His voice.

18. *Thou shalt go with the elders of Israel unto the king of Egypt, and thou shalt say unto him, The Lord, the God of the Hebrews, calls us to go three days' journey into the desert, and to sacrifice there to the Lord our God.*

They ask *to go into the desert to sacrifice there unto their God;* for the desert of naked faith must be traversed before arriving at pure sacrifice. The road thereof is long. People desire this sacrifice at once; but they arrive at it very late, and few there are who attain to it.

19. *But I know that the king of Egypt will not let you go but by a mighty hand.*

20. *And I will stretch out my hand, and will smite Egypt with a vast number of wonders which I will do in the midst thereof: and after that they will let you go.*

Nevertheless God knew *that Pharaoh would only let His people go by a mighty hand;* and yet He sends Moses to speak thus to him, to show that we must always try gentle ways before rigorous ones, and that extraordinary means must only be used at the last extremity when all human forces are useless.

21. *Ye shall not go out with empty hands.*
22. *But ye shall despoil Egypt.*

The Lord is not content to give freedom to these souls, He also *enriches* them *with the spoils* of the others who will not enter into His pure way, verifying what He has said by Jesus Christ, His Son, that *to him who hath shall be given, but from him who hath not, shall be taken away even that which he hath.*

CHAPTER IV.

1. *And Moses answered and said, They will not believe me, nor hearken unto my voice.*
2. *And the Lord said unto him, What is that thou hast in thine hand? And he answered, A rod.*
3. *And the Lord said unto him, Cast it on the ground: and Moses did so, and it was changed into a serpent.*

This distrust and resistance of Moses shows us, indeed, that in the most advanced states we may commit infidelities and resist God. To depend upon signs more than upon the word of God, is so great a fault for an advanced soul that, if God were not so good as He is, this would merit us being rejected for ever. Abraham, a man of an admirable faith, at the word of God alone, is upon the point of committing a parricide; and Moses, after several commands from the Lord, fears to undertake a good action. Even miracles do not assure him; for although advanced persons may, through infidelity, desire

10. *Then Moses said unto the Lord, Hear me, I pray Thee: I have never had great fluency of speech, and since indeed thou hast begun to speak unto thy servant, my tongue is still less free, and more tied.*

Lord, *I know not how to speak,* my voice being a voice of silence, and also, *since thou hast spoken unto me, I have less freedom of speech:* for it is the property of the Word of God to absorb our own, and, according to a prophet (Zech. ii. 13), "*When the Lord comes forth out of His sanctuary, all flesh must remain in silence before His face.*" When God speaks to the soul, everything in it must keep silence, in order to listen to Him. But if everything ought to be silent before God when it is His pleasure to speak, it is also necessary that everything speak for Him when He commands it.

11. *And the Lord answered him, Who hath made man's mouth? Who hath formed the dumb, and the deaf, him that seeth, and the blind? Is it not I?*

Is it not God who ties and unties the tongue? The more ignorant a person is, and the less fluency of utterance he has of himself, the fitter is he in God's hand to be made use of as He pleases. So, after God has made known to Moses that facility of expression on spiritual things does not reside in the natural, but in the Divine power, He assures him that He will speak by him.

12. *Go, I will be in thy mouth, and I will teach thee what thou shalt have to say.*

All apostolic persons, sent of God, have this advantage, that *God speaks by their mouth,* and *teaches them what they are to say:* for being abandoned to Him in all things, He does not fail them in time of need. St. Paul has clearly expressed it for us: "*Are ye willing,*" said he, "*to experience the truth of Jesus Christ, who speaks by my mouth?*" (2 Cor. xiii. 3.)

13. *I pray thee, O Lord, said Moses, send him whom thou art to send.*

Moses' desire was conceived on behalf of Messiah, whom he regarded as the true liberator not only of this people, but also of the whole world; nevertheless all desires, even the most just and holy, ought to be banished from an abandoned and annihilated soul; for it ought to wish nothing but in the will of God, who brings things to pass in their time. Thus the mark of its annihilation, is this impotence to will or desire anything, and we cannot come out of this total death to all desire, without much displeasing God.

14. *And the Lord was angry with Moses, and said to him, I know that Aaron thy brother, of the race of Levi, speaks well. Behold, he cometh forth to meet thee, and when he shall see thee, he shall rejoice with all his heart.*

15. *Speak thou to him, and put my words into his mouth. I will be in thy mouth and in his, and I will shew you what ye shall have to do.*

16. *He will speak for thee unto the people, and he will be thy mouth, and thou shalt conduct him in all that regards God.*

Although God's anger was not raised by Moses' apparently unjust requests, yet *He is angry with this desire;* for the former requests were made with simplicity, and in quite a natural manner, but he could not desire anything without coming out of his state. Thus did God cease here to be willing to speak for him, and for this infidelity gives him a human mouth. Oh, how much it is of consequence not to issue out of that blind *abandon* in God's hands under pretext of good desires! This, however, does not prevent God, without considering this infidelity of the shepherd, from giving all that is necessary for the sake of the flock.

After Moses' fault, God yet continues to assure him that *He will be in the mouth of his brother and in his own;* and that he also will be his brother's shepherd. Aaron is placed between Moses and the people, and Moses between God and Aaron.

22. *Thus saith the Lord, Israel is my first-born.*

Israel is called *the first-born of God*, to teach us that interior souls have the preference in the inheritance of heaven; which, however does not exclude the others, for there are many roads which conduct to the heavenly country. But this one is the most glorious for God, and the most advantageous for souls.

25. *Zipporah said to Moses, Thou art a bloody husband to me.*
26. *And she left him after saying, Thou art a bloody husband to me, because of the circumcision.*

Zipporah, not knowing that the unions which God forms between souls are only for the cross, calls Moses a *bloody husband*, for she knew that so holy a man could not be united to her without her having a share in his sufferings; therefore *she leaves him because of the circumcision*, this first of all his crosses, which was only the beginning of the rest, and already caused her to fear retrenchment and mortification. Few souls are faithful to keep company together reciprocally in the way of blood and the cross.

31. *The people believed, and understood that the Lord had visited the children of Israel, and that he had looked upon their affliction; and bowing their heads to the ground, they worshipped him.*

None *believe* more easily than interior *people*, their whole way being founded upon faith. It was for this reason that Moses and Aaron had no difficulty in making known to the Israelites the designs of God, and in making them enter therein. It is not the same with the people of reason and signs, they do not immediately give themselves up, but only yield to force.

CHAPTER V.

2. *And Pharaoh said unto Moses and Aaron, Who is the Lord, that I should obey his voice, and let Israel go? I know not the Lord, neither will I let Israel go.*

Pharaoh had, indeed, reason to say, *that he knew not the Lord.* It is not the proud who know Him, but only the humble, who serve Him in the simplicity of their heart. This manner of speaking, *Who is the Lord?—I know Him not,* denotes an arrogance worthy of a thousand hells. The libertines and great minds of the age speak thus, when they are warned of anything concerning their salvation. Oh, they have no wish to obey God, speaking to them by the mouth of His servants, for *they know Him not.*

> 8. *Ye shall cause them to make the same quantity of bricks that they made before, without diminishing ought thereof. For they are idle, and therefore they cry, Let us go and sacrifice to our God.*

Is it not to-day that these interior persons are accused of being *idle*. Directors of little experience, and those people who are not acquainted with the mystic repose, seeing a soul given up to contemplation and the prayer of silence, and desirous only of *sacrificing itself to God* in the simplicity of its heart, say one to another, *Let us load* it with practices, and fatigue it, for all its devotion is but idleness. But God knows well how to draw out of their hands these souls whom He has chosen for His repose, and to hide them in the secret place of His countenance from the disturbance of men.

> 9. *Let them be overcharged with labours, and be compelled to finish them, that they may amuse themselves no more with lying words.*

Let them be overladen with exterior works which we enjoin to them, *that they may no longer stop* at their illusions, nor their interior *words*, which are but *lying words* and deceits. Oh, audacious men, who, like Pharaoh, tax the servants of God with illusions and ravings, fear ye not that God may punish you like him?

> 14. *And those of the Israelites who were set over the works of their people, were beaten with rods by the taskmasters of Pharaoh, who said to them: Why have ye neither yesterday nor to-day produced the same quantity of brick as ye did before?*

They add severity to threats, and often *blows,* to oppress these poor souls, who, under the bad treatment they receive, put their whole trust in God: they overcharge them with impossible labours, and if they do not perform them all, they are accused of disobedience. Console yourselves, interior friends of God, the more you are to have part in His Divine life, the more you must be exposed as a butt for the opposition of men.

15. *Then the officers came to Pharaoh, and cried unto him, Why dost thou thus treat thy servants?*
16. *There is no straw given unto us, and they command us to produce the same number of bricks as before. We are beaten with rods although we are thy servants, and they unjustly distress thy people.*

These poor souls, overwhelmed with labours by these unenlightened directors, *cry* that these practices are insupportable to them, at least in so great a number; they complain moreover that they can easily overburden them with methods, but cannot impart to them the facility of performance, which is indeed taken away from them by their burdens; that they get no rest, and that there are rigours for them that are not for others.

17. *Pharaoh answered them, Idleness destroys you, therefore ye say, Let us go to sacrifice to the Lord.*
18. *Go then to your work, there shall be no straw given you, and ye shall produce always the same quantity of bricks.*

To that it is replied that their interior is *idle*, that they love only to remain in repose before God in a spirit of *sacrifice;* and without being listened to, they are overwhelmed with penitences and labours of the active way, which they can no longer bear.

20. *And they met Moses and Aaron, who stood near, waiting until these Israelites should come out from Pharaoh.*
21. *And they said unto them, Let God look upon what ye do to us, and let him judge between you and us. Ye have rendered us of an abhorred savour before Pharaoh and his servants; and ye have put a sword into his hand to kill us.*

They seek those who have led them under the favour of grace to enter into the way of sacrifice, and they say to them in their consternation, Ye have caused us to enter into a way of death, for those persons who previously conducted us with something of kindness, have now nothing but rigours for us, and your acquaintance has been to us like a *sword of death*.

But these spiritual fathers, addressing God with urgent prayers for this afflicted people, haste to draw them out of these tyrannous hands.

22. *And Moses returned unto the Lord, and said unto him, Oh Lord, why hast thou afflicted thy people? Why hast thou sent me?*

23. *For since I have presented myself before Pharaoh to speak to him in thy name, he has distressed thy people still more, and thou hast not delivered them.*

These few words which Moses says to God are a prayer of a tender heart and a true shepherd, who complains to God even of Himself, because He *does not deliver* this poor *people* from the tyranny immediately, as he had imagined. Oh, Divine promises, how far from our imaginings is your fulfilment usually removed! The moment of Providence which discovers you, brings to light so many other things in addition to what we had imagined. Thou hast promised in a few words to deliver this people; and even to the saints who were the ministers of this great work, it seemed that Thou wast going to perform it immediately. But by how many miracles and strange providences will this deliverance be accomplished? And of all those who will have been delivered from Egypt with so many marvels, two persons only will enter into the promised land! Who will penetrate the profound decrees of God? Ah, how good it is, and how beautiful, that they are hidden from the creature until they issue from the bosom of the Creator, at the very hours and moments He marks out for them.

CHAPTER VI.

1. *Then the Lord said unto Moses, Now shalt thou see what I will do to Pharaoh.*

God answers Moses out of His infinite goodness, accommodating Himself to the weakness of His creature when it acts in simplicity. Does it not seem as if the Lord made an excuse to Moses? *Now*, said He, *thou shalt see* what I will do. Oh, simplicity! truly thou art the language that God loves—thou dost not seek so many other things and inventions which please Him not.

> 2. *And God said unto Moses, I am the Lord,*
> 3. *Who appeared unto Abraham, unto Isaac, and unto Jacob, as the Almighty God, but by my name Adonai was I not known to them.*
> 4. *And I have established my covenant with them, promising to give them the land of Canaan, the land in which they dwelt as pilgrims and strangers.*

I appeared indeed *unto Abraham* in naked faith, *unto Isaac* in pure sacrifice, and *unto Israel* in perfect *abandon, as the Almighty God;* they have not been ignorant of My omnipotence in all these ways in which I have conducted them, but they have not known Me by the greatest of all My names, Adonai, which signifies the Supreme Sovereign, and denotes that *I am that I am:* for as I have chosen thee as the legislator not only of the common people of Israel, but much more of My interior people, it was necessary that thou shouldst have more knowledge of my ALL BEING, and of the nothingness of the creature, so that, as much by thy experience as by My inspiration, thou mightest be able to instruct the souls that are destined for annihilation. This profound knowledge, My dear Moses, has been reserved for thee as a great prince of the mystic people and of My beloved annihilated ones, and as the liveliest and most perfect figure of Jesus Christ My only son, the chief and elder brother of all those who by their mystic annihilation honour my redoubtable name of *Adonai*, and who by confessing and accepting their nothingness, perfectly worship the sovereignty of my Being. Also shalt thou see greater effects of my power than thy fathers did, for by thee shall I accomplish, with unheard of miracles, what I only *promised* them.

> 6. *Wherefore say unto the children of Israel, I am the Lord, who will draw you out of the prison of the Egyptians, and will deliver you out of bondage, with my stretched out strong arm, and with my great judgments.*

Nothing touches God's heart so much as to see His dear abandoned ones *captives*, and groaning under the yoke of bondage: *I will deliver them*, He says, *with my stretched out arm.* This expression, His arm, denotes that He will employ extraordinary power.

> 7. *And I will take you for my people, and I will be your God, and ye shall know that it is I that am the Lord your God.*

The Lord assures these abandoned souls that *He will take them for a people* peculiarly His own, and that *He will be their God* in a particular manner, declaring to them moreover that *they will know* by experience that *He is the Lord their God.* For as there are no people that give themselves to God more than those who abandon themselves wholly to Him without exception or reserve, so God gives Himself to them more than to any other people. He never suffers Himself to be conquered in this amorous gift, but gives Himself in a surpassing manner in this life to whomsoever perfectly yields himself up to Him.

> 9. *And Moses spake so unto the children of Israel; but they hearkened not unto him by reason of their anguish of spirit, and their exceedingly hard labours.*

There are many who obey the way of God when it is full of sweetness and accompanied by miracles, but who find it hard to do so when it brings only the cross. This is an infidelity often committed by persons who are commencing.

> 12. *And Moses said unto the Lord, Behold, the children of Israel will not hear me, how then will Pharaoh hear me?*

Moses' excuse appears just enough, alleging that if *the children* who are in the presence of their father refuse to obey because of the cross, still less will the wicked and enemies obey in what is contrary to their own interests.

CHAPTER VII.

> 1. *The Lord said unto Moses, See, I have made thee a god to Pharaoh: and Aaron thy brother will be thy prophet.*

Annihilated souls are as gods to princes even, for as everything in them of the creature has disappeared, there must necessarily remain only God. The interpreters of these persons thus annihilated are their *prophets*, for they speak only the words of God, uttering on behalf of others the words pronounced by these souls who have become as God by the total annihilation of themselves.

12. *The magicians having each cast down his rod, they were changed into serpents; but Aaron's rod swallowed up their rods.*

Some persons of evil and erroneous doctrine desire to *counterfeit* the spiritual ones, and do what they do: but the spirit of God absorbs everything, distinguishes the false from the true, and truth soon *swallows up* lies.

CHAPTER VIII.

17. *And Aaron stretched out his hand with his rod, and smote the dust of the earth, which became lice throughout all Egypt.*
18. *The magicians not being able to do likewise,*
19. *Said to Pharaoh: This is the finger of God, but Pharaoh's heart remained hardened.*

All the marvels that God performs on behalf of interior persons serve only to *harden the hearts* of their enemies. Sometimes the most wicked are forced to confess that *it is the finger of God* that works these miracles, whilst the hearts of the others remain hardened.

23. *And I will put a division between my people and thy people.*

God *separates His people* from those who are not willing to be His; and whilst the persecutors suffer the grievous pricking of the lice of their vanity and malice, which leave them no rest, these fortunate souls dwell content in the abode of peace.

CHAPTER X.

22. *And Moses stretched forth his hand towards heaven; and there was a frightful darkness over all Egypt for three days.*
23. *But the day shone where the children of Israel dwelt.*

The day of the wicked is changed into *horrible darkness* when God stretches forth the hand of His judgment to place them in His truth, which shows them by a just experience that all their pretended light was but darkness, and that the more they thought themselves enlightened in themselves and before men, the more were they ignorant before God. But the just, being united to God by faith alone, dwell always in a true *light*, which, far from diminishing or being eclipsed, increases to a perfect *day*. Who would dare to express the profound truths which God discovers to the souls of faith, and how much they are divinely enlightened when they seem to have lost all light? It must be left to be judged by those who have some experience of it. That which is drawn from the source of God is always truth, God being Truth Itself: that which is drawn from the creature's source by the senses or reasonings, is very often error, for man by himself is nothing but vanity and lies. The infallible method then of entering into truth and dwelling there, of increasing, dying and living in it eternally, is to trust oneself only to God for all things, and to believe them such as they are in His eyes.

CHAPTER XI.

5. *And all the first-born in the land of Egypt shall die.*

The first-born of Egypt are the figure of sinners, who usually bring forth nothing but sin; and the first-born of the children of God are the interior souls. The sinners wish to destroy the interior; but God, on behalf of the interior, humbles the sinners and *slays* sin.

The ministering angels of God's vengeance, by the might of

His power, *put to death the first-born* of the world, whom men esteem so highly, and in whom they place a vain trust; but His dear interior friends are secure under His protection; and although He permits them to be maltreated by carnal men, to purify their love and to augment their crowns, yet they are not smitten in His wrath, but only visited by His mercy: for it is these children of God, much more than the children of men, who put their trust under the shadow of the wings of the Lord.

CHAPTER XII.

3. Let each one take a lamb for his family and for his house.
5. This lamb shall be without blemish.

Interior persons can be distinguished only by the sign of God, and this sign is the blood of *the lamb*, with which they are marked; for having no longer any merit of their own, they possess everything in Jesus Christ; and it is in His blood and by His blood that they are preserved. It is this which causes them to hope against hope, for their despair of themselves sends them happily to put a perfect trust in God.

This *lamb is without blemish;* because that in Jesus Christ there never was any sin, and it is His justice which obliterates our injustice.

7. They shall take of his blood, and shall put some of it upon the two side-posts, and upon the upper door-post of the houses in which they shall eat it.
8. And they shall eat of the flesh in that night, roasted with fire; and unleavened bread with wild lettuces.

It is not enough that we be washed and *marked with the blood of the Lamb.* It is necessary also that His people should *eat of His flesh;* for it is that which makes them grow and be fruitful, and which is to fortify them to pass through the long and frightsome desert of naked faith, which, although full of freedom, and accompanied by a thousand heavenly sweetnesses sustaining the soul in this rude pilgrimage, is nevertheless more

Chapter XII.

difficult to bear than the first captivity; because of self-love, preferring to be burdened with labour, in making bricks (that is to say, works of little value), rather than to be free and employed in conquering heaven (the promised land and God Himself), and foregoing the satisfaction of seeing its work.

Wild lettuces, which are bitter, represent the mortification in which the soul of faith must be exercised; for it enters into the desert of faith only after having passed through all the mortifications possible, according to its strength and vocation. *The unleavened bread*, made without much preparation, denotes the nourishment suitable to the simple state, which is without any preparation, but also without any corruption of self-love, for the creature has but little share in it.

Moreover, this flesh was made ready *at the fire* and *roasted;* for it represented the consummation of charity in Jesus Christ, who is all fire; and charity is the fire of pure love, with which we are to be set on fire by eating this lamb without blemish.

9. *Ye shall eat the head of it, with the feet and the entrails.*
10. *Ye shall reserve none of it till the morning; if there remain anything, ye shall burn it with fire.*

As this *eating* of the pascal lamb of the Jews was the figure of the sacrifice of Jesus Christ; (for what Christian does not see in this roasted lamb that is to be eaten the shadow of Jesus Christ giving himself as food in His sacrament at the time of His passion?) it was also the sensible representation of pure sacrifice, by which the soul must be consummated into God in the desert of faith.

Now this sacrifice allows of *no reserve:* it must be entire; and for this reason it must be a whole burnt-offering, reserving not the least thing whatsoever. Everything must be consumed and devoured, not only *the flesh* and all that there is outwardly with regard to the creature—not only the faculties represented by *the head*, and the affections signified by *the feet*, but also whatever there is most interior in the depths of the soul, its very centre and the highest point of the spirit; everything must be destroyed, so that there may not remain anything whatever, inwardly any more than outwardly; and it is the most interior things that are signified by the *entrails*.

But if this sacrifice, so necessary and so strongly recommended, is recognised as the most perfect of all, oh how much it is combated in the practice!—oh, how difficult it is!—oh, how much it costs a soul before it can surrender itself to it! And, again, where will any one be found who *reserves nothing?* Nevertheless, all these half-sacrifices can never be the sacrifice of the holocaust, which is what God has peculiarly reserved to Himself, to be entirely consecrated to His glory alone; therefore, it is called pure sacrifice. It is a deplorable thing that so many great souls, who have allowed themselves to be sacrificed in so many things, *reserve* almost *all the entrails* for themselves, at least part. Oh! if they knew the glory which God draws from this pure sacrifice, and the advantage which must accrue to them from it, how much more generous would they be in abandoning themselves without reserve! But they are not willing to comprehend it, although God Himself suggests it to their heart, and those that are most instructed in these secrets tell them something of it; for people take for loss that which is gain, and for gain that which is loss. To lose all for God Himself is to gain everything: to lose God even with regard to ourselves, so far as He can be ours, in order to let Him take in us a sovereign glory, without mixing our interest in anything of it—oh! that is the supreme felicity, and the most sublime witness of pure love!

This, then, is the state and disposition of pure sacrifice; all the other sacrifices are sacrifices in which the creature desires to have some part; they are all interested in something, and the creatures wish to be reckoned in them; but pure sacrifice is God's sacrifice, reserved for Him alone: it is the Divine sacrifice: it is the sacrifice of Jesus Christ—model of all the rest—in which He wills that everything be destroyed. Oh, spotless victim, it is in thy total immolation that all pure sacrifices are comprised! and as thine is the original of them, it is also their power and spirit, and all their perfection.

11. *Behold how ye shall eat it. Ye shall gird your loins; ye shall have your shoes on your feet, and your staff in your hand: and ye shall eat it in haste: for it is the Passover, that is to say, the passage of the Lord.*

The loins girded denoted the purity of the obedience to God's will, which is the girdle that happily binds us: without it all purity is but impurity; and outward purity of the flesh is but the figure of interior purity, which is that of the spirit. Now,

Chapter XII.

interior purity consists in conformity to the will of God, and the more eminent this conformity, the more pure the spirit. The will of the creature is first of all rendered conform to that of its Creator; then it becomes uniform, and afterwards it is transformed into the very will of God; and it is then that all self-will is so dead, destroyed and passed into the Divine Will that its name is changed, being no longer called anything but the will of God.

The *covering of the feet* is in this place taken for the sign of pilgrimage, and not for the affections; for if it was necessary for Moses to take off his shoes to approach the burning bush, how much more is it necessary to do so, in the sense of purifying ourselves from our affections, in order to eat of the lamb? But here *the shoes on the feet* represent pilgrimage, as well as *the stick*. They eat the lamb *in haste*, as a sign of the passage that is to be made. Now it is certain that the consummation of pure sacrifice, which is annihilation, is the disposition near to the passage of the soul into God; and the soul is no sooner arrived at the degree of annihilation answering to God's design, than from that moment *it passes* into Him, and He Himself becomes the fulness of this immense void.

All the other voids, which are only the voids of the faculties, are filled by graces conform to the disposition of the subject, and the extent of their void; but annihilation can only be filled by God Himself.

And here is the admirable order which is observed in diverse voids and in their fillings:

God first of all empties the soul of all sin: and, in proportion as He does so, He fills it with His gifts and graces.

Then He empties this same soul of His gifts and graces— at least, in a perceptible manner (for it no longer possesses them, save imperceptibly, and as if it really had them not), in order to fill it with Himself. And this void of graces serves to take away from the soul a limited quality and natural contracting, which renders it incapable of being dilated and enlarged: for it must be known that all God's graces, however withheld they may be, are always proportioned to the capacity of the creature, the receptive property of which is hard and contracted, opposed to the penetration of the Divine life.

Sin dwelt in this creature thus bounded and straightened. When God comes into it by his grace, He drives this sin out of it in a manner even gentle and quiet; then, in proportion as this vase is emptied of its evil liquor, God infills it with the unction of His grace, which causes a lively pleasure even in the most severe penitences. But when it becomes necessary to purge the soul of its central rust, and take from it the filth that remains in its root from the infection of sin,—this filth and rust may indeed accord with grace, but they are incompatible with God,—therefore, it is necessary that this soul be placed *in the fire*, in a fire more subtile and more devouring, which causes it to undergo a most grievous operation. This fire burns briskly, and it seems to sully the soul instead of purifying it, which easily leads people to be mistaken, because the beauty of this work can only be seen when it is accomplished, just as we do not see the workmen desirous of producing the metal, whilst it is all penetrated with fire in the furnace, and covered with dross and earth. It is necessary then that the fire take away the radical rust of the soul in such a manner, either in this world or in the other, that there remain no impurity therein.

In this crucible God takes away from the soul all that He had filled it with, however exquisite it may be, which causes it to experience nothing now but grief and pain without sweetening. In proportion as this fire takes away and consumes the rust of this soul, it takes away also an opaque quality, limited and contracted, which is no other than the selfhood, which, freezing and fixing it in itself, hinders it from flowing into God. And it is this which causes these great pains, the soul being seized in the most sensible and living part of itself—to wit, in its proprietary fund or root. The more subtle and slender this propriety becomes, the more difficult it is to root out; but as soon as it is wholly consumed, the soul, finding itself delivered from its contracting (tendency), and no longer retaining anything of itself, falls into annihilation.

Then it is so supple and pliable, that in place of this hard and constrained quality—which was caused by the propriety, or, rather, was the propriety itself—it has contracted an easy disposition, capable of being extended almost to infinity. It is then that it has attained to the purity of its origin; for God created it thus supple and pliable, and fit to be stretched out by Himself and in Himself; but sin rendering it proprietary, at the same time rendered it hard and resisting, and incapable of being enlarged, until God, the Restorer, causes it to return into the purity of its creation.

When, then, this faithful soul has arrived at the total loss of its propriety and restriction, then it is fit for union, or rather for intimate unity, and to be lost into God. But as God can always communicate Himself to infinity, so can He every day enlarge this soul more and more, and give Himself always more to it.

It is certain that so soon as all propriety is banished from the soul, and thus it is annihilated, at the same moment it is filled with God; for He leaves nothing void in it; and as He fills the void of the faculties with His gifts, He also fills this void of the essence with Himself. The void in part can indeed be filled by some created gift, but the total void can only be filled by the uncreated All.

And this capacity increasing every day by the operation of God Himself, who enlarges the soul in proportion as He infills it, and fills it in proportion as He enlarges it; there is not a moment of emptiness in such a soul. So is it true that it can always advance in its annihilation—that is to say, in its emptiness, and thus increase its fulness; not on its part, for it cannot perform anything of that, but on God's side, who incessantly works in it.

Such was the disposition of the holy virgin from the moment of her conception. She had no selfhood; she was conceived with a supple soul, enlarged and fit to be always more so; she was from this moment filled with God. Nevertheless, she increased in this fulness in proportion as she extended into a greater void, so that when the angel called her full, she was so indeed; and she was also infinitely empty. And this void which was in its greatest extent—so much so, that no pure creature will ever arrive at it—was the immediate disposition at the incarnation of the Word in her. This is why she rightly said that God had looked upon the lowliness of his handmaiden —that is to say, that God having looked upon the profound abyss of this nothingness of Mary, which infinitely surpassed the void of the most holy creatures, He was as it were constrained by this immense void to come and precipitate Himself into her, in order to fill it with Himself; and as no Divine fulness in the creature was to be equal to this one, so no void has ever been more extended or more destroyed than the one which served God thus. When God desires to come Himself to fill it, all that is not God must give place to Him. Thus the holy virgin does not say, that the Word chose her for His mother on account of any virtue that was in her, but only in the sight of her great emptiness. It is necessary, then, that all the souls who are to arrive at the apostolic state, which is that of the production of the Word in them after their annihilation, be in this emptiness more or less, according to the design of God, as all saints in glory must be in this same void more or less, according to the degree of their elevation in God.

It will be objected here, that the holy virgin has not passed through the losses, weaknesses, and other trials which God makes use of to annihilate other souls. This is true, for these states are destined to the latter, to enlarge them in proportion as they make them lose their proper and contracted quality which they all derived from Adam. But the divine Mary was placed, from the moment of her conception, in perfect enfranchisement from all propriety by the pre-eminence of original grace, although not yet in all the perfection of annihilation; for it could always increase until the end of her life in proportion as she was able to be more filled with God, or rather more absorbed into Him, the void of the creature requiring to become so much the greater, the more the fulness of God is superabundant; but for all those who have contracted the propriety in Adam, whether they have only the selfhood derived from him, or whether they have augmented their selfhood by actual sin, I say that all, without exception, must pass through purgatory, and the loss of the gifts of grace and virtues, in the manner previously explained; in fine, by total loss and perfect annihilation, according to their degree, in order to re-enter into God, and arrive at the purity of their origin.

It costs mortal pains to those who have much of propriety, and in whom this hereditary infection is most rooted; and also those whom God destines for the greatest extent of annihilation; as a thing can only be enlarged with much difficulty when it resists greatly, or when it is desired to stretch it excessively, as happens in making gold-leaf by repeated blows.

This operation of smelting is most grievous at the beginning, when the soul still retains much hardness and it seems to be torn in pieces. But when it allows itself to be torn and stretched, this is done more quickly.

It is very remarkable that the faithfulness of this state does not consist in retaining and preserving the graces of God; but in suffering ourselves to be stript of them without resistance, according to God's will. The fidelity of this degree is passive, abandoning ourselves fully to God's operation. During the time of our being clothed with the virtues and filled with heavenly gifts, there was necessary an active fidelity to labour therein with our whole strength; but when the signal of stripping is given, we must suffer it by submission to the Divine workings.

But it is so difficult for the creature to submit to these that there is nothing in it that does not resist them, and seek to be sheltered from them as much as possible. And although people are convinced of this truth, they sadly fail in practice beyond all that can be imagined. Nevertheless, the more the soul resists, the more it prolongs its pains; so that many, through unfaithfulness, never arrive in this life at annihilation.

Therefore it has been necessary that souls, in other respects of an eminent sanctity, should pass through purgatory, in order to finish in the other life an operation, to which they could not surrender themselves in this. There are others whose lives are passed in building and destroying, not being able to suffer a void in themselves, and filling up immediately by their own industry what God would do there. They never acquire perfection; for they continually desire to acquire everything and to lose nothing. The philosophers even recognise it in the truth that the generation of one thing is the corruption of another: and the divine life is never given to a soul until it has lost its own. But almost no one gives himself up to this. Those who have experienced it will understand me perfectly.

15. *Ye shall eat of unleavened bread for seven days. From the first day there shall be no leaven found in your houses. And whosoever shall eat of leavened bread from the first day until the seventh, shall perish in the midst of Israel.*

The *seven days* signify seven years, or a considerably long time, that the soul usually passes through in losing little by little its own inventions, before entering into the desert of naked faith. Those who, during this time of stripping, preserve their own methods of propriety, are commonly *cut off from Israel*— that is, they never attain to being of this perfectly purified interior people.

23. *The Lord will pass through to smite the Egyptians; and when he seeth the blood upon the lintel and the two side posts, he will pass over the doors of your houses, and will not suffer the destroyer to enter to smite you.*

There is nothing to fear for those who are *marked* with the seal and *blood* of Jesus, for His faithful abandoned ones, who place their confidence only in His blood, and who by the loss of all self-righteousness find themselves happily obliged to despair entirely of themselves. They are thus even more in safety than if they possessed all things; for they are marked with this blood, and this blood forms all their merit. Therefore an angel in the Apocalypse cries unto those who have God's commands to smite, Touch not those who have this seal on their forehead.

24. *Ye shall keep this law inviolable, and it shall be for everlasting for you and your children.*

26. *And when your children shall say unto you: What meaneth this religious worship?*

27. *Ye shall answer them: It is the victim of the passage of the Lord, when he passed over the houses of the children of Israel in Egypt, smiting the Egyptians and delivering our houses. Then the people, bowing their heads to the ground, worshipped.*

Keep this law inviolable for yourselves and for your children: What does this mean, if not that it can hardly be understood of any but of abandoned souls, although it is the most just in the world, and must be observed *for ever*. *And when your children shall say unto you*, What manner of glorifying God is this? losing all merit and self-interest, to be clad only with those of Jesus Christ, in which all our hope must consist. Ye shall say unto them: This is the *pure sacrifice* of *the Lord*, which He has reserved unto Himself alone, and the mark *of the passage* of the soul into Him by the loss of all propriety. *Then the truly in*terior people *shall bow their heads*—that is, shall submit to it, and *shall worship* this so just a law, which takes all from the creature to restore all to God.

40. *And the children of Israel had dwelt in Egypt for four hundred and thirty years.*

41. *After which on the selfsame day all the host of the Lord went up from Egypt.*

From the time when the captivity was accomplished, *on the same day*, it was necessary to *come out* of this land to begin the road of the desert.

Chapter XII.

43. *And the Lord said unto Moses and Aaron: Such is the worship of the Passover: No stranger shall eat of it.*

The worship of the Passover—that is, the state of the soul in this mystic passage, is of *such* a nature that none of those who are not fully abandoned can *eat of it*. A nourishment so bitter and difficult, a state so denuded, cannot have relish and sustenance for strangers that are not in the same way. Thus we must not be surprised if they cannot relish or comprehend it; but for the chosen people it is the delicious food.

44. *Every slave that is bought shall be circumcised, and then he shall eat thereof.*
45. *The foreigner and the hired servant shall not eat thereof.*
47. *All the congregation of Israel shall keep it.*
48. *And if a stranger desire to join you, every male belonging to him shall first of all be circumcised and then he may celebrate it.*

He who has been bought by these chosen souls as the price of their prayers, and whom God on their behalf has rendered like to them, shall eat of it. But the *hireling*, who seeks his own interest in something, cannot eat of it, no more than he who still negotiates and hopes for gain. So pure a food is not for them.

All the congregation of the abandoned children shall celebrate this sacrifice. If a stranger desire to join them—that is to say, to enter into the same state, let him first cut off all that he still retains of his old practices; and he will be associated with them, and his children even by this retrenchment, will enter with them into the same state, and *will eat* of the same food of the passage of the Lord.

49. *This same law shall be kept equally for those who shall be born in the land, and for the strangers who sojourn with you.*

There shall be but one law for him that is *born* in this way—that is to say, who by a rare felicity has entered into it from his infancy; and for him who for some years may have followed another road, but happily comes into this one at last. The mystic annihilation is the indispensable passage for both.

CHAPTER XIII.

13. *And every first-born of your children ye shall redeem.*

All our productions belong to God. He has acquired them by right of creation and redemption, without which there would have remained to us nothing but non-being and death. The *price* by which the *first-born are redeemed* well expresses the dependence of all our works on God, and the continual homage that we owe to Him, which is an entire disappropriation, by which we recognise, as says St. Paul, that *it is in Him we live, and move, and have our being.*

17. *The Lord did not conduct them by the way of the land of the Philistines, which was near; Lest the people should repent if they saw war, and return to Egypt.*

Those who pass through the desert of naked faith have not to undergo such great temptations from devils; because they have many other things to endure, and because also being conducted by means of a great loss, if temptations began to attack them at the beginning of this way, it would lead them to resume their practices, and to turn back; by reason of their having been only a short time gone out, they would not yet be sufficiently confirmed in the way.

18. *But he caused them to take a long circuit through the way of the desert, near the Red Sea. And the children of Israel went up thus in arms out of Egypt.*

When they have advanced into the desert, war astonishes them no longer; because it is no more they who fight, but the Lord in them. In the wars of the passive way [but luminous] people resist forcibly and with violence on account of the luminous grace sustaining them. But in naked faith it is not so; for in the beginning of this nudity, the soul being yet feeble would return into the practices of the passive way of light and perceptible and savoury love, in which, perhaps, it might allow itself to be conquered by an emotion caused by sin. The wise director then conducts his people *through the desert* of faith, *near the red sea*, quite another trial from war, but more sure, although longer and more painful.

Chapter XIV.

21. *And the Lord went before them to lead the way, in a pillar of cloud by day, and a pillar of fire by night—to be their guide day and night.*

22. *And the pillar of cloud by day and the pillar of fire by night was never taken from before the people.*

When the soul has entered into the desert of naked faith, and by a total *abandon* allowed itself to be conducted to God, He Himself undertakes the conducting of this soul, and that with so particular a care, that He leaves it not a moment until He has conducted it into the promised land, unless through infidelity it comes out of this *abandon*. He is as a cloud to it *by day*, so that too much light may not inconvenience or stop it; for the soul is easily amused with distinct lights, therefore God conceals them from it, so that nothing may hinder its progress. The same cloud also serves for refreshment, so that the sun's brightness may not inconvenience the mystic soul, sensible love rendering it heavy and more sluggish in its course; just as the heat of the summer enfeebles the body. God takes all this away, and shuts it up, as says St. Denis, in the sacred darknesses of faith: under favour of which, as a cloud, the desert can be passed through more easily. But as in this same desert *night* is as frequent as day, and much more frightsome, God, who tempers the heat of the day, also dissipates a little the darkness of the night. This takes place in the manner mentioned, and is what causes souls to persevere in this frightful desert. This conduct *never fails* on behalf of the true abandoned ones.

CHAPTER XIV.

10. *And when Pharoah drew nigh, the children of Israel lifting up their eyes, beheld the Egyptians following them: and they were sore afraid and cried unto the Lord.*

11. *And they said unto Moses, Were there no graves in Egypt? Why have you brought us here to die in the wilderness?*

The first trials of souls in the desert of faith proceed more from fear than fact. It is true that before entering into the red sea, they are smartly pursued by their enemies, and with such strange force, and in so extreme a conjuncture, that there are very few of them sufficiently abandoned not to regret their first way. They see themselves on one side ready to fall into the hands of their enemies; and on the other, on the point of being drowned in the waters of the red sea. In this extremity how certain would not death appear to them! Alas, they say, was not our first slavery more pleasant than this death? And since we have come into the desert only *to die* there, was not death as good in the other way as in this?

12. *It had been better for us were we the slaves of the Egyptians, than to come to this desert to die.*
13. *And Moses answered the people: Fear ye not, remain firm, and ye shall behold the marvels that the Lord will perform this day; for the Egyptians whom ye now see before you, ye shall behold no more for ever.*

No, no, dear friends; be not afraid. Death, I confess to you, is inevitable in appearance; ye cannot of yourselves be delivered from it, your own strength having been taken from you; ye will find no help in any creature. But God alone well knows how to make a road for you through so frightful a sea. Let your only care, then, be not to issue out of *abandon*. The extreme distress of the soul thus pursued on all sides leaves no room for it to remember the miracles which God has wrought on its behalf. All is dark with it. It sees only death near, and it is then that a Moses is needed to aid in the traversing of so dangerous a passage. The anguish is beyond all that can be expressed, and everything is painted with the image and shadow of death.

Oh fidelity, how necessary thou art in so rude a passage! Courage, dear souls, when you have passed the red sea *ye shall no more behold the enemies ye now see* at its entrance; but follow, I adjure you, on this so pressing an occasion, the counsel of Moses, the true director in this way, which is to *remain immovable*, like rocks, as if it concerned you not; and to take good care not to stir, however little, under any good pretext whatever.

14. *The Lord shall fight for you, and ye shall hold your peace.*

It belongs to the *Lord* to *fight for you*, and you to *remain in*

Chapter XIV.

[handwritten: similar to death of my marriage — required Boldness]

repose. Many people break down at this place, which is the cause of their not passing beyond; and not having the courage to cross the red sea, nor to remain constantly exposed to all that God ordains, they stop there and never advance. Oh how necessary it is for a director to have charity and patience with these persons, to bear all their complaints which the fear of their loss draws from them!

15. *And the Lord said unto Moses: Wherefore criest thou unto me? speak unto the children of Israel to go forward.*

God never causes his power and goodness to shine forth to greater advantage than in the extremity of need. In this so frightful a passage, courage and *abandon* only are necessary; and this so profound a sea, which is to engulph all the others, will be found dried up for the true abandoned ones, who find life where the others find death. It needs us only to go *forward* in this way without stopping, boldly surmounting all the perils that we meet there.

16. *But lift thou up thy rod, and stretch out thine hand over the sea, and divide it, so that the children of Israel may walk on dry land through the midst of the sea.*

A *division* must be made, that it may be possible to *walk over dry shod*. It is necessary that the spirit be separated from the senses; and it is here that division is made, after which the soul walks in a blind *abandon* and happily passes the sea. That which is the rock of destruction to the others, is to it the port of safety.

19. *Then the angel of God, which went before the camp of the Israelites, went behind them: and also the pillar of cloud which was at the head of the people,*

20. *Stood behind them, between the camp of the Egyptians and the camp of Israel; and on the one side the cloud was darkness, and on the other it gave light during the night: so that the two armies could not come near each other all the night.*

One cannot sufficiently admire the grandeur of the faith by which God desires these souls to walk in entering into this sea, and how much it ought to be denuded of all support. What had these poor abandoned souls, wandering in the desert, to rest on, except the conduct of God, who *walked before them* day and night? Nevertheless this must also be taken from before their eyes, and at this moment they must lose all perceptible Divine succour; and this was the proper disposition to enter into the sea, without other assurance or support than loss itself. Although they now seem to have nothing of God that is known to them, it is certain that He was never protecting them more.

He places Himself between them and their enemies to be their more sure defence. This means, that God takes away from Satan all power over these souls; and all the trials they experience afterwards are no more from those enemies, but from nature, or from God Himself, as will be remarked in its proper place.

21. *And Moses stretched his hand over the sea, and the Lord made an opening in it by causing a violent and burning wind to blow during the night; and the sea was dried up and the waters were divided.*

22. *And the children of Israel walked in the midst of the sea on dry ground, and the waters were a wall to them on their right hand and their left.*

After the Holy Spirit has, by his heat, made a *division* between these two parts—the spiritual and the animal—*the waters* which drown every one *serve as a wall* and rampart for His chosen people; and by these very waters, which naturally cause death, they are sheltered on all sides and guaranteed from every sort of attack. But, mark one thing: that Moses may indeed *stretch out his hand* to give the signal for the division of the two parts; but this division is wrought by no human means; that is reserved for the Holy Spirit, whose *burning wind dries up* these waters in the desert of faith and during the most obscure night. By the ardour of this devouring wind He dries up the sea, for the division of the spirit from the senses, and also the spirit from the soul, can only be made when the soul is reduced to the last state of exhaustion, and in the most extreme *dryness*, caused by the loss of its interior perceptible acts, and of all that there was savoury and powerful in its faculties; this universal drying up causing

23. *And the Egyptians pursued and entered after them into the midst of the sea, and all Pharaoh's horsemen, and chariots, and horses.*

27. *And when the Egyptians wished to flee, the waters came before them, and the Lord enveloped them in the midst of the waves.*

It may happen that souls still living in themselves should believe themselves able to pass dry shod through this red sea; but they will be taken in it, and will find themselves *engulphed in the waves.* The signal to pass it is known when the director stretches out his arm to give the command, or give assurance of the Divine call; and when the Lord has so dried up the soul that He has reduced it to nothingness in itself, or when He Himself, with absolute authority in place of direction, causes it to pass, the soul having fully consented to everything it may please Him to do with it, whether it knows it or not.

CHAPTER XV.

1. *Let us sing unto the Lord, for he hath triumphed gloriously; the horse and his rider hath he thrown into the sea.*

It is truly on issuing out of the red sea that the soul is in a state to *sing to the Lord* a song of thanksgiving, but a new song and a song of purity, which is sung before the Lamb, crying with a loud voice: "It is to our God that sitteth upon the throne, and to the Lamb, that is due the *glory* of our salvation." It is then that the faithful abandoned ones know the happiness of their deliverance; for until that time, although they had seen a great many miracles of an extraordinary Providence, their eyes were not sufficiently opened to see all these marvels in God Himself, and they were not in a state for singing this new song, thus it had not yet been inspired. Then they know to attribute all to God, and to faithfully render to Him all the glory of what He has done on their behalf.

2. *The Lord is my strength and song, and he is become my salvation. He is my God, and I will publish his glory; my father's God, and I will exalt him.*

The soul which has been faithful enough to abandon itself to God without limits and without reserve, knows on issuing from this blessed shipwreck that it is *in God* that all *its strength* lies, and not in created supports nor in itself. It refinds in God all that it conceived it had lost; and ravished with admiration it cries: I have lost all strength of my own, and thus I have found that God was all *my strength*. I have lost all power of *praising* Him, and He Himself has become my *praise* and song. I have risked and lost my salvation in so far as founded on some possible good viewed in the creature, and it is for that that *He Himself has become my salvation*. Oh it is now that I can say that *He is my God*, and that I honour Him as God. Now I know that He is the *God of my father*, therefore will I exalt Him.

11. *Who is like unto thee, O Lord, amongst the mighty ones? Who is like unto thee, who art glorious in holiness, terrible and worthy of all praise, and who performest wonders?*

This lover, now better instructed, no longer esteems so much the power and holiness of other mighty and holy souls, for they are not strong and holy as God. Thus he says: Behold *amongst these mighty* and prudent ones, is there a *power like that* which exists in God alone? Where is the holiness that can be compared to the magnificence of that which is all united in God? Is there anything which merits *praise*, if not what God performs?

13. *Thou hast in thy mercy conducted the people which thou hast redeemed, and thou hast led them by thy strength even to the place of thy holy habitation.*

This soul, seeing itself delivered from the pressing dangers to which its *abandon* had exposed it, affirms that it has been by the goodness of God alone, and it is He who *in His mercy conducts His interior people*. Thus what at one time appears a rigorous justice of God exercised on His servants, is afterwards seen to be a great *mercy*. This people appeared sold to sin, but thou, O Lord, hast *redeemed* them. *Thou hast led them by Thy strength* into Thyself, which is *Thy holy habitation*.

Chapter XV.

17. *O Lord, thou wilt bring them in, and wilt establish them upon the mountain of thine inheritance, in this most firm habitation, which thou hast prepared for thyself; in thy sanctuary, O Lord, which thy hands have established.*

It is very clear from this verse that the state of *confirmation* in God, or of immovability, represented by *the mountain of the inheritance* is spoken of, for the inheritance is different from the mountain of the inheritance. To arrive into the inheritance is to arrive into God, but to be on the mountain is to be established in God. Therefore it is said: *Thou wilt bring them in*, expressing the entrance into the state. Then: *Thou wilt establish them*, which is the confirmation in the state, and which is well represented by the confirmation in the Christian state given after the baptism, and which is the reception of the Holy Spirit, as the apostles having received it with fulness were confirmed in grace. Therefore scripture calls this mountain a *most firm habitation*, for it is then a fixed and permanent place for the soul that is arrived at it. But it is a habitation which God alone has made; *a sanctuary established by His hands*, without the participation of any creature.

18. *The Lord shall reign for ever and ever, and beyond.*

How can God *reign* for more than eternity? This expression, *and beyond*, means that although His reign over the souls that are perfectly His is eternal and invariable for ever, yet it can always be augmented, as well as the extent of their annihilation can always be increased by the greatest possible extension.

22. *And Moses brought the Israelites from the Red Sea, and they entered into the desert of Shur; and after journeying three days in the wilderness, they found no water.*

It is not without reason that Moses prays God to confirm His people in a state in which they have need of every possible firmness in order to pass through what remains of the interior road, much more appalling than all that has hitherto appeared. But alas! the end of this state is still far away, and perhaps they will never attain to it. When the red sea has been passed, we fancy for a long time that we are at the end of all our miseries; for, having received a new life and enjoying an ineffable felicity, everything seems to be accomplished: but

this proceeds from not considering that having found God is
not yet to enjoy and possess Him, but to allow ourselves to be
possessed by Him. This state demands a great purity of love.
Thus is it an astonishing thing, that of so many persons who
have courage enough to pass the red sea, so few are found
who can venture to pass what follows, as we shall see; for it is
necessary to be freed from all active and passive interest, and
to resume nothing of what we have quitted.

To better understand this, it must be known that in all the
states of the interior life there is a sacrifice, *abandon*, and destitution proper to each state.

In the passiveness of light and savoury love, the soul enters
therein by the sacrifice which it makes of itself to God; afterwards it abandons itself to Him; then it leaves itself destitute
before Him, but for this state only, and according to the
capacity and light given to it.

This destitution of the passive state having attained to its
perfection, the soul issues out of it to enter into the mystic state,
or naked faith. On entering into this state, it finds itself so
different from the other that it is obliged to make a new sacrifice; afterwards it abandons itself to God for the whole extent
of this sacrifice; and then it remains in destitution until it arrives
at the end of this same state.

In the state of loss into God, or the divine life, a new sacrifice is necessary, and greater and more extended than the preceding ones. But the soul finding itself powerless to make it,
on account of its having been wholly melted into God, there
remains no longer any movement of itself, nor anything proper
to it: it sees only that it is being sacrificed, and that the Sovereign High Priest, to whom it has already so many times sacrificed and given itself up, Himself immolates it to His whole
will. It finds itself also afterwards abandoned for this sacrifice;
and at last it remains destitute therein.

When this destitution is consummated, the soul is placed in
the state of pure infancy; for when it entered into God it was
rather placed in the state of innocence, but not yet in the state
of pure and recognised infancy. Whilst man grows, he always
issues the more out of childhood; on the contrary, when he
most approaches his interior perfection, he always returns the
more into infancy, and into the most diminutive infancy, even
until being born anew.

Now I say, that in all these states there are persons who well perform sacrifice and *abandon;* but few, and fewer than can be expressed, who leave themselves destitute; and some do so for one degree, but who fail in another. This is the cause that of so many persons who give themselves to the interior life, there are very few who arrive at their origin, because the greater part withdraw themselves after having given themselves up, or always retain themselves in something. This being assumed, I say that after the *red sea* there is yet a *desert* still stranger to pass through than all that has appeared, because the *red sea* has been passed by sacrifice and *abandon*, which are quick actions and courageous efforts, in which the soul has much share; but the length of the destitution will be afterwards so tedious that the greater part will tire of it. Meanwhile, the soul has no longer here any possession for itself although it is full of God: therefore nothing satisfies it, and it finds itself in a vast *desert without water*. It imagines that it will die of thirst, for the division of the two parts having been made, there fall no waters from the superior upon the inferior, and this is very painful for nature.

23. *And they came to Marah; and they could not drink of the waters of this place, for they were bitter.*
24. *Then the people murmured against Moses, saying, What shall we drink?*

If there flows any *water* from the highest part of the soul, it is so *bitter* that the sensible part *cannot drink of it*, and it is in great distress. Nature then, thus left destitute, falls into such extreme rage and despair, that it suffers itself to break out into murmurings, which it did not do before, therefore the will has no part in it. And it is certain that many do not sin in these outbursts, as much because they take place in the animal nature and not in the spirit, which remains hid and protected in God, as because it is God Himself who delivers them up to these weaknesses after their *abandon*.

It is nevertheless to be feared that nature may at last attract the spirit after it and cause the will to *speak;* which can only happen by issuing out of *abandon*, and can never take place in destitution. The reason of it is, that so long as this will remains united to that of God, and separated from all that takes place in the lowest part of nature, it cannot take any part in it, nor consequently sin. Now, by destitution the will of the creature remains always united to that of God, out of which it cannot come but in withdrawing itself, and issuing out of *abandon.*

25. *And Moses cried unto the Lord; and the Lord showed him a tree, which he cast into the waters; and immediately they became sweet.*

The tree of the cross, looked upon or *cast* into the waters of bitterness, has the power of sweetening them; because in Jesus Christ the cross has been glorified and rendered less severe; and God, in order to relieve these souls in this horrible desert, gives them a little of the sweetness of the cross. This will be difficult to understand to those who have not experienced it.

It must, then, be known that the state of nothingness in the desert of faith, in which the soul has neither pain nor pleasure, is something so difficult to bear, that in order to relieve the soul some suffering is necessary to it; self-love being so envious of possession, that it prefers rather to suffer than to have nothing, and to suffer a very grievous ill rather than feel neither good nor evil. Those who are in this state will confess that I speak the truth; persons even less advanced know it from their experience. There is nothing so frightful as nothingness, and provided we subsist on something, were it the most horrible pains, we are content.

This, then, is the only sweetness that God bestows on souls of this degree, and by suffering even He waters them with some consolation.

25. *There the Lord proved his people.*
26. *And he said unto them: If ye keep my commandments I shall not smite you with all the diseases which I brought upon the Egyptians; for I am the Lord that healed you.*
27. *And the children of Israel came afterwards to Elim, where there were twelve springs aud seventy palm trees; and they encamped near the waters.*

God Himself *proved His people* to see their fidelity, promising *not to smite them with any of the plagues with which He had smitten Egypt,* which were plagues for sinners; although He must still try them by many labours and afflictions, which are common to the just; but from which *the Lord heals* them, turning them always into love and into crowns for eternity.

He afterwards causes them to go into *a place* of refreshment, *where there were springs and palm trees.* As it is God's method to give some relief after the trial of the cross, the soul that is not sufficiently experienced in His ways imagines that it has already obtained the victory; but it does not see that it is the Lord alone that *tries it*, to show that in this state the demons have no more to do, having been for ever engulfed in the red sea. *There are twelve wells*, so that each tribe has some spring from which to refresh itself; but as these twelve tribes form but one interior people, so these twelve springs have but one source in Jesus Christ.

CHAPTER XVI.

2. *In this desert all the children of Israel murmured against Moses and Aaron.*

How great is the feebleness of a nature left to itself and separated from the spirit! Its follies are inconceivable. This is why it is necessary that directors should have an extreme patience to bear with them. A fearful infidelity hinders these souls from remaining in destitution. They cannot bear this so extreme a nakedness. They lay the blame on their directors, regretting the good living they had in the state of passivity of light and sweetness of the affections, in which, under pretext of fervour, they were nourished in a manner yet strongly sensual.

3. *And the children of Israel said unto them, Would to God we had died in Egypt by the hand of the Lord, when we sat by the flesh pots, and we could eat bread to the full! Why have ye brought us into this desert to kill this whole people?*

People of *flesh*, how difficult it is for you to become spirit, and to content yourselves with naked faith! These persons often issue out of *abandon* for some moments, and frequently their will has no part in these extravagances: it is nature alone which, destitute of its spirit, mourns like a brute beast. The enlightened director easily discerns this state.

Many of those who enter therein, and nearly all, are so blind that they regret their *not having died* in the time of their abundance, fancying that at that time their salvation would have been more certain. This word *sat*, signifies the repose they took in their lights and sweetnesses.

> 4. *And the Lord said unto Moses; I shall cause it to rain bread from heaven: Let the people go out and gather what is sufficient for each day, so that I may prove them whether they walk in my law or not.*

O goodness of my God, Thou recompensest with all *heavenly manna* the murmuring of this people. This very recompense, or nourishment, which God bestows upon them, shows clearly enough that the will had no part in their discontent. O directors, who have persons of this sort under your care, have compassion on them; for they are very worthy of it: treat them as God treats them; and above all, take not away from them the holy eucharist. The more feeble you see them, the more ought ye to give it to them, to nourish and strengthen them, this divine strength being very necessary to them. Do ye not see how God desires them to receive it every day as long as their want shall last, in order, says He, *that I may prove them whether they walk in my law or not?* God desires no other trial of these faithful souls in the time of their most extreme destitution than the reception of so great a good. It is true that they are often tempted to withdraw from the holy table on account of their miseries; but let them do it not, except out of obedience. God desires to prove them, and see if they will be faithful to receive Him every day. It is thus that He proves their obedience, and this is the touchstone whereby to know if this state is of grace, to wit, when they obey in spite of the repugnances of nature, and are faithful to tell their repugnances to the one who conducts them.

> 5. *But on the sixth day they shall reserve some of it to keep by them, and they shall gather twice as much as another day.*

There come certain days of repose on which the soul is deterred by God Himself from *gathering* this manna, provision having been made; but this state must pass like the rest; and the same Providence which brings it for some hours, takes it away again to be succeeded by labour and ordinary refection.

Nevertheless, this soul continues to live on its hidden manna, and to receive from it a double grace, this repose in God bringing it more than its own labour.

> 7. *And in the morning ye shall see the glory of the Lord shine forth, for he has heard the murmurings that ye have uttered against him.*
>
> 13. *And on the evening there came up a great number of quails and covered the camp; and in the morning there fell a dew all around the camp.*
>
> 14. *And behold there lay upon the face of the wilderness a small round thing, as if pounded in a mortar and resembling hoar frost upon the ground.*

The patience of God, so admirably displayed on behalf of these souls, well instructs directors how much they also ought to have of it for them. It is a sure mark of a person's advancement not to be astonished or annoyed at seeing such weaknesses, and to judge of them according to truth; in place of which, others unenlightened load them with reproaches and penances, and causing them, in fine, to quit everything, they place before them an invincible obstacle to their perfection.

> 16. *This is the thing that the Lord commands; Let every one gather of it sufficient for his eating, an omer for each person.*
>
> 17. *And the children of Israel did what was commanded them, and they gathered, some more, and some less.*
>
> 18. *And having measured it with the measure of an omer, he that had gathered more had nothing over; and he that had gathered less of it had no lack; but every man had gathered of it according to his eating.*

Oh admirable figure of the eucharist! If we should wish to explain you more, we would but obscure you in some manner. Who does not see here the ineffable mystery by which he who receives only a small piece, *has not less* of the reality of the sacrament than he who receives it under a greater; and he who takes a greater part of it has not more than he who has less, each one receiving neither more nor less than what he can eat of it, to wit, Jesus Christ all entire, all under the smallest as the greatest piece, for in this adorable sacrament, O Lord, Thou givest Thyself wholly to all.

This is also the figure of the Divine state, in which all have the fulness of it, each, nevertheless, according to his capacity; and the little are full as well as the great. Although the capacity of the great is more extended than that of the little and it holds more of God; but it is the same God who is all in all, and all in each of them, and who can alone form their fulness and true satisfaction.

CHAPTER XVII.

5. *And the Lord said unto Moses: Go unto the rock of Horeb,*
6. *And I myself will stand before thee there. And thou shalt smite the rock, and there shall come water out of it, so that the people may drink. And Moses did before the elders of Israel what the Lord had commanded him.*

Self-love appears here by the distress of the thirst which must be undergone on this road. This people so chosen and so cherished *murmur* against God. But God out of His infinite goodness does not weary of performing miracles on their behalf. *The rock gives forth the waters* of grace to relieve them; and God stands over this rock, for He is the source of this grace. It is very difficult to remain fully destitute in pure sacrifice; and where will some not be found who do not now and then withdraw themselves? Yet God causes water to issue out of the rock, as a proof of the immovableness of His bounties towards those very persons who are sometimes unfaithful to Him.

7. *And he called the name of this place Temptation, because of the murmurings of the children of Israel, who tempted there the Lord, saying: Is the Lord in the midst of us or not?*

Moses gives a true name to this people's fault, calling it Temptation, for they said: We shall see *if the Lord be with us or not*. It is not possible to help desiring signs, particularly when one is conducted by this way. It is this which causes us usually only to do and undo, not being able to suffer ourselves to be entirely denuded. This renders the desert so long, and is the reason why almost all die on the road before arriving at the promised land.

> 8. *And Amalek came and fought with Israel.*
> 11. *When Moses held up his hands Israel was victorious, but when he lowered them a little, Amalek had the advantage.*
> 12. *And they placed a stone under Moses, upon which he sat; and Aaron and Hur stayed up his hands, the one on the one side and the other on the other.*

Persecutions are inevitable in all states. The creatures make war on this people, and wish to destroy them; but when Moses lifts his hands, that is to say, whilst we are faithful in remaining elevated to God by abandon and faith, and firm to look only upon God, whatever enemies we may have, we easily carry off *the victory:* and when Moses *lowers his hands*, that is to say, when we relapse into self through reflection, we are immediately vanquished, the creature finding itself plunged into its weakness, is wrapped up in its vain turnings and windings from the time when it consents to regard itself. This is the infidelity of this state. From that time we enter into doubt and hesitation—into pain and trouble—which bring defeat upon everything, and are the cause of Amalek (denoting nature and self love, the only enemies that remain in this degree) having immediately the advantage.

To avoid this disorder, we have but to remain *seated upon the rock*—to hold ourselves firmly in destitution and to dwell in the repose of *abandon*—whilst faith and confidence, *as hands held* up towards God, *sustain* the soul in its distress.

CHAPTER XVIII.

> 19. *Jethro said unto Moses: Serve the people in that which regards God;*
> 20. *And show them the way wherein they must walk, and the work they must do.*

21. *And choose able men, that fear God,*
22. *Whose duty will be to render justice at all times.*

This counsel of Jethro's is an excellent one for directors, and they ought here to learn two important rules for their conduct —the one of Jethro, the other of Moses. First, That their duty is not to meddle with the temporal matters of the souls they conduct, but only to be mindful of *what regards the glory of God* in them and their perfection, leaving the temporal to others when it is desired, as much not to be overtaxed with this burden, which would steal from them the time they ought to be employing in things of eternal consequence, as because God, not requiring that from them, they ought not to interfere therein; and secondly, Let them learn from Moses, by his humble acquiescence in the wise counsel of his father-in-law, that although he was so full of the spirit of God, and Jethro was not even of his people, it is necessary to receive truth and good counsels wherever they come from. God often loves to cause persons much inferior in dignity and grace to impart them, to humble thus the greatest directors, and to show them that it is He alone who is the author of all good light.

CHAPTER XIX.

3. *And Moses went up unto God. And the Lord called unto him out of the mountain, and said to him: Thus shalt thou say unto the house of Jacob, and tell the children of Israel.*

God's providence always gives a director to persons whom He conducts in faith, so that he may declare to them the will of the Lord. So it is necessary that they have a blind obedience to allow themselves to be conducted, for not being able to stop at anything given them out of direction and providence, they must blindly do what the enlightened director teaches them, God usually giving them a faithful guide to conduct them surely in the gloomy desert of faith.

5. *If then ye hear my voice, and keep my covenant, ye shall be*

of all peoples peculiarly mine own, for all the earth is mine.

This well expresses that although all peoples belong to God, yet the interior people is His in a manner altogether particular. God says that this interior people *will be peculiarly His own.* This signifies that if they will allow themselves to be completely annihilated they will become so fully God's that none other than He will have any part in them. No other way than this can obtain this advantage. Thus God says that they will be chosen *from amongst all peoples.* Who says all excepts nothing.

Now, all that God asks of this so dear a people for them to arrive at so sublime a state is only that they obey Him, and remain in destitution. This expression, *keep my covenant,* is as if He said, remain in My union.

6. *And ye shall be unto me a kingdom of priests and a holy nation. These are the words thou shalt say unto the children of Israel.*

The *kingdom* denotes, even according to the letter, the absolute power that God possesses over abandoned souls who resist Him no longer in anything. He is so sovereignly master with them, that it is not possible to be more so. It is not so with others who possess themselves, because that being free with their own liberty and full of self-will, they desire a thousand good things which God would not, and which He grants only to their weakness; but He reigns as a sovereign over those who have no more will of their own. Therefore, when He taught His disciples to pray and to ask that His kingdom might come, that is, that He might reign absolutely over them, He adds, and that His will might be done on earth as in heaven, as if by that they would mean: When that shall be, Lord, Thy will shall be done upon the earth as the blessed do it in the heavens, without resistance, without hesitation, without exception, and without delay. For this reason in the Gospel these two requests are comprised in the same verse.

The Lord adds to Moses that His people will be *a priestly kingdom,* for this kingdom is formed of priests and apostles. Moreover, that they will be unto Him a truly holy nation, because all the malignity of man being destroyed in them, there will remain nothing therein but the holiness of God. Then they will be holy *for* God, and not for themselves. Thus God does not say simply, Ye shall be a holy nation, but *Ye shall be unto me a holy nation.* And *behold,* He adds to these directors, *these are the words ye shall say* unto My dear abandoned ones.

8. *And all the people answered with one voice: We will do all that the Lord has commanded.*

This consent, given by the whole people so unanimously, expresses the gift and sacrifice that the souls make of themselves for the ways that are proposed to them. God is so good that He always acts thus towards those whom He desires to introduce into the ways of obscurity and crosses. He first proposes them to them, and asks their consent, for although He is sovereign ruler, He governs with a great reserve, as if He respected our freedom. But, alas! how rare it is to find those who abandon themselves fully when the state has arrived. Almost all then forget their consent and their sacrifice. It also happens that the fervour and promptitude with which these persons make their sacrifice are the cause of their forgetting their weaknesses and miseries, and *replying,* like this people, *We will do all.* But if they then considered their impotence and abandon, they would find the former persuading them that they can do nothing of themselves, and that by the latter they are stripped of all will to leave themselves entirely to God. They should rather then say: "Let the Lord cause us to do everything, and we will do it, for our trust is in Him, as well as everything else, and of ourselves we are but feebleness and sin." This confidence and leaning on one's self being a secret presumption, is always followed by some fall, either great or little, according as as it is more or less extended.

9. *The Lord said unto Moses: Lo, I come unto thee in the darkness of a cloud, so that the people may hear me when I speak unto thee, and that they may believe thee in all things.*

The darkness of a cloud shows that God desires His interior people to believe upon faith alone, that it is He who speaks by the direction, and not upon signs.

10. *Go unto this people, and sanctify them to-day and to-morrow, and let them wash their garments.*

Chapter XIX.

This *sanctification* which God desires is a new purity, in order to enter into a new state of a new law of pure love.

Moses, who had passed the state of death, is introduced on to the mountain where God is, who is the origin of this state of pure love. He being already purified, is conducted even to its source.

> 12. *Let none amongst you be so bold as to come up upon the mountain, nor approach the border of it. Whosoever will touch the mountain will surely be put to death.*
> 13. *The hand of no man shall touch him to kill him, but he shall be stoned or pierced with arrows.*

But for every other one, it must cost him his life only to *approach the mountain or to touch it*, as the Lord Himself says: *No man shall see me and live.*

But how shall he die? Ah, *it will not be by the hand of man;* it will be *by the arrows* which Thou wilt discharge against this heart which cannot yet love Thee purely, O God of my heart, without losing his own life. Thou wilt crush him *with stones*, because that his heart, not having suffered itself to be destroyed and melted by so many bounties, as it was Thy desire, is but a heart of stone; and it is necessary that, as Thou hast expressed it by a prophet, Thou shouldst take from him this heart of stone in order to give him a heart of flesh to love Thee purely, a heart pliable and easy to be handled, a heart pure and new.

> 16. *And it came to pass on the third day in the morning that there were thunders and lightnings, and a thick cloud covered the mountain, at which all the people that were in the camp were afraid.*

People persuade themselves that the Word of God is all sweetness, and that is true if it is considered in itself, or when it is accompanied by a tender effusion of graces, which causes it in the beginnings of the spiritual life to be all sweet and most agreeable, but for souls of this degree, alas! it is full of terror, and has nothing but bitterness. Therefore, it was heard by St. John in the same manner, and when he receives the new name, after hearing this fulminating word, he was called Son of Thunder.

18. *And all the mountain of Sinai gave forth smoke, for the Lord had descended upon it in fire; and the smoke went up like that of a furnace: and the whole mountain caused terror.*

When God appeared unto Moses the first time, He suffered him not to approach the fire in which He was without taking off his shoes; and to-day He introduces him into the fire itself, on account of the purity of his love, which has increased almost to infinity. When He formerly appeared to this faithful minister it was also in the fire, to impart to him His charity and pure love. Now that He desires to give the law of pure love, He appears also to the children of Israel *in the very fire* of love, since He is love itself. It required no less a fire to kindle so many hearts.

But how comes it, O my love, that Thou appearest here so *terrible?* Ah! it is to those who see Thee only outwardly and in the effects of Thy love, which, looking at things superficially, appears all cruel towards the souls that are devoted to it; but sure it is that inwardly and in itself it is all agreeable to the well abandoned heart.

19. *And the sound of the trumpet increased also, little by little, and became stronger and louder. Moses spake, and God answered Him.*
20. *And the Lord came down upon the top of Mount Sinai, and called Moses up to the top of the mount, and Moses went up.*

O admirable conversation! God speaks to the soul, and the soul hears Him! The soul speaks to God, and God also hears it! But there is much of other commerce between God and the soul of which there must be no witness. To accomplish this, God causes this chosen soul to *mount up to the summit of the mountain* of love, upon the highest degree of pure charity. It is received into God Himself, but in a manner so sublime and so ineffable that all expression falls far short of the reality. It is then that all that remains in the exterior itself, or lower part of man, is changed and renewed by the purity of this love. It is then that this man is rendered divine, not only within, but even outwardly. O sacred fire! Thou has the power of renewing the whole earth. These souls, or rather this soul alone from amongst so many millions of saints, not only ascends this mountain, but even goes up *to its very summit;* for it was necessary that he should be provided with this pure love, both for himself and others. He must draw it up from this source of fire, so as to be as a furnace capable of furnishing and distributing the holy fire to so great a people. O Moses! thou hast indeed changed thy state! Once, in thy humility of holy practices, thou didst deem thyself unworthy to speak to a king and to the people of Israel, and now, in thy profound annihilation, thou hast neither pain nor repugnance to *ascend* to the highest degree in God, to speak to Him so familiarly, and to be His chosen vessel full of Himself. It is annihilation which causes man no longer to look upon himself or his meanness, and being below all lowliness, he is by that above all height.

24. *And the Lord said unto Moses: Go, get thee down. Thou shalt come up, thou, and Aaron with thee. But let not the priests or people break through to come up unto the Lord, lest he destroy them.*

Ah! how good it is to be united to such holy souls as these! They obtain for the one person that is joined to them what they possess for themselves. Although all the people were united to Moses as children to their father, yet Aaron was so in a particular manner, being connected with Moses paternally, no other than he being so. There are also persons whom God joins after this two-fold manner in paternal union; and all others that are united to them, though they are their children, are not, however, equal to them in the ministry, whatever they may be. For there were many *priests* after the order of Aaron, but *Aaron* alone *went up with* Moses, whilst the others dared not even touch the mountain. Yet Aaron was not in every thing equal to Moses, nor raised to the same degree: the communication from God Himself into God Himself in so sublime a manner was for Moses alone.

CHAPTER XX.

2. *I am the Lord thy God, which have brought thee out of the land of Egypt, out of the house of bondage.*
3. *Thou shalt have no other Gods before me.*

5. *Thou shalt not worship them, and thou shalt not render to them the worship that is due to me. For I am the Lord thy God, a mighty God, and a jealous God, avenging the iniquity of the fathers upon the children unto the third and fourth generation of them that hate me.*

God, desiring to submit man to His law, represents to him at first the graces He has bestowed upon him, so that he may not find this law difficult, and may possess a lively confidence that this so good a *God*, who has *brought him out of bondage*, will not put him anew under the yoke, but that, on the contrary, He will give him the necessary grace and strength to keep His divine precepts, as He clearly promises in another place. *I will put*, says He, *my Spirit in the midst of you, and will cause you to walk in my precepts, and keep my statutes, and do good works.* He will thus Himself accomplish His law in those who, abandoning themselves perfectly to Him, allow Him to act in them without resistance.

For this reason His first command is *to have no other God before Him*, that is, to rest on no foreign strength in order to observe His law, but on His alone, for as He is *a mighty God*, who can do everything by His sovereign power, He is also *a jealous God*, allowing no one to presume to share with Him this same power, nor to attribute the observing of His commandments to any other strength than His own, not to fidelity, nor effort, nor industry, nor anything whatsoever. Provided that we remain in this justice towards God, robbing Him of nothing of His own, the law becomes easy, because we no longer look upon it in itself, in which case we would find it very difficult, but we regard it in God, when it is seen with the Divine power surmounting every difficulty.

Therefore, the Lord adds, *All them that hate Him.* [This word *hate* must only be taken here for a turning aside, for all those who violate the law of God in something do not mean to hate him.] Those, then, who turn aside from Him to regard themselves, and who thus render themselves the slaves of the law, oh! it is those who commonly sin against the law itself; and their fault, arising only from their having fallen into a subtle and secret idolatry, attributing God's strength to themselves, the Lord does not pardon them anything, and allows this law to be extended over all their works. And this is the cause of these persons being so constrained and narrowed, to

Chapter XX.

wit, for God calls their sins to account, *even to the third and fourth generation,* that is to say, that all their works are enslaved by the subjection of their turnings to themselves.

6. *And showing mercy unto a thousand generations of them that love me and keep my commandments.*

But in those that *love,* oh! love alone is the fulfilment of the law, and God bestows *graces* on them by *thousands.* This word *graces* is here taken for the remission of a thousand things pertaining to the law, which God does not regard; for, viewing the uprightness of their hearts and the desire they have of pleasing Him, He is content with the love of the law, delivering them from its bondage. Therefore, it is said that there is no fear in love, but perfect love casteth out fear; for the soul is so engrossed with the love of its God that it can only look upon this same love, and think of nothing else, and by the excess of this sovereign love, whilst forgetting the law, it fulfils it perfectly, penetrating its spirit through the letter.

8. *Remember the Sabbath day, to keep it holy.*
10. *The seventh day is the day of repose, consecrated to the Lord thy God.*

To remember repose is to remain in it; and there is no other *sanctification* than that of resting in repose itself, for it is *the repose* of God in Himself—of God in the annihilated soul, and of the soul in God.

These three kinds of repose are different, and must be explained. The first is that of God in the soul when it has arrived at union with God's will, at the mystic state, and when He dwells in the soul and rests there, as the Son of God assures us: *If any man love me,* said He, *he will keep my word, and my Father will love him, and we will come unto him, and make our abode in him.*

The repose of the soul in God is after the resurrection, by which it is received into God. Then it finds its perfect repose in Him, its pains and troubles being passed for ever; for previously God rested fully in the soul, because it was void of sin, and its will was conform to His own, but the soul did not yet find its repose in God, since it walked by a road full of uncertainties, pains, and disturbances. It finds its true repose only when it has arrived into God, where it dwells in a tranquil and lasting state, subject no more to any vicissitudes. It finds there, however, still a repose, and there is yet something for it, since this repose is perceived, and is really a repose of the creature in its God, perceptible and recognised as such.

But the repose of God in Himself is the repose that He takes in a well annihilated soul, in which everything of the creature having disappeared, there remains God alone, who rests in Himself; no more for this creature, who, having entirely passed into God, has no repose different from His; for having resumed, by the perfect annihilation of the creature, all that belonged to Him, He remains all in all, in the terms of the great apostle, and this is the repose of God in God.

18. *And all the people heard the thunderings and the sound of the trumpet, and saw the burning lights and the mountain covered with smoke, and they were seized with fear, and stood afar off.*

19. *And they said unto Moses: Speak thou with us, and we will hear thee; but let God not speak with us, lest we die.*

The soul that sees God coming near, fears *death* very much, well knowing that it is necessary to die to see Him. From the time when the state of death begins, which lasts for a long period, it enters into strange fears, and would willingly say: I would prefer to go no further than to pass through such rude trials. *It keeps itself aloof*, and endeavours to defend itself from death, thinking that it even approaches God when it loves to remain in its estrangement; and deceived as it is by self love, it prefers to preserve its own life rather than suffer itself to be carried away by a holy death, which would happily resuscitate it in God. This leads it to say to the director (much more by its real resistances than by its words alone): *Speak to me thyself;* for so long as it is only thou who speakest to me, and I keep to the words of man and human means, or, at least, comprehend by reason, I shall not die, but to go upon the word of God alone, and under His particular conduct, in the obscurity of a naked faith, I cannot resolve to do it, *for fear of death* and loss.

20. *Moses answered the people: Fear not, for God is come to prove you.*

This excellent director assures his people that there is yet no occasion for *fear*, since this is not the place of death, but only a *trial* which God desires to make of His interior friends, to see if they have the courage to enter the way of death.

21. *And the people stood afar off, and Moses entered into the thick darkness where the Lord was.*

This people, though already well advanced in the interior way, yet *stood afar off*, because they feared death; *but Moses*, who had already passed through death and been resuscitated in God, could die no more, therefore he is not afraid: God was no more a stranger to him, being as much Moses himself as He was God Himself, according to the unity of the Divine life, so that what caused death to the others gave life to Moses, on account of his mystical state of resurrection in God. He *enters*, however, here only *into the thick darkness where God is*, to teach us that whatever manifestation God makes of Himself in this life, it is always an obscurity for the creature, which can have only a limited knowledge of it, bounded and covered with the veil of faith.

CHAPTER XXIII.

20. *Behold, I send my angel, that he may walk before thee, and keep thee in the way, and bring thee into the land which I have prepared for thee.*

God never fails to give us this *angel* as long as it is needful for us. This is the director who *keeps us in the way*, but he can only *bring us into the place prepared for us*, after which, God Himself is the conductor.

21. *Respect him and obey his voice; and beware of contemning him, for my name is in him.*

The Lord bids us *respect* this director, *obey him*, and not reject him, *for His name is in him*—which means that he represents His person, bears His word, and acts by His authority.

23. *My angel shall go before thee, and shall bring thee into the land of the Amorites.*

He again repeats this, to better show that direction is necessary until we are arrived into the promised land, which is the state of repose in God alone.

CHAPTER XXIV.

1. *God said unto Moses, Come up unto the Lord, thou and Aaron, Nadab and Abihu, and the seventy elders of Israel, and worship ye afar off.*
2. *And Moses alone shall go up to where the Lord is; but the others shall not come near; and the people shall not go up with him.*

Aaron had, indeed, been upon the mountain, which was a great advance compared with the state of the people; but to arrive at the summit was reserved for Moses alone, for no other had attained to so sublime a state and so pure a love. He was the fountain from which the source was distributed to others.

4. *And Moses wrote all the words of the Lord.*
5. *And he sent young men from amongst the children of Israel to offer burnt offerings and to sacrifice peace offerings to the Lord.*

He wrote the words of the Lord, for he must leave them to posterity. God causes His servants to write what He has communicated to them of His Divine and hidden truths, so that they may remain, and that many may profit by them.

Moses also sends *the youngest of the children of Israel to sacrifice to the Lord peace offerings*. It is the property of young souls thus to sacrifice; their sacrifice is only peace and sweetness. It is not the same with advanced souls; they must offer *burnt offerings*. But as, amongst the children of grace, there are two kinds—those newly come into the spirit and the way, and others who have again become children by the excess of their advancement in the same way—so Moses distinguishes two sacrifices—the one of peace, suitable for the first children, and the other, of burnt offerings, proper for the last.

6. *And Moses took half of the blood and put it in basins, and he sprinkled the other half upon the altar.*

7. *And he took the book of the covenant, and read it before the people, who said, We will do all that the Lord has said, and we will be obedient.*

8. *Then taking the blood, he sprinkled it upon the people, saying, Behold the blood of the covenant which the Lord has made with you, that you may fulfil all these things.*

When *Moses read the law*, he remarked that the people promised to keep it with much promptitude and assurance; but, like an experienced director, he well recognised that there was in that a secret presumption, because they relied upon their own strength, and did not entertain sufficient distrust of themselves, in order to look for all their fidelity from the goodness of God. *He sprinkled* then *upon them the blood that was in the basins*, for this was the figure of the blood of Jesus Christ, to represent to them that all the strength needed to fulfil this law depended upon this blood, and that they must be washed and arrayed with it, assuring them, moreover, that every covenant between God and men is established in view of this blood, and that there could be no other.

15. *And Moses having gone up, the cloud covered the mountain.*
16. *And the glory of the Lord abode upon Sinai, covering it with a cloud for six days; and on the seventh day God called unto Moses out of the midst of this darkness.*
18. *And Moses passing through the cloud went up on to the mountain, and remained there forty days and forty nights.*

Moses was in God, but the whole *mountain was covered with darkness* for the others. This state is terribly dark for those who are not in it; and they have difficulty in believing this little that can be told them of it, whatever sign they may have, until experience has arrived.

Although Moses had already been so much with God and conversed with Him in so eminent a manner, and He had gratified him with so singular a familiarity, which causes a doubt whether he has not seen in this life the Divine Essence for some moments; yet it was still necessary for him to wait *six days*, and, as it were, in a kind of purgatory, before entering so near God, and treating so familiarly with Him. Oh how pure God is! *On the seventh day God called unto him from the midst of the cloud;* and Moses having entered therein, *went up entirely, and stayed there forty days and forty nights.* He returns from it at last, altogether renewed and transformed, and always more deified. God proceeds by degrees, as well in the communications of Himself, as in those of His graces, extending the creature's capacity little by little, and not all at once; for it could not bear such an operation. See how Moses takes no step by himself, and makes no advance by his own movement; but he does things just as God causes him to do them, and punctually as they are commanded. This is the fidelity necessary in the whole passive state, but above all in annihilation, in which a soul dead to itself ought thus to apply itself to everything God desires of it, without anticipating or resisting Him.

CHAPTER XXV.

8. *They shall make me a sanctuary, and I will dwell in the midst of them.*

10. *Ye shall also make an ark of Shittim wood.*

This *sanctuary* represents the fund and centre of the soul, the dwelling-place of the Lord, in which is wrought the superessential and inexplicable union, and where the adorable Trinity resides and discovers itself. It must be kept for the Lord, and for that reason empty of everything else, so that the Lord may *dwell* and manifest Himself there: this holy place is for Him alone.

The *ark* was in this sanctuary; because from it there was to issue the oracle of God's word. Until now, God had spoken to His people, as it were, from a distance, and without remaining in a certain place; from henceforth He desires to speak and *dwell in the midst of them*, and to make Himself known and heard in the sanctuary of the centre of their souls.

Chapter XXV.

17. *And thou shalt also make the mercy seat of pure gold.*

The pure and fine *gold* denotes the purity that this centre of the soul must possess, that God may appear and deliver His oracles there; and how much, before serving as the *mercy seat*, it must be purified by the fire from all earth and impurity, and have been tried by the hammer.

18. *Thou shalt make moreover two cherubim of gold, which thou shalt place at the two ends of the oracle.*
20. *Their wings shall be stretched over the two sides of the mercy seat, and they shall cover the oracle, and they shall look one upon another.*

Naked faith and total *abandon* are the *two cherubim* which *cover* the *ark* of the oracle, that is to say, forming the *mercy seat*, from which God delivers His oracles. Faith covers the soul, hindering it from examining itself and seeing anything of all that is proposed to it. *Abandon* hides it also on another side, preventing it from regarding itself to view its own loss or advantage—obliging it to blindly abandon itself; but this faith *and abandon look upon each other*, as do the two cherubim upon the cover of the ark; for the one cannot exist without the other in a well regulated soul; and faith perfectly responds to *abandon*, while *abandon* is submitted to faith.

22. *And there I will give thee my commands, and will commune with thee from above the mercy seat.*

The Lord means here, that from this time it will be from this centre and fund of the soul as from His *oracle*, and no longer from the faculties, that He will make Himself heard. Experienced persons will comprehend this difference of the Divine communications, and which will be found elsewhere explained, —as much as it is possible to throw light upon an inexplicable thing.

40. *And look that thou make everything after the pattern that has been shown thee on the mount.*

This *pattern* is God Himself, in whom exist the eternal ideas of all things; and Jesus Christ, His Word, who expresses them. It is necessary that everything that is done for the sanctification of souls be regulated after this model.

CHAPTER XXVI.

33. The vail shall divide the sanctuary from the holy of holies.

God desires *the sanctuary* to *be divided from the holy of holies*. The *sanctuary* is the centre of the soul, and the *holy of holies* is God Himself. They are united and divided; they are united, in that the centre is in God, and God is in the centre; and they are separated by a difference of state; for to possess God in the centre is something very great; but for God to dwell in Himself for Himself, is a degree still more sublime. We have already explained (chap xx. 8) what it is for God to be in us, us in God, and God in Himself.

This *vail* of division between the sanctuary and the holy of holies also represents the substantial distinction which exists eternally between God and His creature, with the inexplicable unity of love and transformation, which is wrought by the annihilation of the soul in itself, and its reflowing into God. God remains God really distinct from the transformed soul, although the deified soul by this ineffable union becomes one same thing with God—John xvii. 21; 1 Cor. vi. 17.

CHAPTER XXVII.

21. Aaron and his son shall prepare the lamps, that they may burn from evening to morning before the Lord. This worship shall be perpetual amongst the children of Israel.

The *lamp* of charity must always be ardent, and *shine* without interruption in the presence of the Lord.

CHAPTER XXVIII.

30. Thou shalt grave these two words on the breastplate of judgment: Doctrine, and Truth.

These three things may be distinguished in the mysterious

Chapter XXVIII.

breastplate: judgment, doctrine, and *truth.* *Judgment* is something less sure than doctrine, since it depends on the person who judges, and it is an application he makes of the doctrine to the thing of which he judges. *Doctrine* is more sure than judgment, being the use of the knowledge and experience by which we judge; but *truth* is above them all. And because it is to the last that judgment and doctrine relate—as it is also their source—it is necessary to pass through these two degrees to enter into truth. Now that was graven upon the breastplate, to show that our reason is exercised by judgment; that it submits to, and is instructed by doctrine; but that it receives all its light from truth. Judgment is found in us; doctrine is communicated to others to attract their obedience and submission; but truth dwells in God, and we must be in God to be in truth; and it is for this reason that the Holy Spirit is called the Spirit of Truth.

36. *And thou shalt make also a plate of the purest gold, upon which thou shalt grave these words :* HOLINESS BELONGS TO THE LORD.

It was necessary that God's name be graven upon the forehead; for this name is the all of God; and is HE WHO IS, or, rather, all HOLINESS BELONGS TO HIM WHO IS.

38. *This plate shall be always upon his forehead, that the Lord may be favourable to him.*

Now the soul bears this name upon the supreme part, denoted by *the forehead*, because it cannot, without attaining to a most eminent state, know the all of God and the nothing of the creature such as it is. Many think they have this knowledge, who have it only superficially. Annihilation alone can bring experimental conviction of it.

Why does Scripture add: "*that the Lord may be favourable to him*"? It is that God cannot be opposed to a soul placed in the truth of the all of God and its own nothingness. By this justice which it renders to its Creator, it draws down upon itself His most benign regards. And it is this truth which it bears in figure upon the breastplate, and in reality *upon the forehead*: for the truth of God, as God, can only fall under reason in a superficial and figurative manner, but is really graven upon the supreme part of the soul, where it was placed at creation, from which it was effaced by sin, but is re-established with increase by Jesus Christ in annihilated souls.

CHAPTER XXIX.

21. *Thou shalt take of the blood that is upon the altar, and of the anointing oil; and thou shalt sprinkle it upon Aaron and his garments, upon his children, and their garments.*

It was necessary that the priest that was to be consecrated to God be anointed. Now *the oil* of the consecration was *the unction* of the Holy Spirit, which He sheds Himself over apostolic persons by His divine infusion. *The blood* that is sprinkled upon them teaches us that they can have no authority over souls but by Jesus Christ; and that it was in His blood that from that time all things were accomplished,—all holiness and priesthood being consecrated by the effusion of this blood.

25. *Thou shalt receive all these things from their hands; thou shalt burn them upon the altar as a burnt-offering for a sweet savour before the Lord, for it is his oblation.*

All other sacrifices have something of self-interest mixed with them; they are offered either to obtain pardon for sins, or to be delivered from pain, or to appease the wrath of God, or to entreat some grace from His goodness. All reserve something to themselves, and are still imperfect. It is only the *burnt-offering* where everything is consumed. It is this perfect sacrifice which represents annihilation, and is wholly for God alone. Thus it is called, *the sacrifice of the Lord sending up a sweet savour before Him.*

CHAPTER XXXI.

18. *The Lord gave unto Moses upon Mount Sinai the two tables of the testimony, which were of stone, and written by the finger of God.*

God *graves* His law with *His finger upon stone* when the soul has arrived at the Divine immobility; then it no longer has the law otherwise than graven upon the heart. This law is then imprinted upon it in such a manner that it becomes, as it were, natural to it. Then the soul is like a rock, on which this law is *written*, but written *with the finger of God*, so that He Himself fulfils it in it at His pleasure. And this soul being then in pure love, it is by that in the perfection of the law, and in its most real fulfilment, love being the perfection of the law (Mat. xxii. 40). It is, then, by it that the soul, perfectly submitted to God, without thinking on the law, follows it faithfully in every point; for it is united to the will of God, and transformed into it above every law by perfect charity.

CHAPTER XXXII.

1. *And when the people saw that Moses delayed to come down from the mount, they gathered round Aaron, and said to him: Come, make us gods that they may walk before us; for as for this Moses, the man that brought us out of Egypt, we know not what has become of him.*

The only point in which the man abandoned to God, and already so far advanced as we see represented by this people, sins and issues out of his state, is IDOLATRY. But as this may be exposed to the censure of the learned, we must explain it at a little greater length.

It must, then, be understood that as complete, gross, and impious idolatry is committed by denying to the one only and true God the supreme worship due to Him, either worshipping the creature as God, or acknowledging several divinities (which is properly to acknowledge none), so, to divide what is due to God by the sovereign religion reserved for Him, in order to give some part of it to the creature, may be called a partial and secret idolatry; and to do this wrong to the true and only God, is really to WORSHIP IDOLS, and to be desirous of joining some alien worship with His.

Now this is done (over and above infidelity, which is the first and most criminal kind) either with a noted wickedness sufficient to make it a crime—somewhat similar to that of the infidel idolators; as St. Paul says, that there are those who make their god of their belly, and that covetousness is idolatry; or with a lesser fault, called propriety, by which man retains for himself a portion of the worship which he ought to render to God, in order to worship Him perfectly, which is done either by reserving something to himself in the gift that he ought to make of himself to God, or in some point drawing back after having given himself to Him. The criminal idolatry of infidelity into which the Jewish people begin here to fall, and afterwards so often, is the figure of the idolatry of proprietary infidelity, in which are engaged, more or less, all those whose love not being quite purified, is still mixed with self-interest; and all those also who, after making great progress in the way of the spirit by the holy *abandon*, relapse into themselves by drawing back, and by that alone, give occasion for great falls.

This being premised:—Before this time all the weaknesses of this people did not pass for notable sins before God. All their murmurings and complaints were not accounted anything. God had indeed always loaded them with new benefits. But the sin that is committed here causes the soul to issue entirely out of its state, and it can scarcely return without a miracle of mercy. This idolatry is committed when man withdraws his will from the union which it had with God, to stand in a forged state, and to return to his own inventions; tiring of such a state of nakedness, he issues out of his destitution and loss in God, and seeks in the creature's inventions what can only be found in God.

4. *Aaron made a molten calf; and the Israelites said: Behold your gods, O Israel, that have brought you out of Egypt.*

5. *And when Aaron saw it, he built an altar before the calf, and made a proclamation: To-morrow is the feast of the Lord.*

This unfaithful soul withdrawing from God, attributes to the creature, and even to beasts, that is to say, to its own efforts and practices, all the graces it had before received; exclaiming, that it is they *that have brought it out of captivity*—which is to join blasphemy to idolatry. Turning, then, away from God when it belonged the most to Him, it becomes again proprietary, and by this idolatry it falls little by little into all disorders.

Man first withdraws his mind from the sovereign worship

Chapter XXXII.

which he owes to God, and due to Him alone—a supreme adoration, by which he recognises Him above everything; and this first part of the adoration pertains to the Spirit. The other part is the love of preference for God, and is a worship of the heart, from which man turns aside when he loves the creature with a love opposed to that sovereignly due to this Creator. These two parts are essential for worship, and cannot be separated from it; so that if I recognise a sovereign power other than God, I commit idolatry in the spirit; and if I love anything more than God, I commit idolatry in the heart. To withdraw one's spirit from the dependence in which it ought to be with regard to God, and this loss into Him (by which the soul, through a secret and imperceptible adoration, acknowledges His supreme power, lets itself be conducted, and abandons itself to Him, without being troubled about itself, God sufficing it for all things, and the creature failing in everything,) is, in the matter of the interior life, to commit idolatry in spirit. To withdraw voluntarily one's heart from God, in order to love the creature out of God's order, or in something opposed to Him, is to commit idolatry in the heart. By this idolatry the soul becomes again proprietary, both in its spirit and heart, withdrawing them from submission to God (in which they were through *abandon*,) and from pure love, which was the perfect union with the will of God.

Now I say, that the souls of this degree cannot return into the way of sin, nor sin, at least notedly, except in this manner; for as long as the spirit does not issue from its *abandon*, nor the will from its union with God's, whatever feebleness this man may have, he cannot sin; since, if he sinned, he would by that cease to be united to the will of God, becoming opposed to it by his sin; and it is only after having drawn back from this conformity that he sins, the will of God being altogether incompatible with sin. St. John very clearly touches this truth when he writes (1 John v. 18), "*We know that whosoever is born of God cannot sin: but the birth which he has from God keepeth him, and the wicked one toucheth him not.*" To be born of God is to remain attached to Him in unity of mind and heart by a perfect *abandon*. So long as man is in this centre of safety, neither sin nor the wicked one can touch him; but so soon as he comes out of it, he is pierced by the arrows of sin and the wicked one, and it is through propriety that he comes out of it. All persons of experience will understand me.

7. *The Lord said unto Moses: Go, get thee down; for thy people which thou hast brought out of Egypt, have sinned.*

God calls this people *Moses' people*, and not His own, as formerly, on account of *sin*. As soon as the soul that is united to God sins, it is rejected from Him. As soon as this people had begun to commit idolatry they became brutalised, so that they changed entirely; and, losing all intelligence, they provoked God's wrath.

9. *And the Lord said again unto Moses, I have seen this people, and behold they are stiff-necked.*
10. *Let me alone, that my fury may be kindled against them, and that I may exterminate them; and I will make thee the chief of another great people.*
11. *But Moses besought the Lord his God, saying: Wherefore, Lord, is thy wrath kindled against thy people, which thou hast brought out of Egypt with great power and a mighty hand?*

Moses, being innocent, placed himself between God and the people as a barrier to prevent the torrent of His wrath from bursting upon them. Oh what power a fully annihilated soul has with God, and what great things He does on its behalf! Does not God almost seem to entreat Moses? *Let me alone*, says He. The man that is the friend of God prevents His anger from kindling, as if God was not almighty; for a soul that has entirely got rid of itself, and possesses only God, uses in some manner power with Him. The Lord was truly then *the God of Moses*, who besought Him, saying: *Lord, why is thy wrath kindled against thy people?* He brings to His remembrance that they are His people, and not Moses'; and he represents to Him the great blessings He has bestowed upon them, praying that so many graces may not be in vain.

12. *Let not the Egyptians be able to say: For mischief did he bring them out to slay them upon the mountains, and to exterminate them from the earth. Let thy wrath be appeased, and pardon thou the iniquity of thy people.*

The prayers and remonstrances which directors make to God for souls entrusted to them, when they withdraw from their way, are made to interest the glory of God in their return. "Lord,"

Chapter XXXII. 251

say they, "if Thou reject them after their sins, this will bring Thy purest way into discredit, and it will be said of them, 'See how these ways of *abandon* end! They must be worth nothing, since people perish therein; it is not good to trust oneself all to God; it may be carried to excess, and it is much better to labour by oneself.'"

13. *Remember Abraham, Isaac, and Israel, thy servants, to whom thou swarest by thyself, saying: I will multiply your seed as the stars of heaven, and I will give unto your posterity all the land of which I have spoken, and ye shall possess it for ever.*
14. *Then the Lord was appeased, and he resolved not to do unto his people the evil he had thought of.*

He also puts Him in mind of the faithfulness of His promises, by which He had sworn, that if any followed the road of naked faith, of pure sacrifice, and perfect *abandon*, they would arrive at the *promised land*, which is union with God and His true and real possession. But, oh goodness of a God, to stay His just vengeance at the mere word of one of His servants when he is annihilated, and has no more self-interest, and regards in all things the glory of God only! Moses neither complains of the trouble this people cause him, nor of the grief he would have to see them perish, nor of what would be said of him, nor of all that he might be accused of; his only fear is, that God may be blamed. Oh how admirable is a soul without self-interest!

25. *Moses saw that the people were reduced to nakedness, because Aaron had stripped them by this shameful abomination, and had left them naked in the midst of their enemies.*

This expression, *reduced to nakedness*, well delineates the state of this fallen people; for they had already lost their own strength when they were prepared to be conducted into God, this being necessary that they might be clad with God's own strength. In this state, then, in which they sin, they are doubly *stripped*, losing God's strength by their sin, and no longer finding any of their own. This is why it is so difficult for these persons to turn again; for, according to St. Paul, "*It is almost impossible for those who have been once enlightened, who have tasted the gift of heaven, and have received the Holy Spirit, and are fallen, to be renewed again by repentance."* Not that they cannot still be saved, but it is very difficult for them to regain the degree from which they have fallen; because the manner in which they must repent is very different from that necessary for other sinners who have never been perfectly converted, nor advanced in the ways of the Spirit.

Moses seeing his people thus stripped, attributed it to Aaron, for he had *forged* for them the object of their idolatry; but he adds that they have been *stripped by a shameful abomination;* because everything that is foreign to God is but dung; and there is no greater sin than idolatry; and thus it possesses the ignominy of the dung and excrement of other sins; and by this sin, committed in this degree, the unfaithful soul falls into the most deplorable state. For, having been for a long time stripped of its own strength, and being here destitute of the strength of God, it is placed completely *naked in the hands of its enemies*, who take vengeance with pleasure for the long privation of the power they once had over it, not having been able to harm it whilst it remained in God as in an impregnable citadel.

> 26. *And Moses stood in the gate of the camp, and cried aloud, Who is on the Lord's side, let him come unto me. And all the children of Levi gathered round him.*

Moses wishes to see those who, in so universal a sin, have preserved some remainder of what they were, or have not allowed themselves to be corrupted by this general idolatry. He calls upon them *to join him;* and *the whole tribe of Levi*, destined for the priesthood, obey him. These priests of the Most High, who represent the souls of pure sacrifice, remain in their sacrifice, and do not issue out of it in the unhappy fall of the others. Thus do they merit by this rare fidelity, being united to Moses in the office of the priesthood.

> 27. *And he said unto them: Thus saith the Lord God of Israel, Put every man his sword by his side; pass and repass through the camp from one gate to the other, and let each man kill his brother, his friend, and his nearest neighbour.*

But at what a price are these faithful souls distinguished from amongst their brethren! *By killing* all that could lead them to commit idolatry afterwards, *sparing neither brother nor friend*, nor any one dearest to them. By this act these faithful Levites give to those who escape this cruel vengeance the example of the penitence they must make; for they who have fallen in this degree, must mercilessly be sacrificed anew; and without halting for their fall, however glaring and enormous it be, they must give themselves to God, to serve eternally His will, falling into Him alone by the clear knowledge of their impotence, which, causing them to despair, leads them through distrust of themselves, caused by this sad experience of their frailty, although in a state already far advanced, to lose themselves in God; so that, killing all their own strength, and getting rid without pity of the occasion of their fall, they become the murderers of self-love and self-interest, the cause of their idolatry. It is necessary, moreover, by a new and extremely pure sacrifice, to place in God's hands the pardon of their fault, abandoning it to His will, according as it will be the most for His glory, without in any way claiming it, or desiring to be assured of His mercy.

28. *The children of Levi did according to the word of Moses; and there fell of the people in that day about (twenty) three thousand men.*

29. *Moses said: Ye have to-day consecrated your hands unto the Lord, each of you having killed his son and his brother, so that the blessing may be given you.*

Souls that fall in the active way give themselves to the mercy of God; and their trust in it enables them to obtain pardon for their sin by the works of common repentance; but those of this degree must act with disinterestedness, if they would rise again by the repentance proper to them, and would come out of their fall even with advantage, and a notable increase of love. They must offer themselves up to the Divine justice, in order never to be exempt from the punishment they merit; and still further, as those who are enlightened will understand me, by an excess of charity, which—without asking of God the remission of their sins, but only His will and greatest glory—infallibly covers in one moment a multitude of the greatest sins. They thus sacrifice without mercy all self-interest, signified by *the son, the brother, and the friend.*

This kind of repentance has the power of re-instating the soul in the degree from which it had fallen, and properly belongs to this fall of the passive or mystic persons. All other repentances might, indeed, assure their salvation, but never re-establish them in their degree; on the contrary, they would always remove them the further from it, causing them to enter further into, and to subsist the firmer in their self-interest.

Now this manner of repentance after the fall of these souls is something so difficult and so painful to the self-love still living in them, and hurt by their sin, that such persons would prefer rather to let themselves be flayed alive, than to remain faithfully in it, drinking in with deep draughts the penalty of their fault, and allowing themselves to be devoured by the burning heat of their confusion. Nevertheless, this same penitence is so much the more glorious for God, as it is the more annihilating for man; and it is so pure that he has no sooner returned to it, than he is re-established in the state from which he fell, with advantages which he had not before.

It is this repentance that is meant when it is said in Eccles. x. 4: "*If the spirit of the ruler rise upon thee, leave not thy place; for the remedies that will be applied unto thee will heal thee of the greatest sins.*" The place of each soul is where God had set him before his fall; however miserably he may have fallen, he must not leave it; but, resuming his first way, he must continue his course, trusting that if he peacefully remain in his abjection, sacrificed to all God's designs over him, He will apply to him the most sovereign remedies, by which the sins will cease, and he will be healed of them, even with an increase of graces.

And because this counsel is of extreme consequence in so dangerous a step, it is very necessary that directors should well comprehend it, so that, far from being astonished at the falls of the greatest souls, they might sustain them in their desolation, and animate them with a new courage, causing them to hope for a happy return to God, if they are faithful not to stir to return to their former practices, but to love their confusion in order to exalt God's glory so much the more, thus making a peaceful and passive repentance, in the very place of the interior way from which they have fallen. Such was David's repentance, but so happy a one that the Holy Spirit yet continued to speak by his mouth, and dictate to him the psalms after his sin as formerly. Such was the repentance of St. Peter, who did not renounce by his fall **the dignity of vicar of Jesus Christ, chief of the church, and prince of the apostles, which he had** before received, and which he even exercised a few days after with a courage all divine. Neither of these great penitents left the rank which God had given them in His church. This teaches us that neither is it necessary on account of any offence whatever to leave the degree of the interior to which we have attained, since the Divine Physician has remedies suitable for all our evils and states; and, far from wishing us to turn back, under pretext of commencing again by another road, He desires us to double our pace, and giving Him the hand of a perfect trust and total *abandon*, to advance still further. For although sin is the greatest of all evils, it is nevertheless certain that by the confusion it causes us, and the experience it gives us of our weakness, it delivers us (by crushing our own proper existence, and the love of ourselves) from a great obstacle to our annihilation and flowing into God. This is why God has permitted the like falls in many of His saints in order to conduct them afterwards more speedily and surely into Himself alone.

But this repentance of spiritual persons who have fallen is so grievous—for it takes away all assurance rather than gives any—that there are few faithful enough to remain in it; and for the same reason, there are few who after such falls are re-established in their state. But if these persons were firm and constant to bear the weight of this yoke, without wishing to be relieved by their own inventions, oh what advantage for them, and what glory for God!

> 30. *And on the morrow Moses said unto the people: Ye have committed a very great sin. Behold now I will go up unto the Lord to endeavour to obtain pardon for your crime.*

The character of a true shepherd is charity; he begins by reproving the people for their sin, and making it known to them; then he prays God to *obtain their pardon*, offering himself to bear the penalty due to so great a crime.

> 31. *Lord, pardon them this fault.*
> 32. *Or, if thou wilt not do it, blot me out of thy book which thou hast written.*

Oh how admirable is this speech, and what a signal effect of the charity of Moses! *Lord*, said he, *either pardon this people, or blot me out of thy book which thou hast written.* This book is the book of life, in which Moses knew he had been written by his predestination. It is this manner of praying which forces God to pardon; for will not so pure and disinterested a charity obtain all things? St. Paul, this great conductor of souls, did as much when he desired to be accursed for the salvation of his brethren. They both knew by their experience how far the sacrifice of a perfect love could extend.

CHAPTER XXXIII.

1. *And the Lord said unto Moses: Go, get thee out of this place, thou and thy people which thou hast brought out of Egypt, and go unto the land which I sware unto Abraham, to Isaac and Jacob, saying, Unto thy seed will I give it.*

Thou art willing, Lord, in spite of sin, to recompense this ungrateful and unfaithful people, because of the fidelity of thy word, on behalf of the faith, sacrifice, and *abandon* which they formerly practised. But permit me to say unto Thee, that these very recompenses are frightful punishments, since whatever is agreeable to the senses must hurt the spirit.

2. *I will send an angel before thee.*
3. *Ye shall enter into a land flowing with milk and honey. For I will not go up with you, lest I consume you by the way, for ye are a stiff-necked people.*

Thou art indeed willing, oh God, to give them *sweetnesses*, consolations, extraordinary things, as visible *angels, to accompany them* in their way of light, thou wilt do miracles in their behalf: these are the great things which the ignorant souls esteem much; but they do not see the horrible punishment contained therein. It is, that in loading them with Thy gifts, thou deprivest them of Thyself. O horrible threat! Take away all the rest, and give us Thyself, and that is sufficient. This is, then, the punishment with which Thou smitest an ungrateful, carnal, and self-interested people.

We must remark that these words: *For I will not go up with you,* very well express how God grants His gifts in place of Himself; and how often people take for a reward that which is a veritable punishment. He adds that it is *on account of their being stiff-necked* that He will not go with them; for He would be obliged to consume and annihilate them, if He conducted them in the pure and naked way, by which alone we can proceed to Him perfectly, it being seen that they were incapable of this trial.

> 4. *And when the people heard these evil tidings, they began to mourn: and no man put on his accustomed garments and ornaments.*

This people, from whom crime had not altogether taken away the remembrance of the way of truth, acted with great wisdom. They are afflicted at so disadvantageous propositions; and without setting any value on all these gifts, they wish to have no ornaments; to show God that they prefer to be stripped of all goods, in order to have the happiness of possessing Him in the midst of them. This is a proper manner of acting in order to win God.

> 5. *The Lord said unto Moses: Say unto the children of Israel, Ye are a stiff-necked people; if I come up once in the midst of you, I will consume you. Leave at once all your ornaments, that I may know what to do with you.*

God wishes to prove this people, to see if it is really Him, or only His gifts that they long after. He threatens them with Himself in a terrible manner: *Should I once come into the midst of you,* said He, *I will annihilate you. Strip yourselves at once* of all that remains of My favours, *and I will see what I shall do.* How many persons are there who upon a like occasion would say: Let the angel guide us, let Thy gifts remain, and let not God come with us? But this well-instructed people on this occasion act quite the contrary, and in their silence show, that although it costs them something, they prefer God to everything else, stripping themselves immediately of all their ornaments.

But why does Scripture, having previously mentioned *that they had not put on their customary ornaments,* say now, *that they stript themselves of them?* It is to be understood in this manner. They do not put on the graces God would give them in place of Himself; on the contrary, they despise them; **and to show**

Him still further that it is Himself they desire and not His gifts, they strip themselves even of those that remained to them, and which they had previously received, preferring annihilation to everything else, provided that God conducts them.

6. *The children of Israel left their ornaments near the Mount Horeb.*

7. *And Moses took the tabernacle and set it up afar from the camp, and called it the tabernacle of the covenant. And every one who had some difference went out of the camp, to go to the tabernacle of the covenant.*

They had no sooner accomplished this generous stripping than Moses *set up* before them *the tabernacle of the covenant*, as if to make known to them that God would Himself come with them. Thus Moses had no sooner entered into the tabernacle than the Lord appeared Himself there, and spoke in the cloud as formerly.

9. *And when Moses had entered into the tabernacle of the covenant, the pillar of cloud descended, and stood at the door; and the Lord talked with Moses.*

10. *And all the people saw the pillar of cloud standing at the door of the tabernacle, and they also stood at their tent-doors, and worshipped the Lord there.*

It was, then, there that these poor criminals found their refuge, and where they asked of God all that they needed. They no sooner knew by *the pillar of cloud* that God was with them than *they worshipped from their tents*, that is, from the place of their repose; for the thoroughly passive soul knows how to do that in everything without issuing from its repose; and this manner of worshipping is more perfect than any other. They worship from afar, and *standing;* for the perfect worship, made in spirit and truth by faith and love, penetrates all distance, and surpasses every disposition of the body, rising to God above every medium. Although this worship of a spiritual people, penitent in their degree, was already far advanced, yet it did not approach that of Moses.

11. *The Lord spake unto Moses face to face, as a man speaketh unto his friend.*

This chosen and unique friend of God, elevated above everything, *speaks to God face to face*, in the most intimate of all unions—close, essential, and elevated above the faculties. God, having raised the creature's capacity and lowered Himself, that He may have some friendship with it, speaks to it face to face, treating it in so familiar a manner that it may be compared to the way one acts with his most intimate friend, concealing nothing from him, and making him in some manner equal to himself; for intimate friendship renders friends equal.

12. *When Moses returned to the camp, his servant Joshua, a young man, son of Nun, departed not out of the tabernacle.*

It is the custom of *young* souls, beginning to enter into the interior way, to remain continually in prayer: they are so charmed with it that they cannot leave off. A sweet and penetrating love seizing hold of them keeps them buried in themselves; and a strong and lively presence of God infused into them concentrates them so sweetly within themselves as in a *tabernacle, that they cannot quit it.* The wise director, after Moses' example, must leave them in it, for it is not yet time to draw them out.

12. *Moses said unto the Lord: Thou dost command me to bring up this people, and thou dost not tell me whom thou wilt send with me, although thou hast said unto me, I know thee by thy name, and thou hast found grace in my sight.*

13. *If then I have found grace before thee, shew me thy countenance, that I may know thee, and may find grace in thy sight, and look favourably on this great multitude of thy people.*

This prayer of Moses would appear bold, insulting to God, and useless, were it not wholly mysterious. It would be bold; for what mortal man ought to aspire to a clear *vision of God?* It would be insulting to God, pretending that He discovers His countenance, although it is protested that that is not done in this life; and it would be useless, since Scripture says that God spoke to him face to face. But it is none of these. This request of Moses was a just one on this occasion, when he acted not for himself but for so great an interior people. Moses then desires to know, and also his people, if it will be God Himself and not His angel who will conduct them, that they may be persuaded that God alone can conduct them into Himself by the frightful road which they have yet to traverse, and which is so much the more dangerous as it is near its end.

Moses then desired to see if it would be God who would conduct this people, so as to judge by that of their re-establishment in grace, and of the safety of the road which they were going to take. Moreover, he signifies that it is not enough for the conductor to speak to God with so much familiarity—that being a grace for himself; but that he must, besides that, *see God's countenance*, that is to say, that he may have the clear sight and understanding of the words spoken to him, so as to be able to teach them without error.

It is very remarkable that one may have the enjoyment and understanding of a thing for himself, and yet nevertheless want the light and facility of expression to make others comprehend it. Therefore St. Paul has distinguished as two different gifts that of speaking diverse tongues, and that of interpreting them; and amongst the gifts of the Holy Spirit, there is much difference between wisdom, understanding, and counsel. Wisdom is the discernment of the Divine truths with the experimental taste which is given of them; understanding makes them thoroughly understood and more vividly penetrated, such as they are in themselves, with a greater extent and distinction; but counsel is the facility of expressing them correctly for the good of others. For this same reason this so great apostle and director said, that the countenance of God had been discovered to him; "*for us*," said he, "*in whom the open countenance of the Lord expresses his glory as in a mirror.*"

Moses, to show still further that he did not regard himself in this prayer, adds: "*look favourably upon thy people;* for it is on their behalf that I make this request."

14. *The Lord said unto him: My countenance shall go before thee, and I will give thee a place of repose.*

15. *Moses answered him: If thou walk not thyself before us, let us not depart from this place.*

God continues to assure this admirable director of His particular protection over himself, and promises him *a place of repose;* that is to say, that as for him he will always find God, and his perfect repose in Him, and he need not trouble himself

Chapter XXXIII. 261

about other things. But the great heart of Moses, forgetting all self-interest to think only on that of his flock, accepts not this advantage; he continues to entreat his God, protesting to Him, that if he does not see Him going before his people, he cannot suffer them to depart from this place.

> 16. *For how shall we know, I and thy people, that we have found grace before thee, if thou do not go with us, that we may be in glory and honour amongst all peoples that dwell on the earth.*

How shall we hope for pardon? How shall we have advantage over our enemies? How shall we walk in safety if *thou come not thyself with us?* Ah, such a soul prefers to lose all, rather than to lose its God! Oh how to walk under God's conduct is to walk in safety! But all other manner of walking is exposed to infinite dangers.

> 17. *The Lord said unto Moses: I will do that which thou askest of me, for thou hast found grace before me, and I know thee by thy name.*

God *grants* to this charitable shepherd *what he asks*, for He *knows him by his name*, true and legitimate shepherd, full of charity; and on account of his pure and violent love, he cannot refuse him anything. This is what He calls, *finding grace in His sight*. But He only grants him here victory over his enemies—not that He will not also grant him the rest, but He is pleased to make him languish in the pursuit of so great a a good, which merits to be preceded by some difficulties, and to be sought after with an ardent desire.

> 18. *Moses said unto him: Show me thy glory.*
>
> 19. *The Lord answered him: I will make all my goodness pass before thee, and will proclaim the name of the Lord before thee; I will be gracious unto whom I will be gracious, and will shew mercy unto whom I will shew mercy.*

Such a soul is not content with a temporal recompense, or a limited good. Moses again asks with entreaty for the same favour, although under a different expression. *Shew me thy glory*, said he; as if he said, I will not be content until I see Thy glory and what Thou art in Thyself. God, in fine, promises him that He will *shew him all His goodness*, Himself being the sovereign good, and the centre of all goods.

He promises it, however, in a manner seeming to find fault with Moses making so ardent requests, when He says to him: *I will be gracious unto whom I will be gracious, and I will shew mercy unto whom I will shew mercy*. But, oh Moses, let not this apparent harshness repel thee; this will be a greater good for thee than all the preceding caresses: it is, indeed, a sign that the Lord, out of the excess of His love for thee, will grant thee all that thou desirest. When God promises His greatest graces to His servants, He bestows them with a thousand marks of His affection; but He grants the sovereign good in seeming to repel: He drives away whilst attracting; and when He outwardly rejects, it is to introduce inwardly, as when Jesus Christ refuses the Canaanite woman, it is only to hear her with more compassion. The creature must be destroyed in itself before it can be received into God; and it must know that it is from the pure goodness of God alone that it has to look for this ineffable grace, seeing that, as St. Paul adds, while explaining this very verse, *It is not of him that willeth, nor of him that runneth, but of God that sheweth mercy*.

20. *God said unto him also: Thou canst not see my face; for no man shall see me and live.*

God's design in this refusal is to instruct Moses in the disposition necessary for the full enjoyment of Himself. *No one can see Him*, if he be not truly dead to all *self-life*, either of nature or of grace, and of all that is not God. Thus He does not say: No one shall see Me without dying, but *no one shall see me and live;* to make us understand, that to attain to this supreme felicity, one death alone is not sufficient, nor even several, but that there must not remain the smallest particle of proprietary life whatsoever.

There are several spiritual deaths, all necessary for the soul's purification—that of the senses, the faculties, and the centre; and each of these deaths is accomplished only by the loss of an infinity of *lives;* because there are an infinity of attachments and supports on created things in which man subsists proprietarily. In order to *see God*, to be united to Him by the most intimate union, it is absolutely necessary to be deprived of all these lives; and if the holy flame of pure love does not annihilate them all in this world, the purifying fire must devour them in the other.

21. *And the Lord said: There is a place near me where thou shalt stand upon a rock.*
22. *And when my glory shall pass by, I will place thee in an opening of the rock, and I will cover thee with my hand until I have passed by.*
23. *I will then take away my hand, and thou shalt see me from behind; but thou shalt not see my face.*

This place, destined for the enjoyment of God, *is near Him;* since it is in Himself, and is Himself. In order to possess this inestimable good, we must be established *upon the rock* of the Divine immobility; and *when*, says the Lord, *my glory shall pass by, I will cover thee with the hand* of My protection, so that thou mayest be able to bear so great a favour as this, which otherwise would consume thee. Nevertheless, thou shalt only see Me as *through the narrow opening*, or the extremity *of the rock*, which is the most subtle point of the Spirit; and when this majestic state of My glory, which can only be seen in this life like a flash of lightning, *shall have passed, I shall withdraw my hand*, which covered My glory, and hindered thee from seeing it, lest thy soul should be separated from the body, nature being too feeble to bear the weight of so great a good; then *thou shalt see me*,—thou shalt comprehend in some manner by a particular view of My Divinity with which I will gratify thee, that I AM THAT I AM, and that all is in Me: but thou shalt only see Me *from behind*, that is to say, in what can be comprehended by man elevated to the most eminent grace, which is to *see* only as *from behind*, and to perceive the surface of what God is; but God in Himself is absolutely incomprehensible, as St. Denis has said so profoundly: "If any one having seen God has comprehended what he has seen, it is not God that he has seen, but only something that exists by Him, and may be known by man."

CHAPTER XXXIV.

1. *The Lord said unto Moses: Hew thee out two tables of stone*

> *like to the first; and I will write thereon the words which were upon the tables that thou brakest.*
>
> 4. *And Moses rose up before it was day, and went up on to Mount Sinai, bearing the tables with him.*

God looks upon Moses with singular kindness, or rather allows Himself to be seen by him; but it is on condition that His law be graven upon *tables of stone* that will not be broken again; to show that He desires to grave it upon hearts which, by their central immobility, are placed beyond the reach of all infidelity.

> 5. *And the Lord descended in the cloud, and Moses stood with him, and called upon the name of the Lord.*
> 6. *And when the Lord passed before Moses, he said unto him: Lord God, sovereign ruler, merciful and gracious, long suffering, abundant in goodness and truth.*
> 7. *Keeping mercy for thousands, etc.*

The expressions of Moses when he has the happiness of beholding God upon the mountain, sufficiently show the agreeable transports with which a soul is seized in the reception of so great a grace. They also point out to us, how those who are visited by God in their interior centre, feeling these delicious touches, can only allow the fire of their love (with which they are kindled) to evaporate by a thousand and a thousand praises which they offer to their God. Moreover, we learn that it is in these precious moments that the spouse receives the clearest knowledge of God, by the manifestation He makes to her of Himself. She calls Him, *Lord, God, true, merciful, long suffering;* and admiring His Divine attributes, and not being able to praise them enough, she loves them all equally, His justice as well as His mercy, His power as well as His virtue; for, seeking nothing of self-interest therein, she is enraptured that these are the perfections of her God shining forth in Himself, or on behalf of the creatures.

> 8. *And Moses immediately bowed his head to the ground, and worshipped God.*
> 9. *And said unto him: Lord, if I have found grace in thy sight, go, I entreat thee, with us; that thou mayest pardon us our sins and our iniquities, and that thou mayest possess us.*

Chapter XXXIV.

Moses makes use of the occasion of these favours to obtain what he desires. He *worships Him* first; rendering Him this duty of religion: then *he entreats Him* to become Himself the *Conductor of the people, so that*, he says, *Thou mayest pardon us, and mayest possess us:* for the surest mark of pardon for sins is to be possessed by God, and to possess Him also within one's self; seeing that God cannot dwell where sin exists. In proportion as God pardons sins, He must re-enter into possession of the heart, and re-establish it in Him as it was before its death by crime.

> 10. *The Lord answered him : I will make a covenant before all people; and I will do marvels such as have not been seen upon the earth.*

God promises Moses what he desires, assuring him that He will bestow on him greater graces than all he has yet received. When God desires to come into a soul, it must be stripped, by the mystic annihilation, of all its graces; but when He has come, being the author of all graces, He brings with Him such as the creature *has never experienced*, and which, like the ornaments of His inner court, cannot exist without Him.

> 12. *Take heed never to make a covenant of friendship with the inhabitants of this land ; for this would be the cause of thy ruin.*

This counsel is given to spiritual souls, to wit, to have no more commerce with souls that are yet in themselves and walking in proprietary ways, lest they draw them out of their state of loss in God, and by their reflections make them return to themselves, and thus *cause their ruin.*

> 14. *Thou shalt worship no other God ; for the Lord, whose name is Jealous, is a jealous God.*

He commands them again *to worship no other God*, as they had done, for His Name is *The Jealous God.* Oh! goodness of my God, Thou hast an holy jealousy for the heart and spirit of Thy creatures! Thou wilt have them belong to Thee *alone*, and to take good heed of never returning to any idolatry like to that by which they had allowed themselves to be seduced.

> 16. *Thou shalt not give the daughters of this country for wives*

> *to thy sons, lest being corrupted with their gods they also entice thy sons to the same fornication.*

He justly forbids these alliances, and calls idolatry *fornication*. For the soul being God's, must belong to Him alone; and so soon as it withdraws from Him to place itself in something else, it commits *adultery*, as the Holy Spirit declares by St. James (James iv. 4).

> 30. *And when Aaron and the children of Israel saw that the face of Moses shone brightly, they dared not come near him.*

This *brilliancy of Moses' face* was a sensible mark of his reflowing into and sublime transformation in God Himself, the fulness of which overflowed outwardly.

> 34. *When he spake to the Lord, he took off his vail until he came out.*
>
> 35. *But he covered his face again when he spoke to the people.*

This wise conduct of Moses teaches us that persons of this degree ought not to make manifest the secrets revealed to them, nor what they experience, to others not capable of receiving them; for it would only frighten and repulse them. They must be known only to God and to directors, or to those in the same state; for the rest, everything is *covered with a vail*, impenetrable to their spirit, however penetrative they believe themselves; and if this vail were lifted, they could not bear the splendour that would issue from these deified persons.

CHAPTER XXXV.

> 3. *Ye shall kindle no fires in all your habitations on the sabbath day.*

This commandment well expresses in the letter the repose of the souls that God has made to enter into His divine *sabbath*, which is the mystic *rest!* They must not do anything of themselves, but remain simply as they are kept. *To kindle fire* is no other thing than to stir up a little affection in order to keep warm the sensible or perceptible Divine love. This is permitted in other degrees, when it is still necessary to remain in activity, and to maintain one's self by some sign; but this must no longer be done *on the sabbath day*, or repose in God; and he that would do so, would violate the sanctity of the Sabbath, interrupting the Divine repose. Let those persons then who are called to this holy rest, and who are also assured of it by direction, enter and remain therein without fear, religiously respecting the Majesty of God, who desires to be perfectly worshipped in them by silence and repose; remembering that this is the Sabbath that remains to us in the law of grace; a Sabbath which the most chosen people of God must celebrate in this life ever after they are introduced into it, to continue it afterwards eternally in heaven, according to the explanation given by St. Paul (Heb. iv. 9).

5. *Take ye from among you what ye have resolved to offer unto the Lord. Let every one offer it with his whole heart and will.*

These *first offerings* that God demands, are the first good works, and this beginning of the spiritual life which the soul newly born to His love can then consecrate to Him, since it can act of itself. All its actions must be referred to God, without retaining anything of them whatever; and by this voluntary offering of all that lies in its power, God sanctifies and consecrates to Himself all the rest through the free gift which it makes of its *will* to Him, and He takes so strong a possession of its whole self, that He ever afterwards deals with it as a Sovereign. And this is the most certain and the shortest way, or rather the only way of acquiring perfection, to wit, to abandon one's *heart* and all that depends on it to the power of God, that He may do with it as He pleaseth, as it is recommended us in a psalm. Those persons generous enough to do this, having thus got rid of themselves, have shaken off the greatest enemy to their perfection; and being happily placed within the hands of God, they have lost all power over themselves.

But they have lost it only by the voluntary offering they have made of it to God, not being able to make a more holy, just, or advantageous use of their liberty, than in returning it and consecrating it unto their God, who has bestowed it on them. They are, however, always in a state in which they may resume it through infidelity, and there are very few who make a perfect gift of it, the greater part always using some reserve or resumption. But were this perfect sacrifice made all at once, we would be that very instant perfect, seeing that no imperfection can remain where God's will acts and reigns without resistance.

These material offerings then of the law are the figure of the spiritual sacrifices God desires of us; and a hundred thousand times happy are those who penetrate their spirit, love their practice, and relish their truth.

20. *All the children of Israel*
21. *Made their offerings to the Lord with willing hearts, for all that was to do to the tabernacle of the testimony.*
25. *And the women also, skilled in work, gave what they had spun, of hyacinth, purple, scarlet, and fine linen.*
26. *And gave everything willingly*

It is necessary only *to offer unto the Lord* these first fruits of our will, and the free right we have over ourselves, so that He may perform in us *the work of the tabernacle.* God, by means of Moses, in this desert and in the rest that His people take there, instructs all spiritual persons and directors, under these sensible figures, of the way they ought to take to succeed in the work of their Christian perfection; and whoever has light enough to penetrate through those shadows will see it with delight.

The *tabernacle* is the habitation of God; and it is Himself who builds this dwelling place within us, from the time when we have yielded unto Him our rights. As soon as man, by gentle and firm recollection, turns away from the creatures, and lives solitarily with God in the midst of himself, and rising above his own frailty plunges into God to find there all that is needful to him, God begins to perform His work in him; but so bountifully, that He makes use of everything in order to construct His interior palace, making *everything work for good to those that love him, and are called to holiness according to his purpose.* (Rom. viii. 28.) The evil wills of the creatures that oppose them, serve as so many strokes of the hammer to polish the outside of this edifice by the crosses they cause them, whilst God Himself works within, and builds His *tabernacle* there. But it is necessary that everything *be offered freely and with open heart*, thus Scripture says, that *they all gave willingly*, to show that God never violates our freedom, but that He disposes the heart by His love so that it freely gives Him what it has to offer.

CHAPTER XXXVI.

4. The workers were obliged

5. To come unto Moses, and say, The people offer unto God more than is necessary.

The best things have their times and seasons for finishing. Can there be anything better than offering unto God what one possesses? Why then does Scripture say, that they *offer* here *more than is necessary?* The reason is that when we have freely offered ourselves unto God, and have also made an irrevocable gift of our liberty to Him, it is no longer necessary to offer it, since it no more belongs to us; and we would require to resume ourselves in order to offer anew.

It will be said to me, however, that we can always offer new virtues. It is true that we can always offer new fruits as long as we possess the tree. But when we have given up the root, it would be ridiculous to yet wish continually to offer the fruits thereof, since it is clear enough that they belong to the master of the root, and we cannot desire to give them again without rendering ourselves in some manner proprietary.

If good souls often reiterate this donation, as is common enough at the commencement, it is either because it has not been made in all its perfection from the beginning, or to cut off some reservations that yet remain; or to renounce resumptions that have been made through infidelity; or by an amorous out-pouring of the heart, which takes pleasure in ratifying all it has done for its God; or, in fine, by a movement of God Himself, who loves to see this sacrifice of love many times renewed.

6. Then Moses caused it to be publicly proclaimed throughout the camp, that neither man nor woman should offer any-

thing more for the works of the sanctuary. And thus all ceased from offering gifts.

This wise director, well instructed in the mystic science, forbids either *men*, signifying the strongest and most advanced souls, or *women*, representing the weakest and less purified, *to offer any more gifts;* since the offering that has been made of all self is sufficient in order to allow God to act, and to build His sanctuary Himself, according to His eternal design.

7. *What they had already offered was sufficient; and there was even more than was necessary.*

They had already exceeded the command that God had given. The love of self-activity often leads us to give ourselves when we ought to do so no longer. And this would always occur did the true directors not forbid it with as much patience as firmness; or did not God (making use of the right He has acquired over the creature by its free gift), render it powerless to do so, drying up its faculties and exhausting its activities.

CHAPTER XL.

31. *After these things were finished,*
32. *A cloud covered the tabernacle of the testimony, and the glory of the Lord filled it.*

The *tabernacle* is no sooner *finished* according to God's order than He immediately comes to *fill it* with His presence, and to give sensible marks of His Majesty there. This means, that our interior, being prepared up to the point that God desires, He forthwith comes to make His habitation there, although in *the cloud*, that is to say, under the obscurity of faith.

33. *Moses could not enter into the tent of the covenant, for the cloud covered everything; and the majesty of God burst forth on all sides.*

Chapter XL.

But when this interior tabernacle, or the centre of the soul, is filled with God Himself, nothing can enter therein, not even the holiest things. Everything which partakes of the divine resolves itself into God, in proportion as He draws near, and cannot be distinguished; and all that is opposed to Him remains without. For although this *cloud* is not God, yet He is within it. It is necessary, then, that the interior sanctuary be entirely empty, that the Majesty of God may repose there.

LEVITICUS.

WITH EXPLICATIONS AND REFLECTIONS REGARDING THE INTERIOR LIFE.

CHAPTER I.

8. *And the priests, Aaron's sons, shall lay the parts, the head and the fat, in order upon the wood that is on the fire which is upon the altar.*

9. *But the inwards and the legs shall he wash in water; and the priest shall burn them upon the altar, to be a burnt-offering of a sweet savour unto the Lord.*

All these sacrifices of the law are the figures of interior sacrifices, as the apostles themselves have declared (1 Peter ii. 5; Eph. v. 2). But there are several kinds of them, and in all, the creature always reserves something to itself, according as it was figured in those of the law, in which a part of what had been offered to God was laid aside for the priests and Levites. Such are the sacrifices of all the active and passive states, and even the mystic ones at their commencement. There is only the state of pure sacrifice, represented by the *burnt-offering*, which retains nothing, and burns everything, even what seemed most necessary for the subsistence of the proper life; and it is this pure sacrifice which forms the consummation of the mystic state.

CHAPTER IX.

22. *And Aaron came down from offering the sin-offering, the burnt-offering, and the peace offerings.*

All that man can perform for himself is to offer victims; and for others, to sacrifice them and lay them in order, bringing to them, as a priest, the fire of charity. This being done, he has exhausted all that lies in his power, and must *come down* again into himself to allow God to act.

24. *And there came a fire out from before the Lord and consumed the burnt-offering and the fat that were upon the altar, which when all the people saw, they praised the Lord, and fell upon their faces.*

But when the soul has arrived at a certain state of purity, God *sends forth a devouring fire* from His countenance, that is to say, from Himself, who is perfect charity; and this fire *consumes the burnt-offering*, burning all that remained of himself in the man, destroying it, and reducing it to ashes: And this is the consummation of perfect annihilation, which can only be wrought by God Himself, and by the fire of His countenance, which is the purest and most disinterested love.

CHAPTER X.

1. *The two sons of Aaron, Nadab and Abihu, took each of them his censer, and put fire therein, and incense thereon, and offered a strange fire before the Lord.*

God is so jealous of His glory and pure love, that He cannot suffer *a strange fire*, such as is not kindled upon His altar, that is, in Himself. There is no middle point; we either must be on fire with His love, or be consumed by His wrath.

2. *And at the same moment, there went out a fire from the Lord, and consumed them, and they died before the Lord.*

A soul consecrated to its God, and which has devoted itself to Him; a soul whom He has called to serve Him by pure sacrifice, can never admit any strange love, self-love, or self-interest, but it *dies* that very moment, and dies *by the fire coming forth from the Lord:* for the fire of His justice issues no less from Him

Chapter X.

than does that of His love. And this death is caused by its issuing out of its state—this infidelity being a death to the purity of the same state, which happens to it *in the presence of the Lord*, during its life even, ceasing as much to live in Him alone, as it desires to live by itself; and dying to the perfection of the divine life, just so much as it will not die to its own self-love.

6. *Moses said unto Aaron, and unto Eleazar and Ithamar, his sons: Uncover not your heads, rend not your garments, lest ye die, and the wrath of the Lord be kindled against all the people. Let your brethren, the whole house of Israel, bewail the burning which the Lord hath kindled.*

He desires that amongst the priests and Levites, the most consecrated to the Lord, there shall be no mourning for the loss of these persons taken away by God: because he wishes the sanctified souls to enter into the interests of the Divine justice, without regarding any human interest. Did they commit this infidelity even under good pretexts, they would by that, issue out of their state, and would merit the same punishment. An inviolable faithfulness is needed, not to make a resumption in anything after having given one's self to God. The common souls may be afflicted at some loss, out of a feeling of compassion: and that passes with them for a good, and indeed can be so, when it is inspired by charity, or by a reasonable, though human, affection. But those before spoken of, must, in all things, regard the sole interests of God alone.

7. *But for you, go not forth from the door of the tabernacle; else ye shall perish: for the oil of the holy anointing has been poured upon you.*

He adds—If (by some turning back to yourselves, or for some particular interest) *ye only go out of the door of the tabernacle*, which is but for God alone, and in which ye ought always to stand enclosed; if ye stop at some voluntary reflection, *ye shall perish*, and issue out of your state; since having been consecrated to God by the *oil of the holy anointing*, which is the indelible mark of the character of a soul arrived in God, He is not willing that, by a single look, you should share in the grief and interests of the common souls.

CHAPTER XI.

44. I am the Lord, your God: be ye holy, for I am holy.

The *holiness* that God demands of us, is a holiness relating to His own. Now, the holiness of God is in Himself, of Himself, and for Himself; it is therefore necessary that the holiness of these souls be in God, of God, and for God. It must be in God, existing only in Him, otherwise it would be proprietary, and would rob Him of something; and of God, seeing that all holiness that is not received from God, cannot be called such; and for God, as it must refer to Him as to its end and centre, and must serve His glory. The soul then arrived into God has no longer anything in itself, for itself, nor of itself; but by its loss into God, everything is received in Him alone; and that which it possesses is not for itself, any more than it comes from itself. But, as everything has come from God, so has everything flowed there again. This then is the holiness proper to this degree.

45. For I am the Lord, that have brought you out of Egypt to be your God: Be ye holy, for I am holy.

This verse is the confirmation of the preceding one, and further explains it. God declares that He *has brought* this people out of the land of their captivity, which was their own inventions, so as to lose them into Himself. This expression, *that I may be your God*, means, that I may be all in all to you Myself, in Myself, and for Myself. He no longer says, that I may be in you, or in the midst of you: for this would be too little; nor that I may be for you; but, that I may be your God. Not for you, but in Me, and for Me. *Be ye then holy, for I am holy.* Be holy with this holiness, for it is Mine.

46. This is the law of every living animal.
47. That ye may know to discern between the pure and impure.

Ye *shall discern by this law of all that liveth*, that which is either perfect or imperfect; and ye shall also know by it, that the *love* that I exact of you is alone *pure* and upright. It is not that, for souls living in themselves, there is not a law less perfect, which they can and ought to follow, not knowing any other; but for the souls living in God, they must make this difference; because, that which is good for others, would be *impure* for them; and it is given them to know with more light, what they ought to embrace or reject. But the others have not yet the perfect disinterestedness [discernment].

CHAPTER XIV.

14. *And the priest shall take some of the blood of the trespass offering, and shall put it upon the tip of the right ear of him who is to be purified, and upon the thumb of his right hand, and upon the great toe of his right foot.*

This manner of *purification* denotes that the soul that is clean and pure enough to enter into the most advanced way of the spirit, must have *the ear* consecrated to God alone, in order to listen to Him: for here it no longer uses words with God, at least ordinarily, unless He lead it Himself to say something to Him, which very rarely happens. For this reason, the ear is purified, and not the tongue; that it may be silent before God, and be faithful to hear Him. *The thumb of the right hand is purified* moreover, which signifies that all the actions of this soul must be consecrated to God, and be done all in the uprightness of His spirit—God being Master and Author of them, as well as of the affections, denoted by *the feet*, which must be wholly pure, and of holy steps. But the right foot only is consecrated because the soul must carry all its affections to God, without ever turning aside or doing anything for itself out of an interested motive. Therefore David made this prayer: "Conduct me, Lord, in Thy way, and make me to walk in Thy truth." He meant in God Himself: for God is truth as well as charity, from which we ought never to turn aside.

CHAPTER XV.

This whole chapter contains but an *exterior* and legal *purification*, an attention to which would appear unworthy of God, did it not signify His intention to instruct a gross and carnal people, and exhibit also His purity; of this He desired to impart to them a high idea (suited to their state), by this exterior purification, which was that of clothes so often purified and washed, and which, not being able to bestow purity upon the soul, was but an outward sign of what God exacted of this same soul. For God, having established this law of outward purification, on account of the grossness of this people, shows in the Gospel what a little thing it is—reproaching the Pharisees with being contented to cleanse the outside of the cup, whilst within it is full of extortion. The Christians of the present day do the same thing; they are contented with cleansing the outside, with affecting an apparently regulated life; although within, they are full of usurpations and plunder of God: for, if robbing men is accounted so criminal, how much more so is it to rob God? Jesus Christ then has taken care to instruct us how much these exterior purifications, bearing only the figure of the interior, were of little value and account, compared with this interior purification, which consists in taking away all rapines from within, restoring to God the usurpations and thefts that we have committed. He shows us the way, by poverty of spirit, renouncing ourselves, bearing our cross, and following Jesus Christ.

I believe, then, that all the fruit that we can draw from this chapter is, to make apparent to us the purity that God exacts of those who are His, as much inwardly as outwardly, which is but a very gross figure; that we are no longer washed in *water*, but in the blood of Jesus Christ, in which we can plunge without ceasing. This is what we ought to do the very instant we perceive ourselves to have committed some fault, by accident, or even willingly, to make a simple and sincere return to Jesus Christ, more or less active (according to the soul's degree), as its prayer is more or less active, or by a simple return—a plunging into God—into this sea of love—which will purify us from all our filthiness, much more than all the waters in the world.

The offerings after the purifications were *pigeons* or *turtle doves* —showing that the most agreeable sacrifice to God is that of simplicity. A simple soul is immediately re-established in the grace of God, and in His pure love, and as promptly as a straw is consumed in a great fire, provided it does not issue out of its simplicity.

There are two kinds of oblations: the first is simply *offered* to God, and well represents the purification made by simple returns to God after faults of inadvertence or pure weakness. The sacrifice of *burnt offering* which was made of the other turtle dove, admirably signifies the purification of a more advanced state, wrought by holy love, in which the soul always remains like a burnt offering, not only to be purified, but to be consumed in this same love, in which it seems to change form and nature—to have no other form than that of this divine fire —and this is the thorough and radical purification which can only be wrought by pure love.

CHAPTER XVI.

1. *The Lord spake unto Moses after the death of the two sons of Aaron, when they offered a strange fire before the Lord, and were killed.*

Nothing is of greater consequence to a soul drawn to God, than not *to offer strange fire*. Its fire must be pure, clean, upright, inviolably holy for God; without which, it merits *death*.

There are two kinds of strange fire; the one more gross, the other more subtle and dangerous. The first is the attachment to some created thing out of ourselves; riches, honour, fortune, persons, etc.; in fine, all that is not God Himself. The second strange fire is self-love and propriety, which are enrooted and identified in us; it is offering a strange fire to burn our incense upon this profane fire. The *incense* denotes prayer and orison, as the Apocalypse designs it when it says that the four and twenty elders held each a censer before the throne of God, which were the prayers of the saints. Prayer, in order to be perfect, must be produced by pure love, which melts and dissolves, so to speak, the soul, as the gum of the incense is melted and dissolved in the fire, so that this soul melted thus (if I may speak so) by the loss of propriety, which kept it fixed in itself, hindering it from flowing and losing itself in God, and, being perfectly disappropriated by pure love (which alone can do it), is lost absolutely to itself, flowing into God its last end.

2. *And the Lord said unto Moses, Speak unto Aaron, thy brother, that he enter not at all times into the sanctuary within*

the vail before the mercy-seat, which covers the ark, lest he die; for I shall appear in the cloud upon the oracle.

How comes it that God does not desire the high priest *to enter at all times* into the Tabernacle? It was that at that time God might be more reverenced by the people, who, having only low and gross ideas of Him, were also conducted only by terror or extraordinary things—miracles and prodigies. Since the birth of Jesus Christ, this so great and holy God has rendered Himself familiar to men; but alas, how much they have abused Him! Terror is perhaps more advantageous to them than this immensity of goodness. It is thus with evil hearts; but, for good hearts, how much more are they touched by His love, than by all imaginable miracles! But how rare are these good hearts!

It is also to be remarked that God said *He would appear in the cloud upon the oracle.* This is an admirable figure. For it is certain that it is only through the nakedest faith that the soul truly has a perpetual access into its centre, where God dwells. God covers and envelops, so to speak, His majesty with a cloud; everything is done and accomplished in this divine obscurity, in which the soul neither sees, feels, knows, nor discerns anything but a profound silence; but it is certain through faith that this is God; it cannot doubt of it; since He has chosen, as He has said in another place, the darkness for His hiding-place. This adorable majesty, enveloped for the soul with clouds, has something infinitely more august and certain, than all that is discovered by the senses and faculties—as relishes, visions, revelations, ecstasies, and the rest—which are received either in the senses (and these are the more gross) or in the faculties, which are less so, but which are always of very little account compared with these sacred darknesses, which in this life serve for the communication of very God, as the light of glory serves in the other.

3. *And let him not enter therein until he has offered a calf for a sin offering, and a ram for a burnt offering.*

It was necessary that the high priest should be entirely purified before entering into the Tabernacle, according to all the purification of the ancient law, which was done by the shedding of the blood of animals—a more extended purification than that of water, since it not only served (like water) for legal purifications, but also for sins; although this blood had no merit in itself; but all its value was included in that which Jesus Christ was to shed. It was necessary then, that the high priest should be purified by the blood before entering the Tabernacle which was covered with a cloud. Likewise, the soul must also be purified from all its filthiness, in the blood of Jesus Christ, after having been so by the waters of the tears of repentance, in order to be admitted into this cloudy centre, where God dwells. What purification must it not bear! It is only Jesus Christ who can purify the soul to the necessary point. Not only must it be sprinkled with His blood, but wholly washed in it. Adorable Saviour, nothing is done but by Thee; and although Thou art then objectively concealed from the soul, it discovers afterwards, when it is more advanced, that it is Jesus Christ who has performed all these things. "Everything has been made by Him; and without Him has there been nothing made." It is then Jesus Christ who prepares and purifies the soul, until He has rendered it pure enough for it to be lost into God, and hidden there with Him.

After the high priest had offered up the *calf for the sin offering*, the *ram* must be offered *as a burnt offering*. This marks the last purification, which can only be made by this pure and divine love consuming everything, and destroying it so absolutely, that nothing remains. This is why pure love is truly the sacrifice of burnt offering, in which all propriety is destroyed.

> 4. *He shall put on a tunic of linen; and shall have linen breeches, and shall gird himself with a girdle of linen; and with a linen mitre shall he be attired; for these garments are holy; and he shall put them on after having washed in water.*

The *linen* garments with which the high priest was to be clad, very well designate a pure life—simple and innocent outwardly—observing all the rules of outward decency and modesty, so as to edify and not to scandalise the neighbour—concealing the inner, covering it with this vail of simplicity and innocence. Nothing is commoner than linen; nothing is more common than the life of these souls who are simple and innocent, childlike and little.

7. *He shall present two goats before the Lord at the door of the tabernacle of the testimony.*

8. *And he shall cast lots upon the two goats; the one lot for the Lord, and the other lot for the scape-goat.*

9. *And he shall offer a sin offering of the goat on which the Lord's lot fell.*

10. *But the goat on which the lot fell for the scape-goat, he shall present living before the Lord, to offer prayers upon him, and to send him away into the desert.*

These two goats represent that innocent Lamb who has been willing to be offered up for our sins, that admirable *scape-goat*, charged with the sins of His people.

We can also see here a soul purified up to the point, called lost with Jesus Christ in God, who is then placed in the Apostolic state, to aid his brethren; but, moreover, who, like *the scape-goat*, is laden in some manner with their iniquities. After being charged with the curse of those for whom he suffers, he is driven *into the desert*.

There are two kinds of deserts. The first relates to ourselves, and through which we must pass before being able to aid others—the desert of ourselves—this separation and division from all things and ourselves, by dying to and renouncing everything—by quitting ourselves so absolutely that we no more take part in what regards us, than if we existed no longer—leaving ourselves destitute in God's hands, and lost in Him for time and for eternity.

The other desert is that to which the Apostolic man is often banished for his brother's sake. He must bear his weaknesses, be exiled, so to speak, from God, on account of him, bear his different dispositions, be driven into the desert; for he has been made as a scape-goat for his brethren; and this is an extension of the mission of Jesus Christ, and of the Apostolic life.

The lots cast upon the two goats, and the destination made of them by the Lord, marks that all purified souls are not called to the Apostolic life. There are some admirable souls, of whom one has no knowledge, who are sanctified in secret, and who will be known only in the other life; these are the saints *consecrated to the Lord*, as this goat is consecrated.

Chapter XVI.

These two goats also represent two kinds of persons, called of God to be offered up to Him by different sacrifices. Some by the loss of themselves into God, peculiarly belong to Him, and He destines them to the most eminent grace, which is, to be reserved for Him alone, and to be sacrificed to Him without reserve and without there remaining to them any means of preservation. Others are destined for good works—for the service of the people and divine gifts; and the latter save their souls.

This lot clearly enough expresses the singular and efficacious calling of God, for one or other of these two ways. Those destined for holy activities finish their life thus and holily, meriting great crowns before God, as the price of their labours and services they have rendered to souls. But for those who in this life are destined for God Himself, Oh, what their life must cost them, and how mercilessly they must be *sacrificed!* Each one must be faithful to his way, respecting that of the others; and without judging or despising them, we must consider that every one has received his proper gift of God, and that what puts a value upon the states, is the will of God, by which we are there, and the faithfulness with which we remain therein: as it is also what constitutes all our perfection.

12. *And he shall take a censer full of burning coals of fire from off the altar, and his hands full of sweet incense beaten small, and he shall enter within the vail in the holy of holies.*

13. *And he shall cast the incense upon the fire, so that the smoke thereof may cover the oracle that is upon the testimony, and he die not.*

This is another sacrifice here, which is made only in the holy of holies; because it is altogether interior, and the soul must have almost attained to its end before it is offered. It is *the sacrifice of the incense* dissolved by the holy *fire* of love, in which prayer is but *a smoke of incense*, in which the soul as it were liquified in the divine love, does nothing but flow into God, where the sweet smell and smoke of the whole interior unceasingly ascends up unto Him without ever returning below, and where the soul having the honour and glory of God alone in view, with no more self-interest whatever, mounts unceasingly on high. And this sacrifice is of a sweet savour, ascending to the throne of God, who accepts it willingly. This is the sacrifice of thanksgiving of which David speaks, Psalm cxvi. 17, in which the soul has eyes only for God: it would have Him loved and glorified, it knows that He alone merits everything, and it returns all to Him. It is also the sacrifice of entire disappropriation: there remains nothing of the dissolved incense but a faint pleasant odour after the whole cloud has ascended. I believe that this is in the most perfect sense what St. Paul calls the sweet savour of Jesus Christ (2 Cor. ii. 15).

It was moreover necessary, that the *smoke should cover the whole oracle*, that the high priest might not die. In this state, everything is hidden by the obscurity of this fragrant cloud, so that the soul might neither see nor discern anything in God, (all being covered with darkness, and faith being the real light of this life); and might no longer see itself; for to look upon ourselves brings death, as also does curiosity for things God does not Himself discover to us.

> 16. *And let him purify the sanctuary of the uncleanness of the children of Israel, the transgressions they have committed against the law, and of all their sins. He shall do the same thing for the tabernacle of the testimony, that has been raised amongst them, in the midst of the uncleanness they have committed in their tents.*

It seems that the sins of the people sully the Lord's *sanctuary*. This is so true, that the destruction of the Temple was only caused by the sins of the Jews, as they were threatened: "I will profane my sanctuary, I will destroy it and the sabbaths," etc. (Ezek. xxiv. 21.—Lev. xxvi. 31). It was necessary then to *purify the sanctuary from the sins* of the people. But this was not enough: it was needful to purify their habitation and the sanctuary that was *in the midst of them*, without which their sins would have always sullied this sanctuary. It is just the same at the present time. The Church in itself is all pure and spotless as was the Tabernacle; but we pollute it by our crimes. How will it be purified from our filthiness if we are not converted? If we do not purify ourselves, we are by our sins the cause of all the misfortunes that unceasingly happen to it. It is in vain that we say, we wish to reform the Church. Let us all turn ourselves to the Lord; let us reform ourselves, and it will be reformed. It is without spot or wrinkle: it is we who cover it with mud and shame. O Lord, do Thou reform our hearts! This is the only reform needed.

Chapter XVI.

> 17. *And when the high priest shall enter into the holy of holies to pray for himself, for his house, and for the whole assembly of Israel, there shall be no man in the tabernacle until he come out.*

When God ordains *that there shall be no man in the tabernacle when the high priest enters into the holy of holies*, it denotes to us, that when God enters our sanctuary, which is the centre of our soul, we must keep the soul entirely void of all gross and earthly objects, and still more of self; no distraction must enter into this sanctuary, no attachment, nothing, nothing to which the heart may incline.

There are some good souls, who, hearing this, may be troubled at having distractions in spite of themselves, certain vague thoughts which they cannot prevent. Let them not be disquieted; for all these do not enter into the sanctuary; they are only in the court of the temple. God permits these things to deprive us of the knowledge of what passes within the holy of holies, just as He concealed from the eyes of the people what took place in the Sanctuary. When the heart is empty and detached from everything, distractions can do no harm: but those that proceed from attachments must be corrected by cutting away all kinds of ties and affections through a total death to all things.

> 21. *And Aaron shall lay both his hands upon the head of the goat, and shall confess all the iniquities of the children of Israel, all their transgressions, and all their sins, putting them upon the head of the goat, and shall send him away by the hand of a fit man into the wilderness.*

The high priest laid both his hands upon this scape-goat, upon whose head he confessed the sins of the whole people. I seem to see the Eternal Father applying His justice to Jesus Christ, as this priest laid his hands upon the goat: for it is certain that Jesus Christ has felt all the weight of the hands of a God, which is the weight of justice. Job, the most patient of men, desires his friends to have pity on him, for the hand of God had touched him. If this simple touch was so grievous, what must the weight of this mighty hand be!

The confession of sins represents the Eternal Father in applying His justice upon His son, ladening him with the innumerable multitude of our crimes, the deformity of which

He showed to him: Therefore, the Prophet says, "He was laden with our iniquities, and by his stripes we are healed." *They loaded this goat with the curse.* Has this Divine Saviour not been made a curse for His people, as it is written; "He has been made a curse for us," and again, "cursed is every one that hangeth upon a tree." Has He not been driven from amongst the men He came to save? Has He not been in the desert with no other company than the beasts? This was then the figure of Jesus Christ laden with the sins of all men.

> 29. *And this shall be a statute for ever unto you: that on the tenth day of the seventh month, ye shall afflict your souls; ye shall do no work with your hands, whether it be one born in your own country, or a stranger that sojourneth among you.*
>
> 30. *For on that day shall be made your expiation, and the purification from all your sins: ye shall be purified before the Lord.*
>
> 31. *For it is the sabbath of rest, and ye shall afflict your souls by a perpetual worship.*

At this time *ye shall afflict your souls.* This might be taken for a figure of active repentance, were it not added, *ye shall do no work with your hands.* There are two kinds of active repentance: the first consists in afflicting simply the flesh by fasts, penances, austerities, mortifications, so as to reduce this flesh to subjection; the second consists in having, as Scripture says, a broken and a contrite heart, and the regret of having offended so good a God, who merits all our love and gratitude, but which we have only paid with ingratitude.

There is also another repentance which may properly be called passive, in which our soul is afflicted by the privations of perceptible consolations and supports. We afflict our soul to excess, by our reflections upon the graces we think we have lost, because we do not feel, nor even perceive them any longer. It is at this time *that we must do no work with our hands*, and wait in repose until the Lord manifests Himself. It is then that the soul passes beyond all the purifications before spoken of, expressed by *every work*, and from which it must cease: for nature always ardent, seeking out supports, and desiring consolations and something to satisfy it, places itself in a hundred postures to recover what it thinks it has lost:—it only causes itself to be dried up the more.

It is then of great consequence at this time, not to act by ourselves, and to passively suffer ourselves to be consumed by pain, that it may have all its effect, and purify us according to God's design. Our activity prevents justice from acting: it is only an entire rest that gives it room to act: thus Scripture assures us, that after these times of purification, we *shall be purified before God* of all our sins, which can only be by entire disappropriation. There is a great difference between appearing pure before men, and being really so before God. Simple, active purification makes us appear pure in the eyes of men; and truly so; but we are very far from being such in the eyes of God. Passive purification, or entire disappropriation can alone do that.

It is added, *for it is the sabbath of the Lord, and ye shall afflict your souls by a perpetual worship.* It is after being purified before God that the soul enters into this so memorable a Sabbath, which is not our Sabbath or rest, but the Sabbath of the Lord, in which the soul passing into God finds in Him this perfect *rest and perpetual worship;* since it is wholly employed for Him, and by Him, not being able to be moved by any other thing. This worship is made in God Himself for Himself. Might I dare to say that it is the worship of God in God, and not in us? This supreme adoration is as much exalted as the creature ennobled and elevated to God through the loss of itself can render it.

But it will be said to me, if the soul is in this perfect repose, with what can it be *afflicted?* With nothing that regards it. It is this perpetual worship that afflicts it, for it knows what God merits, and the little it renders to Him. It is either God who in this perpetual worship inflicts suffering upon it, either to render it more conform to Jesus Christ, or for others; or it proceeds from so many creatures, to whom it must respond and correspond on account of its pilgrim state. This affliction may indeed invest the soul, but cannot penetrate to the centre —this divine sanctuary which God has chosen for His Sabbath or place of repose.

32. *This expiation shall be made by the high priest, who shall have been anointed; whose hands shall have been consecrated to perform the offices of the priesthood in his father's*

stead; and he shall put on the linen robe, and the holy garments.

32. *And he shall make an expiation for the sanctuary, the tabernacle of the testimony, the priests, and the whole people.*

Who is he *that must make this expiation?* It is this High Priest, this admirable Priest after the order of Melchisedec. It is to Him that it is given to do it, and none can do it but He.; it is He who has been *consecrated by anointing* in the midst of His brethren, and more than them all; for having been made man, He has become our brother: it is He who was sanctified by anointing, that He might sanctify the others, *and who performs the office* of High Priest *in His Father's stead* for the expiation. This has an admirable sense. God the Father owed to His justice the punishment of the guilty: it was necessary, in the nature of things, that our crimes should be punished to satisfy His justice, which would lose nothing of its rights. But this well beloved Son, this admirable Priest has received the anointing for the expiation: He has received upon himself the bolts of His justice, and has shown mercy on men; He has obtained for them a grace of mercy, which would have been a useless attribute in God, were there not some wretched ones on whom to exercise it. Justice has had in Jesus Christ and through Jesus Christ a satisfaction infinitely greater than it could have taken in the punishment of all men. Thus this admirable Priest having made satisfaction, justice has given place to mercy to be shed on men.

Jesus Christ in becoming man *has put on the linen robe and the holy garments.* He has purified the Tabernacle and the people, changing a figurative worship into a most holy one; He has sanctified the people not by the blood of victims, but by His own blood.

CHAPTER XVII.

3. *What man soever there be in the house of Israel, that killeth an ox, or lamb, or goat, in the camp, or out of the camp,*

4. *And bringeth it not to the door of the tabernacle to be offered unto the Lord; he shall be guilty of murder; and he shall be cut off from among his people, as if he had shed blood.*

5. *Therefore the children of Israel shall bring unto the priest the victims they have killed in the fields, that they may be offered unto the Lord, before the door of the tabernacle of the testimony, and that the priests may sacrifice them unto the Lord, as peace offerings.*

Why does God exact so rigorously *that all beasts killed should be offered to Him*, who declares, that these kinds of victims and burnt offerings are not agreeable to Him? For they had truly no value, but what they borrowed from the future sacrifice of Jesus Christ; their value lay not in themselves but in what they signified. God exacts this ceremony to instruct future races in the obligation under which they are of rendering unto God through Jesus Christ what they have received from Him, teaching the Israelites from that time a certain disappropriation proportioned to the state in which they were. For we must not believe that God was otherwise glorified by this prodigious effusion of blood shed *at the door of the tabernacle*, but in so far as that represented this adorable blood which the Lamb without spot was to shed before His Father's eyes for the salvation of His people.

6. *The priest shall sprinkle the blood upon the altar of the Lord at the door of the tabernacle of the testimony; and shall burn the fat for a sweet savour unto the Lord.*

7. *And they shall no more offer their sacrifices to demons, to whom they abandoned themselves in their fornications. This law shall be eternal for them and for their posterity.*

When God desired *a burnt offering to be made of the fat of the victims*, it was to show that He wished the best things in man to be consumed by the holy fire of His love, to be to Him a burnt offering of a sweet savour. It is this Divine fire which consumes all propriety in good.

It is added: *that they may no longer dedicate themselves to demons.* To sacrifice to the demon is to sacrifice to self-love. All works that are not offered up by pure love to God's glory alone, and which look to other than Him, are consecrated to self-love. How is it to be understood what God says, that those men who sacrifice it to the demon, or self-love, *give themselves up to fornication?* It is in the same sense as that which is written: "Thou shalt destroy these adulterous souls that have withdrawn themselves from thee," (Ps. lxxiii, 27). God is the Creator of souls, their Saviour, their Spouse: it is to be adulterous, and to commit fornication, to draw back from God in order to love something out of Him, or not relating to Him. This is why it is necessary for everything to be first of all *consecrated to God*, and afterwards distributed to the neighbour according to His will.

10. *And whatsoever man there be of the house of Israel, or of the strangers that sojourn among you, that eateth any blood; I will set my face against him and will cut him off from the midst of his people.*

This prohibition to *eat blood* is to make us understand that we must not stop at everything carnal, sensible, or sensual; but allow the earth to resume all these things which pertain to it, so that the spirit pure and disengaged may draw near to God, and be united to Him, who is the end of its creation.

CHAPTER XVIII.

2. *Say unto the children of Israel: I am the Lord your God.*
3. *Ye shall not act after the customs of Egypt, wherein ye dwelt; nor after those of the land of Canaan, into which I shall bring you; and ye shall not walk after their laws and ordinances.*
4. *Ye shall do my judgments, ye shall observe my precepts, and shall walk according as I have commanded you. I am the Lord your God.*

God begins this chapter by these words: *I am the Lord your God:* as if He said; it is I who have a right to command you as your Lord and God; hear My words, that ye may obey Me. I have a right to command you in every way; and ye could not withdraw from My obedience without rendering yourselves

Chapter XVIII.

rebels worthy of death. I command you then as your Lord and God, *not to follow the customs of Egypt or of other peoples:* as if He said: Follow not the maxims of the world: for if ye are Mine, ye must no longer belong to the world: quit the multiplicity of Egypt, to enter into the simplicity of My children: cleave only to Me: shun the world My enemy: I bid you follow Me and hear Me, I, who am your God and Lord alone: *ye must follow my ordinances*, walk in My ways, and do all that I command you: that is, lose all self-will in such a manner, that you have no longer any other will but Mine.

> 5. *Keep my laws and my ordinances; and the man that keeps them will find life therein. I am the Lord.*

If ye always do My will, so that ye *keep what I ordain*, and lose all self-will into Mine: *then shall ye find life.* It is by the loss of our own will into God's that we find a true life: for Jesus Christ becomes our resurrection and our life. He who is not with God, dwells in death. Is it possible to live without Thee, oh true, and only life of the soul? Thou art our God, and an Almighty God, to give us a life infinitely more abundant than {what we lose in Adam, when we are willing to die wholly to ourselves in order to live but in Thee and from Thee.

> 27. *All those who have inhabited this land before you, have committed those abominations, by which it has been defiled.*
> 30. *Keep my commandments. Commit not what has been done by those before you, and defile not yourselves by these abominations. I am the Lord, your God.*

All those who have been before you, have defiled this land by their execrable abominations. This is what may be said at the present time, that almost all follow after iniquity and lying, in withdrawing from God. Alas, how much I fear that it will happen to this perverse race to be punished when they least think it! Scourges overwhelm us every day, and we pay no attention that it is for our iniquities. If we *imitate the crimes* of those God has punished so severely, why should we escape the same chastisements? If we wish to escape them, let us turn to the Lord our God with all our heart, with all our soul, and we shall find life: for *He is our God*, who will make us new creatures in Him.

CHAPTER XIX.

2. Speak unto all the congregation of the children of Israel, and say unto them: Be ye holy, for I am holy, I, who am your Lord and God.

God desires His people to be *holy, for he himself is holy.* So soon as we cease to be holy, we degenerate from this quality of the people of God: for there must be some relation between the people of God, and this God so pure and holy. But what holiness does God require of those who are His? Let us not conceive it to be a usurped holiness, to attribute to ourselves what we find only in God Himself. What God requires is an entire exterior and interior purity of heart and mind, so that we may be able to draw near to this so pure a God, whose holiness is so formidable for criminals, as has been mentioned above: for this same Scripture, or rather God Himself who says to us: *Be ye holy, for I am holy*, also says, HOLINESS BELONGS TO HIM WHO IS. We must then leave Him His holiness without usurping it; but become sufficiently pure to approach Him, and lose ourselves in this abyss of holiness, in which, having none of our own, we shall be participants in the holiness of God; not for ourselves, but in Him and for Him. Be holy, oh my God, and purify us in such a manner that we may not be opposed by our impurities to this infinite purity and holiness, which flows in little streams upon the blessed and upon the faithful people of the Lord.

3. Let every one reverence with fear his father and his mother. Keep my Sabbaths. I am the Lord, your God.

God bids us *honour our father and mother;* for they fill His place upon earth, and He has made use of them to impart to us the life of the body—without which we should have been destitute of being, and of the happiness of knowing God. But how badly observed this commandment is! Children despise their fathers, weary of their existence, and kill them a thousand times with grief: the bad treatment that the greater part of fathers and mothers receive from their children, is incredible; nevertheless, it does not go unpunished in this life, for often the children find themselves dealt with as they treated their parents.

God also bids us *keep his Sabbath days.* These Sabbaths of

the Lord are not a simple cessation from outward work, as some persuade themselves; but first cessation from all works of iniquity; then cessation from our own works; that God Himself may operate in us, in order to enter into this true sabbath, which is the repose of the soul in prayer, and afterwards in God its latter end. This last is the eternal Sabbath, a lasting rest, commencing in this life to endure for ever.

4. *Turn ye not unto idols, nor make to yourselves molten gods: I am the Lord your God.*

We turn unto idols when we depart from God in order to turn towards the creature, whatever it be. When we prefer the creature to God, we make an idol of this very creature. Is it not written that avarice is idolatry (Col. iii. 5). We commit idolatry in every disorderly love. What idolaters there are amongst Christians!

5. *If ye offer unto the Lord a peace offering, that he may be favourable unto you,*
6. *Ye shall eat it the same day, or the day after it is offered; and ye shall burn up with fire all that remains until the third day.*
7. *If any one eat of it two days after, he shall be profane and guilty of impiety.*

When the soul has arrived at the central repose, it may then be said to *offer to the Lord a peace offering:* for it is as a victim offered to its God in a passive state, to suffer everything, interiorly and exteriorly; inwardly, God's operations, whether crucifying or gratifying; outwardly, all crosses, afflictions, persecutions; in general, all that happens to us from God, from men, from demons, from ourselves by our imprudences and faults.

How comes it that the peace offering must be *eaten on the same day it was offered, or on the morrow?* It is to teach us that the soul abandoned and at rest in God, is content with the divine moment, without preparing anything for the future. Its sustenance is the present moment of God's order over us. *The remains* must be burned and *consumed by the fire.* What are the remains? After giving oneself up to the divine moment, and preparing nothing for the future, there come turnings and reflections, which must be allowed to fall, and be wholly consumed in this fire of divine charity.

If one ate of this peace offering several days afterwards, he was guilty of impiety. This marks how much foresight for the future is contrary to *abandon;* and how there is a time for profiting by the present light, after which we can no longer succeed in it. This is what Jesus Christ taught: " Profit by the light while it is day." The present moment must then be the life of the peaceful soul.

> 9. *And when ye reap the harvest of your lands, thou shall not wholly reap the corners of thy field, neither shalt thou gather the ears that remain.*
> 10. *Thou shalt not glean thy vineyard, neither shalt thou gather the grapes that remain; but thou shalt leave them to be taken by the poor and the strangers. I am the Lord your God.*

God gave this commandment to the Jews, to turn them from all avarice, and to induce them to *leave to the poor*, a part of what the Lord had given them.

> 11. *Ye shall not steal. Ye shall not lie one to another. And, let no one deceive his neighbour.*

God absolutely forbids *theft;* so that, by learning to preserve equity towards men, and not usurping what belongs to them, we may at the same time learn this equity towards God—robbing Him of nothing, and usurping not His rights. This is why it is also written: *Ye shall not lie one to another.* For he who reckons himself something, whilst he is nothing, is a liar. He who wishes to be esteemed of men, *is a deceiver*. Of all knaves, thieves, and liars, there are none more criminal than the hypocrite; he robs God of His glory; he imposes incessantly on men, desiring to appear what he is not; he deceives himself; he is full of rapine, and of all iniquity.

> 12. *Ye shall not swear falsely in my name: and ye shall not profane the name of your God. I am the Lord.*

There are many people *who swear falsely*—promising God on oath no longer to offend Him, and turning back to it without ceasing; others who use the oath to deceive their brother, profaning God's name to employ it in fraud—these people are condemned already. Hypocrites swear falsely: they have always God's name upon the mouth, to deceive and impose on men, and thus they profane His name, employing it in fraud and deceit.

> 13. *Thou shalt not slander thy neighbour, nor shalt thou oppress him by violence. The wages of him that is hired shall not abide with thee until the morning.*

Calumny is indeed in use in this age. Hypocrites make use of it, thinking to raise themselves up on the ruins of their brother: party people likewise, believing that everything is permitted them, provided they succeed in their designs. Both make use of authority to oppress those they have calumniated; and this is the height of impiety.

The commandment *not to retain the wage of the hired servant*, is a thing to which few people pay attention: by delaying payment, they cause both the workmen and their families to suffer; they oblige them to borrow, and thus ruin them. But if it is so great an evil to delay the workman's wage, how much greater a sin is it to retain his wage from him so that he loses it? There are some who give alms out of the goods of others, causing poor artisans to suffer loss in order that they may perform almsgiving in an ostentatious manner. All that is an abomination before God. God desires equity in all things.

> 15. *Ye shall do nothing against equity, and ye shall not judge unjustly. Thou shalt not respect the person of the poor, nor honour the person of the mighty; but in justice shalt thou judge thy neighbour.*

There is almost no longer any *justice* upon the earth. Judges are either partial, having a party in view they are so strongly prejudiced, that injustice appears to them justice; others allow themselves to be corrupted. It is very rare that a poor man with a good cause can gain it over a rich man whose cause is bad. Would people solicit the judges were it not to instruct them in the state of matters? There are everywhere honest people, and the world is not absolutely destitute of equitable judges, but how rare they are! And how many there are who oppress the innocent, when *authority* gets mixed with it.

16. *Thou shalt not be amongst thy people an inventor of crimes, nor a secret slanderer; neither shalt thou plot against the blood of thy neighbour. I am the Lord.*

There are two kinds of persons *who invent crimes:* those who, committing new crimes, boast of those they have not committed; and others, who invent crimes against their brethren to torment and persecute them, taking away their reputation from them; these are the *secret* and hidden *slanderers,* a thousand times worse than those that slander openly, to which one gives but slight credence; but these secret slanderers give weight to their slander and calumny, and thus render it without remedy. These libel makers who make no difficulty in inventing and publishing the greatest falsities, depriving honest people of their character, and rendering the calumny immortal by their writings. Oh, how severely will all those persons be punished!

17. *Thou shalt not hate thy brother in thine heart: but thou shalt rebuke him publicly, lest thou sin in not correcting him.*
18. *Thou shalt not seek to avenge thyself, nor bear any grudge against the children of thy people; but thou shalt love thy neighbour as thyself. I am the Lord.*

Brotherly correction is a delicate thing, and seldom used. Some correct their brethren publicly, not because they have erred, but because they hate them: others cry out against them, making known to all, crimes that they invent themselves. In order to correct our brother, we must be without passion, and have a right to do so. If we have no authority to correct him, he must be left in God's hands, without decrying him.

We are forbidden to *avenge ourselves.* Who is there who does not avenge himself with all his might, and who does not say that there is nothing more sweet than revenge? To hear and *forget injuries,* are commandments of both Testaments. Who is there that practices them?

This whole chapter is full of nothing else but precepts of equity, that God desires us to keep. It is only to be remarked, that in all the commandments that God gives in this chapter, He adds almost after every verse, *I am the Lord,* for two reasons; first, to awaken the attention of this people, and to keep them in awe; secondly, to mark that He wished to be obeyed, and that He had the right to exact a blind obedience from these nations. For what God desires the most from us is entire obedience, and death to our self-will: and we may believe that when He gives so many ordinances to this people, and these of so little things that it appears even unworthy of this so Great God, to command in detail things apparently so puerile, it is to teach them, and us, this blind and unreasoning obedience. It is sufficient that He who is OUR LORD AND OUR GOD command us to do anything, for us to do it, without regard to the importance of the commandment. For obedience in little things is more perfect than in great things, which bring their dignity with them. Moreover, little occasions are frequent and daily, and do not allow the suppleness of the soul to fall asleep.

The diversity of these commandments, their frequency, their littleness, render, by degrees, the soul supple and docile. Although we are no longer under the law of rigour, God does not the less exact from us our obedience. Men at the present time have but ten commandments, which they violate without ceasing; and the Jews were exact in this multitude of commandments. It is true that they feared punishment, and had not this obedience of love that God exacts of His children.

CHAPTER XX.

7. *Sanctify yourselves, and be ye holy: for I am the Lord your God.*

8. *Keep my precepts and observe them: I am the Lord that sanctifies you.*

God again repeats to the soul that He desires it to be *holy:* to make it understand that it must always advance in purity: which is done in proportion as it issues out of itself to be lost into Him.

But He assures it at the same time, that it is He who sanctifies it; so that it may learn no longer to seek holiness in the creature, nor perfect purity in any created medium; since it is in God alone that it can be found.

26. *Ye shall be holy unto me; for I am holy, I, who am the*

Lord, and have severed you from all other peoples, that ye should be mine.

He adds, that not only will he sanctify them to render them *holy* like the others; but that they will be holy for Himself, and not for them, having separated them for Himself from all other peoples of the land. All other men may aspire to holiness for themselves; but these here are chosen to be holy for God. Thus are they holy with the holiness put on in God and for Himself.

CHAPTER XXI.

8. Let them then be holy; for I myself am holy, I, who am the Lord that sanctifies them.

This commandment of God so often times repeated, well shows that this people must not think they can be sanctified of themselves, nor be content with a middling holiness. He, Himself, desires to sanctify them, that they may possess holiness in all its breadth, which is the holiness of God; since He sanctifies them by His own holiness.

CHAPTER XXV.

55. The children of Israel are my slaves, since it is I who have brought them out of Egypt.

Oh happy captivity that of souls abandoned to God! They are never freer than when they are more in bondage. To be *God's slave*, is to be so dependant upon Him by the gift we have made to Him of our freedom, that we can no longer use this free-will, except by submission to His divine movements. God commands as a sovereign, and the soul no longer resists Him: it indeed feels itself a slave; but it is so sweet a slavery, that it would not be otherwise, preferring it to all the liberty in the world: and the more its captivity increases, the more also does its freedom increase, as the creature can never be more truly free than when it is wholly swallowed up in the will of its Creator.

CHAPTER XXVI.

3. *If ye walk according to my precepts, and keep my commandments, and do them,*

6. *I will·establish peace in your countries, ye shall sleep in repose, and none shall make you afraid.*

By this universal *peace* which God promises to *establish* on behalf of those that keep His commandments, may be well understood the general peace of the passions and faculties, with which He gratifies those who give themselves up perfectly to Him. For some time they labour in the active way, and endeavour to obtain for themselves the peace of the passions by the religious observance of the commandments of God; but without being able to succeed therein. Nevertheless, in consideration of their labour and pious pursuits, God, by placing them in the prayer of quietude of His infinite goodness, gives them not only the peace of some passions, but peace in them all, and adds also thereto the peace of the faculties, which *sleep* with so gentle a slumber, and so strong as a whole, that nothing can *make them afraid:* all the creatures' threats, and everything that can be said against these souls, alleging that they destroy themselves by this way, and that they are idle in it, can no more turn them from it, nor make them change their resolution.

11. *I will set my tabernacle in the midst of you, and my soul shall not reject you.*

This quietude of the whole soul is the disposition for the first union, by which God comes to dwell by a particular presence in the midst of the tabernacle. He, indeed, *sets his tabernacle in the midst of it;* but it is not yet made the Tabernacle itself; for then the union is not immediate, and there are

12. *I will walk among you; and I will be your God, and ye shall be my people.*

God, however, promises this soul not to reject it. He is so good, that He never rejects us, unless we quit Him ourselves first by our infidelities. He *walks* with the soul; and it always with Him: He declares Himself peculiarly its God and protector, and it is an admirable commerce of love.

15. *But if ye break my covenant,*
16. *I will punish you soon by poverty, and by a heat that will dry up your eyes and consume your souls.*
17. *I will look upon you in anger, ye shall fall before your enemies, and ye shall be subject unto them that hate you. Ye shall flee when none pursueth you.*

The soul has no sooner withdrawn itself from the submission it owes to its God, than it falls into a thousand evils. It retires from *abandon* to God, who, fighting for it, rendered it victorious over its enemies, in order to return to its own efforts, where it finds but weakness and falls. It is even so greatly enfeebled by its own strength in which it trusts, that, without fighting, it falls at the very sight of its enemies; it is so filled and troubled with panics after its infidelity, that it *flees when none pursues it*, removing itself so much the more from simplicity and union with its God, the more it advances in its practices, and buries itself in its own efforts. *The drying up of the eyes* stands here for the annihilation of the Divine lights, which are destroyed by an imaginary fire and *ardour* we procure for ourselves; and then the soul is consumed, for we sow for nought, and labour much without fruit.

18. *And if ye will not yet for all this hearken unto me, then I will punish you seven times more for your sins.*

God speaks now to his abandoned ones, who truly do not return to their own practices; but who also do not hearken to Him to quit themselves in the things He desires, and allow themselves to be conducted as it pleases Him, by the impenetrable paths of His wisdom, fearing to abandon themselves too much to God. Then He makes them suffer *seven times more for their sins*, causing them to undergo weaknesses and trials which he would not cause the greatest sinners to suffer: for the punishment or entire purification of sinners, is reserved for the other life: but for these chosen souls, God draws them out of their proprieties by hammer blows, and by the excess of suffering; and thus such extreme interior pains, as are described in the spiritual life, come only from propriety; and they are marvellously well depicted in many parts of Scripture.

Oh that I could explain here what it is *to be punished seven times more*, and how much God causes a light infidelity to be paid with usury, by the appearance of sin, and pain of sin, and often by sin itself; and how propriety, pride, and self-subsistence are something so insupportable before God, that it usually happens that He permits falls to beat down pride, or at least an appearance of fall, this secret being reserved for His judgment alone! Is it not as St. Paul expresses it? "Lest," said he, "I should be exalted by the greatness of my revelations, a thorn in the flesh, a messenger of Satan, has been sent to buffet me"; as if he said; lest I should appropriate to myself the graces of God, an experience of the lowest misery teaches me what I am by myself, and keeps me in an entire destitution in the midst of the greatest Divine gifts.

> 19. *I will break the hardness of your pride. I will cause the heaven to be over you like iron, and the earth like brass.*

The first *hardness of pride* here *broken*, is the self-support the soul had in its gifts, graces, and its own strength. The second, is this *hardness* in it caused by propriety, previously mentioned, which places a real impediment to Divine union. To destroy this pride and propriety, God shuts *heaven* for this soul: it is *rendered like iron* to it: there no longer flows from it a pleasant dew; God has nothing now for the soul but apparent rigours: He seems no more to listen to it, but rather to reject it. It no longer finds any consolation in heaven or earth: for the earth has become *like brass* to it, in which it can no more taste its sweetnesses. Then this soul finds itself in inexplicable anguish, of which experience alone can give a conception.

But I assure those persons who are in these pains, that they come only from their proprieties; and that what they believe to be great trials from God, are proprietary pains that they know not of: let them, however, abandon themselves, quit all resistance, giving themselves up fearlessly and unreservedly into God's hands, not by formal and distinct *abandon*, which still imparts some support; but really, leaving themselves without hesitation to God's will, allowing themselves, moreover, to be stripped of all good without stirring or resisting, bearing all the enemy's attacks with supreme immobility, without even fearing; being assured that God can alone overturn all our enemies. But so soon as we enter on the defence of ourselves, that is sufficient to cause our fall at their approach alone.

23. *But if even after these things ye will not be reformed, and will continue to walk against me;*
24. *Then will I also walk contrary unto you, and will strike you seven times for your sins.*

God continues to assure these souls that *if* they *still walk* in their first *resistance*, not suffering themselves to be conducted by Himself where He desires, He will increase their punishment in this case: He will not be content with not listening to them, and being stern towards them, so that the heaven remains inexorable, and the dew no longer flows upon them; but He Himself will moreover be *opposed* to them. Oh, if it was known what it is to have God against us, and what frightful torment we suffer thereby, alas, to what would we not abandon ourselves sooner than see ourselves reduced to this extremity? Job, feeling the weight of his horrible destitution, piteously complained that God having become *adverse* to Him, he was a burden to himself. But the creature is so proprietary, that it prefers to suffer such strange things, rather than allow itself to be stripped of a virtue to which it is attached: it thinks even to gain merit by suffering so many ills in order to retain it: but it greatly deceives itself; seeing that it loses the real virtue by wishing to preserve its appearance: in place of allowing this appearance of virtue to be lost when it would preserve the reality.

These reiterated blows, with which God strikes this soul, because of its resistance, are weaknesses relating to mortal sins, with which He overwhelms it in order to make it despair of its own strength, and to lead it to abandon itself fully unto

Him. The soul seems to itself to be nothing but pride. All its thoughts, words, and actions, are full of it: it feels more than than ever attached to the earth and clings to it: it believes itself full of impurity from the head to the feet: it is tormented with jealousy and envy against the persons who belong to God with more *abandon:* it loses all mortification, and it seems to itself to be wholly sensual: it can no more rule itself in anything, nor be content; and the more it tries to do it, the less it succeeds in it: hatreds in the imagination, which it cannot conquer, render it desolate; often they would even seem to be directed against God: anger, which seemed dead for so long a time, wakes up; and hastiness rises up every moment.

All spiritual persons who do not abandon themselves, travel this road, more or less, according to the degree of their propriety, and God's design in their purification: and the more a soul has been elevated by the affluence of Divine gifts, the more profound is its fall by the experience of like distresses. I say, that all those destined for the mystic death go this way, (with the exception of some privileged persons, like the holy Virgin, who never having had the life of the criminal Adam, has not experienced the death of Adam): and it is because whatever fidelity they desire to have, they resist without thinking of it, even placing (for they are not enlightened) their fidelity in their resistance, and being astonished at their sluggishness and carelessness for all good, scarcely being able to perform it any longer; and bringing as much cold into holy things, as they formerly had of ardour in practising them.

25. *I will bring upon you the avenging sword of my covenant: and when ye would flee for refuge into your cities, I will send the pestilence amongst you, and ye shall be delivered into the hands of your enemies.*

This *avenging sword of the covenant* is a knife of division which God brings to the soul, so as to separate the two parts, the superior and inferior, without which it would always resist. Oh, it is then that this separation causes the soul to suffer a strange agony! Seeing itself thus pressed, *it flees for refuge into the cities,* that is to say, it seeks some support in exterior actions, in the practice of virtues, in the conversation of the servants of God, in the frequenting of sacraments; but these no longer relieve it, for the grace of this degree is a grace of *death,* and it is to increase their loss; so that it sees itself, although for its greatest good, *delivered into the hands of its enemies.*

26. *When I have broken the strength of your bread, ye shall eat, and shall not be satisfied.*

God *breaks the strength of our bread*, when, instead of finding consolation in the holy communion, we find there nothing but disgust and new pains. It is a great trial for a good soul that has had respect and devotion for this Divine sacrament, to feel that it is no longer satisfied with this heavenly manna; but on the contrary is always more empty.

27. *And if ye will not for all this hearken unto me, but walk contrary unto me,*
28. *Then I will walk contrary unto you also in fury; and I will chastise you with seven wounds for your sins.*

When God sees that this soul, which He desires absolutely for Himself, *yet resists* His voice, He is not content with *walking contrary to it;* but He still augments its pain, and walks against it in *His fury.* Alas! Then it knows not where to turn: for God breaks it in His fury, as Job had experienced it (Job xvi. 10), his pains becoming extreme beyond all that can be expressed. Nevertheless, certain it is that it is only our resistance that causes them, at least, usually; although it is true that God sometimes inflicts them by His power, causing the purest souls to suffer interior griefs, thus Jesus and Mary suffered them, and St. Paul was often consumed by a sorrow and sadness of heart which his zeal for God's glory, and the salvation of His brethren caused him to suffer; but these sorts of pains are so pure and peaceful, that they may be called all-divine. The other pains caused by propriety, are generally accompanied by some trouble and inquietude, being, as it were, a devouring fire, which, by vigorous and profound operation, causes us to feel the rust and impurity that remain to be consumed. It was in this light that the prophet-king prayed God, not to "rebuke him in His anger, nor chastise him in His hot displeasure," (Psalm vi. 1).

Now, the more resistance continues, the more are the pains redoubled; and it is then that God increases the affliction: for the second time there were but exterior blows for sins according to their distinction; but now *there are seven wounds for sins:* what before was superficial, appears here to have won completely to the interior, and to have formed deep wounds. Oh, what a great difference there is between blows and wounds, and how those who have experienced it know it well! they are the same trials in appearance, being made always upon the seven articles of the capital sins before mentioned; but how very different in their penetration.

31. *Then will I make your cities waste, and bring your sanctuaries unto desolation, and I will no longer smell the savour of your sweet odours.*

God goes still further. He brings everything into disorder in this soul. *Its cities*, which are its exterior and interior senses and faculties, are brought into such a desolation, that they *are changed into wastes.* It is necessary, also, that the centre, and most profound part of the soul, *the sanctuary*, be destroyed and annihilated: there no longer remains any image of holiness; and this God who dwelt there inhabits it no more. Ah! then it is that this so holy sanctuary (but which nevertheless served as a medium between God and the soul), is destroyed with nothing remaining of it. Oh what a strange blow does the soul suffer by the loss of this sanctuary! It is nevertheless a good thing for it in its affliction, and a means of correction, too rude in appearance, but in reality too blissful. From that time, there is now no resource for it. Oh who can comprehend it! Nevertheless it is this total destruction of the Divine sanctuary, or the centre of the soul, which soon ends all the trials.

34. *Then shall the earth enjoy the days of her repose, as long as it lieth desolate.*

As soon as the soul begins to *take pleasure* in its distresses, and desolation, and *in the repose* of its uselessness, and nothingness, delighted to be thus in its proper place, and to serve the glory of God by the loss of all self-interest; it is then usually that all its pains cease, and it is well nigh its end. But it is then also that it can cry, that it has been humbled even to excess, and finds its repose in the most extreme bitterness.

42. *And I will remember the covenant which I have made with Abraham, Isaac, and Jacob.*

45. *And I will remember the covenant of their ancestors, whom I brought forth out of the land of Egypt in the sight of the heathen, that I might be their God.*

Then God *remembers* that it is for Himself that He has brought His dear interior ones out of the country of multiplicity, and that they have been destroyed and annihilated by so many purifications and trials. Oh, then, He draws them out of this state of distress; for He is now *their God;* and no longer resisting Him it is for this alone that He has *brought them out of Egypt.*

NUMBERS.

WITH EXPLICATIONS AND REFLECTIONS REGARDING THE INTERIOR LIFE.

CHAPTER IX.

18. *The children of Israel journeyed according to the commandment of the Lord, and encamped when he commanded them.*

It is the property of a fully abandoned soul, to suffer itself to be conducted to God in such a manner, that it takes not the least step except by the movement of His spirit, ready to perform everything, or to quit everything (all being alike to it) according as it feels itself moved of God. And this is all that is needful for it.

21. *If the cloud abode from the even till the morning upon the tabernacle, and was taken up at break of day, then the Israelites journeyed: and if it was taken up after a day and a night, they journeyed immediately.*
22. *Or whether it tarried upon the tabernacle either two days, or a month, or still longer, the children of Israel remained camped in the same place; and when it was taken up they journeyed.*

These faithful abandoned ones regarded not whether it was *day* or *night;* whether they were in light or darkness: they had no set times or measures to take by themselves: but they left themselves to be conducted without hesitation or doubt, *journeying* or *staying* at God's pleasure with an admirable promptitude, troubling themselves neither about their advancement nor repose, everything being equal to them in God's will.

CHAPTER XI.

1. *There arose nevertheless a murmuring amongst the people from those that complained of their labour against the Lord. And the Lord heard it, and his anger was kindled: and the fire of the Lord burnt amongst them, and consumed the uttermost part of the camp.*

It is so strange a thing this nakedness and desert of faith, deprived of all support, that the soul has great difficulty in remaining contented and faithful therein, without repenting of having bound itself to a way so long and so hard for the senses. For although God is its conductor, yet it has nothing to lean upon, for everything is obscure for it. The excess of this pain causes us *to murmur as if we complained* of God. But this is only followed by a greater affliction; for the soul enters into an interior *burning* so strange, that it suffers the pains of death: and this burning *consumes a part of the camp* which is the repose of this soul: but it is only the *uttermost part;* for this is the repose it took in itself, or in the gifts of God, which must be taken away from it, so that it may unalterably rest in God and His will alone.

2. *Moses prayed unto the Lord, and the fire was quenched.*

Moses' prayer, or the simple return of the soul into its abandon, appeases the wrath of God.

4. *A band of people who had come up with them out of Egypt, fell a lusting after flesh; and sitting down, they wept, and having also attracted the children of Israel, they said, who shall give us flesh to eat?*

This other *people that had joined the children of Israel*, represent the feeble souls, and also the inferior part, which, being afflicted at this nakedness, desires something to feed upon. This feeble part *weeps* in a strange manner, seeing itself deprived of its food which it *lusts after*. It dare not, however, ask directly for what it craves; only it says, *who will give me flesh to eat?* Who will give me some consolation as food? It often even draws *with it* the superior part, which takes part in its pain, and thus sins.

6. *Our souls are dried up: our eyes look upon nothing but this manna.*

These unfaithful persons regret their past practices, nourishing their self-love. They pass in detail what they tasted in Egypt (which is a multiplied country) although these were things pitifully low and carnal. If God desires them to advance further, and that the superior part should have little or no share in these complaints, He gives them nothing; so that no sensible relief may hinder them from going beyond everything to press forward to Him alone. But when the will is mixed therewith, He gives them a delicious food that can content them. And these souls, not seeing that it is a punishment for their fault, believe they have obtained a great grace, in which they are much deceived.

People that are still self-interested say that God performs miracles on their behalf, and that He grants them what they ask: beyond that, they add, *our souls are quite dried up*, and there is nothing to sustain us: *We have nothing before our eyes but manna*, being in the obscurity of faith, which suffers us neither to see nor taste anything; so that we see only this same faith which wearies us: for the manna that is given us, although a pure and substantial bread, satisfies neither the taste nor the sight.

10. *The murmuring of the people appeared unbearable to Moses.*

The enlightened director has the greatest difficulty in bearing with the wanderings of these souls, who regret *the onions*, to wit, their low productions, and cannot be contented with so pure a food as that of faith and abandonment to God: this *appears* to him *unbearable*.

11. *And he said unto the Lord; Wherefore hast thou laid on me the burden of this great people?*

He complains lovingly to God of the yoke He has imposed upon him, *charging him with the conducting* of so many carnal souls, who have so much difficulty in following the ways of the spirit.

12. *Have I conceived all this great people, or have I begotten them, that thou should'st say unto me; Carry them in thy bosom as the nurse carries the little child.*

God's goodness is admirable in thus charging certain persons with so great a multitude of spiritual children, who must be carried in the bosom, nourished, brought up, and introduced into the promised land. Oh Lord, how happy are those to whom thou givest a Moses to conduct them. But this Moses has much to suffer. Alas! he is not only charged with instructing and aiding them; but he must moreover bear all their pains.

14. *I am not able to bear all this people alone, because they are too heavy for me.*

15. *If it please thee, I pray thee kill me if I have found favour in thy sight, that I may no longer be distressed by so many afflictions.*

He suffers the pains of death seeing their infidelities: not, however, pains of regret or of trouble, but pains inflicted by the hand of God: so that when proprietary persons approach such as Moses, they cause them to suffer the pains of hell; and it happens but too frequently, that seeing themselves charged with a great people, who through infidelity do not render themselves pliable to grace, they *long for death* or deliverance from these afflictions.

God often releases them in part, associating with them persons who may aid them to bear the yoke; thus He gives here *seventy elders of Israel* (v. 16) unto Moses, to aid him in conducting His people.

18. *Thus shalt thou say unto the people: sanctify yourselves: to-morrow ye shall eat flesh.*

19. *Not for a day only, nor two days, nor five, nor ten, nor even twenty days.*

20. *But for a whole month, until it come out at your nostrils, and it be loathsome unto you.*

God gives this people what they desire, and contents their taste by some sensible gift for some days, and sometimes even for a long time. This causes them to believe that they have accomplished everything, and have entered on a new life, although it is but a state of pure sensuality and self-love. When the Lord says to them, *Sanctify yourselves and ye shall eat flesh*, it is as if He said: since ye will not have the Lord to

Chapter XI.

sanctify you, sanctify yourselves; return to your practices, and ye shall eat flesh, that is to say, ye shall taste the pleasures of the senses that you esteem spiritual; (which is only to satisfy the gluttony of the spirit:) eat of them until ye be so filled that you are *disgusted* with them, and recognise the value of the former food.

21. *And Moses said, There are six hundred thousand footmen in this people, and thou sayest, I will give them flesh to eat for a whole month.*

Móses still doubts after so many assurances of the Divine power: but this is only done for our instruction. God permits such doubts in His servants, that out of them may come the oracles He Himself pronounces in replying to them. Such was that of the Apostles on the subject of the multiplying of the loaves. *There are here*, said they, five barley loaves and two fishes; but what is that among so many? But Jesus took occasion thereby to instruct them, and to perform His miracle.

23. *The Lord answered him: Is the Lord's hand waxed short? Thou shalt see now whether my word shall come to pass unto thee or not.*

But God shows how everything is easy *to the might of His arm*, and that nothing surpasses His power since it is infinite; we do Him wrong when we measure His power by our feeble reason. Thus does He assure us, that *His word*, which appears often so incredible in the mouth of His servants, *will be verified by His works*, and that one day the effects of His power will be seen in the very things that were thought the most impossible.

25. *The Lord took of the spirit that was in Moses, and gave it unto the seventy elders, and they prophesied.*

Whoever is established in God alone, is so bare and disappropriated of all good, that he suffers everything that had been given him to be *retaken* without resistance, being delighted that it should be *imparted* unto others, for he seeks not his own glory, but the glory of God only.

28. *Joshua said unto Moses: My lord, forbid them to prophesy.*

29. *Moses answered him; Why art thou jealous for my sake?
Would God that all the people prophesied, and that the
Lord would put his spirit upon them.*

This extremely pure zeal for the glory of God alone causes *Moses* to give such a beautiful *reply to Joshua*. Persons well annihilated do the same when souls of grace are concerned about their glory; they do not mind if they lose everything for the interests of God and of souls. *Why*, say they, *is any one jealous for us?* We must be jealous only of the jealousy of God, who is jealous but of His own glory. Thus we ought to be jealous only for God's glory. We should, like Moses, ardently desire *that all* had attained to the same state, and *had* the same *spirit of God*. Oh how beautiful are these words of Moses, and how they ought to be livingly imprinted upon the hearts of all those who serve souls by the ministry of the word of God and sacraments! *Would to God that every one prophesied, and that the Lord would put his spirit upon them!* St. Paul had the same feeling when he said: "What then? So that in every way Jesus Christ is preached; and I therein do rejoice, yea, and will rejoice." All true lovers of Jesus Christ ought to be like so many faithful echoes of this voice, which emanates from a disinterested love.

33. *The flesh was yet between their teeth, and this food was not consumed, when the anger of the Lord was kindled against this people, and he smote them with a very great plague.*

Oh poor souls, tasting new delights which ye thought to be great graces, and which, nevertheless, were but the object of your spiritual concupiscence, God makes you purchase this little pleasure very dearly. You are yet all full of these apparent sweetnesses, when He sends upon you out of His mercy and justice *a great* and frightful *plague*. If it was known with what a terrible plague of death God punishes the spiritual gluttony and sensuality of souls, who, after having tasted the manna of pure faith, return to the sensible, people would be terrified. Ah! how much better it is to suffer the first severity of mercy in destitution than to experience that of justice in a favour procured by sensuality of the spirit.

34. *This place was called the sepulchres of concupiscence.* And

having come out of the sepulchres of concupiscence, they came to Hazeroth, where they abode.

As God has only merciful justice for us, even in His greatest severities, this so strange a punishment in these persons is generally the *sepulchre of concupiscence*; for it is by this long and terrible punishment that they lose all carnal desires in the things of God; and that, leaving in this place all desires, *they come out thereof* without delay to dwell in another place more advanced.

CHAPTER XII.

1. *Miriam and Aaron murmured also against Moses.*
2. *And said, Hath the Lord only spoken by Moses? Hath he not also spoken to us? And the Lord heard it.*
3. *Now Moses was very meek above all the men which were upon the face of the earth.*

It is a common thing for passive souls, when they are in the peace of this state, to think they have passed through all the states; and as they have quite a natural desire of speaking and writing of the things of God, they persuade themselves that they are in the degree of consummation. But they are very far distant from it; and although they say that they have the same spirit as Moses (that is to say, as the souls arrived into God alone), and that God makes them hear the same *language*, they deceive themselves greatly.

God, seeing this mistake, Himself takes the part of these persons, so *holy* and so *consummated* in Him; for they have then so great a *gentleness that there is nothing like it upon the earth:* because it is no longer the meekness of the earth, but the meekness of heaven and of God Himself. This *meekness* is not remarked here for nothing, since it is one of the principal qualities that distinguish the souls that are in God alone from the others.

5. *The Lord having called Aaron and Miriam to the door of the tabernacle,*

6. *Said to them, If there be among you a prophet of the Lord, I will make myself known to him in a vision, or I will speak to him in a dream.*

7. *But my servant Moses is not so, who is the most faithful in all my house.*

8. *For I speak with him mouth to mouth, and he sees the Lord clearly, and not by enigmas or figures.*

These words of God contain so clearly and literally the difference there is between these states of passivity and light, and that of God alone, that it is necessary but to repeat the same words in order to have a conception of it. God communicates Himself to the souls of light *by visions and dreams*, under shadows and *enigmas*, which form some division between Him and them; but for the deified souls, He *speaks* to them *mouth to mouth*, and, as it were, essence to essence, by infusion, and not otherwise. And it is this essential word that is infallible, and which can only be received into the essence of the soul, from whence it flows upon the faculties when it is to be expressed. This is what constitutes their difference from the first, whose grace being more in the faculties, is thus sensible, distinct, and perceptible. God adds, that this soul in God *manifestly sees the Lord*, being placed in the truth of God Himself in God; but the others see it only obscurely and under shadowy images.

10. *Miriam became leprous, white as snow.*

This punishment of Miriam shows how God does not fail to smite these presumptuous souls with the *leprosy* of a thousand weaknesses, which *covers* them for seven days. This relates to the seven mortal sins, and (as has been previously mentioned, Lev. xxvi. 24) this is the usual punishment of these kinds of souls.

13. *Moses cried to the Lord, saying, Oh God, I pray thee, heal her.*

14. *The Lord answered, Let her be shut out of the camp for seven days, after which let her be received again.*

God grants Moses this cure of his sister only after she has passed *seven days* in a kind of banishment, that is to say, when she has suffered all the weaknesses that relate to the seven mortal sins, and has borne the confusion thereof before all the people. These souls in their weaknesses are known as such of every one; and this is what causes their real abjection, and is the sure antidote of their presumption.

CHAPTER XIII.

2. *The Lord said unto Moses:*
3. *Send men that may search the land of Canaan, which I give to the children of Israel, one man out of each tribe, every one a ruler among them.*
24. *They cut down a branch with one cluster of grapes, and they bare it between two upon a staff.*

The land is only known by its fruits. This prodigious *bunch of grapes*, carried by those who had been *sent to search the land*, is a proof of its fertility. Now this fruit is *a grape*, preserving in itself the delicious wine of pure love, not for itself, but for him who expresses it. God has all the glory of it, and the neighbour all the benefit. This *bunch of grapes* marks also the union that souls arrived into God, who is *the promised land*, have amongst themselves; thus the grapes are all united in the same bunch. But this union is founded upon Jesus Christ, who is the grape and *the vine*.

28. *Surely it is a land flowing with milk and honey, as may be known by its fruits.*

There flow from this *land*, which is God, our centre, our origin, and end, rivers of *milk and honey*. The gentleness of the persons who have happily entered therein is without limit; and there flows from them an affluence of divine words wholly mild and agreeable, serving as milk and honey for the little ones.

31. *Caleb said, Let us go up, and enter into possession of the land; for we are able to overcome it.*

A soul full of confidence looks for everything from God's goodness and strength; therefore, filled with courage, he also animates the others. *Let us go*, says he, let us fear nothing, although amongst apparent difficulties; for *we can obtain* by God's goodness what we could not conquer by our own strength; and it is easy for Him to enable us to overcome, according to His promise; "in God shall we do great things, and He Himself shall tread down our enemies."

> 32. *But the men that went up with him said: We are not able to go up against this people, for they are stronger than we.*

On the contrary, souls full of trust in themselves, looking upon it only on the side of their human strength at first despair of ever being able to succeed, and turn aside the others from it, saying that they are too weak to aspire to so elevated a state. It is true that if we take it in the light of our own strength, man can never attain it; but, on the part of *God*, everything is possible, and faith only is necessary for that, according to the promise of Jesus Christ: "If thou canst believe, all things are possible unto him that believeth."

CHAPTER XIV.

> 1. *The people cried with a loud voice and wept all that night.*
> 2. *And all the children of Israel murmured against Moses and Aaron.*

It is strange that they who are full of self-love and trust in their own strength should have so much power to weaken by their false reasonings the faith and trust of abandoned souls, throwing them into such disorder that they even give way to tears and groans for having quitted their first captivity, in which they thought to live in safety, although with great pain. They blame their conductors; they accuse them of being the cause of this loss; and this is a common thing for all the feeble souls who speak to these persons full of self-love, who detail to them sad examples, in order to turn them from this pure way, and to assure them more strongly of their destruction: they spare nothing therein, not being able to suffer people to trust themselves fully to God.

Chapter XIV.

3. *Would to God we had died in Egypt! would to God we had perished in the wilderness, that God had not brought us to this land, for us to fall by the sword, and our wives and children to be taken captive! Were it not better for us to return into Egypt.*

It is a frequent thing for these persons to regret *not having died* in the land of multiplicity, in which they believed their salvation much more secured. They see, however, that there is no means of *returning into Egypt*, for all the passages are shut: They wish, at least, *to die in this great desert of faith*, in which there remains a little hope, not yet being altogether lost.

They well know that God alone can bring them into this land promised to them; therefore they say, *Let not the Lord conduct us there.* They enter into distrust of His goodness and power, and by their infidelity issue out of *abandon*, which causes them an incredible affliction. Oh poor blind ones! You think that so many enemies, whose strength is shown you in proportion as you recognise your own weakness, must be destroyed by your own strength! Ah, how you are deceived! This is why you say that *your wives and children*—that is, your inferior part and senses—are going to remain for ever in a new *captivity*, and that you yourselves are going to *fall under the sword* of sin. No, no, you will never fall if you come not out of *abandon;* and the evil that you do yourselves by thus distrusting God is greater than all those you fear; for in souls of your degree, this is the source of all the sins you can fall into.

4. *And they began to say one to another: Let us make a captain, and let us return into Egypt.*

They are so blind that they still *consult* to *return* to their first activity without considering that this would be impossible for them; and that, no longer having God to conduct them, since He desires another thing of them, they would fall defenceless into the hands of other enemies more powerful than those they dread in the country that God desires to bring them into.

This *captain* is a new director they are desirous of choosing, that he may make them return to their former activities; a director who flatters their own judgment.

5. *Then Moses and Aaron fell on their faces to the ground before the whole multitude of the children of Israel.*

This *prostration of Moses and Aaron* denotes how easily very spiritual persons can give up the conducting of souls committed to their trust. Not so the others; they have a thousand attachments, and endeavour by every means to retain the souls under their direction. The former act in the manner they do, because they are annihilated; and, recognising in themselves neither any goodness, nor strength to aid the souls that God gives them, they resign them without difficulty; but the others act quite the contrary by a strange presumption, believing themselves more fit to conduct than any other.

6. *But Joshua and Caleb, who were of those who had spied the land, rent their clothes,*
7. *And said unto all the company of the children of Israel: The land which we have surveyed is a very good land.*
8. *If the Lord delight in us, then he will bring us into this land, and will give unto us a land where flow milk and honey.*

There are often found amongst the great number of these feeble souls persons both firm and advanced, who sustain the others, and who assure them from their experience of the *goodness* of this land promised to those who abandon themselves purely unto God, and the advantage of being established therein. They add, that it is easy to arrive there if *the Lord delight in them*, that is to say, if He conduct, and they suffer themselves to be conducted to Him, they will not fail to be brought into the land; for the reason why, out of so many persons who come out of the multiplied way, there are so few that arrive into God, and almost all die on the way, is this, that they enter into distrust, and thus slacken their pace and stop, and often issue completely out of the way.

9. *Beware of rebelling against the Lord, neither fear ye the people of this land; for we can devour them like bread. Their defence is taken away from them, and the Lord is with us: fear them not.*

Scripture declares that it is *rebellion* to issue out of *abandon*, and to be unwilling to be conducted to God, coming out of His Divine order, and blind dependence upon Him, to enter by reflections on self-guidance; it counsels us that we must not *be afraid*, but courageously abandon ourselves; for with the strength of God we *we can devour our* open *enemies*, and sin itself, *like bread*, without their being able to harm us; for they can only do so when we issue out of *abandon;* since while we remain in God's hands, all the power and malignity of sin is removed from us; and it, as well as all the demons, remains powerless against us, seeing that the *defence* and power of sin are its sting and malice; and these being taken from them, and God not withdrawing from us, but our will remaining united to His own, there is nothing to fear for us. But it must be remarked that I say so long as we remain united to God's will and in *abandon*, for out of that everything may harm us; nevertheless, we shall never perish except by distrust and want of faith and courage to abandon ourselves amidst all perils, without in the least regarding our own interest, or what may happen there from.

10. *But all the congregation cried out against them, and desired to stone them. And the glory of the Lord appeared above the tabernacle unto all the children of Israel.*

Those under the influence of reflection, and alarmed from their fear, listen not to the wise remonstrances made to them: they even *wish to stone* those that give them so good advice; that is, to wish to convince themselves by reasonings proceeding from the hardness of their heart; but God, whose goodness is infinite, seeing them ready to perish altogether, sends them a ray of His light, which is *the glory* of His majesty quickly discovered to them.

11. *The Lord said unto Moses: How long will this people murmur against me? How long will it be ere they believe me, after all the miracles I have done before them?*

At the same time He justly complains of the *little faith of this people* who doubt, and thus would sink into the abyss, did God not stretch out the hand to them; for nothing wounds His goodness so much as distrust, above all, after having given us so many *proofs of his power* and protection.

12. *I will smite them with the pestilence, and will consume them; but for thee, I will make thee the head of a great people mightier than they.*

13. *Moses said unto the Lord: The Egyptians, out of the midst of whom thou hast brought this people,*
14. *And the inhabitants of this land, learning that thou, who dwelt in the midst of this people, and wert seen face to face,*
15. *Hast killed this innumerable people as one man, will say:*
16. *Because thou hast not been able to bring this people into the land which thou didst promise them, therefore thou hast slain them in the desert.*

God threatens to *destroy* these souls because of their incredulity; but no sooner are they interceded for than He pardons them. Now what is this prayer that His faithful minister offers to Him on their behalf? It is by representing to Him, that it is for His own glory not to suffer them to perish by abandoning them in their wanderings, from which they would all fall, destroyed by real sin (and not apparent) thinking to avoid a peril only imaginary, and falling really into a veritable abyss.

The annihilated man has no more self-interest; therefore, he does not even reply to the kindness that God shows for his person; but being concerned only for the interest of the way of which he has been constituted the guide, represents to God how active persons, seeing those who walk in the way of faith and simplicity fall by some visible disaster, may take occasion thereby to do two things, both unjust to God and to those who abandon themselves to Him.

First, to lay the blame on *abandon* in place of regarding the fault of the creature, which has only fallen from having issued out of *abandon*. They exclaim immediately: Behold what it is to abandon oneself! This way is nothing but deceit; far from having the power of conducting the soul to God, it only *draws* it from the care of itself (which is Egypt), *to bring it to perish in the wilderness* of faith, where, finding itself powerless, having lost the practices that sustained it, it *cannot* be *brought* to God as it hoped, since, on the contrary, He leaves it to perish as a punishment for its rashness. Behold one of the common mistakes in the reasonings of multiplied persons.

The other is, that they always endeavour to persuade people, that those who have unhappily fallen were the furthest advanced, and in the divine state of life in God alone, in which everything is in substantial union, and from which the creature cannot fall away except by a strange infidelity. Therefore they cry out, that they who have thus fallen were of the number of those to whom God *shows himself face to face*, as Moses remarks in this very place ; which is an artifice of the devil to hinder souls from abandoning themselves ; because this holy abandon takes away from him all power over them.

17. *And now I beseech thee, oh Lord, let the greatness of thy power shine forth, as thou hast sworn, saying:*
18. *The Lord is long-suffering, and of great mercy, blotting out iniquity and crimes, and never abandoning the innocent.*
19. *Pardon, I beseech thee, oh Lord, out of the greatness of thy mercy, the sin of this people.*

Moses then prays God for His own glory to draw these souls out of the extreme peril to which they are reduced, so that the others may not have the advantage of thereby taking occasion to condemn this way. He also brings before Him *his mercies*, and how He can as easily *blot out* this sin by His goodness, as He can punish it by His justice. He *beseeches Him to pardon it*.

20. *The Lord said unto him : I have pardoned them according to thy prayer.*
21. *I swear by myself, that all the earth shall be filled with the glory of the Lord.*

God pardons ; but, in doing so, He declares that it is solely for the interest of His own glory that He grants this pardon, so that throughout the whole earth the immensity of His power to happily conduct souls that are abandoned to Him may be known. He *swears by himself* and His own life ; to show by that that He lives in this way, and that it is by it He communicates His life for ever.

22. *But all those men who have seen my glory, and the miracles which I did in Egypt, and who have tempted me now these ten times, and have not hearkened unto my voice,*
23. *Shall not see the land which I promised on oath unto their fathers ; and none of those that have murmured against me shall see it.*

All persons who vacillate and hesitate so much, and who, issuing out of *abandon*, often enter into distrust; who, far from obeying blindly, *tempt God so many times* by their little faith; all these *shqll not see the promised land*—that is to say, shall never enter into this life in God alone, but shall die in the desert and on the way. It is for this cause alone that they never arrive at it. Were they, instead, to allow themselves to be conducted by a blind *abandon*, without thinking of themselves, most assuredly they would arrive at the promised land. But, alas! almost all die on the road; some sooner, others later; but all are deprived of the happiness of seeing it. Not only do they not enter, but they never have a true knowledge of it *by sight;* nor shall they who murmur against the way and decry faith and *abandon* to God, ever have the light of truth to perceive this way and land, that is to say, the repose of the soul in God; they shall never comprehend it in this world.

This figure expresses so clearly and fully the great number of those who through infidelity die on the road of the interior desert, and the small number of those who are faithful enough to arrive at the end, that scarcely in all Scripture will there be found another figure depicting it more naturally.

24. *But my servant, Caleb, because he had another spirit within him, and hath followed me fully, him will I bring into the land which he hath spied, and his seed shall possess it for an heritage.*

Caleb, being of a firm spirit and constant in faith, who had neither hesitated nor doubted, but had allowed himself to be conducted without resistance in blind *abandon*, who had already *seen the land*, and had already been there, coming out of the mystic state to enter into the divine, in which he is yet only on trial and not yet fixed for ever; this *Caleb*, I say, so faithful, *will I bring into the land* which he has spied; I will give unto him this most permanent state in God alone, with which he is already acquainted, and into which he has entered transiently. *His posterity*, the souls of his stamp, who are not distrustful, and who without regarding themselves leave themselves in perfect *abandon, shall have this land for inheritance;* which means that they will possess it in a permanent and lasting manner, and that this state will become so intimate and common to them, and they will have advanced in it in such a manner that it will

Chapter XIV.

appear as it were natural to them; and they will dwell in it as in their inheritance.

Caleb was of the tribe of Judah, which represents the souls strong in Jesus Christ, who is the chief, middle, and end of this family; they possess the courage of the lion, for all their courage is in Jesus Christ, and they have no longer any of themselves. But of all the tribes, there is but that of Judah—that is to say, of all spiritual souls only those who, with a lion-like courage, abandon themselves to God's hands without ever drawing back, arrive into God alone. Nevertheless, this courage is not in them, but in Jesus Christ.

25. *Seeing that the Amalekites and Canaanites are hid in the valley, get ye up to-morrow, and return into the wilderness by the way of the Red Sea.*

Oh, if it was known what hurt is done to interior persons by doubts and distrusts, it would create surprise. These infidelities are the cause of much going back, therefore we see under the figures of this people who *turn back* when on the point of entering this so much desired country, souls retracing their steps and *returning* to the first desert from which they had set out. It is thus with many who pass all their life in doing and undoing, and who, without any notable advance, die at the end of twenty years in the same state, having done nothing but advance and go back; for we must necessarily do either the one or the other in the ways of the spirit.

26. *And the Lord spake unto Moses and Aaron, saying:*
27. *How long will this wicked people murmur against me? I have heard the murmurings of the children of Israel.*

God calls those people *wicked* who speak against the way of truth by which He conducts these souls in blind *abandon;* and He is greatly offended at them. How could those be other than wicked, who are opposed to God and His dearest friends, and who fight against what He esteems the most? However good their intention may be, their zeal is not according to knowledge nor true discernment.

28. *I swear by myself, saith the Lord, that I will do unto you as ye have spoken in my presence.*

This *oath* that the Lord swears *by himself*, shows the magnitude of the offence which has been committed against Him. To doubt His power, is to doubt His Being; and it is to take away from His title of God either to doubt His power or goodness; His power to perform what He promises, His goodness to will it: thus He adds, *I will do unto you as ye have spoken in my presence:* as if He said, Ye shall be treated just as you have trusted yourselves to My power and goodness, and as ye have doubted both.

29. *Your carcases shall fall in this wilderness, and all that were numbered of you, from twenty years old and upward, which have murmured against me,*

30. *Ye shall not enter into the land: Caleb and Joshua alone shall enter.*

Ye *shall all die* on the way and *in the wilderness*, without arriving at the end for which I had drawn you from your multiplied labours; *with the exception* of the children who like simple and young hearts, have not entered willingly into distrust, having only fallen therein out of pure weakness and by the influence of the others; or else, who maintaining their hearts in simplicity, although young and little advanced, have neither doubted nor *murmured*.

Out of six hundred thousand men and more who came forth out of the land of Egypt or multiplicity, *only two* arrived in God alone, all the rest having died on the road for want of faithfulness and *abandon*. This clearly shows that all are called to this way and end, namely, to return to 'their origin (which is God) if they were faithful enough to allow themselves to be conducted there. God calls them all, but very few attain to it. This, however, does not proceed from the part of God, whose goodness is infinite, and who fails not to offer the necessary means to those who are willing to make use of them. Not only does He wish all to be saved; but, moreover, that all should arrive at the end of their creation, which is God Himself; or rather, none can be saved, who arrive not at this end before entering into the enjoyment of salvation: which will necessarily be performed in the other life in each chosen one, if it has not been accomplished in this; for it is the Christian perfection, without which none shall enter into the possession of eternal salvation; nothing imperfect, nor the least *propriety*, being able to enter into God, nor into the paradise of His glory. Those then who do not arrive there, are deprived of it by reason of their want of faithfulness.

Those who find so much mention made here of faithfulness, will take this in an active manner, thinking that this faithfulness lies in taking precautions and observations, and in doing much on their own part. No, this is not the faithfulness of this degree, which consists only in believing and abandoning ourselves—in *believing* that God is all good, and all powerful; all good, never forsaking those that abandon themselves to Him, as He assures us by Isaiah; "Can a mother forget her child, and have not compassion on the son of her womb? yea she may forget, but I will forget you never." If God then has so much goodness for all those that trust themselves to Him, to doubt it is to do Him the worst injury. He is equally *all powerful* to sustain us; "Thou shalt know," He says by the same prophet, "that it is I who am the Lord, and that all those who trust in me shall not be confounded," according as it is said of Daniel, that he received no hurt in the den of lions, for he believed in his God. The second point of this fidelity is *destitution*, never resuming ourselves through any cares of our own, never being anxious or concerned about our state, but remitting to God even our salvation, and our eternity. This is what is called blind *abandon*, looking to no self-interest, but suffering ourselves to be conducted to God, as a blind person is led by his guide.

31. *And for your little children, whom ye said were to be the prey of the enemy, them will I bring in, and they shall see the land which has not pleased you.*

These *little children* are, as I said before, the simple and innocent souls, who, although not far advanced, yet arrive at the termination; for, without following their own reasonings, they suffer themselves to be conducted, like little children, without any concern as to where they are led. They do not sin, since they do not even know what sin is. These persons then, simple and innocent, *whom ye said were to become the prey of the enemy*, will be those that I Myself will lead into Me, and whom I shall cause to enter into the Divine life, in order that ye may know the advantage there is in trusting to Me, and the ineffable happiness ye have despised when I called you to bring you therein.

32. *Your dead bodies shall be spread on the ground, in the desert.*

It is necessary that man be truly *dead* in order to arrive at the promised land, and not only that, but also that he should rot by the experience of his own abjection, according as Jesus Christ saith that "except the grain of wheat fall into the ground and die, it abideth alone." This rottenness then is the death of the grain, and death is the cause of its rottenness. And *these dead bodies* that rot *in the desert* are thus the figure of a frightful death and rottenness, which must be passed through interiorly in order to find a new life in God.

As for the unfaithful souls, God does not show them the promised land in this life, but *their bodies* being *dead*, they must remain *in the desert*, which is to perform their purification in the other world, and to serve as an example in this one, by the death which has surprised them before attaining to their perfection.

But the true mystic sense of this passage is, that God causes those who resist Him to pass through a death and abjection much more strange than the others who suffer themselves to be led without resistance; and, as they commit many infidelities, they remain in this state of death and rottenness without ever coming out of it in this life. This is well expressed by the *dead bodies* that lie *spread on the ground, in the desert*, and it is as if God said to those that resisted Him, Ye shall be stretched by the sleep of death, in your own corruption, without ever coming out of it, whilst those whom I have withdrawn have happily issued from it, having believed and trusted in Me.

33. *Your children shall wander for forty years in this wilderness, and they shall bear the penalty of your infidelities, until the dead bodies of their fathers are consumed in the desert.*

The *children* are those who, through feebleness, have doubted, hesitated, and participated in the fault of the others. All must, without exception, remain for a long time in the way of faith, and not come out of this obscure *desert* of the mystic life, until all *rottenness is consumed*, for nothing of this rottenness can enter into God; it is indeed the road by which it is necessary to pass to arrive in Him, but nothing of it whatever can dwell there. It must then be wholly consumed *in the desert*, and be all reduced to ashes by total annihilation, which forms the end of every way, for it leads to the goal.

This rottenness is no other than the corruption proceeding from ourselves through the bad smell *of the dead bodies of our fathers*, that is to say, of the flesh, which has been corrupted by sin in Adam, for it is necessary, as says St. Paul, that "the body of sin be destroyed," and "we have the hope of being delivered from the bondage of corruption, to participate in the liberty of the children of God." And as all spiritual men have sinned, either by themselves, or in Adam, it is necessary also that all pass through the corruption and rottenness, caused either by their own sins, or by the dead bodies of their fathers. This is very evident.

> 34. *According to the number of the forty days during which ye searched the land, a year will be reckoned for a day.*

It is easy to see by this passage that, as has been said above, the observation of the land was nothing but the disposition towards the permanent state which it precedes, according to the usual conduct of God. Therefore it is said that *forty years will correspond to forty days*, and *that a year will be reckoned for a day*.

> 40. *And they rose up early in the morning, and went up to the summit of the mountain, and said, We are ready to go to the place where the Lord hath commanded us, for we have sinned.*

Those who recognise that they *have sinned* through a resumption of themselves, commit a second fault as untoward as the first, it is that they wish to *ascend* to God again by their own efforts, and fancy they are able of themselves to arrive at their end; they strive then to *ascend even to the very top of the mountain*.

> 41. *But Moses said to them, Wherefore transgress ye the command of the Lord, since it cannot prosper?*
> 42. *Beware of going up, for the Lord is not with you, lest ye fall before your enemies.*

But the enlightened director, seeing their error, warns them wisely *not to go up lest they fall before their enemies*, for those who place themselves in states of their own accord, perish there, God not being with them.

> 44. *But they, being infatuated, went up even to the summit of the mountain. Nevertheless the ark of the covenant of the Lord and Moses departed not out of the camp.*
>
> 45. *And the Amalekites and Canaanites that dwell upon the mountain came upon them, and smiting them and hewing them in pieces they pursued them even to Hormah.*

Those persons who desire to enter by their own efforts into the ways to which God does not call them, are so *blind* that in spite of advice they yet continue to introduce themselves therein. But neither God nor directors conducting them, they are *wounded by their enemies*, and are obliged to return with a thousand wounds.

Whence we ought to learn two great truths, first, that God alone can conduct souls in His ways; second, that we must not interfere therein, nor on the other hand excuse ourselves or hesitate when God calls us to them. Fear and rashness, distrust and presumption, are almost equally punished in this people. We must suffer ourselves to be conducted to God, following step by step His divine movements and obedience, without anticipating Him or drawing back, but by a total abandon leave ourselves as God desires, suffering patiently the retardment caused by the fall, drinking in with deep draughts the humiliations which it brings, and being well pleased that God should be satisfied throughout the whole extent of His justice without wishing to diminish any of it, content to remain all our life in our low degree, without aspiring or labouring to draw ourselves out of it unless God do it Himself, and then leave ourselves to be led as a child where He wills.

CHAPTER XV.

> 26. *It shall be forgiven to all the people of the children of Israel, and to the strangers that dwell amongst them, seeing that this people have sinned through ignorance.*

God shows here pretty clearly the difference that there is between interior persons who are His chosen *people*, and others who have not this advantage, namely, that the former commit sin only through *ignorance* and frailty, their will remaining united to God's, so much so that they would rather die than offend Him, and this is so true that when they think that what they have done is sin, they suffer thereby a mortal grief; moreover, did they sin deliberately, they would thus issue from their state, and from the conformity, union, or transformation of their will into God's, according to their degree.

God not being able to bear sin, should the will become guilty, that very moment it would necessarily be separated from God, which would place these souls in a hell, feeling assured of their sin being voluntarily committed. But so long as they remain in their *abandon*, in their resignation, in the union of their will to that of God, in a general sacrifice of themselves and of all that regards them to His good pleasure, generously preferring His glory to all self interest, in a lively experience of His pure love, and in an entire abandonment to His conduct, believe me, they have not sinned voluntarily although they may have fallen into appearances of sin, for all the fruits of grace, and of a pre-eminent grace, are incompatible with crime. Thus, although they assure you themselves that they have sinned, yet you will see that when in confession you ask them if they have a distinct knowledge of having sinned deliberately, they will, when pressed thus, say that they do not know of it. It is certain that grace exists in these souls, and that their will being retained in God, although under mystic darkness, is entirely separated from all that takes place in the inferior part.

29. *There shall be but one law for all those who sin through ignorance, as much for the inhabitants of the country as for strangers.*

This *law is also for the strangers* who have intercourse with the people, that is to say, for those who join themselves to the advanced spiritual ones, and who enter into the same state although they may not have been raised to it, and for all persons less advanced who sin unwittingly.

30. *But whoever shall sin presumptuously, whether he be born in the place or be a stranger, he shall be cut off from his people, for he hath rebelled against the Lord.*

Scripture confirms what has been said before, namely, that so soon as these souls *sin presumptuously*, as much the advanced ones, who from their birth have preserved the love of God, and who have entered early into this way, as well as those who, after growing old in other ways, have at last placed themselves in this one. So soon as they sin voluntarily, they must issue out of their state, and from being in conformity as before, they now become enemies, and thus are *cut off from the people of God*, being separated from those who are only that through the union of their will with God's. This does not, however, hinder these sinners from repenting and being saved, but they no longer belong to this chosen *people*, who may indeed have wretchedness, and may commit faults through frailty, but who never can deliberately will to displease their Well-beloved, and consent to be His enemies, since by this they would issue out of the union with this so dear a people, whose proper quality is love.

It is then that there is verified what St. Paul says, that it is almost impossible for those who, having once tasted God and have since quitted Him, ever to return to Him, at least in a like degree to what they were before their fall. It is even more difficult for them to be converted than it is for great sinners, for no offence wounds the Well-beloved so much as to see a soul, on whom He has bestowed so many blessings, and to whom He has given to taste of the innocent pleasures of His love, voluntarily quit it, withdrawing from His arms where He held it embraced for so long a time, to delight in outward vanities and declare itself His enemy. To think of this alone horrifies one, for then the will is a thousand times more wicked, and the spirit more perverse, than they ever were, having separated themselves from the Sovereign Good after knowing and tasting Him, which the others have not done. Thus there is more malignity in the disobedience of those who have had the more knowledge of God, and the more experience of His bounties; and the surest mark of their fall is, that they withdraw from their way to give themselves up to outward pleasures, even decrying it, and publishing abroad that they have known its errors, and abandoning themselves in fine wholly to sin; in place of which the others being united to God, and faithful to remain in His way, it must not be thought that they sin easily, although there may be seen in them the appearance of sin. And so long as they remain supple and obedient, abandoning themselves to God in spite of their miseries; so long as they are humbled by them, and desire not to offend God, although they may suffer extremely thinking they have sinned, yet assuredly there is no crime.

CHAPTER XVI.

1. *At that time Korah, Dathan, Abiram, and On,*
2. *Rose up against Moses, and two hundred and fifty others with them, of the princes of the congregation and chiefs of council.*
3. *And gathering themselves together against Moses and Aaron, they said to them, Let it suffice you that all the congregation are holy, and the Lord is in them. Wherefore do ye lift yourselves above the people of the Lord?*

It is a strange thing that the punishment they had just received upon the mountain for having desired of themselves to ascend higher than was permitted them, did not prevent them from following their presumption, and from wishing to encroach upon the charge of Moses and Aaron. It is common enough for the more advanced persons, before God calls them to this employment, to be desirous of mixing themselves with the conducting of others, fancying that they are better able to do that than those whom God has chosen for it. It is an error of the spiritual life, which slips into it even from its commencement, to be desirous of labouring for others unseasonably; and it is only a false fervour that leads us to undertake the aiding of them before we have received the talent and vocation to do so successfully. Many fancy themselves capable of conducting in the way of the holy who have scarcely entered therein themselves; and wishing to impart to others the graces that have been only given for them, they themselves lose the fruit, and cannot succour others with them. We must not set about helping the neighbour while we desire it, and have not the experience of divine things and the calling for it, for it is necessary first of all to be founded and established in the interior life.

Jesus Christ, our perfect model, passed thirty years in the hidden and unknown life (applying himself to continual prayer and remaining annihilated before his Father during a period so long that he might have been able to have done an infinity of good to the world), before employing himself visibly for the salvation of men; in order to teach us, by his example, to allow all eagerness to assist the neighbour to die out, and which is generally wholly natural, and to dwell in silence and repose until the time and moment has arrived when God will give us His word and command to labour for the salvation of souls, should He design to make use of us. As for Apostolic employments, I dare affirm that the permanent Apostolic life can only be given when the soul has arrived in God, and that in an eminent degree. This does not, however, prevent obedience from engaging therein, but when it is by obedience, God supplies what is wanting to the state, and He knows well how to do it, so that those who work according to His command produce all the fruit that He intends.

Some persons, even very spiritual, hearing me speak of the permanent Apostolic life, will take that for a certain ardour which passive souls have of assisting others; they possess within themselves so great a good that they would communicate it to all the earth. But these persons are infinitely far from the state of which I speak, which can never arrive until the soul be dead and resuscitated in God, and well advanced in God alone, where everything is found in divine unity. Then it enters into the Apostolic life permanently, by substantial effusion and by essential union, where it is God who acts and speaks in it without its anticipating or resisting Him, nor participating in any thing of its own in what is said or done by it, imitating thus the manner of speaking and acting of Jesus Christ, who said, "I can do nothing of myself," and "I judge according as I hear," and also of the Holy Spirit of whom He says that "He will speak not of himself, but that he will speak all that he will hear." This must be understood thus.

The Persons of the Trinity as united in the Divine Essence are there all equally, and they speak and act by themselves as speaking and acting outwardly by one same essence in perfect unity, but as distinct Persons they receive each other, the Son the Father, and the Holy Spirit the Father and Son, by their eternal emanation.

Now I say that it is necessary for the soul to pass by Jesus

Chapter XVI.

Christ, and by the Trinity in distinction, before arriving in God alone, who is the essential and indivisible Trinity, everything being found re-united in the one Essence, in perfect unity, so that after having been united in Jesus Christ distinctly, and to the personal Trinity, according to the operations appropriate to the divine Persons, everything must be re-united in the point of Essential Unity, where all personal distinction is lost, and where we remain hid with Jesus Christ who is our life, in God, as St. Paul had experienced it.

The reason of this order observed in this reflowing is, that the soul having come out from the unity of the Divine Essence by the Trinity of Persons, and this Trinity having been communicated to it by the graces and merits of Jesus Christ, it is necessary also that in order to return fully to its origin, it should proceed by Jesus Christ, its mediator and chief, to the Trinity of Persons, and by it to the Unity of the Essence, where everything is reduced into perfect unity in the fulness of the divine life, and in unalterable repose.

But when the soul has become re-united in this essential point of God alone, it makes itself known outwardly by its deeds as the divine Persons by their operations; and thus it is multiplied in its actions, although it is perfectly one, simple, and indivisible by itself, so that it is one and multiplied, without, however, multiplicity preventing unity, or unity interrupting multiplicity. This must not be understood solely according to thought, sight, sentiment, conformity, or resemblance, known as such by the creature, but by a real and permanent state, although it usually is not known to the soul (that has the felicity of having attained to it), as in itself and for itself, but it is given to it to know it and express it as in others and for others.

In this state, however, it is not the creature which comes out to speak and act and produce the effects of the Apostolic life. The soul has no part therein. It is dead and perfectly passive, or rather perfectly annihilated to every operation; but God, who is in it essentially in most perfect unity, where all the Trinity and personal distinction is found re-united, comes out Himself by His operations without ceasing to be everything within, and without quitting the unity of the centre, He diffuses Himself over the faculties, performing by them and with them, sometimes the office of the Word, instructing, acting, conversing; sometimes the office of the Holy Spirit, sanctifying, setting on fire with love, melting the most secret places of hearts, and speaking by the mouth of this creature, which remains perfectly passive to all that God the Word, and God the Holy Spirit operate in it and out of it by its organism, whilst this soul (void of all propriety and distinction, not only of persons, but of itself), dwells essentially united to God in the centre, which is God Himself, where everything is in the perfect repose of the essential unity of God, whilst also the same God acts by it in distinction of Persons. All this is wrought without the sight or knowledge of this creature, which is entirely incapable of making this discernment, and which knows its words and actions only when they appear, as it would those of another person. But God reveals this mystery to whom He pleaseth.

Now when the Word *(Verbe Parole)* speaks by this soul, He can only speak by it what He spake Himself whilst living upon the earth, so that this soul makes use of the words of Jesus Christ and of Scripture without seeking them or thinking that it does so. The reason is that Jesus Christ being Himself His word He can never speak but what He has spoken. And this speech multiplied outwardly is found re-united in the Word, and the Word in God, without personal distinction or multiplicity, but in the perfect unity of the essence, as St. John expresses it, "The Word was in God, and the Word was God." *The Word was in God*, behold the personal distinction; *the Word* was God, behold the unity of the essence.

This is then what I call THE APOSTOLIC LIFE, namely, the state in which the soul being dead to everything, and perfectly annihilated, retaining nothing of itself, God alone dwells with it and in it, and it is sunk and lost in Him, living in its centre only from its essential life, but issuing outwardly in its personal life, by distinction of deeds and not of knowledge. This is shown us in the great Apostles who were confirmed in the permanent state of life and apostolic employments only after the reception of the Holy Spirit with fulness, which caused in them an entire void of themselves, and so great a suppleness to all that God desired to operate by them that it is said "it was not they who spake, but the Spirit of their Heavenly Father that spake by their mouth, and St. Paul declares that it was Jesus Christ who spake in him. Every one who is enlightened, or who has attained to this state, will understand me well.

I say moreover, that few persons attain to this state, and that very holy souls die in the consummation in God alone, without God having personally, and by effects, come forth in them. A particular calling is necessary for this, and when it arrives it in no way draws the soul out of its perfect unity in God alone: as neither Jesus Christ nor the Holy Spirit were drawn therefrom, although they act in a different manner outwardly: so that it is certain that on account of the essential and indivisible unity, when the Word acts outwardly, the Father and the Holy Spirit also act indivisibly with it, and when the Holy Spirit acts the Father and Son do so likewise, for they are indivisible in their operation with regard to the creature. This however does not prevent this perfect unity reduced into God alone, from changing names according to the multiplied effects proceeding therefrom, nor does it prevent as real a distinction of the Persons, as it is true that the Essence is one in itself, and according to the relation which the operations bear to the different properties of the Divine Persons, they are distributed amongst them differently: fertility and power to the Father, wisdom and providence to the Son, goodness and love to the Holy Spirit, and these are all united in God alone, where all is power, wisdom, and love.

These apostolic souls in whom this is wrought have neither movement nor tendency, however little, to assist and speak to the neighbour, but God furnishes them with everything by His Providence, and puts His words in their mouths as and when it pleaseth Him.

This being established, it is easy to see that there are very often some who commit faults similar to what is remarked in this part of Scripture, when, finding themselves in the passivity of light and love, they often take as from God what proceeds only from their own fervour, and there may be and there is often a deception. But in the state that I speak of here there is none, and can be none except by coming out of the state itself.

These persons say often, like *Korah:* We are as fit as the others to help the neighbour, since *all* that is in us is *holy;* but the sequel and experience will well show that though they be holy in themselves and for themselves, they are not yet holy enough to perform the office of priest and shepherd on behalf of others, this being reserved for those whom God has chosen for this employment.

It may also be known from this why so many workers, labouring much in the church of God, produce so little fruit. It is that they either meddle with it themselves without being called, or because they are not sufficiently established in Jesus Christ, nor united to Him in order to bring forth by Him great fruit.

4. *And when Moses heard it he fell on his face to the ground.*

Behold the true character of an apostolic man: not only does he never think of conducting any others than those whom God has entrusted to him, but besides he is ready at the slightest signal to quit everything, and far from disputing he gives way immediately, being ready never to mix himself in anything.

5. *And he said to Korah and to the whole congregation, To-morrow in the morning the Lord will make known those that are his, and will choose the holy ones for himself: and those that he will choose will come near to him.*

This reply of Moses, and this manner of speaking, referring everything to what *God* will *make known* concerning it, is admirable. He says that God Himself will cause it to be known who are His, and who are these *saints* whom He has *chosen* for this ministry: but by what sign will they be distinguished?

6. *Thus do ye: Let each of you take his censer, you Korah, and all your company.*
7. *And to-morrow put fire therein, and put incense thereon before the Lord, and whomsoever the Lord will choose he shall be recognised as holy. Ye are much lifted up ye sons of Levi.*

One can scarcely distinguish these persons except by *fire* and by pure charity, which having God alone for its object, as He is its end, sends up to Him an agreeable *perfume*, and mounts up straight to Him without turning, for having no longer any propriety they retain nothing for themselves, and return directly to God all the glory of what He does in them and by them as a perfume of an excellent odour. Now he whom God *chooses* to help others, in receiving from Him the odour of His *perfume*, is truly *holy*, since possessing nothing in himself, he must necessarily be filled with God, and consequently be holy.

These words, *Oh sons of Levi!* uttered by inspiration, denoted the grief that Moses had for these souls more than all the others, for being more advanced their fault is the less pardonable. It is as if he said to them, Oh! ye who were destined to perform what

Chapter XVI.

I do, ye who were to have been soon introduced therein, ye who have been marked out for these divine employments, how have ye done such a thing when ye ought to have recognised your dignity as much superior to that of the others! This manner of speaking equally makes known Moses' gentleness and charity, and his discernment.

8. *Moses said also to Korah, Hear me sons of Levi.*
9. *Does it seem to you a small thing that the God of Israel has chosen you from all the people, and has made you come near him to serve him in the ministry of the tabernacle, and has employed you in his sacrifices in presence of all the people?*

He addresses himself principally to Korah as the author of this faction, and by him to all the others that might be in the same degree with him. Moses then is pained at their fault, because the state from which he saw them fallen was so elevated above that of the others, and he reproaches them so simply and justly, " But *did it seem* too *little* for you *that* the *God* of souls *had separated* you from everything common and earthly, that He had cut off from you all that could hinder His most intimate communications, *that he had* afterwards *made you come near him to serve him in the tabernacle*, that is to say, to sacrifice to Him in the centre of yourselves, and also to serve Him in this state in the things of the interior only, by which He was disposing you for afterwards aiding souls? He did more, for you had already the power of helping them by your sacrifices and prayers, and you were as mediators between God and the people."

10. *Has he made you come near him, you and your brethren the children of Levi, that you may aspire to the sovereign priesthood also?*

Has the Lord bestowed upon you so many graces, *on you and on all the sons of Levi* who are in a like degree with you, that you may aspire to be *sovereign priest*, wishing to mix yourselves with the giving of the divine oracles, which is the final state of the shepherd and to which you have not yet been called, and daring to attribute to yourselves by a great crime what is only due to God, even to meddling in a thing for which He has not chosen you, for in order to be the oracle of God it is necessary to be annihilated so as to mix therein nothing of one's own, and to say only what God says.

> 31. *Hardly had Moses ceased speaking when the earth opened under their feet.*
> 32. *And the earth opened her mouth and swallowed them up with their tents and all that belonged to them.*

This is the punishment merited by those who of themselves put their hands to what God does not desire of them, and who desire to be conductors of others through presumption and self-sufficiency, namely, *that the earth* which seemed to be *under their feet*, that is to say, all the earthly things which they seemed to have trodden under foot and to have been far above, and all sensualities, *re-open* and receive them into their womb. Then they are overwhelmed by the very things they had surmounted, and this earth and sensuality engulf them even to *their tents*, denoting the place of repose, showing that the centre and the will are enveloped in this fall.

> 35. *At the same time there came a fire from the Lord and consumed the two hundred and fifty men who offered incense.*

But *the fire* of love *which comes from God* and tries all things and all works, burning what is combustible, and sparing what is not, *consumed these men* who desired to do what God asked not of them, for all their works merited fire, being only proprietary works, as says St. Paul, that "the fire will try each man's work." But the works of pure love, being exempt from all propriety, cannot be consumed, and their fire burns only for God, being consumed for His glory, whilst the others being proprietary are consumed by the fire of propriety and cupidity, which, robbing God of what is due to Him, attracts *the fire* of His wrath and not that of His love, for the fire of love remounts speedily to Him from whom it came, with the same purity with which it set out, but the fire of justice does not re-ascend until it has consumed the propriety opposed to it.

CHAPTER XVII.

> 8. *Moses found that Aaron's rod, which was for the house of Levi, had budded, and that the buds were blown, the*

flowers sprung up, which, as the leaves spread, were changed into almonds.

God causes *Aaron's rod to flower*, to serve as a perpetual sign that it is necessary to be like it to become an apostle. *His rod had budded*, that is to say, out of its substance there had sprung a germ of life. This is what is done when, from the mystic ashes, as from a dead wood, there is reproduced a new life by the interior resurrection. But it is not enough for this rod to bud (denoting that it has resumed life again and is full of sap), it must, moreover, *flower* (which is a more advanced state after the resurrection), *and bear fruit*, and its leaves must spread out, meaning that the soul is placed at large, so that its works are no longer restrained, and in fine its *fruits* must become ripe. All this admirably represents the interior seasons of a soul in as advanced a state as this. After winter, the time of the mystic death—just as this rod was dead—spring resuscitates and causes it to bud and blossom; summer forms the fruits and gives them increase; and autumn brings them to maturity. This is a very visible picture of the resurrection of the soul in God; its renewal in Him; its confirmation in this state; and its outward extension in perfect freedom, and with the fruits of the season serving as nourishment and sustenance for other souls.

9. *Moses brought out all the rods from before the Lord, and showed them to the children of Israel, who recognised them; and each tribe took its own.*

10. *And the Lord said unto Moses, bring back Aaron's rod into the tabernacle of the covenant, that it may serve as a sign to the rebellious children of Israel.*

The Lord desires this *rod to be kept* (representing the authority and power that these apostolic persons have over those submitted to them), as *a mark* of the state in which those ought to be who are called to the guidance of others. It is necessary, I say, that they have flowers and fruits in maturity, and their leaves all spread out, before attempting to lead.

CHAPTER XVIII.

20. *The Lord said unto Aaron, Thou shalt possess nothing in*

> *their land, and thou shalt have no inheritance among them.
> I myself shall be thy portion and inheritance in the midst
> of the children of Israel.*

O happy *portion* that of apostolic souls! Whatever *inheritance* of holiness the others may have, it is a holiness mingled with *earth* and propriety; but as for the heritage of the *house of Levi*, which is that of apostolic persons, there is no longer anything for them, neither in heaven nor in earth. God alone is *their inheritance;* God is their portion and their possession; and God is to them all things in such a manner that He alone moves them and acts in them. They claim nothing, and have no inclination for anything whatsoever, for they possess the same inheritance that is possessed in heaven, namely, God Himself; and most really, although yet under the vail of faith. Souls who do not permanently possess God are continually desiring, looking for, or sighing for something or other in the degree of their estrangement, but the former souls have no longer any tendency or inclination. They are in expectation of nothing, not even of eternity, for they possess, in an excellent manner, the God of eternity; and possessing the Sovereign Good, nothing is wanting to them, and it is on this account that they no longer desire anything.

But it will be said, should these persons not earnestly desire at least not to lose God by sin? Ah! if they could still think of that, they would be occupied with their own interests, and with something less than God. Thus they would not be in the state whereof I speak, in which we repose in God through a perfect *abandon*, without care or uneasiness about what concerns us. It belongs to God to prevent them from offending Him, and they could not be occupied with anything out of Him, however holy it might be, without coming out of their state of loss in God. Whoever says loss means more than a thousand oblivions. It is possible sometimes to recollect something that has been forgotten, but what is wholly lost can never be refound. That which has only strayed can be found, but what has been lost in God cannot be found without coming out of God. Thus, if this soul could think or fear of losing what it possesses, or could look by itself on what it possesses, by this very thing it would issue from its state as long as these dispositions subsist. God alone and nothing else.

It will be said to me again, that if this soul has some care, it is for the glory of God. To this I reply, that it is incapable of thinking of the glory of God out of Him. God's glory is Himself; this is sufficient without its being able to think of it. The whole business of this soul is to no longer exist. God is its glory; it is His to provide for it. This is not the business of this creature, which has no more occupation, for it is not.

CHAPTER XX.

4. *The people said to Moses and Aaron, Wherefore have you brought all the multitude of the Lord into this desert, that we and our cattle should die there?*
5. *We can sow nothing; there are no figs, nor vines, nor pomegranates, and what is worse, there is not even water to drink.*

This encampment of the people in the desert of Zin signifies advancement in the desert of faith, which appears so much the poorer as it is the more purified, for the soul loses its supports the more, and everything that could give it some assurance out of God. This soul bewails its poverty, beholding itself stripped of the best things, even to no longer being able to make use of the most excellent *fruits* of the church, namely, the sacraments and holy practices. *There is*, it says, *no place where we can sow*, since we can do no works by ourselves. The church seems to have no more fruits for us since we are deprived of all it has of the most holy, the sacraments (from which God well knows how to wean souls when He desires to carry their stripping further). For us there are *neither figs* (signifying the sweetness found in doing good works); *nor vines*, which would enable us to taste of the grapes of virtues; *nor pomegranates* (representing charity by their fruits). We appear deprived of all these great goods. Moreover, *there is no water*, the water of all sensible grace being dried up for us.

3. *Would to God we had perished with our brethren before the Lord.*

It is then that there are felt the pains of death. *Why did we not die*, say they, in our abundance? This is what is said every time they enter a new desert and a more denuded state: for it must be observed that each state has its degrees, and each degree a beginning, progress, and end. Thus the country of faith is long, and one passes there from desert to desert, from nakedness to nakedness, and the last desert is always the more terrible, so that one comes out of one stripping to enter into another, the latter appears always new, and the preceding one seemed even to have great blessings compared with the poverty of that which follows. And what is strange, those who have attained to this point, although they have received so many graces, and have seen so many miracles performed on their behalf, can never be persuaded that they will arrive at the end. And as, when they are in the repose of the union of the faculties—although this is but the beginning of faith—they fancy themselves at the end, and think not that there is anything else to possess; so when they are in naked faith, and in this stripping, they do not believe they will come out of it, and think not of going on to the end. It is the quality of the little courageous to be cast down by the slightest obstacles, and to despair of the enterprise where they think they cannot succeed.

7. *The Lord said unto Moses,*
8. *Take thy rod and gather together the people, thou and Aaron thy brother, and before them speak to the rock, and it will give forth water.*
9. *Moses took the rod which was before the Lord, as he had commanded him.*

God seeing that this people have not strength enough to pass so bare a state, commands Moses to *speak to the rock,* for it was time for this people that the rock should *give forth water,* since all must drink of the living water of this rock before entering into other states, as has been said before (Gen. xxix. 3). This living *water* drawn *from the rock* is the grace merited by Jesus Christ, who forms the refreshment of those who are in this desert, through the conformity they have with his states, not by thoughts, sight, or light of them, but by a real resemblance, although imperceptible, God hiding it from the soul in order to make it walk with more faith, and consequently with more purity. Now here it is no longer necessary to use the *rod* in order to strike, for *speech* is sufficient to cause this water to come, which is Jesus Christ; since being the speech of the

Chapter XX.

Father, this same speech only was necessary to communicate it to these souls.

It is for this reason that apostolic persons produce it in souls by speech, and not by the rod of direction; for it is no longer their authority that acts here, but the divine infusion shed abroad by them by means of speech. This is why Jesus Christ has not desired to reproduce Himself in His Sacrament by other means than that of speech, for speech alone can produce the Word, who is the speech of the Father, and whom the Father produces in speaking.

It is then in faith that the soul enters into conformity with Jesus Christ, without thinking of Him as distinct from it, nor looking upon this relation. In the passivity of light there are given many knowledges of Jesus Christ, which nourish and recreate the soul; but here it has no light of Jesus Christ, and although it never was more like Him, yet it never perceived Him less. It continues to enter into His states by a true conformity, without thinking of it however, bearing them all entire until by Jesus Christ Himself it arrives in God alone, where it will be hid with Him, until it has the power of reproducing Him, and, as it were, incarnating Him anew in souls by its word. For the soul having become God in some manner by participation, has the power of the speech of God, which is entrusted to it to cause the Word to be born in others. Speech essential produces the Word-God in Himself, and speech substantial, received into the soul, produces the Word in others. I will explain myself. God, from all eternity, begets His Word by His speech, and in time, His same speech in Jesus Christ produced the same Jesus Christ in the holy sacrament. Thus this divine speech, out of the mouth of an annihilated soul (although then it is only mediate and not substantial), who performs the office of priest for interior communications, produces the Word in the souls to whom it speaks; and this is why so many conversions are made by the simple speech of these persons. This is clear in St. Paul, who says, "my little children whom I bring forth again with pain until Jesus Christ be formed in you." It is by speech, without doubt, that he brings them forth to the Saviour, as he clearly says in another place, "I have begotten you in Jesus Christ through the gospel;" and it is by this very speech that JESUS is formed in us, God rendering it powerful and efficacious to carry Him into hearts, and to make them conform to Himself.

10. *Moses gathered together the multitude of the people before the rock, and said to them, Hear now ye rebels and unbelievers, believe ye that we can fetch water out of this rock?*

11. *And raising his hand he struck the rock with his rod, and the water came out abundantly, so that all the people and cattle drank of it.*

This is a fault usually committed by those who conduct, namely, not to be content with the simple word of God, which is given them according to the want of souls at the moment they consult them. They always wish to use, as formerly, old methods and general maxims of direction, and the more they have seen them succeed well, the more they cling to them. But this is a thing extremely displeasing to God, as much because He desires to be the absolute director of the directors themselves, as because He alone knows the wants of souls according to the designs He has over them. Therefore the apostolic conductor must, in all things, give himself up to the movement of the Spirit of God.

This shortcoming is here visible in *Moses*, and however perfect he was, God permitted him to fall into this infidelity for the instruction of other directors. As he had been accustomed to perform great wonders by striking *with his rod*, and that had never failed him, he wished to do the same here in order to draw water from the rock. But God not having commanded it, although He had ordered him to take the rod in his hand as a sign of his authority of direction, he added of himself *the striking of the rock*, of which God had not spoken. He even doubted that it was not sufficient to speak to the rock if he did not strike it also, to perform this great miracle; and thinking he did well, he mixed together the work of God and his own operation.

Moses' fault was this, that having been told by God to take his rod, but to *speak* to the rock, in place of speaking he struck it, and thus did not glorify God, which he would have done had he used speech alone. The reason why it displeased God was, that he desired to show before the eyes of the whole people that what was of the old must pass away, and thus to take away from them all support in this miraculous rod. In fact, from this time Moses' rod did no more miracles. The second reason was, that God wished to make known that Jesus

Christ was to perform all His miracles by speech, He who was the Father's word, and that there was to issue from Him, as from a living rock, torrents of grace which He was to shed abroad upon the people. Miracles belong more to the old law than to the new. Thus Jesus Christ seeing that the people being accustomed to miracles, were influenced in their faith almost entirely by them, came to teach us the secret of faith, which must rely purely and simply upon His speech.

12. *And the Lord said unto Moses and Aaron, Because ye believed me not, to glorify me before the children of Israel, ye shall not bring this people into the land that I will give them.*

It is strange that a little fault, or a leaning on anything whatsoever in souls so advanced, should be punished so rigorously; and that God should show Himself so angry at it! He does not, however, take away their grace nor cause them to come out of their state. He does not say to them, ye shall not enter into the promised land, since Moses having had the essential communication, and having seen God face to face, had nothing more to possess for himself; and being in God in so eminent a manner, he could not enter into an inferior state: but God says to him, *ye shall not bring this people into the land which I will give them*, thus showing that He took away from him from that time the supreme grace and perfect success of direction; and that although he had himself passed into the states leading to the most consummate perfection that can be attained in this life, he would not however have the advantage of conducting his flock to the perfection of its origin.

It is thus that God punishes the directors who desire to mingle their own industry with His word, for this industry can indeed cause the water of grace to flow, but cannot give the living water of Jesus Christ, and produce it in souls—this industry hindering this divine production, which the Word of God alone can produce, and that all alone. God also complains here that this infidelity has prevented Him from being *glorified before the people*, as he would have been, if without striking the rock His word alone had been trusted.

25. *The Lord said unto Moses, Take Aaron, and his son with him, and bring them to Mount Hor.*

26. *And strip Aaron of his garments, and put them upon Eleazar, his son.*

God *takes from Aaron his priestly decorations*, in order to divest him of the character of his priesthood, and to degrade him. But this is the figure of the stripping of the spirit of direction. This is a common punishment for those who conduct others and commit like faults. God afterwards gives this spirit of direction to others, for it is never lost. He no sooner takes it away from him who loses it through his infidelity, than he *puts it upon* another, and often *one of his spiritual children*.

14. *At that time Moses sent messengers to the king of Edom, saying,*
17. *Let us pass, I pray thee, through thy country.*
18. *The king replied, I will not let thee pass by my country. If thou comest there, I will go out with my army against thee.*
21. *Therefore Israel withdrew from him.*

Often interior souls would do good in some *countries*, and dwell or pass there for that purpose; but the demon, seeing the great fruit that these souls produce in those they converse with, *opposes* with all his might *this passage*. He *arms* everything to hinder it, and blinding people, he leads them to *refuse* themselves their own good fortune. It is surprising how much is done to hinder these souls from having any communication in the monasteries. The princes of the church arm themselves against them without knowing them. Slander deploys all her arrows, and the world comes with armed hand against these persons, who think not of defending themselves, desiring only to do good. Therefore God often makes His people take another road, or sometimes He arms Himself, and combats so as to make a passage for them; or He even casts the former out from their pulpits and thrones to establish His servants in their place.

CHAPTER XXI.

1. *And when king Arad the Canaanite heard that the people of Israel were come by the way of the spies, he gave*

battle against them, and having gained the victory, he carried off a great booty.

It happens often and almost always that God, by a stroke of His providence, makes use of the creatures to strip these souls of their *booty*. This booty is the honour and self esteem that they have of themselves, and also what others have of them. They lose then all the esteem of the creatures, that being a good that must be destroyed. For it is not enough to be guilty of a thousand weaknesses towards God, which render us criminal both in His eyes and our own, as happened so many times to this people; but they must also appear the same in the eyes of men, and our infamy must be known to all. This is what happens when the creatures carry off our spoils, triumphing over our loss. It is then that people say, behold this abandoned people whom God sustained! He has made them fall into the hands of their enemies. Thus the creatures who overwhelm this interior people by slander, enrich themselves with their *booty*, taking occasion to boast that their way is much superior, and that it is far better to act as they have done, with energy and prudence, than to proceed by this *abandon*.

2. *But Israel vowed a vow unto God, and said to him, If thou wilt deliver this people into our hands we will destroy their cities.*

3. *And the Lord heard the prayer of Israel, and delivered up the Canaanites to them; and they utterly destroyed them, and razed their cities to the ground.*

But *Israel*, or the abandoned souls, have no sooner shown God by a new *abandon* that if they ever again return to their first reputation, they will retain nothing for themselves, and that they will take good care to appropriate nothing; on the contrary, that they *will destroy the cities* in which self-love is fortified. They have no sooner, I say, witnessed their readiness to do this, than God gives them the advantage over their enemies. The Lord destroys them by a blow of His hand, and at the same time brings to view the malignity of slander, and the innocence of His people.

4. *The people were wearied by reason of the length of the way, and felt faint because of the labour.*

5. *And they murmured against God and Moses, saying, Wherefore have ye brought us out of Egypt to die in this wilderness? we have here neither bread nor water, and this light nourishment is loathsome to us.*

There happen similar weaknesses almost the whole length of the desert of faith, because of its obscurity. Feeble souls *weary, are disgusted*, and afflicted; they say continually that *so light a bread tires them*, that is to say, so spiritual a food. But God, wishing to save this people and not to destroy them, punishes them immediately for their weaknesses.

6. *Therefore God sent fiery serpents among the people, and they bit the people and made many of them die.*

He *sends serpents* whose envenomed tongues sting them, and give them *mortal wounds*. These thrusts of poisoned tongues are a thing hard to bear, and so much the more severe as those who suffer them, feeling themselves guilty of many things, bear all the confusion of them both outwardly and inwardly, both before God and men.

7. *And they came to Moses and said to him, We have sinned in murmuring against thee and against the Lord, pray unto him that he take away these serpents from us. And Moses prayed for the people.*

Then these poor souls, all in confusion, frankly confess *that they have sinned*, and that it is by their own fault that they have drawn down upon themselves this just punishment. That if they are not guilty of what is insinuated against them they are so of many other things. They go then to their director and tell him that they know their own wretchedness, all that has happened to them and what they deserve, but that they cannot do anything either in withdrawing themselves from their weaknesses, or in delivering themselves from these wounds, but that he can accomplish with God what he wills. Then *he prays* for these afflicted souls, and God instructs him as to the means to employ to cure their wounds.

8. *The Lord said to him, Make thee a serpent of brass, and set it up on a high place, and every one that is hurt that looketh upon it shall not die.*

God commands a *serpent of brass to be made*, for the remedy of this evil must be found in the evil itself. This serpent was *of brass*, brilliant as fire and thus resembling those who gave the children of Israel these *burning* wounds. Nothing so much causes the soul to die to itself, and draws it so greatly from the chagrin and ennui of the road as the sight of its feeblenesses and the remembrance of what is said of it. This much advances its death. For when weaknesses are not followed by slander it passes more lightly, but when slander awakens the remembrance of the terrible state we bear, it renews the pain and renders the thing unbearable.

The *sight of the serpent* raised by the command of God, which is the mark of His will, calms and *cures*, as also does the union with what Jesus has suffered, when the soul can look upon it, which God sometimes causes to happen, giving it suddenly, and in the light of faith which passes as a spark, a simple view of His crucified and outraged Son. At other times He awakens in the centre of the soul the love of the cross, and this restores life to it. Whoever has the experience of this will confess that it is as true as it is beautiful, and that it is really experienced in souls as it is depicted under the veil of these figures, although apparently they may seem to be far removed from it.

33. *Og, king of Bashan came with all his people before the Israelites to fight against them.*
34. *And the Lord said unto Moses, Fear him not, for I have delivered him into thy hand.*
35. *And he was defeated with all his sons, and all his army passed under the edge of the sword until all were slain.*

God delivers up to these souls Og, who is the demon, *with all his people*, for far from being subjected to him they rule over him, and they would not even fear though all hell should be armed against them, not that they believe they have the power of conquering him, of this they do not think, but it is Our Lord who has vanquished him for them, and they have conquered in Him, so that now, without any labour on their part, they find themselves freed from these enemies who even fly before them. These souls with one word, and by their approach alone, cast down the demons, for the Lord *has delivered them into their hands.*

CHAPTER XXII.

5. Balak, King of Moab, said to Balaam,
6. Come and curse me this people for they are mightier than I.
12. God said to Balaam, Go not with them, and curse not this people for I have blessed them.

Is it not to-day that people desire to make the prophets, that is to say those who fill the place of God, speak against His interior people, and too often there are found some of these persons feeble enough to allow themselves to be won over. But God, who is master of all, knows well how to prevent it. *This* interior *people is stronger* than all the others, for their strength lies not in their arms nor in their own defence but in God.

28. The Lord opened the mouth of the ass, and it spake.

Often although the will of man be determined upon a cowardly action against the interior people, when it is on the point of being executed God causes quite the opposite to be *done* and *said*.

31. God also opened Balaam's eyes and he saw an angel standing in the way and holding a naked sword in his hand, and falling on his face he worshipped.

Then the animal and exterior part finding itself powerless to execute what is desired of it, is the cause of the soul *opening its eyes* to see the danger to which it was exposed, which obliges it at the same time to do quite contrary from what it had resolved.

CHAPTER XXIII.

7. Balaam said,
8. How shall I curse whom God hath not cursed? How shall I defy whom the Lord hath not defied?

This is the manner of speaking of those persons who are enlightened by their faults, as Balaam himself afterwards confessed that it was by his fall that his eyes were opened. They remain after that intrepid, changing nothing of what is God's order, blessing what they are desired to *curse*, and exposing their life for the defence of the truth.

9. *This people shall dwell alone, and they shall not be mingled amongst the nations.*

They *shall* always *dwell alone*, although in the midst of all the world, for their heart being separated from it they are always alone with God. Therefore they are not reckoned amongst the nations, not being a people of the earth but the chosen people of God, and reserved only for Him.

10. *Who can count the dust of Jacob, and know the number of the generation of Israel? Let me die the death of the just, and let my last end be like theirs.*

This man, established in the truth through his fault, knows well the advantages of the interior persons. His manner of speaking so well expresses that of a soul returned from its wandering, and which has a sincere regard for those it wished to afflict. *Who can count*, says he, *the dust* of this people? He compares it to dust on account of the innumerable multitude promised to Jacob under the same simile.

But this also means the humiliations that this people must bear, which will be but *dust* in appearance, but which will be an innumerable dust and will compose the people of God. *Who can know the number* of their virtues and all the graces which God bestows upon them?*

Oh how happy they will be *at death!* since they will be then so much the more elevated in glory as they are now abased. Oh that I may *die the death of the just!* It is this death which fears nothing, for they are just from the justice of God, not being able to attribute to themselves anything of all God has placed in them, but abandoning all, and regarding it in Him alone. All the justice of man is but filthiness before Him; as Isaiah has clearly expressed it, "All the works of our justice are but as filthy rags." *Oh that my end might be like to theirs!* Oh that like them I may be stripped of all self-righteousness, to have only the righteousness of God! then would my death be like unto theirs, seeing that by this stripping of all righteousness man is placed in his end.

19. *God is not as a man that he should lie, nor as the son of man that he can repent. Will he not do then what he has spoken? and will he not fulfil what he has resolved upon?*
20. *I have been brought to bless, and I cannot turn away this blessing.*

This addition to what has been already said shows how the justice of man is varying and *changeable*, but that which comes from God is not, and *can never lie;* therefore those whom God has clad with His justice can never incur His curse, for then He would curse what is His own. To be cursed of God they would require to lose first His justice, rebecoming proprietary without which they remain immovable in their blessing.

21. *There is no idol in Jacob, nor statue in Israel. The Lord his God is with him, and the cry of the king's victory resoundeth in him.*

By *idols* is understood propriety, which is banished from the interior people; and by *statues* is denoted lying, which covers itself with the mantle of truth. This interior people then is as much removed from disguise and duplicity as it is removed from propriety. The love of ourselves gives birth to lying, and pure charity is the mother of truth. *In this* innocent *people*, then, *there is found neither* propriety nor lying. Therefore *the Lord* their God *is with them*, not being able to be separated from a soul no longer proprietary. For He Himself fills up the void caused by its renouncing its propriety.

It is on this account that *a cry of victory resounds in them*, because existing of themselves no longer, and God alone being in them as Sovereign King whom nothing resists, this cry of the *king's victory*, causes itself to be heard *in them*. Observe it is the king's victory and not the victory of the people, and that this king is not out of this people, but in the midst of them. O beautiful difference! So long as man can work by his own efforts, and fight with his own arms, the victory is attributed to him. When God walked before him it was said that the Lord fights for him, and walks at his head. At that time the union is yet only in the faculties. There still remain some enemies whom God Himself destroys, the soul being passive to His operation. But here the cry of the king's victory is continual in this soul; God having taken possession of its centre, He is victorious king, and this centre chants unceasingly the *victory of its king*. It even makes it *resound* by great *cries*, for there are no more combats to sustain. When the union is yet only in the faculties, although God is victorious, walking at the head of the army, it always costs something, and the victory is often gained only after some wounds. But here it is not the same; the victory is without combat, and it is permanent and durable, as the Sovereignty of God in this soul is immoveable.

23. *Surely there are no augurs in Jacob, nor soothsayers in Israel. It will be told in their time to Jacob and Israel what God hath wrought.*

The augurs and soothsayers denote those who are in the state of light, infinitely inferior to this state, since then the soul yet possesses itself. O how far removed that is from the state of faith and perfect *abandon!* When it will be recognised, either during the day of the same faith or in eternity, *this people* (who have been conducted by the way of faith and abandon), *will be told* with admiration of the marvels *God has wrought* in them. This expression points to a great astonishment, as it is said in the book of Wisdom, that the wicked, beholding the just saved with so much glory, will be seized with amazement, and troubled with a great fear, saying to themselves, madmen that we were! their life appeared to us folly, and their death shameful, yet behold them raised to the rank of children of God, having their lot with the saints.

24. *Here is a people that will rise up like a lioness, and lift themselves up like a lion.*

This disappropriated *people rise* with boldness *like the lion* and *lioness*. They elevate themselves by the movement of their faith and interior state, for it is founded on God, who is the highest elevation they can attain to. They are so assured of their victory that they can fear nothing, for all their strength is in the lion, even of the tribe of Judah; and having become one with Him, *they rise up like* Him, invested, as He is, with the strength of God.

25. *He shall not lie down until he eat of the prey, and drink the blood of the slain.*

He shall not lie down in death, nor by any feebleness, *until he has eaten his prey*, that is to say, until he has devoured all the bitternesses and obstacles he may encounter. Although the soul be advanced in the mystic life, and may have been stripped of many things, and of the property of its own strength, there yet remains to it another propriety; it is, that it appropriates to itself God's strength, and this usually happens. We know that we are stripped of our proper strength, but we find ourselves yet strong in God; but expecting nothing of ourselves, through the conviction we have of our nothingness, we look for much from God, by a subtle desire that this void should be filled by Him. But the true annihilated one existing no longer, has neither strength in himself, nor in God; but God alone is strong, God alone is mighty, God is everything. This is a degree much further advanced.

Now this soul being thus raised again by the resurrection, and reclad with the strength of God, *will lie down no more* through sin, and even it shall not die until it has *devoured its prey*, namely, what remains to suffer in the states through which it must yet pass, in order, from strength in God, to arrive at the strength of God. There are no more victories to gain, but there are things to be eaten and *devoured*. It is no longer a thing that is to be destroyed. No, it is something that must pass into us, and must necessarily be swallowed. We must *drink of the blood*, even to the last drop, without allowing anything to escape. Ah! if one could express what that means, but it could not be comprehended. I pray the souls that are at this stage not to spare themselves, and not to fall away or resume themselves in anything. For they must consummate all God's will, however horrible it may appear, as one is horrified at drinking blood; so that it may be said, imitating Jesus Christ, "Holy Father, I have finished the work that Thou hast given me to do;" and the more that these persons will devour and consume these things, the more God will swallow up and consume them in Himself.

It is necessary to eat and devour the whole will of God, and suffer ourselves to be watered by all bitternesses, before being devoured by God, and passing into Him by a state of transformation. It is necessary that the will of God should be passed entirely into ourselves, and become, as it were, natural to us (as what one eats and drinks is changed into our substance), before God eats us. God's eating is the reception of the soul into him—the finishing of its annihilation by its consummation into Himself, which is as the digestion of things eaten. Then this devoured and digested soul, radically annihilated, passes in its substance by transformation into God alone, where it dwells in Him, lost for ever. Then there remains only God alone, in perfect essential Unity, and the personal Trinity in its operations, as much outwardly as inwardly, as was said before (chap xvi. 3).

CHAPTER XXIV.

1. *Balaam, seeing that it was God's will that he should bless Israel, went no more as formerly to seek auguries, but turned his face towards the desert.*
2. *And lifting up his eyes he saw Israel reposing in their tents, according to their tribes, and the spirit of God came vehemently upon him.*

Persons who have recognised the goodness of the passive way, and have already entered therein, are yet some time in seeking lights represented by *things divined*, that is to say, perceptible, as if they desired some knowledge of the future; but whenever they comprehend that the most ample blessings of God are for the people who walk in faith, then without going any more to seek for these lights, they *turn themselves* to *the side of the desert* of faith. One can indeed turn towards this desert of one's-self, aided by grace; but we cannot enter therein except God introduce us. To turn one's-self towards the desert is nothing but to abandon one's-self to God, so that He may make us enter therein if it be His will; and to quit all our lights procured and sought after, in order to remain in this stripping and *abandon*, waiting for God to do what it pleaseth Him.

It is then that this soul has *its eyes* opened to *see this people of* faith in the stripping and desert of naked faith, *reposing in their tents*, that is to say, in this same nakedness of faith; for there is a great difference between being in tents and reposing in them. We are in the tent when we are introduced into the desert of faith; but we only repose there when we are far advanced in this same faith, so that we *dwell* there without difficulty and are content.

This people then rested in their tents *according to their tribes*, that is, each according to his degree; seeing that there is no state that does not contain several degrees, some being more advanced, and others less so, according to God's design and their faithfulness: for it is certain that of many souls who walk in the same ways, some are much more advanced than others.

Now, when this interior man, depicted here under the figure of *Balaam*, had abandoned himself to enter into the way of faith, quitting all his distinct and perceptible lights, immediately *the spirit of God came upon him with vehemence,* that is to say, It came with impetuosity to conduct the soul, which being willing to allow itself to be stripped of all natural and acquired light, of all seeking after supernatural knowledges, abandons itself to It without reserve; from that moment It seizes upon it, and becomes its only mover.

4. *Thus saith he who has heard the words of God, and who has seen the vision of the Almighty, he who falleth and his eyes are opened.*

Man is no sooner stripped of his own lights, and reclothed with the Spirit of God, than he is placed in truth; and it is then he is in a fit state *to hear the words of God,* which are words of truth taking away everything from the creature and attributing all to God. Then also he sees *the vision of the Almighty.* He does not say that he saw in vision the Almighty, but that he saw the vision of the Almighty, this state here being above visions, and even above the sight of the power of God out of God; but he saw *the vision of the Almighty,* which means that he saw things as God sees them, and in the truth of God Himself, who knows His sovereign power and the infinite feebleness of the creature; in fine, he recognises in an indistinct manner the all of God and the nothingness of the creature.

Scripture also observes that it was *by the fall that his eyes were opened.* Oh happy fall, producing so many goods, and which, drawing souls out of their pride, opens their eyes to see their own feebleness and the strength of God!

5. *How beautiful are thy pavilions, O Jacob, and thy tents, O Israel!*

He continues to show how his eyes have been opened to the truth. *How beautiful are thy pavilions, O Jacob;* as if he said, oh perfect *abandon* (represented by Jacob), how lovely are thy pavilions! for these pavilions are no other than the repose in *abandon*, which is entire destitution. Oh what a beautiful thing is this state of destitution to those that know it! Not to issue out of one's *abandon* in the extreme trials through which we must pass is something; but not to come out of the repose in this *abandon* when these same things take place is what enraptures God's heart. This belongs to His servants; for it is quite possible to remain in *abandon* without being in repose, being, on the contrary, agitated by doubts and troubles, and pierced with mortal griefs: but to remain as well in *the repose* of this *abandon*, as in *abandon* itself is a rare perfection.

But if these pavilions of Jacob are so beautiful, *the tents of Israel* are not less so. *Israel*, as has been said, is the strength of God. Oh beautiful thing, to have lost all proper strength by the very experience of our weakness, and to have entered thus into the strength of God! But it is a much more beautiful thing to dwell in repose in this strength in the midst of all our feeblenesses. The more the soul sees itself miserable, the more it knows that it is only its God who is strong: this is a beautiful thing: but to remain *in repose* stripped of all strength, and covered with all weaknesses, being content that God alone is strong, without coming out of this repose to regard one's weakness and to wish to remedy it, glorifying thus by one's infinite weakness the infinite strength of God, this is what cannot be too much admired.

6. *As valleys filled with forests; as gardens by the river's-side are well watered, so are the tents which the Lord has established, and as cedar trees planted near the waters.*

He compares, moreover, these souls *to valleys*, because of their annihilation, but which are *full of forests*, seeing that the more they are void of themselves, the more God fills them with His sublime communications. They resemble *the garden* of the Spouse, being *watered by the waters* of His grace; they are near the rivers, for they approach the source, which is God, their only origin. They are *as tents,* on account of their great repose; but they are tents *which the Lord has set up*, for this is a repose which He Himself has made and continues to make, which is taken but in Him alone, above everything mediate; and this is what renders it invariable, depending no longer on anything subject to change, but strengthened upon the Divine immobility. They are in fine like cedars on account of the uprightness of their heart which has only God for its object, and of the odour of their simplicity. For the qualities of the cedar are to be perfectly straight and of a pleasant smell; and they are *planted near the waters,* since candour and simplicity have always a gentle, fresh, and agreeable air.

7. *The water will flow from his bucket, and his seed shall extend like many waters.*

Out of the *reservoir* of this soul, which will be filled from the source, there *will flow* a superabundance of grace upon the others, who being inferior to it will be aided and as it were watered by it. And *its seed,*—the children of grace that God will give it, *shall spread as abundant waters,* which, dividing into a thousand branches, accomplish a thousand goods upon the earth.

8. *God has brought him out of Egypt; his strength is like to that of the unicorn. This people shall eat up their enemies, they shall break their bones and pierce them with arrows.*

The *bringing out of Egypt* is the enfranchisement from propriety which reigns so powerfully in a carnal country. The *unicorn* is also a figure of the strength of God, as it is said in a psalm "With thy help shall we overturn our enemies, and by the power of thy name shall we tread on those that rise against us."

God having then taken away from this soul all propriety, and being Himself in it, consumes by His Divine power all that could harm it or prevent it from attaining its latter end. *To break their bones*, is to destroy self-love (its most dangerous *enemy*) even in substance; and to *pierce* its adversaries *with arrows*, is to exercise towards them an all-generous charity when even it is most ill-treated, confounding them so much the more as it renders them more good for the evil it receives; which is innocently to pierce them by the splendour of its virtues, as it is written, "The arrows of the little children have become their hurt, and the malice of their tongue has been turned against them."

9. *He couched, he slept like a lion, and like a lioness that none dare awaken.*

It is then that it reposes and *sleeps like the lion and the lioness*, being established in the repose of the strength of God; and being permanently there, it comes out no more, for neither demons, nor men, nor sin, nor any creature *dare arouse it* from its repose in God alone when thoroughly established therein.

16. *Thus hath he said, who falling has his eyes opened.*
17. *I shall see him, but not now; I shall look upon him, but not nigh. There shall be born a star from Jacob, and there shall arise a sceptre out of Israel which shall smite the princes of Moab, and destroy all the children of Seth.*

This person who *by falling has had his eyes opened*, confesses that he *shall see* only *from afar* what is to happen to these interior souls, as much because that can only be known in God, above everything mediate, as because their consummation will be accomplished only by passing through impenetrable states; and in fine it is not now the time for him to know it. There will arrive a time when being dead to himself, he shall behold it.

From this abandon carried to the point that God desires, there *will spring the star of Jacob*, which is the speech of God, producing the word when the soul is transformed in God, as has been said. *And the sceptre shall arise out of Israel.* This is the absolute power of the strength of God, and which will destroy everything that could hinder the production of Jesus Christ in souls, and this will be done by the same Jesus Christ, who is sceptre, star, speech, word, repairer, and destroyer of all opposing strength, who overturns and destroys all that leans upon the power of the creature, so that it will only be God's strength that is valiantly maintained, and it will be maintained in souls through the same word by whom all things have been made.

23. *Alas! who shall live when God doeth these things?*
24. *The Hebrews even shall be destroyed at the end.*

This man sighs grievously, recognising these interior marvels yet distant from him, and knowing already that in order to see them wrought in himself by the power of God, it must cost him his life. Oh, he says, *who* can view God's operations, producing His word by the expression of His speech in souls, while there yet remains a breath of the self *life?* This is wholly impossible, since it is even necessary that the *Hebrews* of the Lord, and the holiest souls, *should perish at the end*, so that there may be but the reign of God alone.

CHAPTER XXV.

1. *Israel dwelt then in Shittim, and the people began to commit whoredom with the daughters of Moab,*
2. *Who enticed them to their sacrifices, and they did eat of them, and worshipped their gods.*

It is a strange thing that the most advanced souls, until they are permanently in God, can always sin. Amongst such holy souls there are yet found some cowardly enough to return *to idolatry*, which is, as I have said, the only sin (with that of lying) that they commit. But it is to be remarked that this happens to them only on account of conversing with strangers, attaching themselves willingly to multiplied persons, and even with the wicked, by natural friendships and by amusements, which bring them into the same way.

4. *The Lord said unto Moses, Take of all the chiefs of the people, and hang them up against the sun, so that my fury may be turned away from Israel.*

The fault being here voluntary, God causes *all the chiefs* to be punished for it, for it is the superior part that must bear the penalty. It is necessary that it should *be hanged upon a gibbet*, for God not willing to receive it, although already come out of its own land, it remains, after having resumed itself through its infidelity, *suspended* between heaven and earth; finding nothing upon earth to support it, for God does not permit it to rest there; and moreover, finding no access to heaven, which was the place of its repose and peace. By this suspension between

Chapter XXV.

heaven and earth, it suffers very great pain—the pain of purgatory, by which the soul, being out of itself, and not finding God to be received into Him, suffers a torment like to being hanged upon a gibbet, which cruelly afflicts it and suffocates it.

These chiefs of the people are hanged *against the sun;* because it is to be no longer propitious for them, and because they will find that its light striking them sharply on the eyes, will only serve to augment their pain. This is what happens to these fallen persons, who are still more afflicted by the remembrance of the favours they have received of God, and by the impression of His truth that remains to them.

Behold the punishment of souls who resume themselves and return to propriety in this degree—very different from the first penalty for idolatry, of which we have treated before (Exod. xxxii. 3). This punishment alone can *appease God,* and even cause the soul to re-enter a higher degree.

6. *One of the children of Israel joined himself publicly to a Midianitish prostitute.*
7. *And when Phinehas saw it, he rose up from among the people and took a sword,*
8. *And pierced them both together; and the plague with which the children of Israel were smitten, was stayed immediately.*

The cause of this kind of falls is voluntary reflection, and the desire of withdrawing from God to return to one's self. Scripture calls this *fornication,* for it is to take away one's self from God to give one's self again to one's self, and this proprietary ME is no other than an infamous carrion and villainous *prostitute,* a rebel against God. But the generous director comes to *slay* this sin *with his sword,* drawing the soul out of its propriety; and this being done everything *ceases,* since the propriety being destroyed, these persons can no longer suffer like pains, which they suffer only from propriety, more or less, according as it is more or less strong.

10. *The Lord said unto Moses,*
11. *Phinehas, son of Eleazar, has turned away my wrath from the children of Israel, in that he has been zealous for my sake, so that I should not exterminate the Israelites in my jealousy.*

12. *Say unto him, therefore, that I give unto him the peace of my covenant.*

13. *And that the priesthood will be for him, and his seed of a surety for ever, for he hath been zealous for his God, and hath expiated the sin of the children of Israel.*

It happens often providentially that some amongst the people, who were only to them as brothers, perform with regard to others the office of director, making known to them the cause of their misfortune, and tearing from them their propriety. Now as this is not done through a false zeal, nor to aspire to the direction, but only for God's glory, as Scripture declares and distinguishes it in a marked manner on behalf of Phinehas, there is merited by this the grace of general and ordinary direction. *I give him the priesthood*, saith the Lord; that is to say, I choose him director and apostle, *for he has been moved with my zeal*, and not his own. This has prevented Me from *consuming the children of Israel through my jealousy*, and for My own glory, seeing that Phinehas has himself espoused My interests, and has slain propriety.

God punished Korah and his adherents because they wished to meddle with the direction, seeking therein only their own glory, for the maintenance of which they desired to establish and preserve their self-love. But Phinehas is rewarded, because he puts his hand to correcting only through the movement of the spirit of God, and for His interests alone, and in consideration of his having slain self-love.

CHAPTER XXVII.

12. *The Lord said also to Moses, Get thee up into this mountain Abarim, and there look upon the land which I will give to the children of Israel.*

13. *And when thou hast seen it, thou also shalt go unto thy people, as Aaron thy brother has gone.*

God still left Moses for sometime in this world to conduct His people in the desert; but on account of his infidelity God only lets him *see from afar off the promised land*, without his

Chapter XXVII.

having the consolation of seeing his people established there in perfect security. He must *die, as well as Aaron*, the spirit of direction having been taken away from them on account of their infidelity, to be given to others.

15. *Moses answered God, saying,*
16. *Let the Lord, the God of the spirits of all men, set a man as chief over this multitude:*
17. *Lest the people of the Lord be as sheep without a shepherd.*

He prays God without thinking of his own interests, being indifferent to everything, and perfectly content to die without introducing the people into the promised land. Such a soul can see nothing out of the will of God; and being stripped of all self-interest, it thinks only of the glory of the Lord and the interests of His children. Therefore he *prays* Him to appoint a person having His Spirit *to conduct this people* in what remains of the road until they have arrived in Him; otherwise, says he, these souls will wander like sheep without a shepherd.

18. *The Lord said unto him, Cause Joshua the son of Nun a man in whom the spirit rests to come unto thee, and lay thy hands upon him.*

God told Moses to take him, into whom He had made *the spirit* of direction pass, and that he would conduct the people; but also *to lay his hands npon him* by a kind of consecration, in order to transmit to him what God wished to communicate of grace and discernment by his organism.

20. *And thou shalt give him the necessary commands in presence of all, and a portion of thy glory, so that the whole multitude of the children of Israel may obey him.*
22. *Moses did what the Lord had commanded him.*

Thou wilt finish explaining to him My will, and thou wilt leave him as an inheritance thy authority and *glory, so that he will be listened* to by all those whom he is to conduct.

Moses obeyed willingly, divesting himself not only of authority, but also *of the glory* he had acquired. Many souls, when far advanced, easily resign their authority to another; but there are not found so many willing to give up on behalf of others, the glory they have acquired in their government. If afterwards, those who conduct have great success, the former conductors attribute it to themselves, and desire it to be understood that it proceeds only from the things which were well commenced having been faithfully followed up; but if some misfortune should happen, that is thrown upon him who succeeds to the conduct, because, say they, he does not follow up well the footsteps of the former government. Oh how few there are who, stripping themselves of authority, equally strip themselves of the glory of it! It was in this that Moses was most faithful, and the example of all the faithful, for it is said, that *he did as the Lord had commanded him.*

DEUTERONOMY.

WITH EXPLICATIONS AND REFLECTIONS REGARDING THE INTERIOR LIFE.

CHAPTER I.

30. *The Lord God, who is your guide, will himself fight for you, as he did in Egypt before your eyes.*
31. *In the desert ye have seen it yourselves, how the Lord your God has borne you in all the way that ye went, even as a man doth bear his young son, until ye came to this place.*

God is the soul's guide so long as it is in the passive way, keeping Himself before it, and making it walk after Him. He *fights also for it* in this same state against all its enemies, to make a passage for it. But *in the desert* of faith have we not seen Him, all we who are there, or have passed it, Himself *carry* the soul *in His arms* (to make it redouble its speed) *as a father* (but a Father all full of tenderness and love) carries his little children? This expresses most perfectly the charity by which God carries souls (when they have abandoned themselves blindly into His hands) through all the so dark and painful ways through which it is necessary to pass to *arrive* at Himself, and be received in Him alone.

Again, this marks admirably how God's protection and assistance correspond to the various degrees of *abandon*. When the soul is only being born, God only begins to call it as from a distance, conducting under His orders this people by the medium of man and of direction, until it attains to the coming out of Egypt. When *abandon* is more advanced, God Himself comes to be its conductor; which appeared, when the people having entered into the desert, the Lord went before them in His cloud. But when *abandon* becomes most blind and most perfect, then God Himself takes this so dear a people *in His arms* and *carries them* with as much speed as safety into the true promised land, which is the transformation into Himself.

It must also be observed that, as it is natural where there is more assurance and signs, there is less faith and *abandon;* and that, on the contrary, where there is to be more faith and *abandon*, there must necessarily be less assurance and signs, so when *abandon* is yet feeble and imperfect, God does not do so much on behalf of souls, for they find plenty of supports out of Him. But in proportion as they blind themselves and detach themselves the more from everything to trust in Him alone, He makes them walk by more unknown ways, to exercise so much the more their faithfulness, and at the same time to take a more marvellous care over them, and in fine, when they seem to themselves to be quite lost, and being in a vast and frightful desert without any light of hope, one would say that everything failed them, and that so impenetrable paths can only end in their perdition, it is even then that God holds them in His arms and carries them with more speed and safety into Himself, enraptured that they hope in Him against all hope, and trust in Him without any appearance of success.

CHAPTER IV.

7. *There is no other nation so great that it has gods so near to it as our God is nigh to us, and present to all our prayers.*

It is certain that there is no other way in which the soul can have its *God so near it* as in this one, since He is more in it than itself, and it needs nothing else to make itself heard than to turn towards Him by a simple regard of amorous faith according to its degree.

12. *Ye have indeed heard the voice of his speech, but ye have seen no figure.*

We can indeed *hear* God's speech, which is His word, and even His *voice*, but we cannot *see* in Him any *figure* or image representing Him, for everything that presents a figure cannot

Chapter IV.

be God. This is why there are so many mistakes in the way of lights and visions.

This also shows the necessity there exists for the stripping of all forms and images, whether sensible or intellectual, in order to arrive at pure contemplation and the intimate union, nothing sensible nor distinctly perceptible to the human spirit being sufficient to bring the soul into God, since He is infinitely above all that.

15. *Ye saw no figure in the day that the Lord spake to you in Horeb out of the midst of the fire.*
16. *Lest being seduced, ye make some idol to yourselves or some statue of man or woman.*

For one true vision there are a great number of false ones. The human mind pictures to itself many things, and the imagination forms images like to those that have been seen. Therefore in the way of faith these are no longer mentioned, because all the sensible is taken away from it to render it more pure, and because also these would amuse the soul and prevent it from advancing, keeping it always in itself in what is sensible and distinct, which is opposed to faith.

24. *The Lord thy God is a consuming fire and a jealous God.*

God is a consuming fire, leaving nothing proprietary in the creature without reducing it to ashes. When He comes into a heart He must destroy, consume, and annihilate everything else in it. *He is* also *a jealous God.* Oh if people knew what God's jealousy is, and how He desires no one with Him, however great and holy, it would terrify them! There is nothing that He does not set His hand to to render Himself absolute master, and to destroy all the obstacles that prevent Him from being so alone. He cannot agree with anything whatsoever, no virtue, no holiness can be found in company with Him. He is jealous; that is to say everything. And as He is the most worthy to be loved and faithful of all beloveds, He is also the most jealous and most ardent of all lovers. Therefore He calls Himself at the same time *a consuming fire,* so as to reduce to ashes all that is opposed to Him.

28. *And there ye shall serve gods formed by men's hands.*

Moses announces to his people, that if they do not suffer themselves to be consumed by this fire, but desire to live on supports and figures, they *shall serve gods that are the works of men's hands*, that is, that they will be subjected to the labour of the active life to procure themselves good and holy things.

29. *But if there ye shall seek the Lord your God, ye shall find him, if only ye seek him with all your heart and in all the affection of your soul.*

Nevertheless, he assures them, that in the midst of their activities they *shall find God*, provided, however, they *seek Him in their heart*, which is the place He desires to be found: but this will only be amongst all the crosses and afflictions that accompany this state; crosses, however, sweeter than all sweetnesses. It is in the heart that we must seek God with all our heart, and it is in thus seeking Him that we find the God of the heart.

32. *Ask yourselves of the times that are past, which have been before you from the day the Lord created man upon the earth, and from one extremity of the heaven unto the other, if ever such a thing has been done or seen?*

33. *That a people should have heard the voice of God speaking to them out of the midst of the fire, as ye have seen and heard.*

Scripture assures us that there is no other way than that of the interior, nor any other people than the abandoned people *who have* ever *heard the voice of God*. This voice is the Word; and it makes itself heard *out of the midst of fire*, for it issues out of the brazier of charity and pure love. The soul alone can hear this speech formed in the midst of this sacred fire, and which in burning the heart instructs it in the Divine verities.

35. *So that ye might know that the Lord himself is God, and that there is none other than he.*

Who are they that can hear Him and live? They are those who being mystically dead, are raised again to God, and made alive to die no more; for then they hear this word without dying; and this word which once caused them death, now procures them life. Now all these states take place, and are wrought so that the soul may know that it is *only God alone* that *is God*, and that there can be no true life out of Him.

CHAPTER V.

2. *The Lord our God made a covenant with us at Horeb.*
3. *The Lord made not this covenant with our fathers, but with us, who are now alive.*

This covenant which God had *made* with Moses and the people of Israel, and which *he did not make with their fathers*, shows the extent of the Divine power, and the magnificence of its bounty. For although He had raised Abraham, Isaac, and Jacob to His greatest favours and so high a perfection, and they had even given such authentic signs of their faith and love, yet they had not had so firm a covenant. This is the magnificence of my God, who could not elevate one creature so much, but He could yet discover Himself more to others. He measures not His so peculiar graces according to their merits, for who had been holier than these admirable patriarchs? Was not this people of Israel much inferior? Ah, it is to show His power so much the more that He takes pleasure in bestowing favours always greater and more reserved, often even much more to sinners than to great saints who have always lived in righteousness.

4. *He has spoken with us face to face out of the middle of the flame, upon the mountain;*
5. *And at that time I was the mediator and arbitrator between the Lord and you, to announce to you his word.*

As Moses was drawn from the peril of the waters, which was a kind of shipwreck, to be the conductor of so great a people, it happens likewise very often that God takes persons whom He has drawn out of the deeps of sin to make them signal conductors of souls. There is yet another reason for these so particular favours, and for this so close a covenant which God makes with Moses, and not with Jacob, Isaac, and Abraham: it is that these fathers and patriarchs were only called to the spiritual generation, and not to the office of shepherd; thus they had no need of so intimate an alliance, for it was not necessary for them to have so extended an experience of interior ways.

It must be observed that there are three kinds of souls—first, those to whom God gives a multitude of children, but far removed, and which are yet in the germ of their seed, as the Christians were contained in the blood of the martyrs: these are sanctified by God in Himself, as much as it is possible, having only designed them for this distant production; and He grants them out of His goodness a great number of children, of which they have but very little knowledge. There are others who do not bring forth in Jesus Christ, and yet continue to perform the office of preachers, and to aid souls already formed which God sends them, who gives them also the lights and knowledges necessary for this design, and instructs them in what to say. There are, lastly, others destined to beget souls, to bring them up, to conduct them in all the ways, and to bear them up to the most consummated state, God for this rendering them universal apostles, who bring forth, baptise, catechise, give milk and bread, and medicines according to need, and who, like Moses, conduct through the passage of the desert of faith, even to God.

It is to these great souls that God must give a double grace; and without regarding their demerits, He makes them enter into a real experience of everything, so that they may not only aid others by their lights, but even *bear them in their womb* by a veritable experience. To bear a soul in one's womb is to have experienced all that it suffers; therefore Moses said to the Lord (Num. xi. 12), "Have I brought forth all this great people whom I must bear in my womb?" God *makes*, then, with these persons the most particular and most intimate *covenant* that ever has been, for they are destined for generation and education, and bearing up to the consummation. Generation is accomplished by bringing souls out of Egypt, or multiplicity; education conducts them in the desert of faith; and consummation introduces them into the promised land, which is their end. It is, then, these souls that God unites to Himself in a closer manner than any other, showing Himself to them, face to face— that is to say, joining them to Himself, essence to essence, and at the same time placing them in the truth of that which He is, so that they may not be deceived in helping others.

But although God has made this essential union, He yet con-

Chapter V.

tinues to make the father and shepherd walk by the way in which He conducts the others, sparing them in nothing, so that their experimental light may leave them neither doubt nor hesitation. For however enlightened a person may be, even in divine light, if he has not passed along all the way, he can never truly know what it is. The reason is, that one is apt to be deceived in the recital of things, and the tongue cannot sufficiently express what the soul experiences; moreover, the experience of others cannot make itself fully understood, nor place the soul that is conferred with, in the truth, because persons are different, and God never permits them to make known all that they are; so much the more as they do not well know themselves—above all, in the mystic states—in which their interior is much concealed and they can say less of it.

A person who has an evil similar to another's, will comprehend much better what it is, than he who, without having experienced it, only brings it to light, the light of experience being quite different from that of sight alone; as also those persons who have suffered the same evils, are more in a state to give the preservatives and remedies for them, and to know by what is told them of them, their beginning, their progress, and their end, and, in fine, the present state of those who consult them. These same conductors also serve as arbitrators and *mediators*—arbitrators, to decide clearly what is of the will of God; and mediators, to conduct souls to their last end.

24. *The Lord our God has shown us his majesty and his glory. We have heard his voice out of the midst of the fire, and have seen to-day that, although God hath spoken to man, nevertheless man remaineth alive.*

God *shows His glory* to souls when they are in the passive way of light, He even *speaks* to them, *and they hear his voice out of the midst of the interior fire* which kindles them; but all this is wrought in leaving them their life. They have seen and heard all this, and yet *are still alive*, for these states here demand not the death of the soul, being graces proportioned to its capacity. They think, however, that being here they have passed through all the interior states; and, rejoicing in a living light, and in a great felicity, they persuade themselves that all the states of death of which they hear are either already passed for them, or are only chimeras; they are even offended, and make no difficulty in saying that they have arrived in God without having passed through the frightsome deserts and the most extreme trials of which they have been told something. Oh how greatly they deceive themselves, and how much difference there is between communications leaving life, and those that operate death.

The first *speech of God*, and the communications accompanying it, are graces acting in the faculties, which maintain the fire of love in the will, and cause an increase of *life*, and not the death-blow; but the second word makes itself heard in the centre, and it causes death; for it is this word that is "*the voice of one crying in the wilderness: Prepare ye the way of the Lord, make his paths straight;*" for it is God Himself who is to come, no longer by His gifts, but by Himself; and He must come not into the faculties, but into the centre by the essential union. Now this word, which is to precede so great a state, must be a word of death, veritably causing the total death of the soul to itself, as it is necessary for the body to die in order for us to go to Heaven, and for it to rot and be raised again at the last day: for it is likewise necessary for the soul to die to everything in order to enter into Heaven, which is God Himself.

It is, then, in this light that the interior people said that the first word of God had not taken away their life, since they can hear it and also with it see *God's glory* and yet live.

> 25. *Why then shall we die, and will not this burning fire consume us? For if we hear once more the voice of the Lord our God, we shall die.*

Charity having reached a very eminent point, and its conflagration having become very great, it is necessary that this soul should die by the consummation of *this* very *fire*, which is no no longer a moderate fire that can warm without reducing to ashes, as it did formerly, but which has increased so greatly that it must consume everything, and nothing escape it; there is no shelter from it, it is necessary to die; and *if God speaks* by this second word so burning, the soul must perish by its flame, which not only melts the soul (as the spouse once felt it), but makes it die and annihilates it. The figure of this is clearly enough expressed by St. Peter, who says, that "at the end of the world the elements shall melt with fervent heat, and the earth, and the works thereof shall be burnt up." It is necessary that this fire prepare men for the open day of eternity.

The day of time is seen and felt from the time the new-born infant has its eyes open, although it must be advanced in life to distinguish its light; so when the soul is brought forth to grace, it enjoys the beauty of it from the time its eyes are opened, but it cannot distinguish this light of grace until it has already advanced. All that is the temporal day, demanding neither death nor the consummation of the fire. But in order to enter into the eternal day, which is God Himself, the fire must consume everything, either upon the earth or in purgatory; and this is real and incontestable; for, in order that God may give Himself, and that we can enter into Him, there is necessary an all-divine purity taken in Himself, which absorbs and annihilates everything there is in the creature, either impure or of self, or straitened, which hinders what is purely divine in it from flowing into God. This, St. Paul calls an absorbment of everything mortal in us by life, in order that all mortality be swallowed up of life. So that grace as a created gift, however elevated it may be, causes not death; but God Himself, author of grace, eternal day, light of glory, source and essence of life, must necessarily cause death before receiving the soul into His eternal day, which is Himself.

31. *But thou, remain here with me, and I will declare unto thee my commandments, my laws, and my ordinances, that thou mayest teach them to them, and that they may observe them in the land which I will give them for inheritance.*

There is another time when one can hear the voice of God without dying, and that is when one is already dead; as in heaven the blessed will see God, having been raised to die no more, and having been made like unto the angels. This is why Moses could speak to God and receive His oracles, and *remain constantly near Him*, having been dead and raised again mystically.

CHAPTER VI.

5. *Thou shalt love the Lord thy God with all thy heart, with all thy soul, and with all thy strength.*

God commands us to *love Him with all our heart;* meaning, to admit no affection, however holy and elevated it may be, neither of self, nor foreign, except for Him alone, and in Himself. So long as we do not love God above all interest whatsoever—whether virtue, salvation, or eternity—it is certain we cannot love Him with all our heart, since it is possible to love Him more. And who can doubt but that it is to love more generously, to love without any interest, than to seek in one's love something of self? Natural light alone teaches it to all, who believe themselves more beloved as they see no pretension to any advantage, but only a manifestation towards them of most disinterested good will. He, then, who loves God from interest, does not love Him *with all his heart*, although he loves Him from the heart, since he loves his self-interest along with God.

Whoever loves his own soul with God, and fears to lose it, who takes care of it, and loves to see it decorated with God's gifts, and enriched with great merits through self-affection, *does not love God with all his soul;* since he wishes still to take care of his soul in his divine loving, and he bends back on it a part of the love due entirely to God.

He who excepts something, and who does not lose everything for his God, does not love Him *with all his strength*, since he may love Him yet more strongly, abandoning himself fully to Him without any reserve. He who says, *with all his strength*, means a sovereign love, which goes as far as the capacity of the soul; and it must not be thought sufficient to sacrifice to God through a pure love one's temporal life and strength, if we do not also offer up our eternal life and strength.

O precept of PERFECT LOVE, hardly wilt thou be found accomplished under the heaven in all thy extent! and yet thou must be fulfilled in all thy perfection before entering into the paradise of heaven. This complete accomplishment is usually only found at the gate of heaven, after an entire purifying of the soul has given it birth, either in this life or in the other; and so soon as it is in this fulness and consummation out of this life, the entry of paradise must be opened to it, nothing now being able to retain a soul, which loves in this purity, from flowing for ever into God, who is truly become its God and its all, since He has become all its love.

6. *These precepts which I give thee to-day shall dwell in thine heart.*

It is no longer upon the stone that they are imprinted, it is too hard and too material to contain them. They must be *graven on the heart*, for it is only the heart that can receive this lesson. The language of love is learnt from love itself, and it is love that teaches love. Oh Love-God! it is Thou alone who can teach us to love Thee purely; it is Thou alone who teachest to the faithful souls the pure laws of Thy love, wholly exempt from all self-love, and which those that love themselves cannot understand. Truly, that is the law of the heart, known only by the heart, and not the law of stone, which, by reason of its resistance, cannot contain a law rendering the soul so supple and pliable to all God's will, whatever it be and whatever it cost; for the heart that loves, forgets all self-interest to think only of the friend. It is this law that tears away all our proper heart from itself to give it wholly to God, and that it may repose solely in Him; this, earthly love has comprehended in its laws, saying, that the heart is more where it loves than where it beats. God has given Himself to man as a witness of His love for Him; and man abandons himself all to his God to give Him proofs of his love; and when this perfect state has been attained to, we can no more distinguish whether God is our heart, or our heart God.

15. *For God is jealous, and the Lord your God is in the midst of you.*

What? God is, then, *jealous* of man's heart? Yes; he wishes it entirely, and not a half. Jealousy cannot suffer a companion, were it even a king; God will have none, not even of the best things, and it is this jealousy that leads Him to strip the soul and to make it pass through so many strange states, so that, remaining divested of all natural good and supports, it may be void of everything, and be thus in a fit state to lodge the love of God. To love only for one's-self, the virtues, gifts, and favours of God is not to be worthy of Him. Oh! is God not enough worthy to be loved to give Him all our heart, and great enough to occupy it entirely, without our wishing to retain something with Him.

It is in order that we may love Him with this sovereign love, and to guard Himself our heart, that He *dwells in the midst of us*. We must then be jealous for God, tearing from our heart without mercy all that would desire to lodge there with Him. Happy he who knows the generosity of the divine love! However great and beautiful things he thinks to know and publish of it, he will never know it if he does not experience it; and he only experiences it when it draws him out of himself to place him in God by the mystic transport, which can only be known by those in whom it is wrought, much surprised as they are to commence only then to discover the true disinterestedness and the pure generosity of love, which they believed they had comprehended for many years.

Whoever is placed in truth, knows and experiences God's jealousy so well that he allows himself to be proprietor of no good, however little; and if he did appropriate or retain to himself the least thing, Oh, with what horrible chastisement would this infidelity be punished! Those who have experienced the jealousy of a God could tell things of it that would make one tremble with fear; and the more He desires a heart for Himself, the more is He jealous of it. The Bridegroom is more jealous of His Bride than of His handmaidens, and when He admits a soul to His nuptial bed, O God, He suffers it to have nothing in the world, and tears all from it without mercy.

CHAPTER VII.

6. *Ye are a holy people to the Lord your God, and the Lord your God has chosen you to be to him a peculiar people amongst all the peoples that are upon the earth.*

This language of pure love and perfect charity is heard only by those who have advanced to an excellent degree of charity and naked faith; thus Scripture says that this people of love are *a holy people to the Lord.* This is a people holy for God and not for themselves, for they cannot wish the least holiness for themselves, nor any virtue. Were they to see themselves clad with anything appropriated to them, they would desire it to be quickly torn away, and would have the same horror of it as they would have of the devil.

O holiness, thou art only in God and for God! The sight of this truth will cause the saints, stripped of all other holiness, to see in heaven God's holiness alone, and will make them cry for ever, HOLY, HOLY, HOLY. For as in this abode of glory

Chapter VII.

everything will be in pure and clear truth, all will be thus reduced into perfect unity; and this pure truth and perfect unity being only God Himself, holiness, which is composed of it, can be seen no more out of Him. And as all the blessed shall have received it from God alone, by Jesus Christ His Son, so will they all render it again most faithfully, and without power to preserve an atom thereof, to God alone by His Son. This St. Paul has expressed when he said, that "Jesus Christ must deliver up His kingdom into the hands of God and His Father, when He has put down all principality, all power, and all virtue; and when all things shall have been placed under His power, then the Son Himself shall be subject to Him, who has reduced everything under His feet, so that God may be all in all."

If a soul set on fire of this pure love were to see itself clothed with a holiness for itself, it would go, when placed in truth, to the depths of hell to be rid of it, having attained such a point that nothing is more insupportable to it than propriety, and it would rather accept anything else than suffer the least infection of it that it can recognise. It is on that account that this *people* is *holy to the Lord*, since being no longer proprietary, all their holiness is for God; and it is this that produces perfect charity, giving all to God, and taking away everything from the creature. But as this is rare, Scripture says, that this people of charity is the people *God has chosen to himself* (not for its graces, gifts, and favours), so that it may be to Him a *people peculiar* in love *above all the peoples of the earth.*

7. *The Lord has not joined himself to you, and has not chosen you, because ye were in greater number than all the nations, since ye were of all the fewest in number.*

8. *But it is because he has loved you.*

God *has not united himself* to His dear interior *people, because they are greater*, or more *numerous than other peoples;* since, on the contrary, they are the *smallest* in number, and the least in the opinion of men, on account of their stripping and annihilation, but He has united Himself to them *because he has loved them.* Yes, this people so small, so much a nothing in appearance, are loved by their God; and they are loved gratuitously by Him, without regard to their little merit. Is it not just that God should also be loved by them at the expense of everything?

9. *Ye shall know that the Lord your God is mighty and faithful, keeping his covenant and mercy with those that love him and keep his commandments, to a thousand generations.*

Scripture is admirable in its expressions. In order to show this soul which strips itself of all interest of salvation or holiness and of everything else, in order to love God purely, that God loves to see it lose everything for that, it assures this soul that its God, to whom it is abandoned, is *mighty and faithful;* mighty to draw it out of peril and to prevent it from falling, and too *faithful* to suffer it to be deceived when it abandons itself to Him without reserve, and hazards displeasing Him only to wish to please Him too much. Its love is not out of order, except that it loves beyond all rule; and God keeps His faithfulness even to the end with those that love Him.

CHAPTER VIII.

2. *Thou shalt remember all the way by which the Lord thy God made thee pass through the wilderness for forty years, to afflict thee and try thee, to show what was in thy heart, and if thou wouldst keep his commandments or not.*

How frightsome is the wilderness of faith, and how tiresome the length of its way! Moses brings to the *remembrance* of this people what happened to them at the end of this way, and tells them to forget it not, so that they may thus be confirmed in the assurance of their state. He desires them to *remember the road* they took, and how they were *afflicted and tried* for so long a time because God wished to see *what was in their heart;* as if He said, I wished to see if there remain anything in thine heart that could hinder My dwelling there. All these pains and abjections through which these souls pass are caused only for the purpose of emptying their heart, that God alone may refill it.

3. *He has afflicted thee by famine, and given thee manna for food.*

Chapter VIII. 379

One of the greatest pains of the soul in this wilderness is *famine* and hunger, having been formerly so full and being here so empty. Were it given anything whereon to feed, even the most bitter in the world, it would find it sweet. It cannot be believed what this hunger of the soul caused by its self-love is: it destroys it and devours it, so that the pains are a relief to it, because they nourish it yet with something it feels, and which is a support to it. It is in this sense that Job said, that a soul thus enhungered finds bitter things sweet, and nourishes itself on food that once would have horrified it. God then *afflicts* these souls with this hunger in the wilderness of faith, but at the same time He *feeds* them *on manna*, which is so spiritual a food, that the soul finds therein nothing contenting it. This manna is a certain sustenance unknown and invisible which the soul does not distinguish on account of its purity; nevertheless, it is a sustenance which prevents it from perishing, for were it not supported (although imperceptibly) in so denuded states, it would quit everything.

3. *Neither thy fathers, nor thou knewest this manna, but it was to teach thee that man does not live by bread alone, but by every word that proceedeth out of the mouth of God.*

It is certain that so long as the road of faith lasts, the soul *does not know of* the imperceptible support. The *fathers* even, however holy they were, had not known it so that they could speak of it, God not permitting it to be declared to souls; for if the greatness of this state could be made known to them, they would never allow themselves to be lost, nor would they ever come out of themselves. But if they have had some slight transient acquaintance with it, God takes away from them all the certitude of it by the most extreme reverses, so that they can lean upon it no longer. But, says Scripture, God makes the soul pass through these so terribly denuded states, *to make known to it that man does not live by bread alone,* namely, the gifts and perceptible graces serving for it as sensible and distinct sustenance; *but* that he lives much more *from God* Himself, which is signified by *every word that proceedeth out of His mouth.*

It must be remarked that it is not said simply by the word of God, which might be understood as to everything known and comprehended **as** of God; but *by every word proceeding out of*

His mouth. Now this *speech which proceeds from his mouth* is His Word and Himself in essential unity, without means or medium of communication.

The *speech of God*, taken simply, is a mediate speech, received as a medium and in the faculties, by means of forms and images rendering it distinct and comprehensible; but the *word proceeding out of the mouth of God* is a substantial and immediate word issuing out of God Himself. The former is the word of God received out of Him, and the latter is the word of God dwelling in Himself, and which can only produce God.

In confirmation of all that I have advanced, Scripture does not say by every word that *has proceeded* out of the mouth of God,—for the word that has proceeded from God being out of Him, is a means and a created gift; but it expresses itself in the present tense, every word PROCEEDING out of the mouth of God, to show that it is this immediate word alone that is the word of God, and to mark by that the eternal and always real moment of the generation of the Word, who proceeds unceasingly out of the mouth of His Father, and who is never out of Him, as the Father says to Him always, "Thou art my Son, this day have I begotten Thee." God from all eternity begets His Word, and He begets Him unceasingly in all eternity by His immediate speech, which not being able to cease, finds in this Son its infinite termination equal to its principle, who is Speech-God; and this immediate speech proceeding from God and terminating in God, produces by a reflection of love between the Father who speaks, and the Son who proceeds from Him as speech, the Holy Spirit-God.

This could not be otherwise, since what has no other beginning than God, nor other termination than God, must necessarily be God: and it is clear that God producing it totally from Himself, as well as in everything equal to Himself, it is terminated in an immense God, who, by His infinity, receives as much as His Infinite principle can give Him. It must be, then, that this flux and reflux of all an immense and infinite God received into a God with the same qualities, should also produce a God of the same grandeur and immensity; and as this Speech-God is wholly Himself, it must terminate in Him, for did it terminate out of Him, it would thus be annihilated, since He reserves to Himself nothing but what is communicated and given to His Word; so that everything is refound in the unity of essence, and it is this that forms the trinity of persons in the unity of the Divine Essence. A production of all God received wholly into God, and sent back again wholly to this same God, forms the ineffable mystery of the TRINITY. God interiorly sending (so to speak), and communicating totally, is called the Father: God receiving all God from God Himself, is called the Son, and of the reception of all God, and of the amorous regard of God communicating, and of God receiving and returning everything to the same God, proceeds God called the Holy Spirit. All this is veritably one same essence, and cannot be otherwise, being the same God communicating Himself, receiving, sending back, and proceeding.

This is found in the soul whom God favours with His immediate communications through its annihilation; taking no longer anything to itself of what God communicates to it, He communicates Himself to it: and by means of this same annihilation there being no longer anything mediate, God receives the return of His communication; and after receiving it, He sends it back to Himself as pure as it issued forth; and it is this that produces the Holy Spirit, whence proceeds this perfect charity. For it must be known that God being immense and infinite, nothing can limit Him, and He fills all void by His immensity. Now, as He has nothing bounded or limited (and if He had anything finite He would not be God), there is also no void in which He does not perform this eternal generation of the Word; since if this was not the case, there would require to be a place which could contain God, or a void where the Word-God was not; which is equally absurd, since God would not then be infinite.

God then of necessity produces His Word in all creatures thus. But sin covers up and prevents the sight of these divine productions in such a manner that God forms them of necessity, and not with pleasure, in those rational creatures who have been infected by sin, and they do not at all perceive this mystery of eternity which is wrought in them, it being only revealed to the just souls in proportion as they become empty and annihilated, so that although God, even the Trinity, is in hell as well as in heaven, nevertheless He is there in a different manner, namely, He is present in hell out of the necessity of His essence which fills everything by its immensity, and not willingly from love and pleasure. But in these souls here spoken of, God forms these eternal productions as He pleaseth, without resistance on their part, and in a manner as agreeable as in the blessed, although they only know it by effects, and by lively and short illustrations which are given of them.

4. *The raiment with which thou hast been clad has not been worn out by the length of time, nor have thy feet been hurt for these forty years.*

It is surprising that although the soul passes through such strange states its *raiment is never worn out.* This raiment is *abandon* and the conduct of providence. *Abandon* serves it for a garment, and the more wretched it sees itself and the more God destroys it the more does it abandon itself to Him, without power to do otherwise. Now this *abandon* remains entire and *is not worn out*, although everything else perishes. The cloak is the conduct of providence, for the more a soul abandons itself the more does God take care of it, although often in a manner which, by covering it, loads it heavily: but no matter, whilst it remains in the way of faith, and does not issue out of it, these things *are never worn out* although they may be as old as ourselves, since they introduce the soul into the way and accompany it therein even to the end, without, during so long a road and time, either growing old or feeble.

Moses also observes to this people that *their feet have not been bruised*, for although they may often fall, yet for all that their feet are not hurt, unless they issue out of *abandon*, but as long as they remain abandoned and do not resume themselves whatever distress may happen to them, in spite of the weaknesses into which they fall in this frightful desert on account of its great nakedness, and although the senses, left to themselves, commit a thousand faults, caused by feebleness and surprise, yet all these hurt not the feet, for the affection of the soul is in no way harmed by them, it remains always firm and fixed in its God by an invariable and inviolable attachment, denoted by *the shoes* that are not worn out in the desert, and without being troubled at everything that takes *place outwardly.*

5. *That thou mayest consider in thine heart that the Lord thy God has instructed thee, as a man teacheth his son.*

God *instructs* these dear abandoned ones by their experience, *as a father instructs his son,* and *they consider in their heart* this excellent lesson when they have advanced, not knowing it by the lights of the spirit but by the inclination of the heart, and by the remembrance of experience, which remains so vividly imprinted in them that it leaves them no doubt of it. Man may indeed not know it whilst he is on the way, on account of the pain and incertitude of the road, but when he has arrived he cannot doubt but that the road by which he has walked is the true one, seeing that it has conducted him so straight, although across rocks and precipices and a thousand apparent perils, upon the brink of which he must walk without assurance of not falling therein, on the contrary, ready at every turn to fall, the darkness always enveloping this way.

6. *And that thou mayest keep the commandments of the Lord thy God, to walk in his ways and to fear Him.*

The soul is led thus to make it *walk*, without resistance, in the *will* of God, and to oblige it to obey Him with an inviolable fidelity although it may cost it something: and it is by this *abandon* to God's will, above all self interest, that it will be conducted to its end, which is God.

7. *For the Lord thy God will bring thee into a goodly land, where there are brooks, quiet waters, and fountains, and where mighty rivers and depths spring from its plains and hills.*

This is *a goodly land* since it is God who is essential goodness. A land *where there are brooks, quiet waters, and fountains*, since all sources are in Him, and to be in God is to be in the source, but a source of *rivers* by the abundance and impetuosity of His communications, a source of *calm* and *tranquil waters*, a source of useful *fountains*, agreeable and refreshing. By these three kinds of waters Scripture expresses all springing waters, to show that the soul arrived in God through the emptiness and loss of all good, and through the drying up of every other water in this dry and arid desert, finds itself all filled with these very waters, but in their spring and source, and with the fulness of God Himself. Thus the soul, having lost all gifts and every grace, every facility of doing good, every acquired virtue, returning afterwards to its end, finds everything in its very origin, not in rivulets of communications, but in fulness of source; and by losing everything for God alone, all is given back to it in an eminent manner with God alone, since the graces of God and all His greatness are with it—not for the soul, which no longer takes anything of it, but for God, being rich with His riches.

There are not only springs in God, but there are bottomless *depths* and mighty *rivers*, of which something is shown to this soul. There are depths in which it is lost never to come out; there, being contained in the abyss itself, it is made one in it, and in this essential union there issues out from it (as from God, it existing no longer, but God being in it and for it) rivers, waters, and fountains, to be distributed outwardly according to the need of every one. But it is necessary for this that it should have arrived not only at the land, God,—in which it lives and drinks as from the spring—but, moreover, it must be sunk, lost, transformed in God, in order that there may flow from God by it rivers, waters, and fountains; because these all *issue out of* the immense *plains* of the Divinity, *and from the mountains* of His power and grandeur.

8. *A land of wheat, barley, and vines, of fig-trees, pomegranates, and olives; a land of oil and honey.*

Scripture here particularises the Divine perfections which the soul possesses in God, and which are admirable fruits in Him. Goodness in man is of very little account; but in God, it is admirable. Charity out of God is insignificant, limited, and contracted; but in God, it is God Himself. In fine, all the good that we have lost for Him are found all gathered up and contained in Himself, as well as all the virtues, designated by all these kinds of fruits and trees, by the *oil* and *honey*.

9. *Where thou wilt eat thy bread without any scarceness, and wilt enjoy abundance of everything; a land whose stones are iron, and out of whose hills thou mayest dig brass.*

When the soul has attained to its origin, it *eats its bread without any poverty*, because everything that comes from God immediately, and all the virtues in God, being God, are deficient in nothing, but are all perfect; so that then it *enjoys* them without scarceness or defect. Not only that, but everything in it is useful; *the stone*, which out of it would be of no use, gives in it *iron* of the strongest and most necessary kind; and all metals and

and riches come out of its mountains: this is a confirmation of what has been said under diverse similitudes.

10. *So that when thou hast eaten well and art full, thou mayest bless the Lord thy God for the excellent land which he has given thee.*

Experience alone can make this known, therefore Moses said *when thou hast eaten*, that is to say experienced, *thou wilt be filled* with the fulness of God Himself, which fully satisfies the soul. Oh then *thou wilt bless the Lord thy God for the good land which he has given thee.*

14. *Beware lest thy heart grow proud, and thou forget the Lord thy God who has brought thee out of Egypt and out of the house of bondage.*

The only danger there can be in these states consists in souls coming to regard themselves full of so many riches, and attributing to themselves something of them, and delighting in it even to *forgetting* their former captivity and vileness. All this is to be feared for them: this sin alone caused the fall of the angel from heaven to hell, and it is this sin alone that can cause this soul to issue out of God and to be precipitated into hell. Therefore Moses is desirous that if this so advanced a people should be unfaithful enough to look upon their *elevation* in themselves that they should at the same time look upon their *former* captivity, out of which they never could have come had God not drawn them Himself, and by an effect of His absolute power.

15. *It is he who led thee through this vast and terrible desert, where there were fiery serpents, scorpions, and vipers, where there was no water, and where he brought forth water out of the hard rock.*

He desires them also to remember how *it is he* alone who *led* them through so great and *terrible* a *wilderness*, full of *fiery serpents*, for the demons are all filled with fire and fury to destroy the souls that are in this desert. They journey the whole length of this road, surrounded by sins and the rage of their enemy, how then could they have come out of it if God had not brought them? So much the more, as this wilderness was so dry that *there was not* a drop of *water* other than what God *brought forth out of the* hard *rock:* this water which is found in so great a desert is the hardness and insensibility of naked faith which does not permit this soul to think of so many perils, nor to recognise them such as they are, being immovable as the rock is in defending itself, but this water which serves it for sustenance amongst inevitable dangers is given only by God, since it is He alone who not only delivers from perils and from all enemies, but it is also He who imparts to the souls this advantageous firmness so that it may neither be stung nor terrified.

16. *Who fed thee in the wilderness with manna, which thy fathers knew not, and who, after having afflicted and tried thee, had pity upon thee at the latter end.*

All this really takes place in this manner and in the same order. After God has tried the soul by all the demons, miseries, and sins, and by all its enemies represented by these venomous beasts, and whilst all this time it has been deprived of all succour of sensible, distinct, and perceptible graces, of all refreshment and nourishment, having only for support the water of its firmness and insensibility, which appears to it a final reprobation and impenitence, He *gives to it* also *manna*, which is a secret and hidden support and not apparent to it, but by which God prevents it from wholly perishing. He feeds it also upon His sacred body, which however gives it no consolation, although it sustains it: on the contrary, the soul thinks it entirely profanes it, and would rather be deprived of it, so that the nakedness and distaste which it finds in this kind of nourishment augment its pain the more. But although this appears thus to the interior senses and faculties, nevertheless the divine sacrament yet continues to be a great sustenance, although wholly spiritual, unknown, and concealed from the soul.

After, I say, all these trials, God comes Himself to *afflict* this soul and to lay His heavy hand upon it. Oh the terrible affliction of this! It is beyond all expression. *Let God come himself to combat a leaf which the least wind driveth to and fro* (Job xiii. 25). Ah! this is what cannot be expressed. Often this rash leaf thinking to do well, and not imagining that it is Himself, the Strong Armed, wishes to defend itself, and these defences serve only to cause it inexplicable griefs. This poor leaf must then at last bend, yield, and fall to the ground, and be in fine consumed by God Himself. All the other trials which preceded were nothing to this one; for God who sustained this soul in an unknown and imperceptible manner, repelled the burning darts of the demons, the stings and bites of sin, and having rendered the soul very firm and insensible, these merely grazed it, or at most terrified it without doing it any hurt: but this other *trial* of which I speak can come neither from nature nor demons; it must be God alone, who mercilessly causes this rock to bend like a leaf, overturns it, and in fine annihilates and consumes it, and it is solely the operation of God. Serpents may, by their envenomed wounds, cause death, but it is only God who has the power to destroy, consume, and annihilate this soul in His vast bosom, and in fine transform it in Himself.

This operation, being the most subtle and powerful of all, is the least sensible, because it is neither in the interior senses nor in the faculties, but in the most profound centre and supreme part of the soul. It is only God who can perform it, and He does it by causing the centre to suffer, purging it radically from all propriety and dissimilarity, in order, by annihilating it, to lose it into Himself, which causes this operation, although the most insensible of all, to be nevertheless the heaviest. But God, after having thus *afflicted* this soul, and having overwhelmed it with His own weight, after having destroyed and consumed it, *consoles it at the end*, which means that He only consoles it when it is in its end, which is Himself. And when the soul has arrived there it knows that what appeared to it formerly a rigorous justice was a great *mercy*.

17. *That thou mayest not say in thine heart, It is my power and the might of my hand that hath gotten me all these great riches.*

18. *But that thou mayest remember the Lord thy God, and that it is he who has given thee this power to fulfil his covenant.*

There is nothing in Scripture which does not express and confirm all this. It is, it says, that thou mayest not attribute any power to thyself that God destroys thee thus, and that thou mayest not say, *it is my hand that hath done* all this, that is to say, I have *acquired these great riches* by my labour, my cares, and my fidelity, *but that thou mayest remember* that all strength lies in God and all weakness in thyself, and that it is He alone who has performed this great work. Thus such a soul is far removed from attributing anything to itself, God enclosing so great things in earthen vessels, that the power may be attributed to Him, and not to man, who seeing only his own earth and vileness cannot appropriate to himself anything.

CHAPTER IX.

1. *Hear me, Oh Israel! Thou wilt pass this day over Jordan, and wilt find a people stronger than thou.*

3. *But the Lord thy God will pass before thee as a burning and devouring fire to destroy them.*

This *passage of Jordan* signifies the issuing out of the soul from itself to be received into God. It must pass through its enemies. God goes before as a *devouring fire to destroy* and consume all their strength.

4. *But when the Lord thy God shall have destroyed them before thee, say not in thine heart, Because of my righteousness the Lord hath brought me into this land to possess it, and these nations have been cut off for their wickedness.*

The thought that offends God the most of all, consists in the soul beginning to believe or imagine that *it is because of its* innocence and fidelity *that God has performed* on its behalf so many wonders, and that *the others* have been deprived of them on account of their sins. Ah! God has no regard for our *self-righteousness* to do us so many great mercies, since His end is to destroy our self-righteousness. But it is necessary that the soul remain fixed without regarding itself, viewing everything in the power of God and nothing in itself, without examining anything; for all self-righteousness must be destroyed in order to attain to this point. It is not then for our righteousness that we arrive at it, and God destroys in us all self-righteousness only that we might not believe that it could give us entrance into Him.

Chapter IX.

5. *For it will not be for thy good works, nor for the uprightness of thy heart that thou wilt enter into the land to possess it.*

Moses seems by all these repetitions not to be able to show too often that no *work*, no *uprightness*, nor any self-righteousness can procure so great a good. For if anything can obtain it it would be, more than anything else, *uprightness* and integrity, but even this perishes, and God as Himself cannot be possessed by any good, nor by any intermediate means.

6. *Know then that it is not for thy righteousness that the Lord thy God has put thee in possession of this good land, since thou art a stiff-necked people.*
7. *But remember, and never forget how thou hast provoked the anger of the Lord thy God in the wilderness, and how thou hast always been rebels against the Lord from the day when thou didst depart out of Egypt until now.*

He again shows them, and recommends them most particularly *not to forget* that they have not ceased to sin and to *provoke the wrath of God* from the time when He brought them out of the active state. And in the remainder of this chapter he represents to them in detail all the sins they committed on the long road of the wilderness.

Oh wisdom, oh profundity of the word of God! The sight of our sins and of our infidelities without number, ought indeed to persuade us that it is not through our own merits that He has chosen us for interior states, and for the purity of His love, the more as, since He has penetrated us with His liveliest lights, and gratified us with the mystic ray, we have not ceased to be ungrateful and rebellious against Him. God acts thus, then, before making the soul enter into Himself: He shows it in detail all its infidelities and offences, which overthrows it, and casts it even into the abyss.

At the end (v. 26) Moses concludes by confessing for God's glory alone, that He has acted thus with so much goodness towards His people, because they are His, and are *His inheritance*, and He has *redeemed* and conducted them by His *mighty power and outstretched arm*, that is to say, because He has chosen them gratuitously, to signalise on their behalf His power, His wisdom, and His love.

CHAPTER X.

9. The tribe of Levi has had no part nor inheritance with his brethren, for the Lord himself is his portion, as the Lord thy God hath promised him.

To be *the inheritance of God*, is to be given up to Him, and to be conducted by Himself, as was this abandoned people; but *to have God for our inheritance*, can only take place when the soul is entirely annihilated. Therefore, these souls wholly confirmed and annihilated, *have no part* in the sensible graces or perceptible goods of the others, *God* alone being *their portion*, and their hereditary portion, as David, that great mystic, experienced, when he sung with truth, "*Oh God, thou art the God of my heart, and my portion for ever.*" This is also what has been experienced in a peculiar manner by the family of Levi, the family of high priests and annihilated ones.

14. Behold the heaven, and the heaven of heavens is the Lord thy God's, the earth also, and all that it contains.

By the *heaven* is meant the faculties elevated and united to God; and by *the heaven of heavens* is signified the centre where God dwells. He says, then, that not only is the union formed in the faculties, and that they are God's, but that the centre also, the heaven of heavens, belongs to Him by essential union. For as man's spirit is well called his heaven, so the supreme part of the spirit is very well denominated the heaven of heavens; and the word *behold* expresses that it is a state already arrived.

17. The Lord thy God is the God of gods, and the Lord of lords, the Great God, mighty and terrible, who regardeth not persons, nor taketh reward.

As the heaven of heavens is God's, it is there also where *the God of gods* dwells as in his lofty Zion, which is reserved for Him. This well expresses that it is not only God's graces that dwell there, and which are often taken for God Himself, but it is the God of gods, the God of all that, and the author of all these sacred gifts, who dwells in the heaven of heavens. He adds that it is *the Lord of lords* Himself, *this Great God*, strong, mighty, terrible, such as He is in Himself. But this God, who giveth Himself entirely, *regardeth not persons* nor gifts; everything personal and proper must be destroyed and annihilated; likewise also must we be emptied and cleared of all his gifts; then it is that God receives into Him the nothing, but were it not so, it would never be received there.

21. *He is thy praise and thy God, who has done these wonders and marvels which thine eyes have seen.*

God Himself has become the *praise* of this soul: He praises Himself in it, and it has no other praise than Himself, who, after having performed *great* and terrible things in it, becomes in fine its praise, as to Him alone all the praise is due: and *its eyes behold it all*, full knowledge of it being given it.

CHAPTER XI.

10. *The land whither thou goest to possess it, is not like the land of Egypt, from whence thou camest, where after sowing the seed, waters are brought to water it as a garden.*
11. *But there are mountains and plains which drink in the rain of heaven.*
12. *And the Lord thy God careth for it continually, and his eyes watch over it, from the beginning of the year till the end.*

This difference between the *lands of Egypt* and the promised land is admirable: the former, representing the multiplied state, need to be *watered like gardens*, and this watering is no other than this good activity, without which these lands would produce nothing; but not so with the latter. *There are* souls elevated like *mountains*, others agreeable and fertile like *plains*, but both being perfectly passive, labour not to water; they drink in only *the rains of heaven*, not being watered by earthly waters, but by heavenly ones. And God unceasingly *looks upon* this land without abandoning it for a moment, and *his eyes are upon it from the beginning even to the end*, without ceasing for one instant to regard it.

Oh happiness of a soul which, in the cessation from all self-labour, remains exposed and in waiting to receive the rain of heaven! Such a soul is never confounded in its expectation, for God is never a moment without guarding it by the care of His próvidence; He *watches* for it when it rests. Is not the work of a God preferable to that of the creature? Abandon, abandon, and leave God to act!

> 13. *If then thou observest the commandments that I give thee to-day, thou wilt love the Lord thy God, and thou wilt serve him with all thy heart, and with all thy soul.*

All the graces and commandments which God gives us tend only to cause Him to be *loved with the whole heart*, because of the jealousy He entertains for this heart, which He desires all for Himself. He asks only love. Oh, pure love, how rare thou art! Thou costest all the cares and labours of a God; thou costest all the sufferings and frightful strippings of the creature! Oh pure love, where art thou to be found? In God alone, and thou canst not be in the soul unless God alone be there. Thou art in Him, thou issuest from Him, and thou returnest into Him; but out of Himself, considered as the principal, centre, and termination of this love, there is nothing but impurity.

CHAPTER XII.

> 8. *Ye shall not act then as we do here this day, every man doing that which seemeth right in his own eyes.*

Moses means that these dear abandoned ones when they have arrived at the promised land will no longer there do the same things as in the desert of faith, nor as fruits of their own uprightness, nor with difficulty or restraint, for having attained to a divine state, which is a state of innocence, they will do all that is *just*, no longer because it *seems to them* such, nor by reason of their own righteousness, but because they shall then be moved by the righteousness of God Himself, and they will thus act in entire freedom; for although they are to perform

Chapter XII.

more things in the promised land than they did in the desert, as Moses declares to them by the enumeration which he makes in this chapter, nevertheless they will perform them in unity and repose, as God does all things, for they will perform in God and by the gentle impulse of the law of His love, which although multiplied in its effects is perfectly united and peaceful in its principle.

He has told them before that it was not for their righteousness that they would be introduced into this land, for this righteousness being proper to them was not pure enough to enter therein; but the righteousness which is to bring them into it is the righteousness of God Himself, which is exempt from all deceit, for the soul having been placed in truth, which is the eternal law (just as the people of Israel were ruled by the law of God given by Moses), it can judge of things only as God judges of them; thus all that is right in the eyes of God is right in its eyes, which now see things only with God's eyes; this is the cause of its being free from mistakes and of its living in full liberty, although men think otherwise of it.

9. *For ye are not as yet entered into the rest and inheritance which the Lord your God will give you.*

The reason why they have not as yet received this freedom and divine righteousness is that they have not yet arrived *at the rest and inheritance of the Lord;* but when they shall have *entered* therein, oh then they will find nothing that can straiten them, everything being done with an admirable freedom and the greatest purity, because everything is done in God.

10. *That ye may enjoy a perfect rest in the midst of all the enemies that surround you, and dwell there without fear.*

12. *There shall ye eat and rejoice in the presence of the Lord your God, ye and your sons, your daughters, your men-servants and your maid-servants, and the Levite that dwelleth in your cities, for he hath no part nor inheritance amongst you.*

There they will possess great peace even *in the midst of all their enemies*, who will not dare to come near them. Then *they will dwell without fear*, being, as it were, placed in a permanent state. They will be *in a joy* and freedom wholly innocent, and their rejoicings will be made before God: *the sons and daughters, men-servants and maid-servants*, will all have part in this joy of innocence; *the Levites* also, who are the most eminent persons and the leaders of others, *and who dwell in the same cities* with them, will share in this pleasure; and this joy they will have in common with you, since it is the only thing that remains to them, to share with you. David had experienced that when he said, "All they that are in thee, O Lord! are as persons ravished with joy."

17. *Thou mayest not eat within thy cities the tithe of thy corn, of thy wine, and of thy oil.*

18. *But thou shalt eat them before the Lord thy God in the place which the Lord thy God shall choose, thou, and thy sons and thy daughters, thy men-servants and thy maid-servants, and the Levite who dwelleth with you; thou shalt refresh thyself and be filled before the Lord thy God, in all the works of thy hands.*

How many things are there *not permitted in the cities*, that is to say, in the presence of men, which one can nevertheless do innocently before God: St. Paul has well experienced it, (1 Cor. ix. and x.) It is in this sense that Moses says, *thou shalt not eat the tithes within thy cities;* by this word *thy* is meant the souls that are still in possession of themselves, and by *cities* those persons that are offended: the *tithes* denote lawful observances, which are all united in love. How many things would appear hurtful to feeble and unenlightened souls, and would offend them, which nevertheless are in truth but the purest manner of fulfilling the *law !*

But this is only known to souls of this degree who are divinely enlightened. We must render ourselves weak with the weak in order not to offend them. All things are lawful to Paul, but all things are not expedient; all things are permitted to an Apostle, but all things do not edify.

It is necessary also that these tithes be eaten *with joy, and in the place which God has chosen;* it is He who does all things, who gives certain laws to the soul and delivers it from them; and this rejoicing will be universal, extending to the superior part signified by *the Levite*, and to the inferior denoted by the male and female *servants*. In fine, we must *be filled* with the goods of the Lord, *and be refreshed in everything that we do,* acting with a holy freedom which God Himself gives, free from returnings or vexations.

20. *When the Lord thy God shall have enlarged thy border, as he has promised thee, and thou shalt have desired to eat flesh according to thy longing.*

God, having enlarged and greatly *extended* the soul, places it in a new liberty, by which it may *eat* with safety what previously would have caused its death. In the wilderness the people were punished in a terrible manner for desiring *flesh*, and here they are permitted to eat of it as much as they desire, without any evil happening to them; on the contrary, they are exhorted to do so with joy, and in the presence of the Lord. Oh! Scripture decides it, when it says that the first time they *lusted* after it, (Numbers xi. 34); therefore the place of their punishment was called the tomb of concupiscence: but here they are very far removed from eating it in this manner; they eat it only because it is permitted and ordained to them; they eat it to do the will of God and not to satisfy their sensuality; thus they eat it with joy, all lust and malignity having been taken away from them. These souls can no longer think of mortifying themselves, but they make use of everything innocently and without scruple in the name of God. "Let him that eateth of all things not despise him that eateth not, and let him that maketh a scruple to eat not condemn him that eateth" (Rom. xiv. 3); for the Lord has numbered him amongst His own, amongst the number of those who, being perfectly His, find His good pleasure in all things.

CHAPTER XIV.

1. *Be ye the children of the Lord your God. Ye shall not cut yourselves, nor shave yourselves, on account of the death of your friends.*
2. *For ye are a people holy unto the Lord your God, and whom he hath chosen from all the nations that are upon the earth to be unto him a peculiar people.*

Moses commands this people to be like little *children*. This is the character of these innocent souls, to be without malice. He forbids them at the same time to wound or *cut* themselves, for children do not these things, but they live from Providence, receiving what happens to them, and seeking nothing. The reason why he gives them these commands is, because they are *people holy unto the Lord their God;* as if he said to them, not being holy for yourselves, you have nothing to do with these marks of affected holiness; but being holy *for God,* ye must be holy as He desires, that is, be children, since He declares that this is what He loves the most, and it is that you might become children that *he has chosen you from all the nations of the earth to be his peculiar people.*

CHAPTER XXVI.

18. *The Lord hath chosen you this day to be unto him a peculiar people.*
19. *And to raise you above all the nations which he hath made for his praise, for his glory, and for the grandeur of his name; that ye may be the holy people of the Lord your God, as he hath spoken.*

He *raises this people to-day*, that is to say, in His eternal day, as has been explained above, that they may be *peculiar to himself* alone; therefore He renders them more excellent than any other, and *than all the nations which he hath made for his praise, for his glory, and for the grandeur of his name.* All the other good and holy ways are made for the praise of God, and people labour therein for His glory and to bless His holy name; but His praise, His name, and His glory are less than Himself, and are not Himself in that they are out of Him. But these annihilated souls, without thinking either of praise or of glory, are *the holy people of the Lord,* for they have lost all things in order to render to Him a perfect homage to His holiness by their lowliness and misery, to His strength by their weaknesses, to His justice by the loss of their own self-righteousness. The others render glory to God by praising

Him with all their might; but these are the saints of God through their own destruction, for all self-holiness is lost in them, in order that the holiness of God may alone exist there. They are not holy for men who know them not; they are not holy for themselves, believing themselves full of sin, and sin itself. They are not holy for praise, honour, and glory, nor for any of those things which appear of some note, since far from that, they possess only abjection, contempt, and confusion for their lot.

CHAPTER XXVII.

9. *Hearken diligently, O Israel, this day art thou made the people of the Lord thy God.*

It is only at the moment of the going out from ourselves, that we are truly *made a people to the Lord*, although until then we may have been always consecrated to Him by the life of His grace; since it is in this *day* that the soul, losing all propriety, finds itself disposed to be received into God. It becomes also peculiarly His people in that, having gone out from itself, it resists Him no longer; for every soul resists God just as much as it remains in itself, and it becomes to Him so much the more supple the more it comes out.

CHAPTER XXVIII.

9. *The Lord shall in thee establish a holy people to himself if thou keep the commandments of the Lord thy God, and walk in his ways.*

Not only will they be *a people* to the Lord by transient disposition, but they will be *established* in this state; and it will be *for himself* that God will render them firm in His *holiness*, if they do His will and are faithful to *walk in his ways*.

12. *The Lord will open unto thee the heaven as his richest treasure.*

To open the heaven as his richest treasure is to give communication of all that is in the heaven, as much the possession of Himself as the knowledge given only in heaven, or to souls who have attained to this state.

15. *But if thou obey not the voice of the Lord thy God,*
19. *Thou shalt be cursed in thy comings in and in thy goings out.*

But he that quits so beautiful a way, and who, by a frightful infidelity, goes out from his God, *shall be cursed* from that moment *in returning* into his propriety; and cursed in his going out, by withdrawing himself from his God by a calamity similar, in some respects, to that of Lucifer.

20. *He shall smite thee with famine and with want; he shall break and consume thee on account of thine own inventions, by which thou hast withdrawn thyself from him.*
21. *He shall add thereto the scourge of the pestilence.*
23. *The heaven shall be as brass above thee, and the earth under thy feet shall become as iron.*
25. *The Lord will suffer thee to fall before thine enemies.*
26. *And thy dead body shall be the prey of all the birds of the heaven.*
28. *He shall strike thee with madness, with blindness, and with frenzy of heart.*

Thou shalt then be overwhelmed by all the evils possible, being, as it were, in a hell in which sin and the demon will take vengeance upon thee; sin will cling to thee like *the pestilence*, and all the other woes will follow, so that thou shalt be delivered up to all *thine enemies;* thou shalt suffer all the evils of guilt and punishment which will fall upon thee. *The heaven will become as brass for thee*, no longer being willing to hear thee; so that thou wilt scarcely be able any longer to pray or be converted. O woe! woe! In place of the dew of grace, there is nothing now but dust. Then these souls *fall before all their enemies*, who kill them by mortal sin. Everything comes little by little, and from bad to worse. What were only wounds become *deaths*, for afterwards there come *blindness* and obduracy in this state, and also *madness of heart*, which is despair.

CHAPTER XXIX.

4. *The Lord hath not given you until this day a heart to know, nor eyes to see, nor ears to hear.*

It is true that although one walks in the way, one cannot *know* all these things, nor be *enlightened* as to them or *comprehend* them, until one has arrived at the termination. All that might have been said regarding them previously, could not be comprehended by the person while he was on the way; but he has no sooner arrived than he is astonished to see how his *eyes* are opened, how his *heart* perceives, and how he has an understanding of all things.

26. *God will cast those out of the land who serve strange gods.*
28. *He will drive them out in his wrath and fury, and in his extreme indignation, sending them into a strange land.*

By these are meant those who have resumed themselves, and becoming again proprietary, will have withdrawn themselves by their wickedness from the dominion of God, to conduct themselves in their own ways; and who, preferring self-interest to *abandon*, will have quitted the place of repose to return to the care of themselves. These will, from that moment, be *cast out by God in his wrath, and sent into a strange land*, into a place where there will be no more rest for them.

CHAPTER XXX.

2. *If thou return to the Lord, and if thou obey all his commandments, with all thy heart and soul, as I command thee this day, and also thy children,*

3. *The Lord thy God will bring thee again from the place of thy captivity; He will have compassion on thee, and will gather thee together again from all the places whither thou wast before scattered.*

Moses, however, affirms that if these criminal and rejected souls begin to *return towards God, and to obey him with all their heart*, He will draw them out of their captivity. If these persons are with difficulty converted, it does not arise on the part of my God, who being all love and mercy, "wills not the death of the sinner, but rather that he should turn and live." I say again that the difficulty of their conversion comes not from the part of God, who holds always His arms open to receive those who are willing to return to Him; and as, says St. Augustin, when we cast ourselves into His arms, we must not think that He withdraws them and suffers us to fall. Oh no, it would be impious to think so, for it was for that that He died with His arms extended upon the cross; but this difficulty proceeds from the soul, which being established in a state of consistence, can only be moved with great difficulty. Moreover, having been for a long time in a state of inability to distinguish itself from God, on account of its intimate union, it cannot, in any way, either turn itself away from God, nor return to Him; and through long usage, it can scarcely now change its conduct, although it has really fallen.

This is, then, what renders these sorts of falls and repentances equally so difficult, namely, this establishment and state of consistence in God which makes the heart scarcely pliable either on one side or another.

And the soul can only issue out of it in two ways; either by the pride of Lucifer, which leads it to attribute to itself the power and might of God, taking complacency in its state, and regarding itself vainly, whence it is carried away even to attributing to its own strength or merits what God does in it and by it. And as these unfaithful persons imitate the evil angels in their fall, having fallen from so eminent a degree of grace and holiness, they imitate them also in their impenitence, their conversion being rendered so much the more difficult, as they have sinned with the more ingratitude and the less feebleness.

The other manner of going out from God is by resuming one's-self, and voluntarily withdrawing one's-self from His dominion in order to re-enter into one's own conduct, and becoming thus proprietary. Behold, then, the two kinds of sins by which these souls commence their disaster; the wandering of the mind by pride and vain complacency, and the wandering of the will, rendering one's self proprietary, and withdrawing from the dominion of God. This is then the source of all the other sins they commit afterwards. It thus may be easy to see that it is most difficult for them to do this voluntarily and to be lost. This is why there are few or no examples of souls arrived at this point who have fallen; but it is sufficient that it may happen, for us to be on our guard.

What then causes these souls to have so much difficulty in returning to God after their fall, comes from their being established in a state of consistence, and remaining content in the evil as they were rendered firm in the good. And this is also what has caused the impossibility of Lucifer's conversion. They can no longer turn themselves towards God, on account of the unity which they had with Him, and through which they have lost the habit of turning. But what renders the thing almost impossible is this, that these persons desire to perform their repentance from the active side, as formerly, and those who conduct them desire it also, which is as impossible as it is useless. It is necessary then, O directors, that without tormenting such souls as these with active penitence, you make them enter solely into a sight of their own humiliation, as far as they are capable of it, leaving them to drink deep draughts of the wrath and indignation of God; teaching them to remain submitted to His divine justice, content never to be pardoned if such be His will, without distressing themselves as to whether they will be pardoned and re-established in grace or not. Since they have fallen from so high a degree, and have lost so many graces, it is necessary that, stripped of all self-interest, they should remain exposed thus to the extremest blows of divine justice. They must not make any effort to return to a lower manner of prayer than that to which they had attained at the time of their fall, not even although the directors exact it of them; for it is just as impossible as to make a man re-enter his mother's womb, and besides the fact that they would never succeed in it, they would, moreover, by it be hindered from advancing. Retaining them then in their degree, O fathers of these souls, abandon them without mercy to divine justice, permitting them not the slightest deliverance or departure from it. O frightful repentance, and how few have the courage to abandon themselves to it; and even how few directors have the courage to leave to it those souls who have been committed to them! This is what has caused so much devastation in the spiritual life after the falls, for want of applying the suitable remedies. People are offended with the feeble ones, and despair of the poor fallen ones. But if souls were faithful and courageous enough to suffer themselves to be burned and consumed by divine justice, they would, in a short time, be re-established in a state perhaps more elevated than that from which they had fallen, as God promises by His prophet, for the consolation of this kind of penitent ones—" I have turned my face from thee for a moment in the time of my wrath, but I have looked upon thee afterwards with a never-ending mercy."

The reasons why this sort of repentance is the proper one for souls advanced in the passive way, are (besides what has been already advanced), firstly, that nothingness is the immediate disposition for the supernatural, the fulness of God being distributed only into the emptiness of the creature. Now persons thus fallen from a high degree, having been in an eminent supernatural state, and who are to be again re-establised therein, need for that the most supernatural communications, and consequently must remain in nothingness through the acceptation and love of their abjection, and by their eternal abandonment to the disposition of God, in order to be in a state to receive them; otherwise, wishing to fill themselves anew with practices and self-inventions and efforts, they would thus place a new obstacle to the richest graces necessary to raise them and make them enter anew into their degree, just as any form gains admittance more easily into a subject empty and bare than into another where there is something to empty or purify.

Secondly, it is certain that the more the soul renounces its own interests to sacrifice itself to those of God, so much the more is it disposed to a more speedy and advantageous conversion, for nothing touches God's heart more, leading Him to show great mercy, than to see His poor creature rather accept all the blows of His justice than retain any self interest, or not sacrifice itself unreservedly to His glory; and even from the time when it is really in this disposition it is perfectly converted, it being impossible for sin to exist with so heroic a charity, and that grace should not be found in a heart burning with so pure a love that it accepts all that can be accepted for

Chapter XXX.

the interests of God throughout the whole extent of His will, justice, and power. As this then is infallibly the speediest and most perfect conversion, and as moreover this soul is capable of it, seeing that these are fruits of the state from which it has fallen, and it has still a facility and kind of habit of performing these renouncements and sacrifices so intensified, it is necessary to conduct it by this way, and to teach it not only to abandon itself entirely to God, who alone can apply the needful remedy for its ill and show His glory thereby, but also not even to desire this remedy, preferring the good pleasure of God to the cure of its mortal wound. This is then the most sovereign remedy for so great an evil, nothing being in anything more sure, nor more in order than when it is left the most fully to God.

Persons who read this will perhaps think that this penitence is not conformable to the fall; and that it is not a pain and grief, and does not afflict the soul. But if they had the experience of it they would confess that nothing in the world equals this pain. It is the purest purgatory, or even hell, according to the degree in which God places them, and which is an inexplicable torment. Oh how much more skilful God is in purifying than any creature, and how very different the punishments of an avenging God are from all the inventions of the justice of men! Such a soul would rather suffer all possible torments than remain as we have said, (faithful and without stirring) under the hand of divine justice. All the penances that it could be made to do, even the most extreme, would solace it and form a refreshment for it.

It is necessary well to guard against allowing these things to be done to it, for this would draw it still further from its state, and would prevent it from being re-established therein. It is natural that one should rise where one falls, and thence continue one's way, without wishing to return to the beginning in order to rise, or retrace all the road because one has fallen before finishing it. Moreover it would not be a penance for this soul to burden it with mortifications, this would rather be a refreshment. This is easy to conceive. The pain of austerities and outward penances afflicts the senses but consoles the spirit; now as in these souls the senses are in a great measure dead, as much because that having exhausted all the penances and mortifications possible for them, they have become almost insensible to them, as because the senses being separated from the spirit have no more vigour, so that they scarcely feel pleasures and pains; it is no longer by the senses that their penitence must be measured, but that the punishment may be more grievous for them, and also proportionate to their fault, it must be a punishment of the spirit, all their sin being of the spirit.

Now in order that this pain of spirit may be lively, profound, and equal to the fault, it can be inflicted only by God Himself. Whatever, then, is done to the senses, would be an amusement and support for the spirit, diverting it from its pain. But when the spirit finds itself overwhelmed under the weight of divine justice, and sees itself without succour and support, abandoned by the senses, which solace it in nothing, ah! this is a frightful torment, and such as experience alone can make understood. It is a fire penetrating even to the marrow by its activity, and I affirm that of a thousand persons who have fallen, there will not perhaps be found three willing to suffer themselves to be devoured by divine justice, in all its extent, without resuming themselves sooner or later; above all in sicknesses, or near death, for then one desires to make all sorts of efforts to be assured of salvation by self-activity.

But it is certain that it is not necessary for these souls to do more at death than at another time; on the contrary, it is at this time that one must abandon one's-self, with more courage, to divine justice, to bear even its weight through all eternity. Oh! that is the purity of disinterested love, unknown by self-love, but known, esteemed, embraced by pure love! A person happy enough to die thus would render to God an ineffable glory; and without passing through any purgatory (for what can there remain to purge in a soul possessing no more propriety, and arrived at so heroic a charity?) would be elevated to the highest degree in the heavens; in place of which, when people resume themselves at death, they cause God to lose a very great glory, and they lose also an eminent happiness; not that the person is not saved, but he must, in the other life, finish the payment of his cowardice.

This is of more consequence than it is possible to tell, and I pray that those persons into whose hands these writings may fall, will give particular attention to it.

4. *Although thou shouldst have been driven to the poles of heaven, from thence will the Lord thy God bring thee;*

Chapter XXX.

5. *And he will take thee again and bring thee into the land which thy fathers possessed; and he will bless thee, so that thou shalt be multiplied greater than thy fathers.*

Should a soul be happy enough to enter into the disposition which we have just named, although it had been rejected of God, and removed from Him, by the enormity and long duration of its fall, as far as the *poles* are distant from one another, He would again call it back and re-unite it to Himself. He would even give it a more ample *blessing*, and a grace more abundant than what it had before its fall, because of the purity of the love with which it had acted towards Him.

6. *The Lord thy God will circumcise thy heart, and the heart of thy children, that thou mayest love the Lord thy God with all thy heart, and with all thy soul, and that thou mayest live.*

God Himself *will cut off from this heart* all that had contributed to its fall, so that this person *may love* Him always *with all his heart* without resuming himself any more, and *may live again* in Him for ever, with a life more abundant, considering the degree in which he was before his fall.

9. *The Lord shall return to resume in thee his delights amongst so many goods, as he rejoiced in thy fathers.*

He *takes his pleasure* in this soul that has returned to Him, and dwells there with *delight*, because it is more exempt from self-love than ever, and its fall has been to it the occasion of having still greater estrangement from, and hatred of, itself, and also more confidence in and love for God.

11. *This commandment which I make unto thee this day, is not above thee, nor far removed from thy knowledge.*

This way is not, as almost every one thinks, a thing so *difficult* or *distant;* that is, so rare, and extending to so few persons. All are capable of it, since for this it is only necessary to have a heart well submitted to God, and the principal part of the work depends on His grace, which is equally powerful to perform it in all those perfectly abandoned to it, and faithful to allow themselves to be pursued, destroyed, and annihilated.

But the cause of so few souls being desirous of entering therein is self-love, which leads souls to regard themselves, and to resume themselves, to take care of themselves, and to fear to abandon themselves to God, thinking they do better conducting themselves than in blindly trusting themselves to God.

12. *It is not in the heaven that thou shouldst say, who among us can mount up to heaven to bring it unto us?*

Almost all excuse themselves in this manner from entering the way of faith. This is *too high* for us, they say, it is only good for the heavenly souls. Moses knowing well that this would be the most dangerous temptation, for it is covered with the veil of humility, distinctly warns them of it. For all persons who are at a distance from so great a good, think they are perfectly right when they say, 'we are not worthy of it, we dare not aspire to it, it would be a presumption.' I say, however, that this is not the true humility, but a pusillanimity; and that if it were true that these souls could have all the advantages of the others without risking anything, oh with what open heart would they not receive them! It is not the graces that they flee, nor the merits and crowns dependent on them, but it is that there are pains and incertitudes to be borne in order to attain to them, along with the stripping of sensible and luminous gifts, which they fear to lose.

Moreover, it will be acknowledged that all persons who practice the humility-virtue, are far removed from the humility which causes annihilation. By the humility-virtue the more you think you abase yourselves, the more you make yourselves something, believing that you are and exist, and act with strength and vigorous virtue, since it is certain that in order to abase one's-self one must be elevated and be something. A man who lowers himself or prostrates himself on the ground, must be standing or raised up; but he who lies all his length can no more abase himself, since he is in his last abasement. The more, then, that these souls think themselves abased by their humility-practice, which is, moreover, very good for a time, whilst the soul is yet incapable of anything else, the more they remain assured of their elevation; because the depth of the fall marks the height of the elevation, and also in their centre it is a spiritual elevation that they subtilely seek in this humiliation. Thus the humility-practice, as a virtue, cannot

Chapter XXX.   407

enter into heaven, but it must pass into annihilation before it can be worthy of God, and filled with Himself and by Him alone. It is not so with these souls of whom I wish to speak. They can neither humiliate nor abase themselves, for the profundity of their lowness takes away all power of abasing themselves, having given up everything. Should they desire to do so, they would require to ascend on high, and thus issue out of their state. They are so persuaded that in order to humble themselves they would require to place themselves above what they are, that they do not see how they could ever desire it, or how any creature could possibly do it.

Truly it is only the Word-God who, by incarnating Himself, has lowered Himself below what He was, therefore Scripture says that He annihilated Himself (Phil. ii., v. 7), and which it says of no creature, not even of Mary. When Scripture speaks of Mary by the mouth of Mary herself, it says, that God hath regarded the profundity of her nothingness, but it does not say that she had annihilated herself, since she was properly a nothing; and Mary has been the most perfect of all creatures, only because she has been lower than any other in the depth of nothingness. The deeper this nothingness is, the more extended it is, and the more extended it is, the more perfect it becomes; and in proportion as this nothingness is deepened, the communication of God is made more abundant, so that Mary, not being able as a creature to go further into the profundity of nothingness, it was necessary that the divine Word should become incarnate in her, it being only the incarnation of the Word which could be a fulness corresponding to this profound annihilation.

For it must be known that the more profound the void is, God distributes Himself there with the greater extent; but as the goodness of God is infinite, He always bestows a superabundant fulness, as it is written, that His redemption has been most abundant and infinitely so (Rom. v., 15-20). Now it would have been necessary for Mary to have been God in order to have, by her annihilation, a void strictly proportioned to the fulness and replacement of the Word. Thus we may truly say that her replacement was most abundant and infinitely abundant, for her void was most profound and infinitely extended.

The proportion, however, between the void of Mary and the incarnation was this, that Mary, although bounded and limited as a creature, had reached the bottom of the whole extent of limited nothingness, and not all the extent of infinite nothingness which God alone can fathom.

To comprehend this it must be remarked that, although void and nothingness are, properly speaking, neither finite nor infinite, since they are nothing, and the privation of all being cannot possess the properties of being, yet they can be measured, in some manner, as to the beings of which they are the void and annihilation; and in a right sense we can say that there is more or less annihilation, according as there was or could be more being and exaltation. Thus, although the death of a prince and that of a slave are each only the privation of a human life, nevertheless that of the prince is much more annihilating than that of the slave, for it causes the loss of a much more noble life. This being laid down, I say that Mary having attained to the most profound nothingness as a creature, and the Word, as Word-God, having exhausted all the greatness of His Father by His perfect equality, without there remaining anything in the Father that does not pass into the Son, who exhausts to infinity the infinity of the Father; there was between Jesus and Mary this proportion (without proportion nevertheless), that Jesus had exhausted all greatness and all God, as Mary had exhausted all nothingness in the creature. This caused the Word, viewing this proportion of void with His fulness, to come and enclose Himself with all His greatness in Mary, it being only He who could fill her nothingness; but He filled it in a manner infinitely abundant.

I say then that it is not properly a perfect humility in the creature to humble itself; but to love its nothingness and to keep itself in it, leaving its God to do all that He desires, and believing that He can do it. Would it have been a humility for Mary to have refused to become the mother of God, and thus to place some difficulty in the way of accepting the divine incarnation? No assuredly, it would have been a subtle and secret pride, which would have led her to perform something by herself, or to excuse herself from what God desired of her. Attachment to humility cannot be a true humility, since it is contrary to pure charity, which ordains that the creature should not reserve to itself anything whatsoever, and that by a total dependence everything should be sacrificed to the sovereignty of God alone. Many err in this point, maintaining their humility by their self-will; and wanting in resignation and perfect renouncement of themselves, they offend divine charity, thinking that they favour humility, which nevertheless is not humility in what agrees not with charity. If light were granted to discern it, it would be clearly seen that where one believes he is humbling himself he is elevating himself; that in thinking to annihilate himself, he seeks his own subsistence; and that, in fine, one tastes and possesses the glory of humility, as a signal virtue, in the acts of humiliation that one practises.

The true nothingness does nothing and opposes nothing. It suffers itself to be conducted and led where it is desired; it believes that God can perform everything by it, (without regarding itself) just as He could do anything with a straw; and there is more humility in believing these things, and in giving one's-self up to them without laying hold of anything, than in excusing one's-self from them. Let us abandon ourselves with courage. If God does not do anything with us, He will render us justice, since we are good for nothing, and this will be His glory. If He perform great things in us, we shall say with Mary that "he has done great things in us, because he has regarded our lowness."

13. *Neither is it beyond the sea, that thou shouldest complain saying, who amongst us can pass over the sea to bring it to us, that we might learn and do what is commanded us.*

14. *But this word is very nigh unto thee; it is in thy mouth, and in thy heart, that thou shouldst do it.*

15. *See, I set before thine eyes this day, life and good, and on the contrary, death and evil,*

16. *That thou mayest love the Lord thy God, and walk in His ways, adhering to him.*

17. *Choose then life;—*

20. *For he is thy life.*

Moses again shows how easy it is to follow this road, saying that it *is* so *near us* that *this word* of life (which discovers it to us) *is in our mouth and in our heart*, and that *he has placed before our eyes death and life, evil and good,* that we may love God; teaching us at the same time that the means of loving Him is to make *a choice*, just and equitable, useful and advantageous.

This choice is to *adhere to God;* and this adherence stands for abandon and the entire conformity of our will with His own: to *adhere* is not to do or to move of one's-self, but to consent to what is done by Him to whom we adhere. This adherence conducts the soul to the highest perfection, as it is written, that "he that adhereth unto God becomes of the same spirit with him," (1 Cor. vi. 17) because by the continuance of this adherence he becomes uniform, even to being able no more to see that he adheres, nor to force himself to hold himself attached, but he lives remaining united to the divine will. This is also remarked in this same Deuteronomy when it says "ye that adhere unto the Lord your God are all alive," (chap. iv. 4) without doubt from the life of Him to whom they are joined. And it is this very *adherence* which communicates to them this *life*, as it is also by it that God will perform in us what appears so difficult.

CHAPTER XXXI.

6. *Take courage and be full of trust; fear not and be not afraid at the sight of thy enemies, for the Lord thy God himself will conduct thee, and he will not abandon thee nor forsake thee.*

Scripture continues to exhort these souls never to excuse themselves from embracing a road so difficult to the creature that leans upon its self-strength, but so easy to God. *Take courage*, it says to them, and *be trustful*. This is not a thing that you are to undertake of yourselves, but *God* Himself *will be your conductor*. Abandon yourselves only to Him and He will never abandon you nor forsake you, even for a single moment. O advantage of abandon! The soul has nothing to do with taking care of itself nor giving itself any trouble about it. In abandoning itself to its God, He Himself conducts it. O sure conduct!

17. *Surely it is because God is not with me that these evils have come upon me.*

All *the evils* that *happen to* men come only *because God is not*

Chapter XXXI.   411

with them, either on account of their having totally quitted Him through mortal sin, or because they withdraw themselves from Him for want of courage in remaining in the *abandon;* resuming themselves after having given themselves up. But so long as we persist in abandoning ourselves to God, there is nothing to be feared, and no evils can attack us.

> 23. *The Lord gave these commands to Joshua, and said unto him, Be strong and of a good courage, for thou shalt bring the children of Israel into the land which I promised unto them, and I will be with thee.*

If strength is needed in souls to suffer themselves to be conducted fearlessly by a way which the greater part conceive all full of precipices, and the mind of man cannot comprehend, much more so is it needed in those persons who are to conduct others therein. Those have not only a particular assault to sustain, and to suffer the fears of their own destruction, but they must moreover bear the terrors and complaints of all the others whom God gives to them to make them enter and conduct them in so frightful deserts which, according to understanding and reason, even spiritually enlightened, are real losses and inevitable abysses. How often do even directors, becoming so convinced of their own destruction, fear extremely to destroy the others, and have lively apprehensions of it; although, when it is a question of giving advice when it is asked, they could not do other than persist in the impenetrable routes of the most naked faith and the blindest abandons? But receiving from heaven only responses of death to all assurance taken in the creature, as much for the others in this degree as for themselves, they must walk with their families in these frightsome deserts, and make their families walk there with them, by an impulse of the incomprehensible order of God, which leads them where they know not, and out of an apparent disorder makes for them the surest of all routes; and at the same time, the most inconceivable to man, for this is peculiar to abandoned souls who have not wished to set limits to their trust in God, nor to their sacrifice to all His will. It is just that He should exercise His rights and make them pass through all the trials which He has resolved to make of their fidelity.

Not only that, but these conductors of souls must bear all the blows discharged against the persons confided to them, and this is another extremely difficult thing. It happens usually that if a director is interior, all the demons and human persons league themselves against him ; and not being able to find anything to reprehend in his morals, they tax his conducting, and wish to make him responsible for all the weakness and follies of those he conducts, which is truly an injustice, since all defects are personal; and if God, not to violate liberty, does not prevent souls from falling, often drawing more glory from their fall, because they are humbled by it, or through other secret but just judgments, how can people desire the director to be the guarantee of all the faults of those he directs? Was Judas badly led under the immediate and visible direction of Jesus Christ? Was not St. Peter the first among the apostles? Why then should people think it wrong that weaknesses should happen to some souls without the directors being responsible for them or blaming the way? So many thousands are seen to perish out of this way and nothing is said about them, yet if a single person commits a fault, which is perhaps only apparent herein, every one murmurs at it, and they attribute a short-coming which is only personal, to the way or the direction.

To the director, then, great *courage* is necessary, and an extreme fidelity, not to leave off conducting these souls to the very end, in spite of these calumnies. Such a man may be assured that *God is with him.* Often even directors, seeing themselves greatly persecuted, lose courage and quit everything, thinking that everything is perishing in their hands, even until they are unfaithful enough to withdraw into solitude. I adjure them in the name of God never to do that; this is what the demon aims at by the persecutions he raises up against them, and they cause God to lose a very great glory which He would take in them, and in the persons they conduct ; besides, they do themselves an inexplicable wrong, and are thus the cause of the ruin of a great number of souls, who for want of conducting never arrive at the prepared place. It could not be believed how much the demon gains by this ; and it is for this he sets up so many batteries ; he even makes use of good souls to succeed in it, leading them under false pretexts and pious intentions to declare themselves against the pure way, thinking they do God a service when they persecute His dearest friends. But God makes use of the same means *to fortify* by the cross His faithful servants in His love, which does not hinder Him from often punishing their persecutors, and opening their eyes at last to His truth, to make them return to themselves.

CHAPTER XXXII.

1. *Give ear O heavens to what I speak; and hear O earth the words of my mouth.*
2. *Let my doctrine spread as the rain, and my speech penetrate as the dew.*

Moses sings a song unto the Lord. The singing of this song is known to very few, for it is necessary to be far advanced in God in order to express it.

This is the *new song* which is sung in heaven before the Lamb, and which was given to Moses at the end of his days in the flesh as a foretaste of that which he was to sing for ever in glory. Blessed is he who receives this song, and who comprehends in some manner in his inmost this song which comes from God Himself, and which is sung in the soul, not by the soul; for it does nothing but receive and render back without ceasing the voice and words placed in it.

Although he renders to his God all glory and honour, he yet avows that all which proceeds *from his mouth* is great and fruitful. It is great, for it comes from God Himself, as *the rain* from heaven; and it is fruitful as *the dew*, rendering the earth fertile. Thus all *the words* of well annihilated souls hit home and produce great fruits from their fertility.

2. *As thick rain upon the grass, and as showers upon the herb: for I will call upon the name of the Lord.*

The soul is in a state *to call upon the Lord* in a new manner; for it calls upon Him no longer for itself, but for His glory alone, powerless to appropriate anything whatsoever; thus its prayer is an extolling of the magificence of God.

3. *Give homage to the greatness of our God.*
4. *The works of God are perfect, and all his ways are equitable.*

Moses feeling what was in himself, and seeing also what was in the people entrusted to him, cries: *How perfect is all that God does;* as if he meant in his transport, Why will not people suffer themselves to be conducted to God, since all that He does is so perfect, and imperfect works are only so because the creature puts its hand to them? He adds that *all his ways are just* and irreproachable, although they appear to the humanly wise as ways of folly, because they are founded on blind *abandon*, which excludes all reason and human power; but by trusting ourselves to God, and losing all self-prudence, we thus acquire all possible prudence. What greater prudence can there be than to resign our feebleness to so mighty a Protector, and to trust our treasure to so faithful a Friend whenever we see ourselves powerless to preserve it, or even certain to lose it if we wish to guard it ourselves, at least in very great danger?

4. *God is faithful, and there is no injustice in Him.*
He is just and upright.

It is to show the solidness of the judgment of those who trust themselves to God when it is said that *God is faithful and without injustice.* As faithful, He will never fail us, being true in His promises; and since He is *without injustice*, He cannot deceive us. This is even strengthened by what is added, that the Lord *is just and upright:* as *just*, He renders back with increase what we give up to Him; as *upright*, we have only to follow Him to walk in uprightness, for He is exempt from deceit.

5. *They have sinned against him, and are no longer his children, being defiled in their impurities. Wicked and perverse generation,*
6. *Foolish and senseless people, is it thus ye requite the Lord?*

Moses, in his rapture of spirit, has no sooner made known to the people of Israel the advantage they have had in trusting to God, than in a spirit of prophecy he speaks against those who wandering from God merit no longer to be recognised as His children; and these are they who will not abandon themselves, or who, having already far advanced by the aid of the holy *abandon*, resume themselves at the time of the most severe and last trials. The broken language which he uses shows the elevation of his spirit in God; and what seems to be wanting in

Chapter XXXII. 415

order is divinely ruled by the Holy Spirit, who speaks by the mouth of this great prophet.

He reproaches, then, *the depravity and folly* of these souls who will not abandon themselves to God.

Foolish and senseless people, he says to them, *is it thus ye requite the Lord?* As if he said to them, Why do ye make a difficulty in rendering all things in general to Him? or why will you entrust Him with only a part of what you hold entirely from Him? This word *requite* is used to mark the restitution of all that we have from Him by gift: now, as it is certain that God has given us all that we are, we ought therefore to render unto Him all that we are; and this is done by the abandon of everything—riches, honours, life, body, soul, salvation, eternity, justice, holiness—in fine, all that composes our exterior and interior. Is it not to be bereft of our senses not to be willing to do this.

6. *Is not he your Father who has possessed you, who has made you, and created you?*

Is not God your Father? Is tenderness and love for you wanting in Him? Is it not He who ought to *possess you*, and do you not belong to Him already by so many just titles? Ought He not to regard you as His own property? And since He has had the power of *forming you*, will He not have that of preserving you, even to producing you anew if He desired? Even though you should be lost, could he not yet save you?

7. *Remember the days of old. Recall to thy memory all the ages of the world. Ask thy father, and he will relate to thee what he has seen; ask thy elders, and they will tell thee what they have learned.*

Remember what you have known in *times past*, so that the experience of the bounties of God may increase your trust. *Ask your fathers and elders* who have walked in these ways what has been their success. For although they appear to you only a frightful desert, and it seems to you that they must only end in eternal destruction, yet those who have happily arrived at the end of a career so long, so painful, and so obscure, will assure you that it terminates at nothing less than God Himself, who is found all alone at the end, by the happy loss of the creature into Him. Do not think that you are the only ones that walk in such frightsome roads ; many persons have passed along them before you, and many others accompany you though you know them not. God exacts from His most faithful abandoned ones trials of naked faith and generous love proportioned to the greatness of the abandon He has placed in them. Be not astonished even if almost all the others seem to walk differently, for the steps of those who will walk themselves and see where they go, although leaning upon their Beloved, are different from the ways of those who let themselves be carried to their Love, blindly trusting to Him. Sustain yourselves a little upon the testimony *of the ancients*, until you can go to God alone by God Himself, without any other support.

> 8. *When the Most High divided the nations, when he separated the children of Adam, he set the bounds of each people according to the number of the children of Israel.*
> 9. *But the portion of the Lord was his people, Jacob was the lot of his inheritance.*

God from the beginning has *separated the children of Adam*, who conduct themselves, from His own children whom He has chosen to be *his people and portion*. Abandoned persons are blessed in being *the portion of God*. From the time when God becomes our sole portion, we also become His, whilst the others remain in part heirs of Adam, as Adam forms a good part of their inheritance ; all is labour both for Adam and *his children ;* all is *bounded* and limited for them ; but all is repose for the Lord and His children ; all is full of liberty, extent, and immensity for them.

> 10. *He found him in a desert land, in a place of horror and vast solitude. He conducted him by long turnings, and instructed him, and preserved him as the apple of his eye.*

But where *has* God *found this people ;* and how has He known them to be his own ? Oh it is *in the desert land*, in the total separation from all creatures, in the stripping of all good, in the privation of all support, in the *place of vast solitude, horrible* alike to nature and the spirit, where the soul finds itself all naked and alone, without being accompanied by anything whatsoever ; ah, then it is that He *conducts it by long turnings and instructs it* in His purest will. *He guards it as the apple of his eye.* These words so well express God's care, and are so fit and proper, that we could not add anything to them without detracting somewhat from their beauty.

11. *As an eagle stirreth up her young ones to fly, and fluttereth over them, he stretched forth his wings, and took him upon him, and bore him upon his shoulders.*

There is not a word in this verse but is ravishing. *As the eagle stirreth up her young ones to fly as she flies*, so God encourages as His children the abandoned souls to follow Him, to abandon themselves, to suffer themselves to be led, therefore He *flutters over them* like the eagle, to animate and encourage His little ones, to defend them, and to sustain them. It is by this fluttering that He gives them His spirit. He *stretches his wings* over them in the first place, to shelter them from the injuries of the time, from crosses, from persecutions, from the arrows of the devil and the flesh. He defends them from all peril, and covers them with His protection, *under the shadow of his wings;* but not content with that, for greater safety *he takes them upon him, and bears them upon his shoulders.*

O too fortunate souls! Elevated as you are upon this Royal Eagle, you look from on high upon all the other birds who fatigue themselves with flying, and who are always in danger of being taken by the kites, vultures, and other birds of prey, and who at most rise but a little way from the earth. But you, O fortunate young eagles, you border upon the heaven without it costing you anything! You rest yourselves, and you fly, and in this flight of full repose, you overtop all the heavens; and although you advance by immense sweeps, yet you are never fatigued, for even your advancement is a perfect repose, and the more peacefully you repose upon these shoulders of your heavenly Eagle the more you advance. O happiness beyond comprehension, but which may be fully experienced by giving and abandoning one's-self to God!

12. *The Lord alone was his conductor, and there was no strange god with him.*

Whence comes the happiness of this soul—a happiness so unlooked for? It is that *God alone has been its conductor*, and He alone, and *no strange help with him*. O poor souls who fatigue yourselves in the multiplicity of your ways, if you knew the happiness of a soul which, without fatiguing itself, rests from all care of itself upon the arms of providence, you would be enraptured at it, and deplore the time you have lost without advancing, although walking with all your strength.

13. *He established him upon a high and excellent land, to eat there the fruits of the fields, to suck honey out of the rock, and to draw oil from the flinty rock.*

The soul thus borne upon the wings of God, mounts upon a *land eminent* both by the height of its mountains, and *the excellence* of its fertility; that is to say, above everything created, be it earthly or heavenly. Above pure intelligences, faculties, and virtues, it passes beyond all, and goes to repose in God alone, where He conducts it Himself upon the wings of His providence and love. It is then that this soul *eats of the fruits of the field*, nourishing itself no longer, but with the most exquisite things—God and His Holy Will. The will of God is *the fruit* of all lands, for all pains which are borne in the other ways are only to arrive at the knowledge and fulfilment of the will of God; but this soul *eats* of the fruits without any more cultivating them, being itself transformed and established permanently in the will of God, without power to come out of it except by an infidelity like to that of Lucifer.

It also *sucks* there *honey out of the rock*. This honey from the rock marks, in this soul, the good qualities of the rock, namely, firmness, hardness, insensibility, and immovability. This soul then is made firm as a rock in the will of God, it has also the hardness of it, for neither all arrows nor blows can make any impression, and are all broken at its feet without piercing it. It is, moreover, insensible to all things corporeal, human, and spiritual, and in fine immovable as a *rock*, so that all the attacks of hell cannot stir it or make it change its state. Behold what it is to suck honey out of the rock. Finally, it *draws* oil from the flinty rock, in that although it is thus firm, hard, immovable, and insensible to every thing, and made firm in the will of God, in which it is invariable, there flows however from this rock an *oil* and heavenly balm, which without this rock feeling aught of it, yet penetrates all that approaches it, and distributes itself efficaciously in the hearts which God sends to it.

15. *This well-beloved people became fat and rebelled; after being*

Chapter XXXII.

well nourished, fattened, and enriched, they have quitted God, their Creator, and withdrawn from God their Saviour.

This whole song is interspersed with interruptions, and broken with transports. After Moses has depicted the fortunate souls who have entered into the nakedness of the desert, and have suffered themselves to be borne to God, he describes the state of those who are conducted by lights and relishes which he calls *becoming fat*. The first have only been carried by God because they were entirely denuded, and the latter, who appear the well-beloved and most cherished, have quitted God only because they were very *fat*. This is clear. *They have become fat*, and afterwards *have elevated themselves*. This is the property of the state of the illuminative life, and of the passivity of light, to fatten the soul by a certain fulness which it communicates to it; and then the soul begins to elevate itself, finding itself, as it seems to it, in a more perfect state than any other, so that being full, it reposes in its fulness, which is as the *fat* and filling up of the three faculties of the soul—the understanding, the will, and the memory—and seeing nothing better, it fancies itself at the end of its course.

Those in this state have much assurance of their salvation, and the goodness of their state leaves them almost no doubt of it. Whence there happen to them two things—first, that they attribute so many graces to their fidelity, leading them to despise the others, who appear more imperfect, although really they are further advanced if they are of the true denuded ones; and thus they forget that it is God who has done this by His pure goodness without any merit on their part. Secondly, reposing in the gifts of God, of which they are full, they forget to run to God alone, and go beyond all gifts to find Himself, so that their very abundance of the gifts of God is to them the occasion of *quitting God*, by the bad use they make of them, and the proprietary attachment they have to them. These persons, who are thus in light, yet continue to be well-beloved of God even to the end (although in a manner very different from the others), God bestowing on them a thousand caresses, for gifts and graces are not incompatible with propriety when it is not a mortal sin; but God alone cannot be found therein, and He gives Himself only to the soul which, in the frightful wilderness, has lost all propriety and support.

18. *Ye have abandoned the God who made you, and have forgotten the Lord who created you.*

God all full of love and goodness for these souls yet cannot forbear thus lovingly reproaching them—*What! ye have abandoned the God who made you;* ye have quitted the end for the means; ye have stopped at the gifts and left the Giver; ye have lain down at the pleasant spot on your journey instead of ascending up to your origin! It must be observed that although God bestows so many graces upon these feeble souls, He does so only with some regret, and on account of their weakness, depriving Himself of the great glory and infinite pleasure which He would have had if these souls, by generously despising all these riches, should go beyond them all to mount up to Him who created them, and to return like rivers into the sea whence they derive their origin.

19. *And when the Lord saw that, his anger was kindled, because his sons and daughters provoked him.*
20. *And he said, I will hide my face from them, and will see what their end shall be.*

The Lord, not wishing to lose these proprietary and interested souls, leaves them His gifts, knowing that without them they would perish. *He sees it,* however, *and his anger is kindled at it,* protesting moreover that since they act thus they will never arrive in this life at their *final end,* which is to enjoy God Himself and not His gifts; therefore, He adds, *I will hide my face from them,* that is to say, they shall remain deprived of the possession of their Sovereign Good, since they have preferred things of so little value to Me. This is also pointed out in what follows.

21. *They have provoked my wrath in that which was not God.*

Wishing to possess what is *less than God,* they have been deprived of the possession of God Himself. Oh inestimable loss!

39. *Know ye that I am alone, and there is no other God than I. I kill and I make alive; I wound and I heal; and none can escape from my hand.*

Chapter XXXII.

This verse teaches us further how much God desires us to be abandoned to Him alone, and to lean on nothing out of Him. It is as if He said, since *ye know that I am alone*, and that there is nothing like to Me, I desire likewise to be alone in you in all that I do there. Who is able to do that which I do? Is there another God than I? It is I alone who can *make* souls *die* to themselves, and no labour of the creature can accomplish it; and it is I alone who can *restore their life*, and after having killed them, resuscitate and make them alive again.

Tell us, Oh Love-God! what inventions hast Thou wherewith to wound Thy most faithful lovers? Ah! how little would they be comprehended by mortal men, even though Thou shouldst tell us them. Thou *woundest them*, Thou sayest, and Thou *healest* them. Oh how deep are those wounds! It is Thou who smitest, and at the same time thou hidest Thyself, and Thou leavest only the pain of the wounds Thou hast made. The soul thus wounded thinks it can never be healed; it defends itself as long as it can from Thy blows; it doubts even if they are from Thee; and when it is Thou who smitest it, it complains to Thyself of the blows Thou givest, as if they came from another, for it knows not that Thou smitest it. Oh if it knew that it was Thou who smitest it it would be too happy, and would reckon as its delights its most cruel wounds! But alas! Thou hidest Thyself, and Thy lover thus wounded cries and bewails bitterly: it thinks that because it is thus disfigured and covered with wounds Thou no longer lovest it; and the horror of its wounds leads it to wish evil to itself, thinking that they have happened to it by its own fault, and that if it had well defended itself this invincible hand would not thus have disfigured it. Console thyself, poor loving one, console thyself; thou knowest not who is thy innocent murderer. If thou didst know it, thou wouldst esteem thyself more happy in being killed by His hand, than to be made alive by any other.

But what does He, this amiable cruel one? *He heals* all the wounds which He Himself has given. For it must be observed that none but He can heal the ills He sends. He heals then His loving one, and that with so much pleasure that it would wish no other thing than to be wounded thus, to have the pleasure of being healed again. God hides Himself when striking, but allows Himself to be seen when He heals, so that the soul knows not for a long time that it is He who has wounded it, yet it cannot be ignorant of His healing it.

But why, Oh Lord, dost Thou heal this soul with so much care? Is it not a species of cruelty, since Thou only healest it to wound it the more deeply, and to kill it altogether? Yes dear souls, this cure which appears so delightful to you must cost you your life. Ah! what a different pain this will be for you. The pain of death is quite different from that of a wound: and when the death blow is given, you will also not know who it is that killeth you.

The poor soul is so blind, that it thinks it is itself that has buried the poignard in its bosom. No, no; *it is* the unknown *who kills* you: and as He has wounded you only to heal you, He kills you only to *make* you *alive* again, but with a life quite different from the one you had before, which was rather a continual death, since you lived only to die; in place of this you die only to live for ever in a new and permanent life. Defend yourselves as long as you please, your defences will only cause your punishment to be prolonged, as He says Himself that *none shall escape from his hand.* No, no; all your efforts will be useless. You can make them if you like, but it is certain that you cannot escape death.

40. *I will lift up my hand to heaven and say, It is I who live for ever.*

These words relating to what has been already said, point out that God kills this soul only because it has a life contrary to His own, this *lifting of his hand* being as it were an oath which He takes; as if He said, I swear the death of this soul because it still lives in itself, and it is necessary that *I live only :* but that I may do so, I must annihilate everything living in it that is opposed to my sole life, and when that is done *I shall live* in it *for ever.*

42. *I will make my arrows drunk with blood, and my sword shall devour the flesh of the blood of those I have slain, and the enemies with bare heads, and those I have taken captive.*

God is not content with killing this soul, as has been said' He pursues it yet after its death to annihilate it, so that there may remain nothing of it. Therefore He says that *he will make his arrows drunk with its blood*; as if he said, By dint of smiting it my arrows will become all filled, soaked, and drunk with blood. This is not all: I wish not only that there remain no more blood to this creature, that is to say, no principle of life in it, as it is said in Lev. xvii. 14, "*the soul of the living flesh is in its blood*," and it was on that account the Israelites were forbidden to eat blood, the source of the self-life being then in the blood, not only must there remain no more of it, but the sword of the Lord *will* afterwards *devour* the very *flesh of the blood*, the flesh formed by the blood and nourished by it. It is not said that His sword will cut this flesh, but that it will devour it, thus denoting annihilation. This flesh is the flesh of the blood. This expression is admirable. God does not say the blood of the flesh, for the blood usually issues from the flesh, but *the flesh of the blood*, to show that He means by that everything appertaining to the self-life. The first is that of the flesh; therefore blood must be drawn from the flesh to weaken it; and this life is the life of sin, which is quitted when one is converted. But this other life which must perish here, is the spiritual life, and the life of the soul, denoted by the blood. Now this life in such souls issues *from the blood;* for although it is a life of spirit and grace, yet it has become a little carnal, and mingled with the flesh by propriety. But this flesh is no longer the reservoir of the blood, where it dwells in a continual and abundant manner, it is only the appendage and remains of it, therefore God by His sword devours this flesh, so that there remains no more of it. The arrows are indeed drunken with blood, but they do not devour it wholly, the sword must finish by consuming *the flesh of this blood*.

But of what blood? the blood of those already dead, as it is written, *the blood of those I have slain*. It is not sufficient to be dead, it is moreover necessary to be annihilated, and also captivity must be destroyed, as it is said of Jesus Christ, that "ascending into heaven he led captivity captive." This captivity is a certain contracting of the soul, hindering its expansion, as it has been said, and which can only be taken away by annihilation. Now this captivity was *from the naked chief of our enemies*. The chief of our enemies is propriety: this propriety had been wholly stripped by death: but there yet remained a certain restriction, rendering the soul captive, because it prevented it from being extended, and it is this that is achieved by the devouring of annihilation.

CHAPTER XXXIII.

2. *The Lord is come to Sinai, and has risen up from Seir upon us. He has appeared upon Mount Paran, and thousands of saints were with him. He holds in his right hand a law of fire.*

The Lord is come to the mountain, which is His throne, and His throne is no other than Himself. He has come from two sides; from *Sinai,* mount of graces, of light and love; but *he has risen up from Seir,* a desert place, and appeared *upon Mount Paran* by a new communication of His graces. *Thousands of saints are with him,* the spirits of the blessed and the annihilated souls. These blessed spirits are very holy, for there is nothing in them but what is of God; thus they are always with Him, for they are holy only from Him. This also marks the magnificence of God, who never comes alone into a soul, but accompanied by an infinity of gifts and graces, and a profusion of heavenly favours, so much the more sublime as they appear less so, and so much the more pure as they are in Himself, and not in the proper capacity of the creature: thus these thousands of angels who accompanied Him upon Mount Sinai were most intimately and for ever united to Him.

The Lord *holds in his right hand a law of fire.* This fiery law is charity, which must consume and annihilate all that there is in man as of man; for as long as there remains something of it, he cannot be holy. It is this law of fire which makes the saints; and no saint can be holy without passing through it. This fiery law burns the heart, and reduces to ashes all self-love, to leave there only pure love.

3. *He has loved the people: all the saints are in his hands, and all those that approach his feet will receive his doctrine.*

God *loves* all *the people,* that is, all the faithful, but it is properly only *the saints* who *are in his hands.* These are the abandoned souls who allow themselves to be moved at His will. They are in His hands for Him to do all that He pleaseth with them. *And those who approach his feet;* those who are nearest and most supple, and whose annihilation has made them His footstool (for God walks over abysses), these are they who *will receive his doctrine* and truth, and who will be instructed in His secrets the most hidden from others, beholding the economy of His providence, penetrating His supreme will above all things, and admiring how it is discovered to the little souls.

Moses admirably comprehends, in these few words, the entrance, progress, and infinite fruits of contemplation and the passive way. God, he says, has loved His people. When *love* advances reciprocally between God and the creature, it renders the souls *holy*, and from the time when they begin to be holy, they also begin to be passive: abandoning themselves with the more generosity, and leaving themselves *in God's hands*, both increase proportionately. The more a heart is holy, the more it is abandoned, and the more abandoned it is, the more it is holy, since holiness cannot be found out of God. This is well expressed when it is said that *all the saints are in God's hands*. He who says all excepts none, whence it is also clear that the more we excuse ourselves from the holy abandon, the further we remove ourselves from holiness, since we wish not to cast ourselves into God's hands, but to lean upon our own, and, as it were, walk upon them; and on the contrary, the most infallible means of soon arriving at holiness is to cast ourselves as speedily as possible into the arms of God, which is no other thing than to trust ourselves blindly to God, and to submit ourselves unreservedly to His will, which is the foundation and rule of all holiness.

But when Moses adds, that *all those who approach the feet of the Lord will learn his doctrine*, might it not be said that he depicts Mary at the feet of the Saviour, where she listens to His speech, and with her all the contemplatives of which she is the example and figure? As all those who remain in repose at the feet of the Lord infallibly learn His doctrine, for listening to Him, they give Him room to teach them; those, on the contrary, who do not enter into this repose will never learn the doctrine of the Lord, since wishing always to speak before Him, and never to listen to Him, they suffer Him not to instruct them; as also stirring unceasingly by continual and violent agitations of their senses and faculties, they leave Him no freedom to unite them to Himself. God being all repose, it is necessary to remain in repose in order to be united to Him; and since His Word is all speech, it is necessary to be all silence to hear Him, and all ear to receive Him. Moses wishes, then, to teach us that it is necessary to be silent, to repose, and to listen, to leave room for the generation of the Word in the soul, which is properly *to receive the doctrine of the Lord,* for the Word is the doctrine of the Father.

> 7. *Hear, Lord, the voice of Judah, and bring him with his people. His hands will fight for Israel, and he will be their protector against their enemies.*

Judah has always been taken for Jesus Christ, therefore the blessing given to this tribe differs from the others. It is uttered in the form of a prayer addressed to God in the name of Judah, that is to say, in the name of Jesus Christ, who prays his Father to bring him with his people into the land of eternal salvation, which is to be given through him to his chosen ones, and to establish him its liberator and defender.

> 9. *Levi said unto his father and to his mother, I know you not, and to his brethren, I do not know you, nor have they known their own children. They have kept thy word, and they have observed thy covenant.*

The tribe of Levi has always been that of advanced souls, chosen to conduct others, therefore they know no person according to the flesh, neither *father, mother, brethren, nor children,* being stripped of every thing natural and human, and all productions and proprieties. These faithful directors have no longer any consideration hindering them from doing the will of God. Thus it is said, that *they faithfully keep all his words, and observe his covenant.* This covenant is no other than abandon, by which the soul, giving itself wholly to God to do His will, God also treats with it, assuring it that He will conduct it Himself and make it do His will, if it remain abandoned to His guidance. Is not this a treaty of alliance by which the creature gives itself freely to its God, and God promises it His protection, and to be its surety in all things? To observe His covenant is to remain in destitution.

CHAPTER XXXIV.

> 10. *There was not seen a prophet since in all Israel like unto Moses, whom the Lord knew face to face.*

It is so rare a thing to find a man so far advanced as Moses, fit to conduct souls to the last degree of their consummation, that Scripture has even acknowledged it. *There are found almost none* who enter into God in so perfect a manner, which is, *to see him face to face* (that is to say, without medium, without support, propriety, or any thing mediate), because of the difficulty men have, and above all, men of some knowledge and reputation, to suffer themselves to be denuded, as it is necessary for the mystic death and annihilation, by which alone it is possible to pass into God.

CPSIA information can be obtained
at www.ICGtesting.com
Printed in the USA
LVHW060727020623
748621LV00018B/222

9 781556 357947